The School and Community Relations

FIFTH EDITION

Don Bagin
Rowan College of New Jersey

Donald R. Gallagher
Rowan College of New Jersey

Leslie W. Kindred

ALLYN AND BACON
Boston   London   Toronto   Sydney   Tokyo   Singapore

Editor in Chief, Education: Nancy Forsyth
Senior Editor: Ray Short
Series Editorial Assistant: Christine Shaw
Production Administrator: Marjorie Payne
Editorial-Production Service: Chestnut Hill Enterprises, Inc.
Cover Administrator: Linda Dickinson
Composition Buyer: Linda Cox
Manufacturing Buyer: Louise Richardson

Library of Congress Cataloging-in-Publication Data

Bagin, Don, 1938–
    The school and community relations / Donald Bagin, Donald R.
Gallagher, Leslie W. Kindred. — 5th ed.
       p.   cm.
    Kindred's name appears first on the earlier editions.
    Includes bibliographical references and index.
    ISBN 0-205-14785-2
    1. Community and school—United States.   2. Public relations—
United States—Schools.   3. Communication in education—United
States.   I. Gallagher, Donald R., 1929–   .   II. Kindred, Leslie W.
(Leslie Withrow), 1905–1986.   III. Title.
LC221.K56   1994
370.19′31—dc20   93-14106
                                                                CIP

Printed in the United States of America
10 9 8 7 6 5 4 3 2 1   98 97 96 95 94 93

CONTENTS

CHAPTER 15
SCHOOL PUBLIC RELATIONS AND THE SCHOOL
CHOICE CHALLENGE   295

PART FOUR: EVALUATION

CHAPTER 16
ASSESSMENT OF THE PROGRAM   303

PREFACE

School-based management, vouchers, total quality management, sexual harassment, decentralization, and choice are some of the issues that have intensified since the last edition of this book. Ultimately, they all have an impact on what goes on in the classroom. They join a long line of issues that come and go in education. But whatever issues make an impact on the educational scene, the need for communications is always on the agenda. And as this century is closing, educators are realizing more and more the importance of formalized internal and external communication programs in schools.

The field of school and community relations has grown over the last half century. This growth is evident in the large number of school systems that offer programs in the field. It is likewise evident in course offerings of colleges and universities where exposure is provided in teacher-education programs and in programs that prepare school administrators. In addition, an overwhelming amount of evidence for such growth is found in the rising number of school publications, television programs, lay advisory committees, school-made videotapes, special events, and various types of exhibits.

This growth has been stimulated to a considerable extent by the cultural changes taking place in society and by the emergence of new and critical problems confronting schools today. It has been stimulated further by a deepening appreciation on the part of educational and community leaders of the necessity to establish better communication between school personnel and citizens and to increase citizen involvement in affairs of the school.

Along with rapid growth in the field of school and community relations has come a strong need for new and clearer direction on how community relations programs should be developed, the ingredients that go into them, and the ends toward which they should be directed. With this need in mind, *The School and Community Relations* attempts to clarify the present situation and chart a course of action that is both practical and consistent with the role of the school as a social institution in a democracy. It recognizes that publicity is inherent in community relations, that an informational service is required for interpreting the school to the community and the community to the school, and that the real essence of a dynamic program lies in citizen cooperation and involvement in the affairs of the school.

The School and Community Relations emphasizes the importance of designing programs around the needs and problems of the school and its special publics. Dealing constructively and effectively with these needs and problems will increase the chances that parents and other community residents will take a positive interest in the school. Well-designed programs can effect a sense of friendliness and goodwill toward staffs, provide adequate financial support for the schools, and develop a sense of responsibility for the steady improvement of public education.

The fifth edition of *The School and Community Relations* updates the 1990 edition and incorporates current developments and concepts regarding school and community relations. Chapter 12, "Radio, Television, and Audiovisual Aids," and Chapter 13, "Preparing Printed Materials," include the latest application of technological changes since the last edition. Chapter 15, "School Public Relations and the School Choice

Challenge," is new and is designed to help school officials market their schools if the need arises; and Chapter 16, "Assessment of the Program," has been expanded to include the latest thinking on school-community relations evaluation. This fifth edition, then, represents a more comprehensive and timely treatment of school-community relations, yet it retains the best aspects of the previous text.

If you are good at discipline, your school will have good disciplinary procedures. If your strength is in curriculum, you will probably contribute to a better curriculum. If your strength is business, the numbers will come out well and you will save the district money. If you can communicate well and establish a solid school-community relations program, you will keep your job, because students will learn better.

If you cannot communicate well and have all of the other attributes listed above, chances are that you will never make it as far as you would like in school administration. If you do not know how to communicate effectively with your key audiences, chances are good that you will not gain support for the programs, curriculum, and discipline that you, as a professional, know are needed.

You probably will not want to do all of the things listed in this text because not all of them will suit your style or work for you. Some of them should, however, because they have worked for others. We urge you to take a look at the roles that you and all of those who work in the schools should play if you are going to provide the best possible education for your community.

A pioneer in school-community relations, Leslie W. Kindred died shortly after the publication of the third edition of this book. For many years, he was instrumental in setting national direction for school-community relations. As our graduate advisor, he graciously invited us to join him in writing the second and then the third edition of this textbook which is now used in 249 colleges, universities, and organizations throughout the world. For this we are indebted.

Appreciation is also owed to publishers and organizations for permission to cite materials from their publications. We especially wish to acknowledge those professionals who supplied information about programs under their direction and who furnished graphic materials from which we made selections. Our thanks to Larry Ascough, Special Assistant to the Superintendent, Dallas (Texas) Independent School District; Rich Bagin, Executive Director, National School Public Relations Association, Arlington, VA; Gay Campbell, Director, Community Relations, Tacoma (WA) Public Schools; Cheltenham Township Schools, Elkins Park, PA: Claudia Cuddy, Adjunct Professor, Communications Department, Rowan College of New Jersey, Glassboro, NJ; Dade County Public Schools, Miami Florida; East Hampton (NJ) Township School; Patricia Fridlund, Editorial Assistant, Tacoma (WA) Public Schools; Anthony J. Fulginiti, Professor, Communications Department, Rowan College of New Jersey, Glassboro, NJ; Lori Gmack, Supervisor, Human Resources, Green Bay (Wisconsin) Public Schools; Haverford Township Schools, Havertown, PA; John Hewlett, Director, Human Resources, West Chester (PA) Area School District; Albert E. Holliday, Executive Director, Educational Communication Center, Camp Hill, PA; Karen Kleinz, Director, Community Relations, Washington School District, Phoenix, AZ; Donald Langlois, Professor, Lehigh University, Bethlehem, PA: Peg Lawlor, Coordinator, Publications Office, New Jersey School Boards Association, Trenton, NJ; Paul D. Longhofer, Assistant Superintendent, Unified School District #259, Wichita, KS; Janet Lottero, Editor, *The Bulletin,* Montgomery

County (Maryland) Public Schools; Gary Marx, Associate Executive Director, American Association of School Administrators, Arlington, VA; Ed Moore, Managing Editor, *Communication Briefings,* Blackwood, NJ; Stephanie Rosemond, Administrative Assistant to the Superintendent, Beverly Hills (CA) Unified School District; Steve Shapiro, Professor, Communications, Rowan College of New Jersey, Glassboro, NJ: Texas School Public Relations Association, Austin, Texas; Philip Tumminia, Vice-President for Institutional Advancement, Rowan College of New Jersey, Glassboro, NJ: Bernadette Voelker, Director, Public Relations, Elkton (MD) Hospital; Kenneth L. Weir, Director, School Community Relations, North Penn School District, Lansdale, PA; and Judith C. Willis, Director of Community Relations, Mesa (AZ) Unified School District.

1

THE IMPORTANCE OF
PUBLIC RELATIONS

In recent years the importance of school-community relations and overall school public relations has grown rapidly. Studies conducted in the late seventies and early eighties by Phi Delta Kappa, the National Institute of Education, the Nation's Schools Report, and the New York State Department of Education have shown that superintendents have been recognizing the value of public relations and communications skills. All of the studies asked superintendents which courses they wish they had taken more of when they were preparing for their administrative careers. In all the studies, communications and community relations were listed as first or second.

WHY SCHOOL PUBLIC RELATIONS?

Why? Because more and more of the administrator's time is spent dealing with people. In most communities, taxpayers are letting it be known that they care about the quality of education and about its cost. The interest in better communications skills has also been sparked by strong teacher associations and unions that provide public relations help for members. As teacher representatives demand more explanations and as the nuances of negotiation become more subtle, top administrators must learn to be comfortable communicating in diverse situations with a myriad of publics.

An administrator may provide excellent leadership for the schools' curriculum and he or she may be a financial wizard; but if that administrator cannot communicate with the school board, a concerned taxpayers' group, or the staff, days in the district will be few.

An indication of the importance placed on community relations skills comes from the sample interview questions published in a book by the American Association of School Administrators and the National School Boards Association. After a category of questions addressing the candidate's philosophy of administration, the second category of seven deals with community relationships. The book suggests that two questions be asked: (1) How do you see the role of your position in developing community support for the schools? and (2) How would you contribute to keeping the community informed? Some of the other questions concern building relationships with staff members, young people, and minorities.[1]

Front-page newspaper stories frequently declare one of the following reasons for a superintendent's dismissal: "He couldn't communicate with the board," "She alienated teachers with some less than prudent comments," or "He just didn't have a good feel for this community." Knowing the public and being able to keep abreast of the community's thinking are major requirements for today's successful administrator. Suggestions on how to accomplish these tasks are offered in Chapter 3.

If school officials aren't convinced that they have a responsibility to communicate because communication helps people learn or because it builds confidence in the schools, they might want to consider another reason: to keep their jobs.

Minnesota, in 1988, offered parents the opportunity to send their children to any public school in the state. This was tried on a voluntary basis with schools during the year and conducted on a larger scale in 1989.

What does this mean? It means that schools perceived as being good will attract more students. Schools that people do not seem to like will attract very few students. Getting to the bottom line, it means that people working in schools that don't attract students will not have jobs. That sounds dramatic, but it probably will be the result because other states are beginning to offer options as Minnesota does.

Why do people choose one school over another? What makes school A seem better than school B? Many people have different theories. Some feel that it is the overall image of the school projected by the school district newsletter and media coverage. Others feel that it is based on the test scores of graduates. Still others think that an aura, evolved over the years, continues, even though in reality the quality of that school has changed.

With the competition for public funds on the local, state, and national levels, it's imperative that educational leaders be effective spokespersons for education. With only so many dollars available, the question facing legislators is whether those dollars should go for roads, bridges, health care, welfare, or education. Impressions are made daily by administrators—impressions that influence legislators' decisions on public education. While state and national associations can provide lobbying leadership, much can be accomplished on a local level by school officials who communicate well in the community. Whether it's speaking in a classroom to explain how public education works (a neglected curriculum item in most schools) or having breakfast with a local legislator, the school administrator constantly affects the public perception of education. Because administrators lead a fishbowl existence in the community, it's important that they understand and support ways of building confidence in public education. Many of these ideas and techniques are of course applicable to those responsible for leadership in non-public schools.

For too many years school officials were reluctant to commit staff and funds to public relations. They felt that "public relations" carried a stigma—that it was perceived as a deodorant for covering up a problem. Although professionals realize that Edward Bernays' statements on the social responsibility aspect of public relations are on target, many taxpayers still equate public relations with puffery—the attempt to make school people look good. Television's treatment of public relations people—usually portrayed as former beauty pageant winners who always smile and make the company look good—has done little to promote the social responsibility role.

Whether a school chooses to call it public relations, public information, community relations, or communications is relatively unimportant. The commitment to better two-way communications with all the audiences served by the schools is, however, important. One of the reasons more of a commitment has not been made may lie in the fact that so few school officials have been prepared to handle public relations responsibilities. In addition, education has in many cases continued its administrative organization with few changes in title or responsibilities over the years. Yet, a role-playing technique that asked thousands of taxpayers nationally to start the first school found that the need to communicate between the school and home was always one of the top two priorities.[2] Many of the commitments now considered almost sacrosanct were not listed as being one of the top five necessities to ensure a successful school.

The importance of communication in the overall school operation is being recognized by more states each year. They are requiring that candidates for administrative certification complete a course in the field of community relations. In 1982 the American Association of School Administrators (AASA) recognized the emerging role played by school-community relations by devoting a general session—one of six—to the topic.[3] Other national and state education associations are committing more and more sessions to the topic each year.

SUGGESTIONS FOR IMPROVING PUBLIC CONFIDENCE

The following suggestions to improve public confidence in educational leaders and in the schools have been adapted from the AASA presentation. The presentation was made by John Wherry, then executive director of the National School Public Relations Association and Don Bagin, who was president of that organization.[4]

Do an Effective Job, and Let People Know About the Successes and Challenges. To increase the chances of doing an effective job in the public relations area, the initial step is to be sure that the schools themselves are doing an effective job. An image reflects that which is: No public relations program can make a bad school look good for very long. On the other hand, an early step in building confidence in our schools is to let everyone know what the schools are doing well, what the problems are, and what's being done to solve the problems.

The public schools have made major contributions to the country; although the schools are far from perfect, more should be done to promote their accomplishments. Pollster George Gallup suggests that one of the biggest challenges facing educators is to let people know about the fine things being done in the schools.[5] Educational historian Ralph Tyler has estimated that 85 percent of the country's adult population was illiterate when the Declaration of Independence was signed. In 1900, 12 percent of the country's population could neither read nor write a simple sentence in English. In 1982 the U.S. Bureau of Census figures showed that only one-half of one percent of the population was illiterate.

In addition to announcing successes, school officials must be ready to admit problems. The more educated, sophisticated populace that pays for the schools will not be fooled for very long by school officials who attempt to cover up problems. When President John Kennedy admitted the Bay of Pigs fiasco was his error, his popularity ratings increased. The same occurred after President Dwight Eisenhower accepted blame for the U-2 incident. Constituents don't expect leaders to be perfect; they do expect them to recognize challenges and explain what's being done to meet them. A leader who admits that mistakes can occasionally be made encourages staff members to assume risks to try programs that will improve the schools. The key is to establish a spirit of honesty and sincerity so the staff and community believe the information being shared.

Despite protestations of educators about the money allocated for schools, the United States and Canada outspent European countries by more than two to one and spent almost four times as much per person than the former Soviet Union in the late 1980s and early 1990s. People in this country recognize the value of education. In the 1973 Gallup poll about public attitudes toward public schools, 76 percent of those surveyed said they felt education is extremely important to one's success. In 1980 the 76 percent jumped to 82 percent. Every two years the National Opinion Research Center at the University of Chicago conducts a national survey about spending priorities. Consistently, the results show that the public feels that education is an area where the country should be spending more. Ironically, that same public generally has little confidence in educational leaders. In the 1980s and late 1970s, only about 30 to 34 percent of those surveyed said they had confidence in educational leaders. From these studies, it might be concluded that the public thinks education is very important; it is just not too sure about the ability of educational leaders.

The quest for excellence must be communicated to all staff members and the public. Only when people realize that school leaders are serious about this commitment will they have more confidence in the people running the schools. As more people consider the possibility of tax credits and vouchers, the private and parochial school choices loom as greater competition for public schools. School leaders must find ways to identify and overcome such problems as ineffective teachers and administrators.

If a commitment to excellence is not made, public schools will most likely find their hard-hit enrollment figures suffering even more. Parents who value education will avoid sending their children to a school where "fifth grade is the bad year because all three teachers should have been dismissed," especially if those parents have a child entering fifth grade.

Related to the question of quality is that of quantity. Just how much can the schools be expected to do? Should the public schools be expected to offer vocational training? Should they teach students how to brush their teeth, drive cars, and become artists? One of the most serious challenges facing educational leaders is to gain a community consensus on what the expectations are for the schools. Only then can school leaders be evaluated on how well the schools are doing.

The Public's Concern About Discipline Must Be Taken Seriously. Year after year, the public's concern about public school discipline is rated at or near the top of the list by the Gallup survey of public attitudes toward public schools. Whether the problem is real or perceived, it exists in the minds of the people who will help determine how much support public education receives.

Discipline means different things to different people, but some agreement on a definition exists. A 1982 series of regional meetings with parents, students, and educators sponsored by the Missouri Department of Education identified the following as the biggest discipline problems: disruptive classroom behavior, student disrespect for authority, student apathy toward learning, and absenteeism and class cutting.

The importance of the discipline factor in school selection was underlined in a study done in Gloucester County, New Jersey, a county frequently used by the Gallup organization as representative of the country. The telephone study asked 100 parents who had always sent their children to public schools a series of questions about schools. Parents were asked whether they would continue to send their children to public schools if tax relief were provided, such as a voucher or tax credit. Only 41 percent said they would continue to send their children to public schools. When asked why, the number one reason given was "discipline."

To address the perception of discipline, a program that involves parents, students, and staff should be developed to build a clear code. There are many examples of strong discipline policies being supported and even cheered by parents and communities. Programs that encourage more people to visit the schools during the learning day can be a giant step in reducing misperceptions about discipline.

School Leaders Must Personalize the Schools More to Enhance the Comfort Of Those Being Served. People make decisions on key purchases based on their personal experiences with the product, whether it be the choice of an automobile, a hotel, or a bank. How people feel about their schools is usually dictated in the same way. It's not so much the newspaper article or the newsletter story as it is the way a secretary responds to a question, or a teacher returns a phone call, or a guidance counselor or principal helps a student who is confused about an important decision.

Teachers who phone students' parents with positive news, principals who invite small groups of parents for lunch, and secretaries and custodians who greet all visitors as if they were board members do much to make people feel good about their schools. Because so few school employees have taken a course on how to deal with the public, an in-service program to share ideas would help. Such a program is ideal in that it meets the challenge of appealing to all employees, inasmuch as everyone must communicate in some way with members of the community.

All employees must recognize their role in public relations. Studies show that people who acquire their information about the schools from board members and employees tend to support the schools more than people who get their information from other sources. One of the problems is that each entity (board members, administrators, and teachers) feels that the job of building public confidence in the schools belongs to another group. Teachers claim it's the board's job, the board says administrators should be doing it, and the administrators point to teachers as the people having the closest contact with parents. If all groups don't recognize the need to contribute in the public relations arena, the kind of confidence desired will never occur.

Staff Morale Must Be Improved. The number one concern of board members and administrators in the early 1980s—when asked on which level the problem in communications was most pressing—was staff morale. In previous years the major public relations concerns had been media relations, newsletter preparation, and community advisory committees. With the reductions prompted by declining enrollment, staffs are getting older. Fewer new (usually younger) teachers are being hired, and something must be done to ensure that new ideas are generated from veteran employees.

One way to determine the level of morale is to ask this question: If you had an idea to improve the school where you work and it would cost nothing to implement, would you suggest it? Only between 20 and 40 percent of the 10,000 teachers and administrators surveyed in schools throughout the country said they would.[6]

Teachers and principals report that they don't suggest ideas any more. When asked why, they note that the ideas are listened to, but that nothing new happens. With the current emphasis on computers and information dissemination, it must not be forgotten that the most precious part of a school is its staff. People need to be asked their opinions, and they need to be told when they do a good job. Chapter 7 offers specific strategies that will help accomplish these goals. Community residents who hear various versions of an incident that occurred at a school tend to believe employees' versions more than other sources. It's vital therefore that employees be kept informed about school news, including impending decisions.

All School Officials Must Use and Insist That Others Use Comfortable Words. Public confidence in school leaders cannot be built with words that people don't understand. The educator who addresses the PTA or sends a memo to thousands of parents does little to enhance the school's image with jargon and multisyllabic words that the audience won't understand. Other chapters present specific ways to avoid the problem. Suffice it to say here that the utilization of maximal learning stations won't necessarily optimize the SAT scores of the multiethnic, multitrack pubescent adolescents permeating the district.

Educators Must Stop Fighting Among Themselves and Start Building Coalitions. The former, almost guaranteed, support of parents is no longer sufficient to gain what educators think they and education deserve. With only about 25 percent (in 1988) of the parents having children in grades K–12, the traditional support base has been eroded. Therefore, educators must work together to gain public and legislative confidence and support.

This working together has many implications; some will require that association leaders rethink their positions. For example, a National School Boards Association president in 1982 asked that board members extend an olive branch to teachers. Many board members applauded; others disagreed. One teachers' association public relations director privately asked a friend of the board group: "What kind of trick is the olive branch?" It was no trick, but the question conveyed the lack of trust in the board-teacher relationship. As the public image of education comes under closer scrutiny, more and more teachers, administrators, and board members are becoming aware of the need to work together. In one urban school district after a teacher strike, a teacher who worked during the strike reported on page three of an interview in a daily newspaper that she was greeted by human feces in her desk drawer every morning for three weeks after the strike. It's difficult to determine how many students the school lost because of that story, but it's not difficult to conclude that the incident and the reporting of the incident didn't make people feel good about their school.

Teachers must work with other teachers, administrators, board members, parent support groups, and the business community to build the kind of coalition that will be listened to by legislators.

Working With the Business Community Is Essential to Attract Needed Support. As the number of parents decreases, school officials must seek other support bases. One excellent source is the business community, which is more interested in the schools' success than a Business-Education Day might indicate. For too many years educators have hesitated to work closely with the business community, perhaps fearing that business people would encroach on educators' decision making. Educators have much in common with business leaders. Both have suffered a loss of public confidence, both desire good relationships with the community, both want graduates with solid skills, and both have children and grandchildren attending the public schools.

Ray Reed, of Rockwell International, encouraged educators to seek the assistance of the business community. He said,

> We won't bite. Come to us and ask for help. We are open, and we are receptive to whatever you would like to do. We want this to be a cooperative effort. We are not trying to infringe on your turf, and we realize the educator has the responsibility to educate our children. If business, industry, the school district, and all other community entities don't work together, our nation is not going to be as strong as it should be and can be.[7]

With the continuing financial constraints faced by school personnel, the possible availability of funds and donated time from business staffs is attractive. (See Chapter 8 for additional ideas on working with the business community.)

Every Effort Must Be Made to Involve Nonparents In the Schools. As fewer people have children in the schools, it becomes necessary to rethink the goals and responsibilities of the schools. If the schools wish to be blessed with support from the community, their leaders will have to focus on services and offerings that appeal to other than those who are directly benefiting from the K–12 programs. Two workable ways to enlist the support of nonparents are through community education and volunteer programs. Both of these programs prompt people to visit their schools and to get involved with the schools. These approaches allow us to start thinking about public education as a K–70 program instead of a K–12 program.

Nonparents, according to a series of studies in 100 school districts, want to know the following about their schools:

- What's being taught
- How the basic subjects are being taught
- How school funds are being spent
- How the school board operates and reaches decisions.[8]

Citizens who have been in their schools for whatever reason consistently have more positive attitudes about those schools. Therefore, any program that fosters school visits or school use is a plus in terms of building confidence in school leaders.

The Communications Program Must Be a Two-way Process. Acquiring feedback allows school officials to know how the community or staff will react to a decision. It is appreciably easier to lead a school district when the thoughts, aspirations, and commitments of the leaders are known. Communication for many years was equated with school officials telling others about the schools. In the late 1970s and early 1980s enlightened school leaders stressed the listening end of the communication process.

When people are asked their opinion, they feel better about the person who asks for it—especially if it's made clear that the opinion will be considered. Whether it's using the key communicators, conducting surveys, or some method recommended in Chapter 3, the need for feedback is vital.

NEED FOR A COMMUNICATION PLAN

A plan must be developed for community relations, or little will happen. Board members and administrators can commiserate for a long time about the need for a public relations program, but it won't happen unless someone develops a plan and makes a commitment. The superintendent—or someone delegated by the superintendent—must be given the time and resources to develop a sound communications program. Some school districts, in an effort to emphasize the importance of the topic, have committed a year to in-service programs for all staff members, to improve communication within the district. If building confidence is important, then that importance must be demonstrated with commitment. If the commitment is not made, chances are that little will happen, and different education factions will be able to look back and say, "We should have made the commitment."

For quite a while most experts and textbooks in school-community relations have suggested that the prime reason for communicating more effectively with the staff and community is to build confidence in the school. There's nothing wrong with that. This confidence is very productive.

Yet some people tend to forget a vital catalyst for the communications undertaking: to help people learn better. This must be remembered. When schools embark on an effective communications program, support comes more easily when the people paying the bill recognize that communications is a key component of better learning.

This means that the public relations effort should entail dealing with people more than dealing with things. This will indeed build confidence and gain support of parents and others. More importantly, it will—through involving people in the schools and in their children's learning—create a better learning atmosphere and encourage students to learn.

Albert E. Holliday, editor and publisher of the *Journal of Educational Public Relations* and former public relations director for the Pennsylvania State Education Department, is a long-time proponent of effective public relations for schools. The following represents his thinking.

Building support, public relations and financial, is essential for the operation of public schools. But it is not, and probably was never meant to be, the prime or sole function of school public relations.

Education must be viewed in terms of a school-community setting, which includes students and teachers, administrators, support staff, board members, parents and other citizens.

Whether a school system is excellent or mediocre depends on how those people work together—how they communicate, relate, are involved, participate and share. A public/community relations program is aimed at focusing on the relationships of all those people, with an overall goal of improving student achievement.

We in the education field are remiss concerning the term *school* (or *educational*) *public relations*. For example, from a group of 100 teachers, board members, administrators, parents, business people and citizens, you would likely hear different definitions of that term, such as these:

- A means to pass a millage campaign
- A vital management function
- A two-way process to communicate with the public
- Something the superintendent should do
- Ways the community and schools can work together
- Getting positive news into the newspaper (and keeping negative news out)
- A means to build public confidence in the schools
- A way to gloss over problems
- A waste of money
- A process to involve the community
- A concept to make schools into learning resources for all members of the community
- Something principals should do when they have time
- A way to make board members look good.

I've heard each of these comments a number of times when I've conducted conferences around the country. Most administrators believe that "it" is necessary, but irritating and time-consuming, especially in states in which the voters have a say at the ballot box on school millage rates and bond issues. Teachers are often mystified by the topic in terms of why it should be of any concern to them. Parents and other citizens view school public relations through the publications and other materials issued by that department. Board members may understand the value of "good" public relations, but are apt to look at the costs for PR as frills instead of a necessity.[9]

Holliday defines school and public or community relations as a "function on all levels of a school system, established as a program to improve and maintain optimal levels of student achievement, and to build and maintain public support."

The function consists of communication with, and involvement of, internal and external publics in the school system. A series of processes and activities, the program is designed to:

1. Promote a positive and challenging school climate in which student achievement and staff productivity are fostered
2. Encourage maximum involvement of parents, at home and in school, in their children's educational development
3. Build public knowledge of the purposes, successes, and needs of the school system, leading to public understanding and support
4. Involve citizens in cooperative learning practices, partnerships, and other means to make full use of human and other learning resources in the community

As seen in the definition, the two main purposes of such a program are to foster student achievement (through establishment of a positive school climate and parent and citizen involvement) and build citizen knowledge and understanding leading to financial support.

To gain support for schools, some educators have adopted marketing techniques. A number of techniques and ideas—all aimed at building public confidence—have been developed in the last few years. One of the most attention-getting has been using the marketing concept to sell the school's story to the public. William Banach and the Macomb Intermediate School District in Michigan use marketing techniques traditionally employed by companies to sell soap, cars, and other products. In essence, the program identifies the audiences to be reached and defines how the public schools can best meet the needs of those audiences with the schools' services. The program offers bumper stickers, refrigerator magnets, pencils, and other gimmicks to keep the school story in front of large numbers of people. Some educators believe that this approach will reap results; others are slow to accept it because it smacks of gimmickry.

Whatever the feeling about marketing, most educators are becoming increasingly cognizant of the need to employ more community relations techniques than they are now using. This book, therefore, is organized to help the reader understand school-community relations and to employ successful communication techniques. The first part outlines the essentials of a school-community relations program. The second part explains the communication process and ways to communicate with the public, as well as how to build sound and constructive relationships during special events. The third part features the various tools used to communicate to various audiences. And the last part presents an assessment and evaluation of the results of a community relations program.

ENDNOTES

1. *Selecting the Administrative Team* (Arlington, VA: American Association of School Administrators and National School Boards Association, 1981).

2. Don Bagin, Glassboro State College, NJ, 1977–83.
3. American Association of School Administrators National Convention, New Orleans, 1982.

4. The National School Public Relations Association exists to assist school officials with their communications and community relations efforts. It is located at 1501 Lee Hwy., Suite 201, Arlington, VA 22209.

5. George Gallup, addressing the Glassboro State College Chapter of Phi Delta Kappa, December 1982.

6. Surveys conducted by Don Bagin and Donald R. Gallagher, Glassboro State College, NJ, 1978–82.

7. Ray Reed, Rockwell International, speaking at the convention of the American Association of School Administrators, New Orleans, 1982.

8. Ned Hubbell, school public relations consultant, Port Huron, MI, 1981.

9. Albert E. Holliday, "In Search of an Answer. What Is School Public Relations?" *Journal of Educational Public Relations* 11 (2nd Quarter 1988), p. 12. Reprinted by permission.

2

PUBLIC CHARACTER OF THE SCHOOL

The development of sound and constructive relationships between the school and the community is a necessary and natural function of a publicly supported institution in a democratic society. This position arises from a consideration of the public character of the school and the legal framework within which it operates. It is also supported by the role of public opinion in the shaping of educational policies and practices. Even though the American way of life is characterized by constant change, these considerations nevertheless form the basis of the decision-making process in the management of public schools, and they exercise an influence on the nature and direction of change.

The position thus established is reflected in the working definition of school and community relations that is presented in this chapter. The definition reiterates the belief that sound and constructive relationships must be developed and maintained with the community by those who are responsible for public education if the school is to meet its obligations to the cause, continuance, and preservation of democracy.

PUBLIC CHARACTER OF THE SCHOOL

Despite the intervention of the federal government in local and state educational affairs, it is evident in the legal structure of the state school system and in the laws regulating its operation that the power to manage schools actually resides in the people. At the state level, the people have the right to support or oppose legislation affecting the education of children, to work for the modification and repeal of existing laws, and to decide at the polls who shall represent them in the legislature.

This right is similar at the local level where fellow citizens are elected to membership on the board of education and are expected to carry out the popular will. To ensure the public character of the board of education, state law prescribes that parents and citizens shall have the right to be heard at a regular meeting of the board or to file in writing their ideas regarding educational objectives, policies, and programs. Regular meetings must be open to the public, and no vote can be taken on school business in private by the board. The minutes of its meetings and records of transactions are public property and may be inspected at any time on request by a citizen. The failure of a school board and its individual members to abide by these and other regulations set forth in the law may result in dismissal of the board and prosecution of the members for misconduct in office.

This concept emphasizes the public character of the school and that the educational enterprise is one of shared ownership. Citizens in the community hold the status of part owners in the schools. They own stock, so to speak, in the schools by virtue of the fact that it is their taxes that support the schools. The dividends received are formal education for themselves and their children and the indirect benefits that flow to society from a literate and well-prepared population in such fields as art, science, industry, and agriculture.

Shared ownership carries with it responsibility on the part of citizens as well as those who administer the schools. People must be supplied with accurate and adequate information about the school system if they are to form intelligent opinions and transmit their thinking to school officials. And to participate as partners in helping the school meet individual and societal needs, they must have access to pertinent facts and ideas and be able to discuss them rationally among themselves and with those who manage the schools.

What citizens feel and how they act influence the selection of school board members, the fixing of tax rates, the passage of bond issues, the nature of curricular offerings, the determination of salary schedules, the provision for special services, and the like. And prevailing attitudes and opinions not only establish the limits of institutional functioning but also shape and guide the operation of policies and practices within the school system.

It is essential to the management of the school that those who are charged with the responsibility for directing its affairs understand the role of public attitudes in a democracy and their effect on the education of children. The school administrative team need not be expert on the subject, but certainly one or more of its members should possess practical insight and understanding of what public attitudes and opinions mean and why people think and feel as they do. Without this knowledge it is difficult to plan strategies affecting school-community relations.

THE MEANING OF PUBLIC OPINION

Public attitudes may be viewed as predispositions, thoughts, or feelings of persons toward something, such as an issue or a policy question that has not yet come into sharp focus. For example, prior to the real onset of the space race there were attitudes toward federal aid to education, instructional changes in the curriculum, foreign language teaching, and science offerings in elementary and secondary schools. These attitudes were suddenly fused into public opinion upon the specific question of strengthening the educational program when the Soviets put the first satellite into space, and swift action was taken to explore ways and means for turning out a better educa-

tional product and to enact appropriate legislation for underwriting essential changes.

Other characteristics are also ascribed to attitudes, the most common being their emotional tone. Attitudes are always accompanied by some positive or negative feeling, and the nature and intensity of this feeling influence an individual's perception of any new situation he or she encounters. For example, a beginning teacher who has had a series of unpleasant experiences with the principal will probably develop a dislike for principals in general despite the fact that another one under whom he or she is now working is sincere and thoughtful. To the teacher this new principal has an ulterior motive of personal gain in acting decently. Such an attitude may persist for a long time, depending on the intensity of the negative feeling and the frequency of constructive acts on the part of the second principal. It is known that attitudes are the result of forces in each individual's environment, such as his or her physical needs, social needs, emotions, perceptions, motivations, and experiences, and that these in turn influence the individual's behavior. Interestingly enough, opinions are defined in a similar way.

Social scientists have not arrived at a standard definition of *attitudes* or *opinions*. Therefore, they are often used interchangeably. But it may be worthwhile to review some of the meanings connected with the term *public opinion*. Occasionally it is defined as any widespread belief or consensus arrived at by members of one or more groups, or as prevailing customs and traditions handed down by previous generations. The term is also frequently associated with the process of developing opinion instead of opinion itself, with fine distinctions drawn between judgments reached by logical methods of reasoning and judgments growing out of emotional states of mind. Attention may likewise be given to the quality of the opinions expressed or to the intensity of the opinions. No doubt these and other variations in the meaning of the term have a place in a detailed study and analysis of public opinion, but they are hardly suitable to guide the work of laypersons and professional school officials. As a working rule, we should think of public opinion as a collection of individual viewpoints held more or less in common by members of a group regarding some person, condition, or proposal. Generally, these points of view concern matters that are controversial or capable of causing controversy.

SCHOOL-COMMUNITY RELATIONS

In view of its background and status in U.S. society, the school has a definite responsibility to furnish taxpayers and parents with complete and accurate information regarding its needs and activities and to develop educational policies and programs that reflect popular interests and desires. How to implement this responsibility effectively is the problem of school-community relations.

The Forerunners

While the necessity for keeping the public informed is as old as the school itself, nevertheless it was not until the beginning of the twenties that a formal approach was made. This began with studies of publicity, especially newspaper publicity, and of the value such publicity had in keeping the school before the people and in acquainting them with what it was doing. During this period at least three books were published on the subject of school publicity,[1] as well as a scattering of articles in professional journals.

Within a few years the term *publicity* was replaced with the phrase *school public relations,* for at least two reasons. First, it was felt that the word *publicity* carried both positive and negative connotations. And second, the realization developed that a more inclusive concept than publicity was necessary for telling the story more fully and for reaching a wider audience. In the mid-twenties, Moehlman came out with the first book in educational administration dealing with school public relations. He defined public school relations as an "organized factual informational

service for the purpose of keeping the public informed of its educational program."[2] The book included chapters on public relations policy, responsibilities of personnel, and the use of such media as newspapers, house organs, annual reports, school newspapers, and oral and written communications with parents. Attention was also given to the importance of social contacts, parent-teacher associations, school buildings, and appraisal of results.

These pioneering efforts were followed eleven years later with another book by Moehlman setting forth the doctrine of "social interpretation." According to this doctrine, "Social interpretation may be considered as the activity whereby the institution is made aware of community conditions and needs and the factual information service whereby the people are kept continuously informed of the purpose, value, conditions, and needs of their educational program."[3] In other words, it is a two-way system of communication through which the community is translated to the school and the school to the community.

The objectives of a program in social interpretation, as set forth by Moehlman, are as follows: "The ultimate objective is to develop continuing public consciousness of the importance of educational process in a democratic social organization, to establish confidence in the functioning institution, to furnish adequate means to maintain its efficient operation, and to improve the partnership concept through active parental participation."[4]

School public relations at present represents an extension of the interpretative point of view. This extension takes into account a change in basic terminology, increased emphasis on communication, and greater citizen involvement and participation in the educational decision-making process. There is a movement now to eliminate the term *public relations* and to use instead the phrase *school-community relations* because the latter is more in keeping with current concepts concerning the involvement and participation of citizens in the educational decision-making process and is less subject to association with undesirable practices in promotion and persuasion for selfish ends.

It has been increasingly evident that the school in a dynamic, changing social order cannot adapt itself to change or make the necessary improvements in its program without involving citizens in its affairs. As pointed out by Sumption and Engstrom, "There must be a structured, systematic, and active participation on the part of the people of the community in the educational planning, policy making, problem solving, and evaluation of the school."[5] It is through such involvement that citizens come to know the school firsthand. They are able to raise questions, obtain information, express ideas, consider proposals, and take positions on critical issues. They become part of the decision-making process that keeps up with social change and brings about educational change.

Citizen involvement ensures a better understanding of what the community wants for its children now and in the future. It likewise provides better opportunities for closer cooperation with local governmental agencies and community organizations which have an interest in education and public welfare. And, generally, it helps to bring about increased use of community resources in the educational program, thereby integrating further the school and community.

Current Definitions

Before stating what is meant by *school-community relations*, it might be well to examine some definitions of *public relations*.

Rex Harlow examined public relations books, magazines, and journals and found 472 definitions of *public relations*.[6] Additionally, he asked eighty-three public relations leaders for their definitions. From all this he composed an eighty-seven word definition that Grunig and Hunt reduced to "the management of communication between an organization and its publics."[7]

Public Relations News defines *public relations* this way:

> Public relations is the management function which evaluates public attitudes, identifies the policies and procedures of an individual or an organization with the public interest, and plans and executes a program of action to earn public understanding and acceptance.[8]

Wilcox, Ault, and Agee cite this definition of public relations approved at the World Assembly of Public Relations and endorsed by thirty-four national public relations organizations:

> Public relations practice is the art and social science of analyzing trends, predicting their consequences, counseling organization leaders, and implementing planned programs of action which serve both the organization and the public's interest.[9]

Leaders in school-community relations and the National School Public Relations Association use parallel concepts in defining *school-community relations*.

In the first edition of this book, Kindred defined it as "a process of communication between the school and the community for the purpose of increasing citizen understanding of educational needs and practices and encouraging intelligent citizen interest and cooperation in the work of improving the school."[10]

We now include two-way communication in this shorter definition: Educational public relations is management's systematic, continuous, two-way, honest communication between an educational organization and its publics.

The National School Public Relations Association (NSPRA) also substitutes *educational* for *school* in its definition:

> Educational public relations is a planned and systematic management function to help improve the programs and services of an educational organization. It relies on a comprehensive two-way communications process involving both internal and external publics, with a goal of stimulating a better understanding of the role, objectives, accomplishments, and needs of the organization.

Educational public relations programs assist in interpreting public attitudes, identify and help shape policies and procedures in the public interest, and carry on involvement and information activities which earn public understanding and support[11]

Holliday defines school public/community relations as "a systematic function on all levels of a school system, established as a program to improve and maintain optimal levels of student achievement, and to build public support."[12] He contends that the two main purposes of a school public/community relations program are to foster student achievement (through the establishment of a positive school climate, and parent and citizen involvement), and to build citizen knowledge and understanding leading to financial support.

Though other definitions might be quoted as a means of bringing out the various shades of meaning associated with the term *public relations,* the position taken in this text is that sound and constructive relationships between the school and the community are the outcomes of a dynamic process that combines the following ideas and practices:

■ A way of life expressed daily by staff members in their personal relations with colleagues, pupils, parents, and people in the community
■ A planned and continuing series of activities for communicating with both internal and external publics concerning the purposes, needs, programs, and accomplishments of the school
■ A planned and continuing series of activities for determining what citizens think of the schools

and the aspirations they hold for the education of their children
■ The active involvement of citizens in the decision-making process of the school so that essential improvements may be made in the educational program and adjustments brought about to meet the climate of social change.

Perhaps another way of expressing the same concepts is to say that sound and constructive relations between the school and community are achieved through a process of exchanging information, ideas, and viewpoints out of which common understandings are developed and decisions made concerning essential improvements in the educational program and adjustments to the climate of social change.

Planned Relationships

Entirely too many programs for the development of sound and constructive school-community relations are sporadic in nature, improperly conceived, poorly planned, and crudely executed. They defeat their own purpose. If a school system wishes to engage in a comprehensive and continuing program of school-community relations, then it must be willing to plan how its character, needs, and services may be interpreted best to the people, how their wishes and aspirations may be interpreted best to the school, and how citizen involvement may be included in the task of educational improvement and institutional adjustment to social change.

ENDNOTES

1. Rollo George Reynolds, *Newspaper Publicity for the Public Schools* (New York: A. G. Seiler, 1922); Clyde R. Miller and Fred Charles, *Publicity and the Public Schools* (Boston: Houghton Mifflin, 1924); and Harlan Cameron Hines and Robinson G. Jones, *Public School Publicity* (New York: Macmillan, 1923).
2. Arthur B. Moehlman, *Public School Relations* (Chicago: Rand McNally, 1927), p. 4.
3. Arthur B. Moehlman, *Social Interpretation* (New York: Appleton-Century, 1938), p. 104.
4. Ibid., p. 106.
5. Merle R. Sumption and Yvonne Engstrom, *School Community Relations: A New Approach* (New York: McGraw-Hill, 1966), p. xi.
6. Rex Harlow, "Building a Public Relations Definition," *Public Relations Review* 2 (Winter 1976), p. 36.

7. James E. Grunig and Todd Hunt, *Managing Public Relations* (New York: Holt, Rinehart, & Winston, 1984), p. 7.

8. Denny Griswold, *Public Relations News,* 127 East 80th St., New York, NY 10021 as cited by Dennis L. Wilcox, Phillip H. Ault, and Warren K. Agee, *Public Relations Strategies and Tactics* (New York: Harper-Collins Publishers, 1992), p. 7.

9. Dennis L. Wilcox, Phillip H. Ault, and Warren K. Agee, *Public Relations Strategies and Tactics* (New York: HarperCollins Publishers, 1992), p. 6.

10. Leslie W. Kindred, *School Public Relations* (Englewood Cliffs, NJ: Prentice-Hall, 1957), p. 16.

11. *Evaluating Your School PR Investment* (Arlington, VA: National School Public Relations Association, 1985), p. 48.

12. Albert E. Holliday, "In Search of an Answer: What Is School Public Relations?" *Journal of Educational Public Relations* 11 (2nd Quarter 1988), p. 12.

3

UNDERSTANDING THE COMMUNITY

For communication to take place with any assurance, those sending the message must study the intended audience. Otherwise, the content, form, and timing of the message may not be suitable for the receiver of the communications. This understanding of the audience is especially necessary when schools are attempting to communicate with the community.

A major step in developing a school public relations program is collecting information that will enable school districts to know the community in which the program will function. Understanding the community makes it possible to plan more intelligently and to reduce substantially the guesswork that would otherwise take place. Pertinent data about the community should reveal the following:

— Existing needs and expectations of citizens regarding public education
— Opportunities and means for effecting better cooperative relations with various publics
— The nature of the power structure and the areas of decision making
— Immediate and long-term problems that need attention
— Gaps that should be filled in order to produce more public understanding of educational policies and programs
— Situations to be avoided due to a past history of conflict
— An identification of those individuals and groups who are friendly or unfriendly toward public education
— The channels through which public opinion is built in the community
— Changes that are occurring in patterns of community life
— Leadership and leadership influence

— The number and types of organizations and social agencies existing in the community.

In order to comprehend all of these factors, the study of the community should be directed at its sociological characteristics, the nature and influence of its power structure, and the way in which people think and feel about education and the program provided by the district. And since the community is constantly changing, continuing studies are necessary in order to keep knowledge current.

SOCIOLOGICAL INVENTORY

Program planning calls for a factual knowledge of the people who make up the community. The more that is known about them, the better the chances are of designing a program that will achieve its objectives. Accordingly, it is recommended that individual school districts undertake a sociological inventory of their communities. This inventory should be comprehensive enough to cover the pertinent characteristics of the population and detailed enough to supply essential information.

All too frequently, however, inventories of this kind lose their value because they become burdensome and ineffective. Those who conduct them include so many aspects of land, people, and culture that they seldom finish the task. There is likewise the possibility inherent in a long and comprehensive inventory of going through the process of collecting data but then not interpreting the findings and using the results. This failure is apt to occur when the quantity of detailed information reaches proportions that make it difficult to handle. Many school systems hesitate about undertaking a sociological inventory because of the time, labor, and money involved.

It is far better to limit the inventory to those selected characteristics of the community that feed directly into the planning process and, as experience is gained or further need arises, to increase the scope and depth of the study at a later date.

In considering what items to include in an inventory, help can be obtained by reviewing various community survey outlines or procedures for studying the community. These include such topics as the geographic setting, customs and traditions, historical background, material and human resources, age and gender distribution, educational achievement, occupational groupings, social structure, organizations and groups, political structure, leadership, power alignments, religious affiliations, housing, population mobility, racial and ethnic composition, economic life, transportation, communication, and standards of living, health, and recreation. Rather than trying to include all of these items, it is proposed here that the number be reduced and restricted initially to those that can be determined in a short period of time and can be used at once in shaping the program and setting up immediate and long-term goals.

It is recommended, therefore, that the inventory concentrate on customs and traditions, population characteristics, communication channels, community groups, leadership, economic conditions, political structure, social tensions, and previous community efforts.

Customs and Traditions

Customs and traditions are the common ideas, attitudes, and habits of people. They may be referred to as folkways, mores, or lifestyles. Significant in regulating conduct and in predicting behavior, they likewise exert an influence in the shaping of social action and in the determination of services rendered by community agencies.

Lifestyle differences found among community groups arise from the impact of race, religion, nationality background, economics, politics, and social-class structure. Thus individuals who live in an urban ghetto and share similar ethnic characteristics may differ sharply in their way of life, their values, their beliefs, and their habits from individuals who reside in a semirural community. Similar differences in lifestyle can be found among groups who reside in various geographic sections that comprise a metropolitan area. One may consist of a group having a predominantly Italian background, another a Polish background, and a third a microcosm of the entire population.

The problem in this part of the sociological inventory is that of identifying and defining the customs of groups in the community. This information is important to the school in guiding its relations with pupils, parents, and others. Nothing evokes a quicker reaction from parents and citizens than the adoption of policies and practices that run counter to their established attitudes, beliefs, and habits. This has been evident on many occasions when new blocks of subject matter, introduced into the curriculum, caused pupils to think or act contrary to the convictions held by parents and relatives. Equally strong reactions are likely if pupils are retained after school on days that have been set aside for religious instruction.

From another point of view, it is valuable to know how change takes place in group patterns of thought and action. What are the circumstances and forces that produce orderly change? Studies indicate that safe and rapid change occurs during periods of emergency when the need to make adjustments is immediate. Alterations in the physical features of a community, like the construction of new highways, the improvement of housing, or the rezoning of land use, open the way for modifying social habits and customs. Significant changes are also possible when members of different groups are given opportunities to discuss and share in the finding of solutions to problems that have an effect on their ways of living.

A note of caution is in order here about stereotyping people and groups. "Stereotyping is the process of assigning fixed labels or categories to things and people we encounter or, the reverse of this, placing things and people we encounter into fixed categories we have already established."[1] We tend to do this with community groups such as senior citizens and yuppies. Not all senior citizens are poor, against education, and ancient in their thinking. Nor do all yuppies send their children to private schools. And not all members of a race have the same attitudes, opinions, or voting patterns.

Population Characteristics

Population characteristics concerning educational attainment, age, sex, gainful occupation, race, creed, and nationality are important in developing an understanding of the community. Publications and services from the U. S. Census Bureau are helpful in getting population characteristics.

In looking at the educational attainments of the population, attention is directed to the years of formal schooling completed by adults. The amount of schooling may be classified as elementary, secondary, and college, unless the exact number of years is wanted. This information is useful in the preparation of printed materials. Vocabulary, style, and layout are fitted to the educational backgrounds of the audiences for whom they are intended. This information is also useful in estimating the best manner of transmitting ideas and factual information to the community so that attention and interest are generated. Another use of educational attainment information is constructing stratified samples of the population for purposes of opinion polling.

Age data should be broken down into convenient classifications and the implications carefully studied. For example, one community may expect an increase in school enrollments over the next five years, whereas another may just hold its own or suffer a loss. Age distribution may also suggest ideas concerning the vitality of the community. A fairly young adult population would certainly be more demanding of educa-

tional quality than a population having mostly middle-aged and older people. Similarly, the younger group would undoubtedly support better financing of the school program, while the older and more conservative groups would resist an increase in educational expenditures. Thus it is possible from age distribution to form working estimates of community reaction to various kinds of proposals.

In addition to educational achievement, age distribution and sex distribution are used as control factors in constructing stratified random samples of the population for purposes of opinion polling. Analysis of data regarding sex distribution may help to create a better understanding of the labor force and to determine the dominant sex in certain groups to whom appeals should be made.

Occupational information on gainfully employed adults may be organized according to the classification scheme[2] used in the U. S. census reports. These data are useful in checking population stability, changing occupational opportunities, distribution of occupational classes, and employment outside the community. Findings influence the selection of program activities. The participation of citizens is additionally considered.

The study of population characteristics should be rounded out with data about race, religion, and nationality. These cultural factors are important to gain an understanding of the community and some of the underlying causes of social tension and conflict. However, the meaning of the data may not always be clear unless the data are correlated with other information. It is well to treat the data statistically and prepare summaries of the findings. These summaries should be used in the planning process, and copies of them should be distributed to key personnel within the system. At the same time, as much of the information as possible should be depicted on social base maps, with separate sections being blown up for use in individual attendance areas. Statistical summaries and social base maps often provide leads to the solution of everyday problems that are associated with school and community relations.

Communication Channels

Since the development of public opinion takes place through the exchange of ideas and information, it is necessary to know what communication channels are available in the community, how extensively they are used, and which ones are most effective for reaching different segments of the public. These questions are sometimes difficult to answer, but they can be worked out by persistent inquiry. It may be found that the public at large relies on radio, television, and daily newspapers for most of its information so that the media are influential in shaping public opinion on some social issues. But the investigation may reveal that members of special groups in the community receive information from a variety of other sources. These may include publications of clubs and organizations, religious pulpits, labor union headquarters, volunteer fire companies, neighborhood newspapers, and foreign-language newspapers. On this last source of information, it is reasonable to assume that parents who speak and read a foreign language in the home may experience some difficulty in understanding report cards, school notices, and school news in local dailies. Where these conditions prevail, it would be advantageous for the school district to employ a number of bilingual home and school visitors, print school materials in more than one language, and prepare news releases for foreign-language periodicals and newspapers.

Community Groups

The American community is a composite of groups of people who are organized around special interests. Some of the groups have little or no influence on community affairs, but others have a great deal. Many are highly cooperative with those who hold similar interests, but a number are in conflict. The variety is tremendous, and the numbers vary considerably from community to community. Informal groups that come into existence because of some common belief or cause may assume many different forms and often blend into a formal type of organization. No sociological inventory is complete without knowing the purposes and programs of these groups and the influence they exert on public opinion.

A number of groups sponsor programs with educational features that parallel the welfare and instructional services of the school. These groups show concern for public education and stand ready to cooperate with school officials. This has been true of labor unions. They have maintained from their beginning a platform in support of free, universal education and the enactment of legislation for increasing educational opportunities. Luncheon clubs, like Rotary, Kiwanis, and Lions, sponsor projects for the welfare of school children. A few national organizations with local branches devote a major portion of their activities to the promotion of better citizenship and the advancement of American ideals and institutions. There is no end of groups that work on problems of juvenile delinquency, recreation, family life, vocational guidance and career education, museums, libraries, aid for handicapped children, and other commendable services. Many offer excellent opportunities for the articulation of their programs with those of the school.

Although cooperation with community groups having an educative function to perform should be encouraged fully, care must be taken to prevent their possible exploitation of pupils. To some, cooperation means the right to insist that the school approve their requests and modify its program to achieve the ends they are working for. To others, cooperation is nothing more than a guise for the privilege of disseminating propaganda in the classroom, promoting product sales and services, and conducting contests for the sake of publicity.

On the other hand, there are community organizations that dominate school politics but are not concerned primarily with educational matters. Composed of small business groups, property and homeowners' associations, and civic improvement leagues for the most part, they take practically no interest in such things as dropout rates, pupil standardized test scores, or the qualifications and selection of professional school personnel. Instead they are concerned about the impact of school policies on the community and take a strong interest in school costs, especially tax increases and bond proposals.

Other community organizations are those known as special interest groups. Many of these are vehemently opposed to each other; even so, they all converge on schools and pressure them to accept their philosophical positions and to alter educational programs. Often they move to change the school curriculum and to censure textbooks and library books. In any inventory of the community, school officials should attempt to identify special interest groups, become familiar with their philosophies, and perhaps anticipate and prepare for their contacts with the schools.

The question should be raised in the course of the survey about the extent to which individuals and families participate in the activities of organized groups, particularly those having to do with civic welfare. The amount of participation is usually a rather reliable index of community spirit. Research in sociology shows that individuals and families who are active in organized group programs likewise take a strong interest in what happens to their community and that those who are inactive or take part occasionally show only slight interest in needed community improvements.

It is a wise procedure to record on file cards specific types of information on all community groups. Each card should show the name of a given organization, past and present officers, membership size, purposes, programs, operational methods, accomplishments, and attitudes toward public education. With this information at hand, judgments can be made about the amount of cooperation and support that will be given for the modification and improvement of education in the local school system.

Leadership

The next aspect of the inventory concerns the status of leadership in the community. Leadership is a relational concept implying two things, namely, the influencing agent and the persons who are influenced. In other words, when persons are influenced to express organizational behavior on a matter of group concern, then leadership has occurred. Even though this concept may seem too simple and may represent a variance from others that could be cited, it nevertheless provides a feasible base for the examination of leadership and the leadership process.

At this point, it might be well to review a few findings from leadership studies without getting involved in too many details. Leadership is not related necessarily to social status or position in the community. An individual usually holds a position of leadership because his or her characteristics approximate the norms or goals of the group. It is equally true that leaders have traits that set them apart from their followers, but these traits may vary from one situation to another. However, all leaders usually have certain characteristics in common, such as special competence in dealing with a particular matter, wide acquaintanceship, easy accessibility, and contact with information sources outside of their immediate circle. Also, they are sometimes members of several community organizations and have more exposure than nonleaders to mass media. These characteristics are acknowledged as important, but they will not necessarily produce leadership. One school of thought sees leadership more as a consequence of an individual's occupying a certain kind of position in the social system, while another view holds that leadership is a situational matter requiring a particular issue and the exercise of influence on others.

In any event, the inventory task is that of identifying individuals who are recognized leaders of community groups and organizations and who have an influence on the attitudes and opinions of the members. Information should be obtained about their personal backgrounds, family connections, group affiliations, business interests, fraternal memberships, social and political convictions, special competencies, methods of operation, attitudes toward public education, and power in the community. Knowing their backgrounds is requisite to approaching group leaders on educational community problems and to determining their value in rendering particular services.

In working with leaders, it must be remembered that they are not always free to express their own ideas or to take independent action. Their behavior is dependent on the nature of their groups and the beliefs and opinions of the members. They are especially sensitive to questions concerning patriotism, private property, economics, religion, politics, and respected conventions. They realize that any radical departure from the feelings and convictions of their followers on matters like these could quickly undermine their own security. Leadership, however, is a reciprocal arrangement in that group members depend on leaders to initiate ideas and execute plans of action. The leaders sense what members think and want, and so they can direct thought along lines that meet with acceptance. In doing this they play a powerful role in the determination of the attitudes and opinions held by their followers.

The study of leadership should extend to neighborhoods in elementary- and secondary-school attendance areas. Every neighborhood contains a number of men and women who are consulted by neighbors and friends whenever questions come up about the school and its relations with pupils and parents. Their opinions and judgments are important determinants of grass-roots public opinion. It is vital to locate these individuals and to involve them in school activities. They become channels through which the school may be interpreted better on a neighborhood basis, and they can do much to win loy-

alty and support for institutional policies and practices.

Economic Conditions

An analysis of economic conditions will provide essential data for obtaining a better understanding of the community. Though a great deal of information about the economics of the community is available in governmental and business reports, the concern here is to get an overview picture. The picture should be limited to generalized findings on agricultural, commercial, industrial, and transportation activities and to employment, employment stability, and wage conditions. Related information on land use, property values, and tax rates should be consulted. Such information is usually available in the school system's business office, which plays an important part in the planning of the annual school district budget. If further data are wanted, attention should be directed to such items as production output, retail stores, levels of income, amount of savings, and standard of living. These details are relevant, as economic conditions determine in some measure the financial support available for public education. Moreover, these conditions affect public feelings toward the school and the means used for trying to bring about closer relations between the school and the community.

Political Structure

For generations the public school has tried to uphold the idea of keeping politics out of education and education out of politics. It has done this on the assumption that the school as a nonpartisan, classless, and social institution should remain apart from the political life of the community. As meritorious as this may seem on the surface, the truth is that the school cannot and should not separate itself from the political scene.

More money is spent for education at state and local levels than for any other single function of government. This fact alone makes education a thoroughly political enterprise. The support received is the product of political struggles for the tax dollar. These struggles involve the interaction of special-interest groups, political leaders, members of legislative bodies, boards and departments of education, opinion leaders, professional educators, and others. Such items as formulae for the distribution of state aid to local districts, the location, size, and cost of school buildings, and the assessment of property tax rates are frequently matters of political conflict and resolution.

If educational leaders are to cope successfully with the problem of getting adequate public support, they need to acquire a sophisticated understanding of political realities. They should seek this understanding through a somewhat detailed study of the political structure and the political process within the local area. It is important that they know who makes political decisions, how they are carried out, and what political instruments are available to them. In some matters, a similar type of study should be extended to state and even national levels.

Social Tensions

Social tensions and conflicts exist wherever people work and live together. Some are normal expressions of human behavior; others are indications of weakness in the social structure. These tensions are evident in the refusal of neighbors to speak to one another, sectional conflicts over the location of new school buildings, claims that the board of education is favoring the better residential part of the district, interracial confrontations, gang warfare in metropolitan centers, the formation of cliques within parent-teacher associations, and open discrimination against minority groups.

The causes of social tensions may be nothing more than personality clashes, misunderstandings, spite, or petty annoyances, but they may also be associated with economic rivalry, cultural differences, social class competition, ra-

cial discrimination, religious conflict, and other major aspects of society. These tensions, no matter what the causes, are disruptive to life in the community.

In the planning of a school-community relations program, the school must be fully aware of the causes of tension and the amount of bitterness involved. If the school is not knowledgeable about these conditions, it is likely to move in directions that will increase the tensions and deepen the cleavages that exist. Its real job is trying to harmonize differences between individuals and groups in the community when the tensions militate against the operation of the school and the attainment of its objectives.

Sources of Information

If the superintendent of schools and members of the administrative team will start the survey by listing questions for which data are wanted, they will be pleasantly surprised to discover how much they know about the community. The answers they provide can then be supplemented from other sources of information. A valuable and readily accessible source is school records. The entry blanks that children fill out when they first enroll in school contain information on family backgrounds. If used in accordance with the Family Rights and Privacy Act (the Buckley Amendment), these records can provide important demographics of a specific segment of the community. When an annual or biennial census is taken in the district, the returns may supply similar information and other items not contained in the previous records. If supplemental data are wanted, they can easily be obtained by means of questionnaires administered to pupils. These sources furnish a good picture of home and family conditions in the community.

There are also numerous sources of printed materials that are available covering practically all aspects of the needed survey. City directories and telephone books contain the names of organized groups in the community. United States census statistics give detailed information on population. If the community is too small for inclusion in the printed tracts, the information can be secured by writing the Bureau of the Census. Most social agencies maintain records that are useful on a number of points. Excellent data are available from the local chamber of commerce. City, county, and state historical societies and planning commissions have documentary materials that throw light on the growth of the community. A review of newspaper files tells an interesting story of happenings, traditional observances, community efforts, group tensions and conflicts, and outstanding leaders. Publications by the Department of Commerce are helpful in understanding the economic life of the community, and the publications of governmental planning boards often prove to be highly valuable sources of broad information. Encyclopedias may be used for biographical information, religious customs, traditional observances, and related items. The minutes of boards of education meetings are sometimes a rich source of data on leaders, group programs, tensions, sectional conflicts, and relations with the community.

Additional information may be gathered through personal interviews with prominent residents of the community. These individuals know a good many of the intimate details of social life that are seldom publicized. Although the reliability of their statements may be open to question, they can be cross-checked when a sufficient amount of information has been collected by this method. The success of these interviews will depend on how well they are planned and conducted.

An inventory should be made of what the instructional and noninstructional staff members know. Those who have lived for some years in the community may prove to be valuable sources of information. This can be done by asking them to fill out questionnaires designed especially for the survey. Comparison of tabulated replies may be used to test the accuracy and completeness of their information.

POWER STRUCTURES

After completing the sociological inventory, attention should be turned to the power structure or structures and decision making in the community. The concern here is that of understanding the essential characteristics of the power structures, the areas in which they operate, and the effects of power decisions on educational policy and the school program.

In every community there are people who exercise considerable control over decisions relating to social, economic, and political matters. They obtain this power for a variety of reasons like family background, financial status, political leadership, social influence, property ownership, or labor connections. Mostly, they are members of informal groups that sustain themselves through mutual interests. And because these relationships can be described as a structured way of influencing community decisions, they are identified as power structures.

A *power structure* is an interrelationship among individuals with vested interests who have the ability or authority to control other people, to obtain their conformity, or to command their services. They are accorded this power because of their involvement in the decision-making process and the influence they have on decisional outcomes.

Types of Structures

Power structures may be categorized by types. One of the types that sociologists seem partial to is known as the *elite* power model. According to this model, the community power structure is pyramidal, the base representing the lower echelons of power distribution and the apex representing the high concentration of power. The high concentration is in the hands of a small, elite group that represents the industrial, commercial, and financial interests in the community. In some instances, though, dominance is derived from religion, political party, race, or some other source.

Those at the top tend to be the same persons who exercise control both over matters of basic public policy and those that impinge on their immediate concerns. These are the individuals to see before any major community project or undertaking is launched.

A determination of who these persons are may be made through using the "reputational" approach. In using this approach, a panel of individuals is selected from among holders of public office, officers of civic organizations, members of professions, and representatives from other sectors of the community. Each of these panel members is asked separately to name persons who in his or her judgment have the most influence in the community decision-making process. Those who are named by panel members are asked in turn to identify leaders, usually a specified number, whom they consider to be the most influential. This process may be repeated again if further narrowing down or refinement is wanted. In any case, this system does make it possible to perceive the hierarchy of power in a community and bring out the identity of persons reputed to be powerful.

Instead of having one elite power group, some communities may have at least two, with each vying for control over important decisions. Generally, in these situations the sides are rather evenly drawn and the structures of the power models are alike. Another type is known as *pluralistic* or *diffused* because it has several centers of power. Those who hold to this categorization do not accept the idea that only one or two elite power groups make community decisions. They believe instead that most communities contain many groups that are highly influential and that each one concerns itself with a different issue or issues. This being so, no two issues are likely to be handled by the same leaders or those who help to determine the final decision. The small group that controls urban development is not the same small group that influences political decisions, or the same small group that makes welfare policy. The nature of the groups may be determined by

studying significant issues that arise and collecting evidence about those who take an active part in decision-making processes.

The last type of power structure is one perhaps that does not belong in the typology being used. Found commonly in rural settings, it is known as the *amorphous* type. In this type, power is basically absent or, better still, latent. It resembles a condition that is controlled by those who maintain the status quo. As expected, no radical experimentation occurs in these communities unless an emergency situation arises.

Power structures vary not only from community to community in interesting and discernible ways, but also at different times within the same community as efforts are made to establish working power arrangements. On this latter point, Sumption and Engstrom describe the evolutionary stages through which a power structure may pass.

> In brief, in new, growing, and developing communities and those with great population mobility, we might expect to find a rather rudimentary pluralistic structure of power. The second stage of development would be characterized by rather specialized power structures in each of a number of issue areas. The third stage of development would be found in the older, more stabilized communities where the power groups would tend to be fused into a single unit. How well integrated this unit would be would depend on a number of factors related to the community.[3]

The factors referred to include such variables as community size, economic base, political alignment, social life, labor unions, and absentee ownership.

General Characteristics

If the school is to deal intelligently with the power structure or structures in the community, it should have some knowledge of the characteristics peculiar to this form of organization. As pointed out previously, power structures are controlled by people of influence who try to shape community decisions in ways that either protect or advance their own interests or do both. Those who constitute the power structure may have few if any scruples about getting what they want. They are usually individuals with high intelligence and real leadership ability; otherwise it is doubtful if they would be able to command the status they enjoy.

Members of power structures are drawn from a wide cross section of community life. They may be professional people, business executives, bankers, labor leaders, land speculators, newspaper publishers, or industrialists. Many of them make it a point to be associated with influential clubs and organizations where they have numerous contacts with others of their kind and where they can use the membership to spread their propaganda and to mobilize popular support for policies and projects they favor. They do this very quietly and without thrusting themselves into the limelight. Typically, they use a secondary corps of influential individuals to handle matters for them and to report on the nature of public sentiment toward their proposals and the effectiveness of the strategies being employed.

Interestingly enough, power structure members are sincerely concerned with the well-being of the community, especially from an economic point of view. They know that if the community moves ahead and enjoys prosperity, they stand to gain as well. It is not unusual for them to assist in bringing new industries into the community, to put pressure on politicians for modifications in the local tax structure, or to secure public funds for such items as urban redevelopment, a new highway, or a recreational area. However, when the public welfare on an issue does not coincide with their interests, they may take steps to swing the decision in their own favor.

Members of power structures find it advantageous to align themselves with political parties and holders of public offices. This allegiance gives them not only an opportunity to know what issues are under consideration but also an oppor-

tunity to influence the decisions that are made. For example, knowing some months in advance of public announcement that a superhighway will be constructed around the borders of the community enables them to purchase land at reasonable prices and to locate motels, stores, gas stations, and other businesses from which large profits can be reaped.

Power structures influence decision making through a system of rewards and punishments. Rewards are given for going along with the wishes of the power group. These rewards may take the form of advancements to positions of higher social or economic status in the community, such as chairing of prestigious committees, and membership in socially prominent clubs and organizations. Often such rewards consist of monetary gains through means of stock options, franchises, land investments, information on public contracts, and so on. On the other side, punishment is meted out to those who do not comply with the wishes of the power group, and this may take the form of a loss of social position, occupational status, and economic welfare. Punitive measures include such examples as the failure to renew a business contract, refusal of membership in a country club, transfer to a position of lesser importance, reduction in purchase of goods and services, or the stirring up of labor troubles. At times the retribution may be handled so cleverly that the victim is scarcely aware of what is happening.

Due to the lack of social responsibility on the part of power structure members, the community and its citizens pay a price for such individuals' influence on decision making. Instances are legion where sound social proposals have been defeated because they ran contrary to the interests of the power structure, whereas socially undesirable proposals were adopted because they represented the wishes of this group. But since power structures are an integral part of the American scene and do influence decisions affecting public education, the school must learn to live with them and to neutralize some of their actions when necessary.

The Schools and Power Structures

How can a board of education and its professional leaders handle incursions of power structures into school matters? As suggested earlier, an assessment must first be made of the structures existing in the community with reference to action of participants in decision making and issue resolution. Some of the questions that must be answered in this assessment, according to Kimbrough and Nunnery, are as follows:

> What significant decisions have been made that influenced community living within recent years? Who were the leaders who exercised the most power in these decisions? What are some impending decisions in the community and who are the persons actively influencing these decisions? How do the leaders work together and compete in exercising power? Who are the persons in the local structure who have influence with state and national power wielders? What major formal and informal subsystems exist? What beliefs about community living and community norms give direction to community leaders? What is the extent of citizen participation in community decision making? What are the latent sources of political power that are not involved in decisions but which could influence decision outcomes if they were active?[4]

There are many opportunities available for acquiring the necessary information with which to answer these and similar types of questions. Among them are continual scrutiny of stories carried in local newspapers, simplified content analysis of public documents, informal conversations with friends and colleagues, utilization of informative contacts through involvement in civic organizations and social activities, attendance at meetings where proposals are under consideration, and long-term observation of selected individuals connected with the power structure. Consistent collection and study of such information enable the board and its professional leaders to understand what they are dealing with and to note shifts taking place in the district's power picture.

Power structure members often take a direct interest in some phase of school operation. On occasion they will try to block proposed changes in curricular policies and programs when these represent a possible departure from the established way of doing things. They will profess a concern for school welfare and progress and will support a millage increase or a bond issue, but usually their interest centers on the financial side of the school where decisions about the spending of money can result in a profit to them. They may try to influence the selection of school building sites or the placement of contracts for new and remodeled construction, for transportation of pupils, and for insurance. They likewise want a share in the thousands of dollars that are spent annually for supplies, equipment, and textual materials.

Perhaps the best protection the school has against power structure pressures on financial and other decisions is a well-planned and carefully implemented program in school and community relations. By taking parents and other citizens into complete confidence about the institution, its policies, its needs, its operating procedures, its problems, and its accomplishments, the school can develop sufficiently intelligent and supportive public opinion to offset the influence of the power wielders.

It has been apparent that properly organized citizen and advisory committees and groups of concerned parents have had a constructive effect on power groups. They have forced them to support needed school improvements in some instances and to withdraw power plays in others. They have demonstrated clearly that an enlightened public can become a force in society that power dealers are reluctant to encounter.

MEASURING PUBLIC OPINION

Measuring attitudes and opinions of taxpayers, parents, teachers, and pupils regarding education and the local school system is a third avenue through which community cooperation is accomplished. Sociological inventory and power structure analysis provide an informational framework within which the community relations program will be carried on. On the other hand, measurement of attitudes and opinions tells how people think and feel about the school system. It also tells what should be done to increase public understanding, support, and participation in the schools.

Opinion Research Technique

Opinion research started in the field of marketing and soon spread to other walks of life. Its reliability has been demonstrated over and over again in predicting election results, ascertaining consumer wants, determining audience reactions, modifying products, and forecasting trends in public thought and action. Schools have been somewhat slow to employ opinion research, despite its proven worth, in the planning and evaluating of their community relations programs. There has been, however, a noticeable gain in the number of school systems either undertaking their own studies of public opinion or hiring commercial firms to do this work for them. Increasingly, they are coming to realize the value of having precise knowledge of the opinions held by a specific group of people or those held by a representative cross section of the population.

Opinion research is indispensable in the planning, conducting, and evaluating of the school-community relations program. It may be used to determine how people get their information about the schools, to learn how citizens judge the quality of their schools and the criteria they employ, to ascertain whether a proposed change will arouse controversy, to discover if a shift is taking place in public opinion, to find out how well the public understands the education program, to locate points of popular satisfaction and dissatisfaction with the school system, to identify problems that must be solved before increased cooperation and support can be expected, and to know the educational goals and aspirations of parents and citizens.

Opinion research can likewise reveal areas of improvement desired by citizens, their relative willingness to support financially the educational program, the nature of misinformation they possess, the motivations behind their defeat of a tax levy or a bond proposal, and the kind of information they want and how they want to get it.

As an extra dividend, opinion research actually stimulates the individuals who are contacted to form opinions about the subject being investigated. Individuals who have not thought seriously about the schools and school programs for some years are forced to do some thinking about them when their opinions are being sought in a research study. Moreover, they feel important for being asked their opinions.

When applied to staff members and pupils, opinion research discloses their attitudes toward the institution and the values they place on its policies and practices. The capable administrator uses this information to improve internal relationships and to make appropriate changes in the management of the school.

Types of Opinion Research

Opinion research comes under many names, scientific and unscientific, formal and informal, and probability and nonprobability. The name is determined by the manner in which the research is carried out. The results of unscientific, informal, or nonprobability opinion research cannot be projected to the total group from which the sample is taken with any statistical assurance. On the other hand, the results from scientific, formal, or probability opinion research can be. The reason lies in how the respondents are selected to participate in the research. Only in the scientific, formal, or probability method is everybody in a population given an equal chance of being selected, the criterion used to determine if the results of a sample represent the thinking of a larger group.

Examples of unscientific opinion research methods are forums and conferences; advisory committees; some consumer panels; key communicators; mail surveys; newspaper, radio, TV, and magazine surveys; and some quota surveys. Among the scientific methods are systematic, stratified, and area or cluster surveys.

The following descriptions of selected opinion research methods—forums and conferences, advisory committees, consumer panels, key communicators, and public opinion surveys—are designed to acquaint school personnel with some of their options.

Forums and Conferences.   Open forums are a method of getting frank discussion by a selected group of persons on some educational topic of current interest to taxpayers, parents, teachers, or pupils. The discussants are asked to state their views on topics such as the construction of a middle school as a new unit in the structural arrangement of the school system, and the reasons for their views. After a specific period of time, people in the audience are invited to direct questions to the speakers or to express their own opinions. An attempt is then made to summarize the entire discussion and to estimate how those present stand on the question. Sometimes this estimate represents the judgment of the chairperson or the collective judgment of an evaluation committee. Sometimes it is based on a show of hands in response to specific questions asked by the chairperson or on the oral and written comments received shortly after the close of the meeting.

Open forums lend themselves well to radio and television presentations. Such forums evoke wide interest if the issue under discussion is one of community concern and sufficient publicity is built up in advance. Interest is added when participants are known and carefully chosen. Open forums are used commonly in parent-teacher association meetings and in high school assemblies with students in charge. Open forums are difficult to defend on the basis of scientific appraisal of public opinion. They do, however, enable school officials to get rough but significant measures of how people think and to discover areas of their

satisfaction or dissatisfaction. These forums have the added advantage at times of releasing tensions and enabling those who are interested to express themselves freely.

Advisory Committees.   The advisory committee concept centers on the idea that a selected group of laypersons, representing a balanced cross section of interest groups, can express the needs and reflect the opinions of the community. Meeting with school officials on a systemwide or on an individual school basis, the members of the advisory committee are asked to suggest what should be done in solving the educational problems that are presented to them. Their recommendations are in no way binding and can be accepted or rejected. This method affords educators a practical device for evaluating group attitudes. Although there is always the danger of assuming that the personal opinions of committee members are those of the group they represent, the danger lessens as experience is gained in using the method and as the personalities of participants are better understood. Moreover, this system familiarizes people with school problems and brings out their reactions before decisions are made. See Chapter 8 for more details.

Panels.   Panels, also referred to as focus panels, are another approach to the measurement of public opinion. This procedure calls for the selection of a panel or jury of laypersons who are interviewed by trained members of the school staff. Panel members are usually either selected to include representatives from organized interest groups or chosen in accordance with criteria for a stratified sample of the community.

Two types of panels have a place in the measurement of opinion on matters involving public schools. One type is highly transitory and may be regarded as a one-shot affair. It is used for observing changes in opinions or behavior caused by a particular action or experiment entered into by the local district. As an example, let us say the system increases class size, or eliminates some extracurricular activities, or establishes experimentally a year-round school. An initial set of interviews is held before any of these changes occurs in order to record attitudes and opinions on the subject at the time. The interviews are held either individually or collectively with panel members. Then, after the change occurs, a second set of interviews is carried out to determine the effect of the change on members' opinions and behavior. Once this is done, the panel members are dismissed.

In the second type of panel, the members serve on a continuing basis. Interviews are held with them individually in order to elicit their opinions on a scheduled series of open-ended questions and to estimate the intensity of their attitudes and feelings. Interviews are conducted informally without reference to any printed set of questions, and the length of the interview is left to the discretion of the parties. When the interview is over, conversational highlights are recorded in private by the interviewer on prepared forms.

Research on the continuing type of panel indicates that such interviews reveal emotional tones in opinions; the nature and amount of information, as well as misinformation, about topics under discussion; the qualifications attached to stated opinions; the contradictions in expressions of beliefs; and some of the reasons underlying favorable and unfavorable points of view. It has been found that repeated interviews with properly selected panel members not only give a statistically reliable measure of opinion but also bring out causes for shifts in opinion. However, repeated interviews with the same individuals over a long period of time may produce mental sets that consciously or unconsciously bias their replies. To meet this problem, continuing panel operations can provide for the rotation of panel members, with a limit placed on the length of time to be served by any one person.

Key Communicator Program.   Another method of getting opinion feedback from a community is through the key communicator program. It calls for identifying those people in a community who sit on top of a hypothetical pyramid of communi-

cations and asking them to pass along information from the schools to the community. Conversely, they are asked to relay information about the community to the school officials. They are usually invited to a luncheon or a get-together to talk informally about the schools. The program can be very effective in identifying and squelching rumors in a community. It can also provide a quick pulse of community thinking on major educational issues. Chapter 8 details the program.

Public Opinion Surveys.   This method of opinion research can provide the most precise results of all techniques mentioned earlier if conducted properly. For this reason more and more schools and organizations are developing solid data bases of community opinions through public opinion polls. Valid results will often silence vocal critics or vehement pressure groups, provide the basis for school officials to make a major decision that will be accepted by the community, and identify community values and priorities for educational programs.

Before surveying a community, a school should give some thought to the method of getting the information on a survey, the sampling technique, the construction and the wording of the questions, interview techniques, the design of the questionnaire, the use of data processing, and the handling of the results.

Methods of Getting the Information.   The four commonly used methods are the personal interview, the telephone interview, the mailed questionnaire, and the drop-off/pick-up questionnaire. In the last method, the survey instrument is delivered to a respondent's home or place of work and a day or so later picked up. Of all these methods the best for comprehensive and usually valid results is the personal interview. The telephone interview is widely used, and the mail questionnaire provides proportionally the lowest returns. Table 3.1 shows the advantages and limitations of all four methods.

The Sampling Technique.   If findings of a survey are to be used to make decisions on budgets,

TABLE 3.1 Advantages and Limitations of Four Methods of Surveying

	Advantages	Limitations
Personal Interview	1. High percentage of returns 2. Information more likely to be correct than that of other methods 3. Possibility of obtaining additional information 4. Clarification of respondent misunderstanding	1. Greater costs in transportation and personnel 2. Trained personnel required 3. Great amount of time needed 4. Guarded access apartments and communities 5. Safety of interviewers
Telphone Interview	1. Inexpensive 2. Short period of time needed to complete survey 3. No cost for transportation 4. Minimal training of personnel	1. Unlisted phones 2. Some families do not have phones 3. Easy for respondent to hang up
Drop-Off/Pick-Up Questionnaire	1. High returns in a short period of time 2. Clarification of respondent misunderstanding 3. Minimal training of personnel	1. Transportation cost 2. Need many volunteers or workers 3. Safety of interviewers
Mailed Questionnaire	1. Mailing costs cheaper than transportation costs 2. Possibility of reaching groups protected from solicitors and investigators 3. Increased candor among respondents	1. Low number of returns 2. Possibility of an irate citizen's collecting many questionnaires from neighbors and answering all of them 3. Total population not represented by responses

personnel, buildings, and programs, the results should be projectable to the entire community or population from which the sample was taken. And this can be done if the sample is selected by random. But random sampling doesn't mean a haphazard selection of respondents. Standing outside a supermarket and selecting every tenth customer won't give you a random sample that would represent the thinking of the entire community.

A sample must represent a larger population if it is to be statistically valid. A sample is to a pollster what a model is to an architect. Each represents a larger entity within a certain degree of accuracy. And a sample will represent a larger population if all the people in the population have an equal chance of being selected.

A properly selected sample of 400 respondents will give you answers that can be projected to a larger population within a predictable 5 percent error. This is true if the population is 4,000 people, 40,000, or 100,000 or more. *The size of the population generally does not determine the size of the sample.* Instead it depends on how close you want the sample to represent the total population and how much time and money are available to do the survey. Gallup believes he can work with a two and one-half percent error in determining what the citizens of the United States think. Therefore, he surveys only about 1,600 people to learn the attitudes of the entire nation. But his sample is valid because every adult in the United States is given an equal chance of being selected. Table 3.2 gives percent of error at the 95

TABLE 3.2 Sample Size for Two Levels of Confidence with Varying Degrees of Tolerance

Tolerance of Error in Percentages (+ or −)	95 times in 100	99 times in 100
0.5	38,400	66,000
0.7	19,592	33,673
1.0	9,600	16,500
1.5	4,267	7,333
2.0	2,400	4,125
2.5	1,536	2,640
3.0	1,067	1,833
3.5	784	1,347
4.0	600	1,031
4.5	474	815
5.0	384	660
6.0	267	458
7.0	196	337
8.0	150	288
9.0	119	204
10.0	96	165
15.0	45	74

times out of 100 and the 99 times out of 100 confidence levels. If the population you wish to survey is fewer than 400 or 500 people, it would be wise to survey everyone rather than take a sample. Attempt to get at least an 80 percent return in order to have the results represent the thinking of all 400 or 500 people.

In order to get a representative sample, you need to work from a list of names (parents, students, employees, graduates, registered voters, or taxpayers). First, divide the number of people you wish to survey (400 gives you about a 5 percent error) into the total number of names on your list. Usually, this interval will be ten or less unless your list is very large. Second, select a starting number by random from one to ten because the interval is ten. This can be done by taking ten 3 X 5 cards and placing one number on each. Select one card. Using that as the starting number, select every tenth name after it as a person to be surveyed. By this method of sampling, known as

systematic sampling, the thinking of those interviewed will represent, with reasonable accuracy, the thinking of a larger population. This is a scientific or probability random sample which can be defended statistically. Usually much criticism of local surveys is leveled at the method of sampling.

In *stratified surveying,* people are selected so that the sample in certain aspects is a small-scale model of the population it is designed to represent. For example, you may be interested in surveying registered voters. As in the systematic method, stratified sampling requires a list from which to work. In reviewing the list, you find that 75 percent of the registered voters did not vote in the last school election and 25 percent did. To stratify the sample of any size, you would choose 75 percent of it from among the nonvoters and 25 percent from the voters by using the interval method described above, thus giving every voter and nonvoter an equal chance of being selected. Assume that a sample of 400 respondents is sought. In order to stratify it as the total list of voters is divided, you would choose 300 respondents from the nonvoters and 100 from the voters.

Area or *cluster surveying* is based on a previous subdivision of the population into areas, the selection of certain of these areas by using a random sampling technique, and the restriction of sampling units to these areas only. For example, the school district is divided into neighborhoods, and a random selection is made among neighborhoods. After sample neighborhoods have been chosen, households would be listed in each of them, and the required number of households would be selected, again using a random probability method. Details of this method can be found in several excellent textbooks and reference manuals on opinion research.

There is, of course, an unscientific or nonprobability random sampling method used in many cases. But you must be careful in what you do with the results. In this type of sampling, you cannot project the results to the entire population. For example, a school district sends a mailed questionnaire to all 11,000 households in a community, and 2,000 are returned. It would be unwise for the board or superintendent to make major decisions based on the answers on the 2,000 returned questionnaires. There is no way of knowing whether they represent the thinking of the entire 11,000 homes in the community. In order for the results to be valid, more than 8,000 questionnaires should have been returned. Such a large response to a mailed questionnaire is highly unlikely. Another unscientific random sampling method is to have someone stand on a busy street corner and interview any one hundred people passing by. The only thing you can do with the results is to say that this is what one hundred people thought. Again, you have no way of knowing whether the sample represents the thinking of the entire community.

Some school districts may use the unscientific random sampling method to start citizens thinking about the schools and to give them a way of "sounding off" about the schools. As a result, some citizens may become more interested and involved in the schools and may help in solving some educational problems. For these reasons, unscientific random sampling may be justified.

The Construction and Wording of Questions. Open-ended and structured questions are the types used in surveying. The difference is that the structured or closed-ended questions have answers to choose from, and the open-ended questions do not. Structured questions are easier to tabulate; open-ended ones can provide information not anticipated.

A survey can be ruined not only by invalid sampling but also by the wording of the questions themselves. Here are some suggestions on how to word questions properly:

- Be as concise as possible.
- Use words and language that respondents understand. For example, a question such as "What is your attitude toward year-round schools?" is likely to be misunderstood. The phrase "year-round" may have different meanings to different people. Does it mean forty-five weeks of school and fifteen days off? Or does it mean two semes-

ters of classes and a semester off? Or does it mean school every week of the year? Most citizens would be unable to answer this question with a valid response.

- Structure questions to provide you with the exact information, not answers, you desire. For example, in the question "How long have you lived here?" you may get answers such as "A long time," "Not too long," or "A good while." These answers are of little value. In such a question, list alternative answers, such as "less than one year; one to five years; six to ten years; more than ten years."

- Avoid leading questions. An example of a leading question is "If your taxes were reduced, would you favor light industry locating in the school district?" The phrase "If your taxes were reduced" is leading. Many people will answer "yes" to any question that will indicate their taxes will be reduced.

- Avoid double-barreled questions, such as "Do you work full- or part-time? Yes—No—" If the respondents work full-time, how do they answer it?

- Avoid ambiguous questions. The question "Don't you think reading should be emphasized in the high school?" is impossible to answer. What does a "yes" answer mean? "Yes, I don't think . . . " or "Yes, I do think. . . ."

- Pretest all questions on a small group similar to the one to be surveyed.

Interview Techniques. In cases where you choose to conduct personal interviews either at the front door or over the phone, interviewers must be recruited and trained. Where can you get volunteer interviewers who will do a good job? One district used young mothers with children not yet in school to do a telephone survey. These young women were enthusiastic about doing something that extended their contacts beyond the home. Senior citizens, parent groups, college students, or community groups can also be helpful if they have proper training.

Each survey situation differs and dictates some variations, but some general rules of interviewing should be followed whether the personal interview method or the telephone interview is used. Whatever the method, interviewers must strive for neutrality, avoiding any possibility of influencing the answers.

Major suggestions for interviewers are as follows:

- In face-to-face interviews, interviewers should dress similar to those people being interviewed to foster better cooperation.
- Interviewers should become thoroughly familiar with the questionnaire, but not memorize the questions.
- Interviewers should follow the wording of the questions exactly.
- Responses to open-ended questions should be recorded exactly as given.
- Interviewers should be friendly and show a genuine interest in the respondent without appearing to be meddling.

At least one training session is necessary for volunteer interviewers. Besides some practice interviewing with each other, the volunteers should be briefed on the purpose of the survey, how the questionnaire was designed, why each question was included, how the interviewees were chosen, and how the data will be processed and analyzed.

The Design of the Questionnaire.   The design of the questionnaire helps respondents cooperate with you without feeling they are being exploited. First, they want to know how long the questionnaire is. If there are too many questions, respondents become frustrated and will not complete the questionnaire. If the copy is crowded and difficult to read, the respondent will give up quickly. If respondents have to work to find the place to check an answer, they will lose enthusiasm. A good rule to follow is to put all possible answers on the right side of the page near the end of the question. (This will make the job of tabulating the results much easier also.)

Whether it is a telephone interview, a mailed questionnaire, or a personal interview, the structure of the questionnaire is basically the same. Each should have an introduction, main section,

and conclusion. The sections should include the following:

Introduction
- A brief description of the purpose of the survey
- The sponsor of the survey
- Instructions on how the questions are to be completed and returned if a written questionnaire is used
- Nonthreatening questions.

Main Section
- Opinion questions that deal with the basic problems the school is attempting to learn about
- Questions in a sequence to provide the respondent with a logical thought process.

Conclusion
- Open-ended questions to get unanticipated information, such as "Are there any other thoughts you have on the East Bank School District?"
- Demographic questions (age, sex, parent or nonparent, length of residency, and so forth)
- A note of thanks.

Use of Data Processing.   Tabulating results by hand takes an inordinate amount of time and is prone to numerous mistakes. With the availability of office computers, it is strongly recommended that data processing be used in determining the results of a survey. It will provide a quick and accurate process of transferring information from numerous questionnaires to a report with total results. Also, data processing will quickly break out information by various demographics, such as the thinking of parents or nonparents, voting or nonvoting taxpayers, male or female, or any other demographic in the survey. If you decide to make use of data processing, be sure to involve the data-processing specialist before the questions and the format of the questionnaire are finalized.

Handling the Results.   If a decision is made to survey a community, a public announcement should be made through radio, TV, newspapers, and the school newsletter. The local citizens and staff need to be informed of the purpose of the survey, the approximate time when it will be conducted, the size of the sample, and that the results will be made public. In these ways, citizens are alerted to the possibility that an interviewer may call on them.

When the results are tabulated, they should be published. Otherwise, people will feel that you are hiding something. One of the surest ways of reducing credibility with the public is to hide the results of the survey. A definite procedure should be followed in revealing the results of the survey. The sponsors (usually the board of education) of the survey should know the results first, followed by those who worked on the survey, employees, and students. Once the internal public is informed, release the results to the media in the form of a news release or news conference. Finally, the detailed answers to each question in the survey should be highlighted in a school newsletter or other external publications. (See Figure 3.1.)

Provided that school officials construct and conduct surveys carefully, results will provide valuable information about the concerns and attitudes of citizens, and in the long term, help schools continue to bridge the school-community gap.

Planning for Opinion Studies

Before detailed plans for making opinion studies are developed, the administrator should answer certain questions to his or her own satisfaction and to that of the board of education. The questions that need to be answered are the following:

Exactly What Is the Problem To Be Studied? Too often individuals are carried away by their enthusiasm for something they believe is important without taking the time to consider just what the problem is and what kinds of facts are needed to solve it. This is evident in some of the questionnaires that school systems have devised for

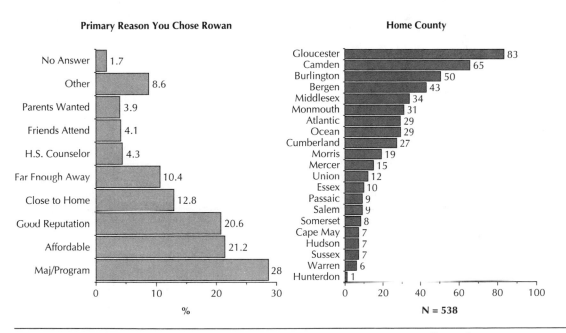

FIGURE 3.1 Graphs Taken from a Freshman Survey Report (1992) at Rowan College of New Jersey. Reprinted with permission.

appraising the attitudes and opinions of parents and taxpayers.

The school administrator will strengthen his or her case and gain board support more readily if he or she has defined the problem and has outlined the exact points to be studied. This is illustrated in the work done by one superintendent who was faced with a steady barrage of criticism about the schools. An investigation of the problem brought out the fact that several individuals were openly declaring that the public had lost confidence in the educational program. With the permission of the board, the superintendent undertook a series of interviews with all persons known to be skeptical and antagonistic toward the schools. From these interviews he was able to determine the exact points around which most of the criticism revolved. He then formulated a statement of the problem and the points needing investigation. The board approved his statement in short order and then voted the money for conducting an opinion survey. They wished to find out whether confidence in the schools had been destroyed and, specifically, what practices were under strongest protest. The results of the survey showed conclusively that the large majority of people believed in the worth of the instructional program and had faith in the competency of the administration. The results showed further that most of the opposition stemmed from a small but articulate minority who misunderstood many of the practices they were complaining about.

Too much emphasis cannot be placed on the advisability of formulating the problem for study in writing and attaching to this statement the reason why this information is required to solve the problem. This becomes not only a matter of record, when approved by the board of education, but also a guide to those who are charged with responsibility for making the study.

What Method Is Best To Obtain the Desired Information? The choice of method depends on the problem and the information needed. Leaving financial consideration aside for the moment, the point is that one method or combination of methods may be more effective than another for obtaining certain types of data. For example, it would be wasteful to conduct an interview poll if the problem were one of trying to get a broad, general picture of how opinion was developing around a given issue. For this purpose, sufficient information could be collected economically and quickly through the open forum, the advisory committee, or the panel methods of measuring opinion. By the same token, none of these methods would suffice for obtaining an accurate measure of public understanding, let us say, concerning guidance services in the school. Actually, the methods brought into play do not have to be costly and complicated when all that is wanted is a general estimate of opinion.

How Much Money Is Required to Conduct Opinion Studies? The answer to this question varies with the nature of the studies made. Large city-wide surveys can be expensive, costing thousands of dollars, and because of costs many administrators shy away from opinion studies without realizing that limited surveys can be conducted on restricted budgets. However, a preliminary or pilot study of opinion often yields satisfactory results and costs very little. Some survey organizations regularly make pilot studies before deciding whether or not it is necessary to engage in a large survey project. The argument on cost falls apart once administrators and school boards understand the need and value of knowing what the public thinks.

How Much Time Is Needed to Complete a Study of Public Opinion? The amount of time will vary with the method employed. The time required is short for the open forum and advisory committee methods, somewhat longer for the panel method, and considerably longer for questionnaires and direct interviews. The last two methods, starting with a definition of the problem and ending with the publication of results, may consume several weeks. This length of time can be reduced with experience in polling procedure. One national polling organization is now able to conduct a nationwide survey and report the findings in less than a day. The significant thing is not how much time is required, but rather learning how to make opinion studies and putting the findings to work in building stronger relations with the community.

Who Should Do the Research In Public Opinion Measurement? Typical school administrators do not have the background or training and experience for this research. They can familiarize themselves with the procedures involved and can learn to apply the more simple ones in their own communities, but they are not competent to undertake direction of scientific polls. If they wish to undertake scientific polls, they should either employ outside experts or else subsidize the training of staff personnel. Although the more convenient alternative is to hire outside experts, this is difficult to sell to boards of education because of the cost involved. The better choice in the long run is to subsidize the training of staff personnel who are then available to conduct studies whenever they are needed. Staff personnel who take over this responsibility should be assisted at the beginning by an expert consultant who can show them shortcuts in procedures, eliminate confusion, and prevent serious errors.

How Should the Findings Be Used? The answers to this question will be governed by the nature of the findings. The findings may show that the superintendent should act at once to solve a pressing problem or that action by the board of education is necessary before anything can be done to clear up an unfavorable situation. They may confirm the soundness of present public relations procedures and the effectiveness of the program or point up the need for studying further a practice that is causing trouble. They may reflect a shift in public opinion calling for follow-up studies to chart direction. They may reveal problems for which immediate provision should be made in the public relations program. They may reveal many other things that are important in guiding relations with the community.

In general, the findings should be published in booklet form for distribution to staff personnel and citizens in the community. Such a publication serves to increase interest in and understanding of the educational program. Discussions built around it afford opportunity for citizen participation in the improvement of school policies and practices.

ENDNOTES

1. Richard L. Weaver II, *Understanding Interpersonal Communication,* 4th ed. (Glenview, IL: Scott, Foresman, 1987), p. 95.
2. See U. S. Department of Commerce, *Standard Occupational Classification Manual* (Washington: Government Printing Office, 1980, reprinted 1990).
3. Merle R. Sumption and Yvonne Engstrom, *School-Community Relations* (New York: McGraw-Hill, 1966), p. 22.

4. Ralph B. Kimbrough and Michael Y. Nunnery, "The Political System and Negotiations in Public Education," *Planning and Changing* 1 (October 1970), pp. 103–9.

4

POLICIES, GOALS, AND STRATEGIES

Developing an appropriate policy and determining attainable goals are early steps in creating and improving a school-community relations program. An appropriate policy describes the rationale for undertaking the program, and it authorizes and usually charges the administration with responsibility for determining the means by which the policy will be implemented. A plan that outlines realistic and valid goals with objectives and strategies to reach them provides a school-community relations program with proper direction. Likewise, it will provide a framework to properly evaluate the total program after given periods of time, such as a year or five years.

NATURE OF A POLICY

To understand the nature of a policy it would be well to start with actual examples and then examine the elements that are contained in them. The following policy was adopted by the board of education in the Dallas (Texas) Independent School District:

> Society has created public institutions to serve the best interests of its citizens. Those interests can only be met by an institution that incorporates the practice of public relations in its truest sense by operating in an open and sensitive manner.
>
> The Board is committed to an ongoing public relations effort designed to help improve the programs and services of its schools. This effort will rely on a comprehensive two-way communications process involving both internal and external publics, with a goal of stimulating a better understanding of the role, objectives, accomplishments, and needs of the District.
>
> Authority is hereby delegated to the General Superintendent to develop and implement public

relations activities which assist in interpreting public attitudes, identify and shape policies and procedures in the public interest, and carry on involvement and information activities which earn public understanding and support.

Another example of a policy is a sample one developed by the Policy Services of the New Jersey School Boards Association:

> The board of education believes that the public schools belong in every sense to the people who created them by consent and support them by taxation; that the schools are only as strong as the intelligent and informed support of the people of the community, and never any stronger; and that the support of the people must be based upon their knowledge of, their understanding about, and their participation in the aims and efforts of the public schools.
>
> The board directs the superintendent to keep the citizens of the district regularly and thoroughly informed through all the channels of communication on all policies, programs, problems and planning of the school district. The board shall invite the advice and counsel of the people of the district at all times, especially at all monthly meetings of the board, except at executive sessions; and solicit the sound thinking and studied counsel of the people through advisory committees selected from the community and appointed by the board to consider those problems which vitally affect the future of our children.
>
> The board of education believes that school district public relations is not solely an information program, but encompasses all aspects of the schools' relationship with the total community.
>
> The board of education believes its school-community communications program should:
>
> A. Promote public interest and participation in the operation of the school system;

B. Gather information about public attitudes toward the school system and its programs and report to the superintendent and the board;

C. Provide an honest, continuous, comprehensive flow of information about the policies, procedures, programs, problems and progress of the school system to the community and the staff;

D. Develop the most effective means of communication with the school system's publics and use available media as appropriate;

E. Develop programs in the schools that will integrate home, school and community in meeting the needs of district residents;

F. Develop and maintain the confidence of the community in the school board and the school staff;

G. Develop a climate that attracts good teachers and encourages staff to strive for excellence in the educational program;

H. Anticipate and forestall problems that are brought about by lack of understanding;

I. Evaluate past procedures in order to make improvements in future communications.

The superintendent shall be responsible for developing programs, techniques and channels for implementing this policy.[1]

An examination of these policies on school and public or community relations indicates that they include the following: the reasons for adopting the policy, the decision to do something or take some form of action for the reasons stated, the general means to be employed in carrying out the decision, and the delegation of authority for carrying out the policy. These elements make the policies sound.

Advantage of Written Policies

Every board of education should have a carefully formulated statement of policy covering school and community relations. The policy should be in agreement with state school laws, the philosophy of the institution, and the traditions and opinions of people in the community. It should consist of a plan of action in which the purposes and general means for their attainment are described in written form or else a statement in which the decision to act and the rationale for it are spelled out clearly.

Purpose is the crucial element in a policy statement because it tells why the policy has been developed and sets the goal to be accomplished. In this respect, the school-community relations policy should emphasize the development and continuance of a strong partnership between the school and the community. By bringing individuals and groups into a dynamic team, ideas can be exchanged, problems examined, practices reviewed, and decisions reached that will enrich the quality and increase popular support of public education.

Practical experience has shown that a number of advantages may be gained when a school system formulates and adopts a policy having the characteristics just described. Simply stated, these advantages are as follows:

Policy facilitates the orientation of new board members regarding relations between the school and the community.

Policy facilitates a similar orientation for new employees—both professional and nonprofessional—in the school system.

Policy acquaints the public with the position of the school and encourages citizen involvement in educational affairs.

Policy provides a reasonable guarantee that there will be consistency and continuity in the decisions that are made under it.

Policy informs superintendents what they may expect from the board and what the the board may expect from them.

Policy creates the need for developing a detailed program in order to implement it.

Policy provides a legal reason for the allocation of funds and facilities in order to make the policy work.

Policy establishes an essential division between policy-making and policy administration.

The policy should be printed, with copies available for all members of the staff and for any resident of the community.

Policy Styles

For the most part, four styles are followed in the makeup of a policy statement: (1) provisions of the policy statement may be set down in broad, flexible language and the details of its administration left to the discretion of the superintendent and his or her staff; (2) the policy statement may include the rationale or purposes for the decision and the aspects, parameters, or limits within which the program is to be designed; (3) rules and regulations or procedures may be attached to the policy statement and thereby become an integral part of it; or (4) the policy may take the form of a resolution on which the board will take legal action.

Policy Development

The development of a school-community relations policy starts with a determination of the end to be served by the policy. This means simply asking why the policy is necessary. The answer to this question may be nothing more than a vague feeling of concern about the nature of the interaction between the school and the community, or it may arise quite naturally from the pressures of outside groups who are seeking change in the school program. The need for a policy might also be indicated by the complaints of parents, the defeat of a bond issue or millage proposal, or the treatment of the schools in the press. No matter how it arises, there must be first an understanding and determination of the reason or reasons why a policy should be developed.

Once the need for a policy has been reviewed with the board of education and the board has authorized the superintendent to work out the details and present them in writing, the door is open for establishing this task as a cooperative undertaking. Under the leadership of the superintendent or a member of his or her immediate staff, invitations can be extended to a cross section of individuals who have an interest in the proposed policy or who will be affected by it at a later time.

They can be asked to serve on a committee for developing the policy, knowing that their recommendations will be subject to board of education acceptance, rejection, or modification.

The members of such a committee might consist of representatives of the board of education, administrators, teachers, parents, and other community residents. The committee should be large enough to produce a rich reservoir of pertinent ideas and information and small enough to permit a suitable arrangement for getting the job done. Not only should the committee have well-balanced representation, but it should also be made up of individuals who are seriously and constructively concerned with the promotion of public education.

The work of the committee calls for the gathering of information, ideas, and opinions about the needs and conditions to be met under the policy. It also calls for the determination of an appropriate rationale or statement of purposes, as well as a decision to act that is in keeping with the rationale or purposes. The committee may decide to outline the general means for implementing the policy decision or to define the essential elements constituting the framework for a detailed program in school-community relations. However the committee handles the content and style of the policy statement, the results should be expressed in writing and transmitted by the superintendent to the board of education for review and decision.

Distribution

After a policy statement has been adopted by the board of education, it should be printed in an attractive leaflet or flyer for broad distribution. Copies should go to all employees of the school system, to parents of all pupils in the system, and to a selected cross section of people in the community. In this way, the nature of the policy has a good chance of becoming common knowledge among the special publics in the community relations program.

Appraisal

In addition to the legislating of a policy in school and community relations, the board of education has a responsibility for appraising its effectiveness. It should require periodic reports from the superintendent in order to determine, first, whether or not the policy is being carried out as intended and, if so, whether or not the results are satisfactory. In accordance with the findings on these points, the board can decide to continue, amend, or repeal the policy.

It makes good sense also for the board to establish an advisory committee for the purpose of reviewing the policy at given intervals of time, say annually. The circumstances and conditions that gave rise to the policy may be undergoing change in such a way as to make the policy obsolete in part or even harmful eventually if continued in its present form. When it is reviewed periodically by an impartial group of individuals, the policy can be kept alive and useful.

GOALS AND STRATEGIES

With a sound school-community relations policy approved by the board of education, a wise school district moves on to determining goals sought and selecting strategies to be employed in trying to reach them. Two different approaches will be outlined here, both of which have merit and, if handled properly, will produce an effective plan. The approaches referred to may be categorized as the conventional approach and management by objectives (MBO).

The Conventional Approach

The use of the conventional approach in program planning involves a number of important considerations and a logical sequence of procedures. They will be enumerated and discussed in the following section.

Program Goals. Goals are expected results, such as what an organization wants its public to

know, feel, or do about itself. Not only do they reflect the viewpoint of the policy statement but they also reaffirm the position taken in the stated philosophy and expected results of the school system.

Kindred, Bagin, and Gallagher give an example of program goals found in various school systems:

1. To develop intelligent public understanding of the school in all aspects of its operation
2. To determine how the public feels about the school and what it wishes the school to accomplish
3. To secure adequate financial support for a sound educational program
4. To help citizens feel a more direct responsibility for the quality of education the school provides
5. To earn the good will, respect, and confidence of the public in professional personnel and services of the institution
6. To bring about public realization of the need for change and what must be done to facilitate essential progress
7. To involve citizens in the work of the school and the solving of educational problems
8. To promote a genuine spirit of cooperation between the school and community in sharing leadership for the improvement of community life.[2]

Using Community Data. At this point in the conventional planning process, attention should be directed at the findings of the sociological inventory, the analysis of the power structure, and the measurements of prevailing opinions and beliefs of various special publics regarding the schools and the educational program. These findings and their interpretation make it possible to block out areas in need of new and of continued treatment. For example, the data might show what additional information people would like to have about certain aspects of administration, special services, or instructional practices. They might indicate the channels through which communication can be carried on more successfully with given publics. Certainly, they can help to delineate areas of most concern to taxpayers and to parents. Long-term and short-term goals can be readily identified and the need for priorities established. It is likewise possible that the data may disclose what values people in the community hold, who makes certain kinds of decisions, and what the educational expectations of citizens are. Data that serve to identify these and other matters of concern are invaluable in working out an efficient and effective school-community relations program.

It is advisable to put in precise written style all of the needs, problems, gaps, and so forth that the data reveal. The more precisely the objectives are stated, the better will be the decisions made subsequently about strategies and means to be used for dealing with them.

Modifying the Goals. The findings may also indicate that some of the stated goals are unrealistic and for practical reasons should be modified. For example, if apathy and ignorance are dominant characteristics of the population in regard to the school system and its educational policies, this condition will have to be changed before a working partnership can be established with the community. Or the findings may show that it would be more desirable to focus attention on the need for guidance, remedial reading, or corrective physical education than try to interpret the work of the board and the administrators to the public. By relating the findings to the goals, it is possible to determine what modifications, if any, should be made before strategies and means are considered.

At the same time, a distinction should be made between long-term and short-term goals. Long-term goals are those that require continued effort over a period of time, perhaps several years, before they can be achieved. Such a goal might be gaining acceptance and understanding of an innovative program some months before a transition from the old to the new takes place. Short-term goals, on the other hand, are those calling for immediate action, such as apprising parents of the necessity for changing the bus schedule at the beginning of the next month, or conducting a three-month campaign for an increase in the tax rate. Short-term goals can be reached and disposed of in a relatively brief period.

Strategies and Means. After the goals have been defined and accepted, thought should be given to the strategies to be followed for achieving them. Those who are doing the planning need to not only identify what has to be done but also select the best possible way of doing it. For example, perhaps the broad line of action should be that of improving face-to-face relationships between school personnel and lay citizens in order to step up the dissemination of school information and correct some of the current misunderstandings about educational policies and practices. The implementation of this strategy would then call for a fairly long-range and continuous effort employing such techniques as internal publications, simulated parent-teacher conferences, interpretation of pupil records, and the establishment of parent advisory committees.

If the goal is one of securing additional financial support in order to bring the educational program in line with the times, there may be alternative strategies to be considered, such as working through community leaders, working through a special citizen advisory committee, making the problem exclusively that of the parent-teacher association, or singling out special publics for a continuing exposure to the importance of additional support in terms of pupil and community welfare. The alternative selected or the combination of strategies to be used would dictate the techniques or means that offer most promise of reaching the goal.

The strategies and means available are influenced by the nature of the audience, the availability of funds and facilities, and the competence of personnel. For instance, an annual report in tabloid newspaper form might be good strategy in one community where the appeal of this kind of format is high, and poor strategy in another area where the appeal is low. If there is not enough money to make a broadside attack on a problem of hostile attitudes toward administrative personnel and distrust of the board of education, it may be necessary to tailor the activities to available resources or abandon the project entirely. Furthermore, school systems do not always have individuals with the knowledge and experience required to use sophisticated devices and equipment for communicating ideas and information to selected audiences. All of these considerations play a vital part in the determination of the strategies and means that are to be employed.

Variations of the Conventional Approach.
Public relations planners have further refined the conventional approach by giving added detail to the process used. Fulginiti, an authority in public relations planning, divides the planning process into nine areas: goals, objectives, strategies, activities, tasks, agents, cost, time, and evaluation. A description of the areas may be helpful in understanding his approach more clearly. He offers these:

Goal—an expected result that may or may not be attained. The *purpose* of the plan, it is a target toward which the organization or school district is moving. Examples of goals follow:

■ To develop public understanding and acceptance of the intermediate unit
■ To make the public aware of the need for a second high school
■ To involve more citizens in the school district's community relations program.

Objective—a specific, measurable subdivision of a goal. Objectives must be attained collectively for a goal to be reached. An objective tells what is to be accomplished. To keep track of objectives, planners label them with a decimal system. The number to the left of the decimal indicates the objective.

1.0 Identify and profile target audiences.
2.0 Assess media relations for the past year.

3.0 Persuade 50 percent of employees to attend the first round of quality circles.

Remember that objectives do not specify *how* the job will get done. They focus on *what* needs to be done.

Strategy—a specific way used to reach a goal. It is the *how* of planning. The available money and the scope of the job govern the number of strategies. Again the decimal system keeps things in order. The first number to the right of the decimal indicates the strategy, as in the following example:

1.1 Conduct a communications audit.
1.2 Interview fifty key communicators.
1.3 Do a content analysis of media coverage for the past year.

Fulginiti points out that these examples of strategies focus on a research objective (1.0 above) so all of them reflect proper research techniques. The strategies in other objectives will correspond to the objective's purpose. For example, appropriate strategies for 3.0 (above) might include the following:

3.1 Develop and distribute a brochure to inform employees about the success of quality circles in other companies.
3.2 Appoint circle leaders who are respected by their colleagues and who endorse the quality circle concept.
3.3 Kick off the first round of circle meetings with an after-hours reception featuring the CEO of a major Japanese firm.

To be truly operational, Fulginiti emphasizes, the PR plan should divide activities into tasks. Consider the activities first. To produce the brochure (3.1 above), a PR person needs to

3.1.1 Interview other firms that successfully use quality circles.
3.1.2 Draft copy for management approval.

Next, divide each activity into tasks. As an example, to "interview other firms" (3.1.1 above), a PR person needs to

3.1.1.1 Identify the firms for interviewing.
3.1.1.2 Develop interview questions.
3.1.1.3 Schedule the interviews.

At this point, the PR plan needs to answer three important questions: (1) Who will do the work? (2) When will it be done? and (3) How much will it cost? The PR manager can estimate the cost of the PR plan by costing out each task and adding.[3]

Fulginiti's variation of the conventional approach emphasizes the need for research at every step of the process to ensure that the strategies and activities taken are going to be productive. When his approach is followed, the final plan is very detailed, well thought out, and ready to be followed over a number of days or months. Fulginiti's process is excellent for short-term planning or for doing projects within a total school public relations program. Nevertheless, his techniques can be effective even if used in developing a total comprehensive community or public relations plan for a school district.

Figure 4.1 gives a slight variation of Fulginiti's approach and shows the partial development of a public relations goal. In these examples, *activities* and *tasks* are used synonymously. Two points need to be explained. The term *intermediate unit* refers to an educational unit in one state that exists between the school districts and the state department of education. It provides educational services to school districts which they themselves could not provide as economically. The other point in Figure 4-1 to be explained is the numbering system taken from Fulginiti's approach to planning. The number before the decimal refers to the *objective,* the first number to the right of the decimal indicates the *strategy,* and the second number after the decimal refers to the activity. With this technique of numbering, the public relations practitioner implementing the plan and working on a goal will know where that activity fits. For example if the school public relations person is working on activity 2.1.1, "Identify publications," she or he would know that it's the first *activity* under the

first *strategy,* under the *second objective* of a goal.

Management by Objectives

A second approach to the determination of goals and the selection of strategies in planning school and community relations programs is management by objectives (MBO).

Developed as a particular way of thinking about management in business and industry, MBO has been carried over and applied, with some modification, to the administration of public schools. In this section, attention will be directed to the definition of MBO, the process involved in implementing the system, the nature and types of goals that are used, the advantages and limitations of this approach, and some examples of its application in the field of educational administration.

Definition and Process. Odiorne, the man most responsible for the development of this system, defines *management by objectives* as "a process whereby the superior and subordinate managers of an organization jointly identify its common goals, define each individual's major areas of responsibility in terms of the results expected . . ., and use these measures as guides for operating the unit and assessing the contribution of each of its members."[4]

As may be noted in this definition, MBO is an attempt to build into management a persistent concern for purpose. This concern is based on the idea that you must have goals to know where you are going and that you cannot evaluate results without some previous expectations against which the results are measured.

According to Odiorne, the MBO system is built around two distinct activities: first, at the beginning of the fiscal year, the manager (or chief administrator) and each of his or her subordinates (or administrative assistants) agree on the subordinate's targets (or goals) of performance for the coming year; second, at the end of the year they

Goals	Objectives
To develop public understanding and acceptance of the Intermediate Unit.	1.0 To identify all current communications methods in the Intermediate Unit. 2.0 To identify internal and external publics and as many influential individuals as possible within those publics. 3.0 To rank all identified publics and research them. 4.0 To develop methods of communication with the most important public.

Objectives	Strategies
2.0 To identify internal and external publics and as many influential individuals as possible within those publics.	2.1 Conduct content analysis of internal and external publications. 2.2 Conduct brainstorming sessions among internal publics and focus groups from external publics. 2.3 File search for names in letters and correspondence.

Strategies	Activities
2.1 Conduct content analysis of internal and external publications.	2.1.1 Identify publications. 2.1.2 Identify general groups in publications. 2.1.3 Collect names of people from publications.

Activities	Agent	Cost	Time	Evaluation
2.1.1 Identify publications.	Tom	– – –	Start Oct. 24 End Oct. 25	Observation

Agent	Activities/Task	Month October 1 2 3 4 5 6 7 8 9 10 11 12 13 14 15 16 17 18 19 20 21 22 23 24 25 26 27 28 29 30 31
Tom	2.1.1	███
Tom	2.1.2	██████
Tom	2.1.3	███████

Agent	Activities/Task	Month November 1 2 3 4 5 6 7 8 9 10 11 12 13 14 15 16 17 18 19 20 21 22 23 24 25 26 27 28 29 30
Tom	2.1.3	████████

FIGURE 4.1 Examples of format in public relations planning.

both look at the targets again and review the subordinate's performance in trying to achieve them.[5]

To accomplish these activities, a series of steps are undertaken as follows:

1. The common goals of each organizational unit are identified. In a school system, some of these units are administration, instruction, school-community relations, and business management. These goals are based upon those for the entire school system.
2. Next, a working organization chart is constructed showing the titles, duties, relationships, and impending changes for each organizational unit. The administrator or supervisor in charge of each unit formulates objectives for him- or herself and for the individuals who report to him or her. It is also the administrator's responsibility to work out performance budgets for divisions within his or her organizational unit.
3. The administrator or supervisor of an organizational unit then asks each subordinate individually to make notes on the objectives she or he would like to accomplish and to set a date for discussing them.
   a. Before the meeting the administrator or supervisor lists some of the objectives that the subordinate should include for the next year.
   b. In the conference that follows, the administrator reviews the subordinate's objectives in detail and offers suggestions or changes.
   c. A final draft of the objectives is typed with one copy to the administrator and the other to the subordinate.
4. A check is made thereafter of each subordinate's goals at stated intervals of time or as promised milestones are reached.
   a. The targets are changed, if change is needed.
   b. Inappropriate goals are eliminated or new targets added.
   c. If necessary, encouragement and assistance are given to improve performance.
5. Near the end of the budget year, each subordinate is asked to prepare a written statement estimating his or her accomplishments compared with his or her targets.
   a. The subordinate also notes the reasons for any variances and lists other accomplishments that were not included originally among the targets.
   b. A conference date is then established for reviewing the written statement. Other pertinent concerns, such as job-related problems, are covered as well.
   c. The stage is set again for working out the subordinate's goals and performance budget for the coming year.[6]

This process is extended downward through the organization so that goals and performance budgets are agreed upon at lower levels between each subordinate and his or her immediate administrator or supervisor.

Goals and Objectives. Before an agreement is reached concerning performance targets for any given position, two things need to be reviewed carefully. The first consideration is the overall goals of the institution. These set the direction for institutional activity and define the boundaries within which specific objectives are formulated. And second, any change in organizational structure, especially as it affects individual areas of responsibility and authority, should be made known so that individual objectives and performance budgets may be shaped accordingly.

After these two considerations have been checked out, attention is then centered on the preparation of specific objectives and performance budgets for individual job positions. In the MBO system, these ends must be realistic and quantifiable with reference to such measures as percentages, weights, ratios, number of dollars, time, and volume. If the quantification of some educational objectives has been tried without success, a descriptive statement is used to point out the conditions that will exist when the objective has been reached. However, there are some advocates of MBO in education who believe that all objectives can be stated in measurable terms.

Usually, specific objectives fall into four broad types. The first type is known as *routine objectives* or those that recur annually. A second type is called the *problem-solving* objective. This type deals with a particular problem that it tries to eliminate or at least to explain. Generally, these objectives are different each year. A third type is referred to as the *creative* objective. Here the focus is on a new and different approach to something that may produce a new or expanded result. The last type is the *personal* objective. This represents effort that leads to the improvement of professional or managerial skills—a career growth.

Each of these objectives is followed then by the steps to be taken in accomplishing the objective.

Advantages and Limitations. The MBO philosophy of management has been instrumental in providing such benefits as those below, according to some of the individuals who have worked with it:

— An open, problem-solving climate
— A greater feeling of participation in the achievement of organizational goals
— A stronger sense of good supervisor-subordinate relationships
— A clearer understanding of the role and responsibilities of managers and subordinates
— An improvement in individual performance because the goals are understood
— A reward system for individual accomplishment growing out of the achievement of organizational goals
— Expanded opportunities for personal growth and development
— Emphasis on priorities at the expense of irrelevant practices
— Establishment of criteria for the evaluation of outcomes
— More effective communication among individuals and groups.

While lack of success in using the MBO system may be due to poor implementation and the absence of sound administrative skills on the part of responsible personnel, nevertheless there are some recognized limitations. They are as follows:

— Administrative background and hard work are required to make MBO work.
— There must be a strong commitment to the system on the part of all involved.
— The process of using MBO must be taught.
— The administrator must be able to assess the actual results instead of activities that seem to suggest the results.
— Real skill is required in the stating of specific objectives and performance budgets.
— Subordinates can undergo a sense of frustration if they are made to feel that increasingly higher goals will be expected.
— Individuals may be evaluated in terms of personality rather than achievement.
— Individuals may become more blame-oriented than problem- or results-oriented.
— Discrepancies may develop between management expressions of values and styles and the behavior of those in lower administrative positions.

Adaptation to Education. As MBO became popular in business and industry, a number of public school systems and institutions of higher learning modified the original design and adapted it to their situations. They developed very structured programs by attempting to quantify many objectives and activities at most levels of administration and learning. Since then some school districts have found that this was not totally functional and have loosened the structure of their MBO plans. A few examples will be cited to illustrate how the basic concepts of MBO are being applied in the educational setting.

In the West Chester (Pennsylvania) Area School District, developing management objectives is an integral section of its "An Appraisal System and Compensation Plan for Educational Administrators."[7] They are evaluated and rated on job performance criteria and achievement of management objectives. Job performance criteria comprise two-thirds of the composite rating of the administrators, and achievement of management objectives, one-third. Among the job performance criteria is the administrator's ability to communicate. Figure 4.2 shows five aspects of communication on which the administrator is evaluated, going from general communication abilities to internal then external communication. The administrator's performance is evaluated by a superior and also assessed by the staff.

The other third of the administrator's evaluation, namely achievement of management objectives, also is related to communication and school-community relations in that the board of education approves a five-year plan and the superintendent develops yearly objectives and passes them on to all administrators. They then develop their own objectives.

Usually the superintendent develops his or her own community relations objectives to strengthen the school district's relationship with the community. These objectives become part of each administrator's plan on which he or she is evaluated. And so, instead of a district community/public relations plan being developed exclusively by the communications coordinator with objectives and activities, all administrators have the responsibility in school communications and community relations. This system is one adaptation of MBO in education and is a sound approach to improving a district's communication program.

Often a school district will develop forms as part of the MBO approach. Figure 4.3 is an example of a form that could be distributed annually to all professional employees. Each employee would be asked to fill it out prior to a conference with his or her immediate supervisor. The form centers almost exclusively on performance goals or targets for the coming year. It facilitates the task of defining what the individual will try to accomplish within the scope of his or her responsibilities and authority. The form is suggestive of

possible ways in which this phase of MBO can be handled.

Figure 4.4 presents an acceptable format for stating goals and objectives. It is also followed by many planners using MBO in business and industry. In this example the objectives are essentially quantified. To facilitate measurement and evaluation, objectives are usually stated in terms like percentages, amounts, weights, ratios, numbers, time, and volume. If quantification has been tried without success, a descriptive statement is used that points out the circumstances that will result when the objective has been reached.

PLANNING CHECKLIST

Good planning is nothing more than a way of determining where to go and how to get there in the most efficient and effective manner possible. However, sometimes a yardstick is needed to measure the plan before it is finalized and put into action. In this way discrepancies may be discovered, omissions noted, and other weaknesses brought to the surface. Such a yardstick is the checklist suggested here. Although this checklist is quite comprehensive, it does not include the principles of communication; they are given in Chapter 6. But aside from these principles, the checklist summarizes the points made in the discussion thus far of the planning process.

■ Program planning represents a process for implementing a legally adopted policy in school-community relations.

■ The larger goals and specific objectives of the program are consistent with the philosophy of the school system and the laws of the state.

■ The larger goals and specific objectives are stated in measurable terms to the extent possible.

■ The strategies selected for attaining the objectives call for the involvement of members of various special publics when such involvement is feasible.

■ A distinction is made in the plan between short- and long-term objectives.

KEY
5 = Always (No significant variation)
4 = Almost always (Some slight variation)
3 = Frequently (Usually, ordinarily, in most cases)
2 = Occasionally (Now and then, infrequently)
1 = Never (Rarely, seldom or not at all)
N/A = Not applicable

IV. COMMUNICATING

Tasks	Performance Criteria	Indicators
• communicates effectively □ □ □ □ □ □ 5 4 3 2 1 NA	- selects appropriate means of communications - writes clear, concise, well-organized reports - makes effective oral presentations	
• communicates with students, staff, district personnel & agencies □ □ □ □ □ □ 5 4 3 2 1 NA	- establishes regular communications mechanisms with students & staff - helps staff understand & respond to information from district offices - provides district offices with staff feedback - maintains appropriate communication with other district administrators, departments and/or other agencies	
• responds to student and staff problems, criticisms and concerns □ □ □ □ □ □ 5 4 3 2 1 NA	- systematically collects student & staff concerns - takes appropriate action to resolve problem situations - communicates results & solutions to problems & concerns	
• promotes teacher/parent communication □ □ □ □ □ □ 5 4 3 2 1 NA	- provides meaningful information to parents regarding student progress - encourages regular staff communication with parents - creates effect communications mechanisms	
• communicates about school/district policies and programs with the community □ □ □ □ □ □ 5 4 3 2 1 NA	- provides information systematically to parents and community - communicates openly with parents and community - utilizes parent/community opinion - interacts with groups to promote positive outcomes - maintains appropriate communications with the School Board - develops communications that reflect & support Management Team decisions and School Board policies	

FIGURE 4.2 Instrument used by West Chester (Pennsylvania) Area School District to evaluate an administrator's ability to communicate. Reprinted by permission.

INSTRUCTIONS TO THE INDIVIDUAL

1. List your major job responsibilities and set forth for each, specific and measurable performance goals for the coming year.
2. Review these performance goals with your supervisor and make any necessary changes.
3. Have four copies of this form completed and signed by you and your supervisor.
4. Distribute the copies as follows: a) original and one copy to your supervisor, b) second copy you retain, c) third copy to the Personnel Department.

Do not use Columns: <u>D</u>id not meet the goals, <u>M</u>et the goal, or <u>S</u>urpassed the goal. These are for your supervisor's use when he or she evaluates your performance at the end of the year. Contribution to the District should be expressed in terms of monetary savings, efficiency improvements to present operating methods, manpower reductions, etc.

PERFORMANCE GOALS

MAJOR RESPONSIBILITY	TARGET DATE	COMPLETION DATE	CONTRIBUTION TO THE DISTRICT	D	M	S
GOALS						

MAJOR RESPONSIBILITY	TARGET DATE	COMPLETION DATE	CONTRIBUTION TO THE DISTRICT	D	M	S
GOALS						

FIGURE 4.3 Form for stating performance goals.

▬ The objectives of the school-community relations program reflect an assessment of need or the gap discovered between what is and what should be.

▬ The program is planned and tailored to the nature of the school and the community with which it is identified.

▬ The communication channels selected for disseminating various kinds of information are appropriate for the audiences involved.

▬ The program calls for a continuing audit of the results it produces.

▬ Each individual having responsibility in the program knows exactly what he or she is trying to accomplish.

▬ The plan includes guides for resolving issues of emotional and intellectual concern to members of the community.

▬ Provision is made in the plan for long-range in-service education of the staff to the extent needed.

▬ Program strategies and activities are adapted to available human resources, funds, and facilities.

Goal	Objectives	Activities	Evaluation
To develop a program of cooperation with community groups within the school district.	1. To identify *all* community groups.	1. Obtain group names from Chamber of Commerce. 2. Contact local libraries for list of groups. 3. Review telephone book for group names.	Tabulation
	2. To gather information about *each* group.	1. Contact each group. 2. Get title, address, phone number, and names of officers. 3. Request information on structure and purpose of each group. 4. Categorize groups according to the nature of each. 5. Put information from #2, #3 and #4 in computer file.	Tabulation of completed group files
	3. To meet with 50% of the groups this school year.	1. Invite six community group residents or leaders to lunch each week. 2. Prepare school district handouts for luncheon meetings. 3. Prepare agenda for each meeting. 4. Get feedback on how the school district can better cooperate with the groups.	Tabulation of number of acceptances

FIGURE 4.4 An example of a partial MBO school-community relations program.

ENDNOTES

1. New Jersey School Boards Association, NJSBA Policy Services, "Concepts And Roles In Community Relations; Goals and Objectives," *School Leader*, Sept/Oct 1992, p. 42. Reprinted by permission.

2. Leslie W. Kindred, Don Bagin, and Donald R. Gallagher, *The School and Community Relations, 4th ed.* (Englewood Cliffs, NJ: Prentice-Hall, 1990), pp. 46–47.

3. Anthony J. Fulginiti, "How to Prepare a Public Relations Plan," *Communication Briefings* (May 1985).

4. George S. Odiorne, *Management By Objectives* (New York: Pitman, 1971), pp. 55–56.

5. Ibid.

6. Ibid., pp. 70–72.

7. This instrument was developed by Professor Donald Langlois of Lehigh University, while he was superintendent of the West Chester (Pa.) Area School District. He indicated that more than 450 North American school districts requested permission to use it.

ADMINISTERING THE PROGRAM

This chapter deals with organizational arrangements and administrative responsibilities involved in the implementation of the school and community relations program. In more specific terms, it discusses responsibilities of the board of education, the superintendent's role in the program, the nature and functions of the administrative team, the relationships and responsibilities of the program director, plans of organization, responsibilities of other administrative and supervisory personnel, the program budget, and the part of instructional personnel in the program.

THE BOARD OF EDUCATION

In thinking about a community relations program, a board of education must constantly remember that the schools are owned and operated by the people. They send their children to the schools to learn, and they pay the bills to keep the schools in existence. By statute people own the schools and elect representatives to govern them. It is only right, then, that they be kept informed continually of the stewardship of their children and their money in the local school system.

How people feel, what they believe, and how they act toward the school, its officers, proposals, and programs can be summed up in the term *public opinion.* Public opinion is that intangible but powerful force in American life that influences all that is done in public affairs. A school board must know something about the nature of public opinion in order to run a good school system. If it fails to do what the public wants, sharp criticism follows. If it moves too far ahead of public opinion, it invites opposition. If board members confuse their own interests with those

of the public, they often stir up resentment and conflict.

Every school board constantly faces the task of trying to satisfy all individuals and groups in the community. This it can never do, but it can operate in accordance with the large middle block of public opinion on many issues it must settle. In doing so, it must likewise recognize that it is always subject to criticism by both conservative and liberal elements of the population.

Many people see the schools personified in the board members themselves. Because the board is the governing body, the public often judges the school system on the manner in which the board conducts itself. Therefore, in its relations with the public a board has a number of important responsibilities.

Functions and Tasks

Many citizens do not know exactly what a school board does or what its duties and responsibilities are. Some are not aware that most board members do not get paid for their services. Others have no idea of the amount of time board members spend on school matters or the number of meetings they attend. Most people understand that the board is ultimately responsible for the schools, but they have little knowledge of terms of office, legal limitations, composition of the board, personal liability of members, relationship to the state and federal governments, and so forth.

Members of the Board

Board members should realize that individual actions—particularly relations with other board members—reflect on the board as a whole. A member should be motivated only by the desire to serve the community and not by some selfish or political reason. Where possible, board members should work as a unit and not as individuals or cliques. This does not mean that there can't be disagreement. Instead it means the board members should recognize the integrity of associates and the merit of their work. Members who resort to personal attacks on other board members at public meetings do the school district and the community serious injustice.

Also, members should understand that it is the responsibility of the entire board to see that the schools are properly run. This means that each member should realize that authority rests with the board in legal sessions and not with individual members.

Legislative Activities

School boards must be aware of the legislative activities of the state and federal governments. Legislation is often enacted that causes school districts serious problems of implementation and many times is of questionable educational value. Before a proposed bill gets too far along in the legislative process, boards should take a position on it and adopt a formal resolution either favoring it or disagreeing with it. The applicable state or federal legislators and officials and the media should be informed of the board's position and the reasons for it.

Board Meetings

The manner in which a school board conducts its meeting has an effect on public attitudes and opinions. A board should follow parliamentary procedures from a well-prepared agenda and show a broad interest in all aspects of education. It should invite and encourage citizens to discuss their views on important questions under consideration and make decisions consistent with the best interests of the school system. It is imperative that a board take public leadership in building

the best educational program possible. Helpful suggestions on what a board should and should not do at a public meeting are contained in Chapter 9.

Policy

The first thing that must be done before a program can be built is for a board to adopt a community relations policy. It is essential that this be put into writing and made available to the public and the profession; it puts a board on record as wanting to make education a collaboration between the school and the community. A policy is the basis for the superintendent and his or her staff to work out the details of the program for the board's approval. The policy statement can be short and somewhat simple. It should say what should be done and reasons for doing it. A clear-cut statement of this kind reduces the chances of misunderstanding, puts up a restraint against impulsive action, and serves as a guide in decision making. (Chapter 4 provides details on community relations policy development.)

Tone Setting in the Community

The board of education sets a better tone for the system when it consults with interested citizens and representatives of community groups on problems facing the schools. Interested citizens have much to contribute to the solution of problems facing a board. Although it can gain much from hearing the views of citizens, it is in no way bound by them. Moreover, those whose opinions are sought usually become strong and loyal supporters of the system. Good ideas and suggestions can also be obtained from groups that have interests in recreation, safety, health, library services, correction of physical handicaps in children, citizenship training, and the like. Consulting these people makes them partners in the job of education and helps to build many bridges of goodwill and understanding.

In daily contacts with people the individual board members are both listeners and ambassadors of the school system. They have wonderful opportunities at family gatherings, through church activities, in fraternal orders, and in everyday business to talk constructively about the needs of the schools, the work of teachers, and the hopes for the future. Through what they say and the way they say it, they can build a desire in people for better education for children.

Individual board members can speak to groups in the community when invited and discuss aspects of the school that need to be better understood in the community. Also, they can help to interpret the community to the school system. This means being alert to the thoughts and feelings of people toward the school system. Pooling such information makes it possible to identify serious community relations problems, catch problems before they become too serious, note changes in public opinion, and determine in part how well the community relations program is operating.

Tone Setting in the School System

The attitudes and actions of the school board affect the attitudes and actions of employees in the school system. The board should take an interest in the welfare of staff members and meet their needs before they become demands. It should recognize the outstanding work of employees; they want recognition for jobs well done. Recognition makes them feel more important, more willing to work harder, and more loyal to the school system. Recognition can be given through letters of commendation, newspaper publicity, periodic banquets, release from teaching for special assignments, and so forth.

The board of education sets a better tone for the system when it consults with employees on problems facing the schools. Employees like to be consulted. They appreciate knowing that interest is taken in their ideas and that they are important to the school system. Personnel studies in industry have shown that production increases when workers are taken into the confidence of

management and feel that they have some part in decisions that are made. The laws passed on collective bargaining in many states have forced a number of school boards to consult with employees on many matters. Those districts that have a history of consulting with employees on work load, sick leave, retirement, supply and equipment needs, discipline, curriculum revision, hiring of personnel, and so forth have found staff morale high, an improved educational program, and fewer and less severe confrontations with employees. With this relationship of staff to administration, everybody is better able to get down to the business of educating the children of a community.

Members of the board should take a day or so a month to visit schools and chat with principals and teachers and other employees. The board should also invite teachers to give presentations on their work at public board meetings. In other words, it should show a real interest in the work being done by employees.

Relationship to Parents

Board members often receive complaints about the school from parents. The manner in which they handle these complaints has a great deal to do with the effectiveness of the school administration. Some board members attempt to answer a complaint themselves without directing it to the appropriate administrator, or they may bypass the superintendent and go directly to the teacher or principal involved. Both of these approaches should be avoided. When a complaint is received from a parent, a board member should always ask if the parent has contacted the principal of the school or the superintendent.

It is wise for each board to develop and adopt a policy on how complaints are to be handled in a school system. Once adopted, this policy should be distributed to all parents and publicized in the newspapers and at parent-teacher meetings. In this way parents will know to whom to complain, and board members will understand their role in handling complaints.

Relations with the Administration

The separation of responsibility between the school board and the administration is not always recognized by the board. Some members have the mistaken belief that it is their duty to actually administer the schools. Some boards spend time dealing with administrative details which should be the responsibility of the superintendent. When boards attempt to manage the schools, they fail to give the necessary attention to their major responsibility—that of seeing that the schools are run properly.

Some boards consider themselves a group of administrators, with the professional staff as its servants. This is a very poor attitude, and it results in a lack of cooperation with the administrative staff when the closest cooperative consideration of issues and problems by the board and the superintendent and his or her staff is necessary. The board and the administration must work in separate areas cooperatively if a school system is to function properly.

THE SUPERINTENDENT'S ROLE

Current conditions in community life have added new meaning to the superintendent's role as the leader in building constructive bridges between the school as a social institution and the people who own and support it. Traditionally, the superintendent's role has centered on such activities as working with the parent-teacher association, establishing rapport with civic groups, becoming involved in community improvement projects, encouraging lay participation on school study committees, supervising the preparation and publication of news stories and literature concerning various phases of the educational program, handling the more serious complaints and criticisms of school policies and practices, and trying generally to bring the school and community into a closer and more harmonious relationship. Although these are desirable activities that have a place in any school-community relations program, they are not broad enough in concept to prepare for problems arising from the growth and expansion of the educational enterprise and the changes occurring in social, political, and economic life.

In both large and small centers of population, the superintendent is faced today with strong demands from organized groups. Among other things, they want a larger and more decisive voice in policy determination, including such things as more functional curricular offerings, improved food services for undernourished children, better racial representation among administrative and instructional personnel, expansion of special services in child and family welfare, lower costs for education, accountability for the educational outcomes produced in students, and increased community use of school facilities. And lined up opposite each demand are powerful and influential groups maintaining a diametrically different position.

Under these circumstances superintendents become mediating agents in matters relating to public education. They must try to reconcile individual and social values, negotiate conflicts between lay and professional interests, and divert the influence of powerful groups into constructive channels. This role calls for a high level of social insight and considerable skill in dealing with people. In reality, superintendents are cast by circumstances into the role of educational diplomats and must spend much of their time dealing with individuals and groups whose influence and power help to shape the quality of educational opportunity in the community.

While carrying out their role as educational diplomats, superintendents must likewise attend to the responsibilities of the office on the more formalized aspects of the school-community relations program. In this regard they are central to developing and putting into practice the several strategies and activities called for in the program. Even though they delegate a substantial part of their responsibility to members of their administrative team, nevertheless they set the tone of the program, stimulate the effort that goes into it, and make the critical decisions it requires. *Unless they show dynamic leadership in pointing the way and setting the pace, it is doubtful the program will be successful.*

As program leaders, they have certain functions to discharge. Their all-pervasive function as heads of their school systems is that of maintaining, facilitating, and improving the educational opportunity for all children and youth in their districts. And correlative to that end are their functions in community relations—decision making, communicating, influencing, coordinating, and evaluating.

Translated into specific types of action, these functions break down into such performance patterns as the following:

- Developing a basic policy for encouraging and expanding constructive relationships between the school and the community
- Assuming initiative in the planning of processes and procedures for keeping the board, staff, and public well informed on school matters
- Helping all personnel connected with the school system become sensitive to the meaning and importance of their contacts in the community
- Ensuring the establishment and maintenance of open communication channels within the school system and between the system and the public
- Developing the structure and working relationships essential to the discharge of community relations responsibilities by administrative staff members and others
- Working with key groups and influential individuals in the community on significant educational policies and problems
- Seeing that key groups and influential individuals are supplied with facts and information that will challenge them to act in behalf of education
- Taking leadership in providing the opportunities required for district-wide involvement of citizens in programs for educational improvement
- Putting board and staff members in contact with groups and individuals whom they are most

likely to influence in behalf of better education and with whom a two-way system of communication may be developed
- Seeing that the evaluative aspects of the school and community relations program are carried out and that findings and their interpretations are submitted for review by the board of education
- Bringing together members of the administrative system and utilizing their experience, knowledge, perceptions, and skills in decision making with regard to various facets of the school-community relations program.

These performance patterns vary among superintendents depending largely on district size and outside pressures. In smaller districts which lack specialized personnel, a superintendent may assume almost total responsibility for technical aspects of the program. He or she may prepare news releases, leaflets and pamphlets, parent newsletters, radio scripts, details of open-house events, and direction of bond and millage campaigns, among others. Though the acceptance of such responsibilities is commendable, usually the more important aspects of community relations are either overlooked or disregarded. These include the development of basic policy, goal definition, and balanced program execution. In larger districts outside pressures sometimes build to a point where the superintendent delegates his or her principal administrative tasks to a deputy and devotes his or her time almost exclusively to the demands of the situation.

THE ADMINISTRATIVE TEAM

As implied in the foregoing discussion, the superintendency has become complicated enough so that those who hold the position depend on the services of specialists in meeting their leadership responsibilities. In fact, the superintendency may be viewed today as more of a team arrangement than a single position. However, there are no standard patterns concerning the composition of the team. It varies with the interest and special abilities of the superintendent, competencies of his or her staff, and community pressures on the school system.

In large urban centers the team may consist of the superintendent, deputy superintendent, associate superintendents, and district superintendents with heads of divisions and principals being invited to meetings from time to time. Or the larger administrative staff, including principals, may be broken into a number of smaller groups for discussion of problems and exchange of ideas on a scheduled basis. In other districts, the team may be made up of the superintendent, directors of instruction, pupil personnel services, business management, staff personnel, research, planning, school-community relations and a representative sampling of school principals.

The team performs two important functions. First, it provides a superintendent with information and ideas that enable him or her to keep the school and community program in proper perspective and to generalize about the larger aspects of it. And second, it brings the expertise of members to bear on the development of program details and operational procedures.

Besides their role as perceptive generalists, superintendents may serve on the team as specialists in one or more task areas of administration. It is common to find them wearing the cloak of building specialists, business specialists, community relations specialists, or instructional specialists. In some instances they retain the same specialties they had prior to becoming heads of their school systems. Occasionally they are forced to assume a specialist's role because of the system's size or the lack of qualified personnel. But as team members they usually pursue a specialty that is appropriate to their training and experience.

DIRECTOR OF SCHOOL-COMMUNITY RELATIONS

Directors of school-community relations are members of the administrative team in many school systems. They are members because of the strategic position they hold and the nature of their assignment. This will be evident in the discussion that follows regarding their status at present and the qualifications required for fulfilling their role successfully.

Title of Position

Directors of school-community relations have a variety of position titles. The titles used most frequently are assistant superintendent, administrative assistant, director of information services, director of community relations, director of public relations, communications director, director of information and public relations, director of information and community relations, director of information and communications, and director of community-school relations. Besides these titles there is a scattering of others like director of publications, coordinator of school information, and public information officer.

These titles represent a shift in concept that has taken place in the last two decades. Where previously the emphasis was on public relations, today it is more on community, communications, and information. These three words are now employed in combination with another term, such as *director* or *officer* in the title of the position.

Administrative Level

The position of director of school-community relations varies somewhat in terms of the administrative level at which it is placed. Only the largest school systems designate this officer as an assistant or associate superintendent with line authority. Usually the person holds a staff position and his or her title carries the word *director, coordinator, officer,* or *specialist* in many instances.[1] As a staff member, the officer reports directly to the superintendent, though in some school districts he or she reports to some other administrator, such as an assistant superintendent, an associate superintendent, or a deputy superintendent.

Some years ago the position of director of public relations consisted primarily of writing news releases and preparing newsletters. He or she was not considered part of the superintendent's cabinet and in fact was told what to do after cabinet actions. Many times decisions were made that created public crises. The superintendent in turn would ask the public relations person to help alleviate the situation. This was an almost impossible job. The best he or she could do was to keep the communication channels open with the public. The public relations person should have been involved in the discussions prior to the decisions being made that caused the public crises. Many now are cabinet officers.

With the public becoming more sensitive to educational costs and to what goes on in schools, it's imperative that the public relations person be a member of the superintendent's cabinet. He or she can help the district administrators understand how a decision will be perceived by the public. Likewise, if the public relations person is to explain, defend, or interpret school district policies properly to the public, he or she must be involved in their development from conception to birth. And finally, this person, with an understanding of citizen attitudes, needs to be a part of the cabinet if the group is to understand thoroughly the feelings of the community.

Size of System

The question frequently arises as to how large a system should be in terms of student enrollment to justify the employment of a full-time director of school-community relations. Although there are no studies on the point in question, a generally accepted rule of thumb is that a full-time director should be employed when student enrollment is in excess of 5,000. Some school districts with 3,000 students, however, have a full-time director of school-community relations. Size, however, is just one criterion. The nature of the community is another. A stable 7,000-student community may not need a full-time director, whereas a problem-ridden 3,000-student community may.

A number of school districts have expanded the office and have given the fulltime director all the responsibilities that are directly or indirectly related to communications. Aside from the usual public and community relations duties, they would include employee communications, community education, adult education, district printing and graphics, editing all publications from district schools, and supervision of telephone operators, among other responsibilities. To meet such responsibilities some offices of communications employ twenty to thirty people.

In districts that do not group all communications responsibilities in one office, the decision to hire a qualified person to head the school-community relations program is contingent on factors other than student enrollment. Some of these factors probably are the financial condition of the district, the nature of existing community relations problems, and the board members' and superintendent's conceptualization of program requirements.

Functions and Responsibilities

Directors of school and community relations have six basic functions to perform in trying to reach the objectives of the program. One or two more could be added but their addition would depend on how the position is viewed by the board of education and the superintendent of schools. The term *function* describes something that is done to facilitate the realization of the objectives for which the program is designed. The functions of the director are *research, advisement, planning, coordination, communication,* and *evaluation.* They make up the structure or system within which the details of the program are selected and carried out. From this point of view these functions are the constants of the program—they do not change. What makes one program different from another is not the functions but rather the activities or variables that come under them. For example, advising the school board and superintendent should be a permanent task of directors, but the nature and subjects of their advisement may differ markedly from one system to another. The same is true regarding evaluation of program results. Here the function remains constant, but the way it is implemented may range considerably in what is done and how carefully it is done.

There are several reasons why directors' activities vary among school systems. In some districts the perception of their role by superiors is broad and balanced, and in others it is narrow and restrictive. Often district size influences the nature and scope of their activities. In small districts, for example, little or nothing may be done with the research function. Sometimes in larger school systems some of their activities will be handled by line personnel or even the superintendent. The amount of money available for community relations is a strong determinant of how directors spend their time and what they do. The nature of their work is likewise influenced by the kinds of problems facing the district and the image of the school system held by residents of the community.

Against the background of functions, several school systems throughout the country have worked out statements describing the responsibilities of full-time directors of school and community relations. These statements represent not only the conceptualization of their role in a particular school system but also the nature and scope of the program they are expected to develop and put into practice. In Wichita, Kansas, for example, the director of communications' major activities are as follows:

1. Interpret policy of the board of education and the program of the school district to the public.
2. Edit the district's staff newsletter.
3. Plan internal and external publications.
4. Supervise and assist the Supervisor of Communications with news media relations and with public affairs programming on the district's cable television channels.
5. Facilitate staff recognition programs.
6. Assist school personnel and board personnel in planning public participation events.
7. Provide school-community relations consulting service to board of education members,

central office administrators, and school principals.
8. Help assess public attitude and keep appropriate school personnel informed.
9. Serve as a source of information to individuals from the community regarding school matters.
10. Serve as a consultant in the preparation of informational materials prepared by school personnel.
11. Serve as assistant clerk of the board of education and assist with agenda preparation, as needed.
12. Provide effective leadership in implementing the school district's commitment to full compliance with civil rights legislation, rules, and regulations.

A somewhat different type of statement was prepared for the supervisor of information for a California school district. It describes the office's major responsibilities as follows:

1. Counsels superintendent of schools, board of education, and others as needed, in matters relating to public relations.
2. Produces district newsletters and brochures (editor, writer, photographer).
   a. Staff monthly newsletter on board of education actions
   b. Staff quarterly newsletter
   c. Monthly newsletter to all parents
   d. Annual report to all residents and businesses in the community
   e. Periodic brochures as needed. Usually two or three a year.
3. Prepares all district news releases and writes magazine articles.
4. Counsels school personnel on writing manuscripts and approves material written by school personnel if it mentions the district personnel, programs, methods, materials, or other related information associated with the school district.
5. Approves requests to use students and facilities for "production" purposes not covered under civic center requests, and acts as liai-

son between the school district and photographers, film and television companies, and other media.

6. Represents the school district as spokesperson to the media.

7. Attends all regular board of education meetings to assist media.

8. Answers general inquiries about the school district and is the contact person in other phases of community relations.

In systems that employ a part-time director of school and community relations, the position is given a range of titles. In many instances, this individual is a central office administrator who reports directly to the superintendent of schools.

The responsibilities assigned to the part-time director are associated mostly with the use of mass communication. They include handling the press, radio, and television contacts, collecting news and preparing press releases, writing community newsletters and staff newsletters as well as leaflets and brochures, developing audiovisual material for community relations projects, producing speeches and reports, and performing editorial services for members of the central office staff. In addition, the part-time director may be responsible for handling citizen inquiries and complaints, a speakers' bureau, and millage and bond campaigns. And some part-time directors prepare the superintendent's annual report, establish contacts with civic groups, disseminate information on federal and state projects, and direct special undertakings like American Education Week.

Professional Qualifications

More and more school systems have established formal requirements for the position of director of school and community relations. In the North Penn School District, Lansdale, Pennsylvania, the requirements call for graduation from a four-year college with a specialization in English and participation in specialized workshops, seminars, and conferences pertaining to community educa-

tion programs and school public relations. Course work in journalism and graphic arts is desirable but not required. Besides education, the director must have administrative ability, a broad knowledge of the school district and community, leadership skills to administer the community education program, an ability to establish effective relations with sources of information and public news media, an ability to compose interesting news and feature stories about school topics, an understanding of the role of public relations in the school setting, an ability to organize effective procedures for dealing with requests for facility use, editorial skills, and management skills related to census efforts.

A Wisconsin school district's requirements called for the director to have a bachelor's degree, with study in the area of communications, including such courses as public relations, journalism, speech, marketing, advertising, graphic arts, radio, television, and writing. Further, the director must have had study in at least two of the following areas: behavioral sciences, education, or related disciplines. His or her previous experience must include full-time employment in a public relations responsibility either with an educational organization or one outside the area of education or full-time employment in mass communications with news, editorial, or program responsibilities. As special requirements for the position, he or she must have an "understanding of the role of education in a free society, the local program, and the responsibility of social institutions to communicate with their publics; understanding of the communication process, which requires a two-way flow of information between the school system and its internal and external publics; ability to collect and interpret information from and for the various publics involved, to write clearly, and to get along well with others; high ethical standards involving integrity, respect for confidences, and loyalty; access to complete information about district problems and plans, including immediate access to research information of the district, and the right to initiate or suggest needed research studies."

Perhaps the most complete statement of standards for educational public relations professionals is the following one adopted and published by the National School Public Relations Association:

STANDARDS FOR EDUCATIONAL PUBLIC RELATIONS PROFESSIONALS

An educational public relations professional is a person who performs public relations functions in a staff or executive capacity with an educational organization.

I. General Standards

General standards for an educational public relations professional shall include:

A. Understanding and acceptance of the role of education in a free society.

B. Understanding and acceptance of the role and social responsibility of public relations for all educational institutions, organizations, and agencies in a free society.

C. Commitment to the improvement of educational opportunity for all.

D. Professional performance and ethical behavior in educational public relations as described in NSPRA's Ethics for Educational Public Relations.

II. Specific Standards

A. Professional Preparation

1. Minimum of a Bachelor's Degree from an accredited college or university.

2. Study in the areas of public relations, behavioral sciences, management, and education.

B. Experience

Standards for experience shall include at least one of the following:

1. Two years' full-time experience in an executive public relations responsibility with an educational organization.

2. Three years' full-time experience (or the equivalent time) in a staff public relations responsibility with an educational organization.

3. Three years' full-time experience in an executive public relations responsibility with an organization outside the area of education, plus one year in a professional capacity with an educational organization.

4. Four years' full-time experience in a staff public relations responsibility with an organization outside the area of education, plus one year in a professional capacity with an educational organization.

5. Four years' full-time experience in mass communications (press, radio, television, etc.) with news, editorial or program responsibilities, plus one year in a professional capacity with an educational organization.

6. Five years' full-time experience in a professional capacity with an educational organization, plus one year in a full-time public relations responsibility.

7. Three years' full-time experience as a college teacher of school public relations or related communications courses, plus one year in a full-time public relations responsibility with an educational organization or three years of significant public relations consultant experience to educational organizations.

C. Demonstrated Ability

Standards for demonstrated ability shall include, in general, a working knowledge of comprehensive internal and external public relations programs, a mastery of basic communications skills, and a sensitivity to the importance of two-way communication.

Specifically, the educational public relations professional shall demonstrate these abilities through the following:

1. Employing effective human relations practices in the performance of public relations responsibilities.

2. Perceiving, identifying, and determining the implications of educational public relations problems.

3. Creating, proposing, and conducting activities designed to solve educational public relations problems.

4. Conducting continuous public relations activities that depend on the na-

ture, structure, and functions of mass media.

5. Planning, developing, and executing specific public relations projects essential to campaigns, interpretation of innovations, or other major activities.

6. Planning, developing, and using feedback processes, including opinion surveys.

7. Identifying and working with elements of power structures.

8. Identifying and working with individuals and citizens groups in the development and execution of the organization's program.

9. Involving staff and/or members of the organization in the development and execution of the organization's public relations program.

D. Professional Growth and Development Standards for professional growth and development require that educational public relations professionals continue to refine skills and expand knowledge through:

1. Maintaining membership and participation in NSPRA and other professional public relations associations and societies.

2. Participating in the NSPRA National Seminar and other recognized public relations seminars, conferences, workshops, and institutes.

3. Pursuing additional study beyond Bachelor's Degree requirements in pertinent areas.

4. Reading, researching, writing, speaking, and consulting in public relations.

5. Seeking NSPRA accreditation.[2]

Professional Assistants

Except in small school systems where it would be difficult to justify the expense, directors of community relations need the services of one or more trained assistants. Without such help it is virtually impossible for them to undertake a comprehensive program or to achieve established objectives. They must instead eliminate all but the most critical parts of the program and then concentrate their efforts on those activities they handle best. A glance at the nature of programs in school systems having only a director indicates that attention centers principally on such things as preparation and release of news stories, development of newsletters and pamphlets, and the maintenance of relationships with some community groups.

Where directors have the right to employ professional assistants, practice shows that they usually select individuals with a background of preparation and experience in editing, writing, and use of mass media. Many come from journalism, radio, television, and motion pictures. Some, however, have specialties in commercial art and others in community relations. If the system is large enough, the office of director may be divided into sections such as an information section, publications section, community relations and community education section, with a supervisor placed in charge of each one. A substantial portion of directors' time then goes into the administration of these sections.

PLANS OF ORGANIZATION

In general, three plans of organization are used to place responsibility for community relations activities and to facilitate the operation of the program. They may be described as centralized, decentralized, and coordinated plans.

Centralized Plan

A centralized plan is one in which responsibility for the program is centered almost entirely in the chief administrative officer and his or her immediate line and staff associates. Those who support this plan of organization point out that the superintendent is the person best known to the people of the community, and is looked to for leadership in matters affecting the welfare of children. Superintendents are expected to supply information on the conditions, needs, and practices of the schools. They enjoy many contacts with important citizens which enable them to keep their fingers on the pulse of public opinion. As a result they know when it is opportune to propose new policies and suggest changes in older ones. Specific assignments can be made and responsibility fixed more easily in the plan. Moreover, the staff is readily available for consultation. The example set by superintendents and their associates can have a wholesome influence on all employees in the system, who may show more interest in their own relations with the public.

Thus in a small school system, the superintendent engages in a variety of activities for interpreting the work of the school and earning the goodwill of the public. For example, he or she may give talks before many groups, join different organizations, participate in community affairs, supply news copy, prepare printed materials, and handle complaints received in the system. He or she may also consult with teachers on community problems and urge them to improve their relations with pupils, parents, and other citizens.

In larger systems superintendents delegate much of this responsibility to other persons. Usually they will delegate it either to an assistant superintendent in line authority or to a director of school and community relations with staff status. The program operates at the top of the system, with comparatively slight attention being given to individual building principals and their staffs. Instead of focusing on the personal side of community relations as an essential part of the total program, emphasis is placed heavily on community group relations, relationships with the community power structure, contacts with commercial media, and the preparation of materials for media distribution.

Although this type of centralized arrangement is found in many large school systems, there are serious weaknesses connected with it. The most serious one is the fact that good community relations can never be achieved solely through the office of the superintendent and his or her immediate associates. They may do excellent work through their personal contacts in the community and through the preparation and distribution of printed materials, but these activities are scarcely effective enough to offset the negative influence of unsatisfactory relationships between individual building personnel and pupils, parents, graduates, and others.

Decentralized Plan

A decentralized plan is one in which responsibility for the program is centered almost entirely in the building principal and in which the individual school is regarded as the natural unit for community relations. This is a common plan in many school systems today. There is justification for it. As an educational leader, the building principal is in a strong position to foster friendly relations with the school's publics on a neighborhood and area basis. Principals are close to the people and have a more intimate understanding of their needs and interests than do the administrative-supervisory officials at the top of the system. Principals can work with the instructional and noninstructional staff in establishing need for the program and conduct in-service training through the everyday situations which arise in the school. Excellent media are available for keeping parents informed and educating people in the service area about instructional aims and practices. Through the principal's efforts, the building can become a community center and activities carried on for the improvement of community living.

Though the decentralized plan is excellent in many respects, it is open to criticism in others. It usually means a neglect of community relations by central administrative officials and a failure on their part to reinforce the efforts of school principals and their staffs. Without central administrative leadership and direction, some principals are incapable of developing sound programs or else they are unwilling to take the initiative. Nor does this plan function successfully in systems replete with dissension among staff and with strong conflict between staff and administration.

Coordinated Plan

A coordinated plan is one in which community relations responsibilities of central administrative officers and building principals are fitted together into an articulated unit. The work of those at the top is planned to complement and reinforce that of the principals and their staffs. Each knows what is expected of the other. Central administrators, especially the director of school and community relations, serve as resource persons in assisting the principal and members of his or her staff. The administrator's advice and special knowledge may be requested in such matters as preparing leaflets and brochures for parents, resolving complaints and criticisms, gathering and writing news stories, and appraising the effectiveness of certain program activities. In many phases of the individual building program, central administrators are expected not only to perform advisory functions but also to share responsibility with the principal and his or her staff. They may share responsibility, for example, in arranging contacts with the news media, selecting a representative panel of citizens for advisory purposes, and assessing the nature of public opinion on particular issues in the attendance area served by the individual school.

In the coordinated plan, the building principals have broad discretionary powers. But they must use them within the structure of the district's philosophy and objectives of education and its policy on community relations. In their leadership role, they involve teachers and other staff members in program planning and operation, beginning with the identification of needs through the evaluation and dissemination of results. And in making special assignments, they try to gear them to the interests and competencies of staff members. In their role as communicators, the principals explain all facets of the program to building personnel and interpret the educational enterprise and its problems to students, parents, people in the school system, and residents in the immediate attendance area.

In some large secondary schools today the principal is assisted in his or her work by either a full-time or a part-time community relations specialist. This person may act as a liaison with community groups, handle news media contacts, prepare news stories and spot news announcements, edit internal and external publica-

tions, involve parents and others as resource persons for classes and committees, prepare and direct tours and observations for visitors, organize special advisory groups, and serve as a clearing agent for inquiries.

If the coordinated plan is organized carefully and the division of responsibilities is understood clearly, it offers an excellent opportunity for developing a comprehensive and well-balanced program that should produce satisfactory results.

RESPONSIBILITIES OF OTHER TEAM MEMBERS

Other central administrative team members, besides the superintendent and the director of community relations, have definite responsibilities in the community relations program. These members include assistant superintendents, district superintendents, and directors of special divisions and departments. Their community relations responsibilities cover the reception and treatment of office visitors, the effect of team activities on the community and district employees, the proper handling of telephone calls, the skillful management of correspondence, and the maintenance of satisfactory contacts with professional and noncertificated personnel within the system. They also serve in a resource capacity to building principals, as was pointed out in the discussion of the coordinated plan of organization. Through contacts with business leaders and others in the community, they have many chances to interpret the school and to create channels for a two-way flow and exchange of ideas and information.

These administrative members are expected in some systems to prepare their own interpretive materials, using the services of the community relations director's staff and special offices of the school system such as that of the audiovisual director. They are also expected to furnish information requested by the community relations director and to apprise him or her of any significant happenings that come to their attention. And in a number of districts, they are assigned responsibility for specific program activities like television programs, sociological studies, special events, and the preparation and application of evaluative instruments.

BUDGETARY PROVISIONS

How much money should a school system spend for public relations personnel, services, and media? Administrators and school board members frequently ask this question. They want to know approximately what their school system will have to pay for a good public relations program. No method has been discovered for calculating this figure, nor is there likely to be one in the future. The cost will naturally vary with the amount of work to be done and the willingness of the system to do it. Therefore, the only practical answer to the question is to first build the program and then determine how much money must be appropriated to operate it.

Determining how much money a program will cost is not easy because many of the activities are interwoven with regular services. However, many methods have been advocated for arriving at a cost figure. One is to take a fixed percentage of the total school budget, say one-half of one percent, and allocate this amount of money for program operation. Another is the so-called project-appropriate method, whereby the budget is based on the estimated cost of the projects planned for the year. A third method is followed in systems having a public relations office with a director in charge. The budget is restricted to this office alone and worked out in the same way as the budgets for research, pupil personnel, accounting, adult education, and similar departments performing special services. Still another method is to make a careful analysis of the program for the year and estimate how much money the board of education must provide. The amount needed can be presented in a separate budget statement or it can be included in the budgets of the several departments and units of the system having responsibilities in the program. A problem in public relations budgeting is determining just what should be included. So many activities in a school district can be considered public or com-

munity relations activities, such as any external correspondence, report cards, the appearance and printing of stationery, telephone costs of all offices, board meetings, appearance of buildings and transportation equipment, special events, community education, adult education, and so forth. Obviously, in many districts budgeting for these activities can't be included totally under the public/community relations section of a school budget. In some larger districts it may well be.

More specifically, the budgets of many public/community relations offices would include such considerations as salaries, telephone costs, postage, stationery, office supplies, printing and publications, graphic supplies, memberships in organizations, travel, conferences, subscriptions to professional publications and local papers; equipment such as cameras, audiovisual items, typewriters, and computers, word processors, and printers; and outside services such as graphic artwork, typesetting, photographs, mailing services, and clipping services. If any special event is the total responsibility of the public/community relations office, it should also be included in the department's budget.

STAFF MEMBERS

Unfortunately, in many school systems there is no organized community relations program. In these situations, some employees sense a responsibility to relate to the public and in many cases do a good job. This group unfortunately is in the minority. Even in districts in which there is a community relations program, there are often staff members who do not know what to do because they haven't been informed by their supervising administrator. If staff members knew exactly what was expected of them, they would undoubtedly carry out their part of a community relations program. Too often a plan is implemented at the administrative level and much lip service is given to it as well as a low priority, and it never becomes a functional reality. Staff members who are enthusiastic about relating the school story to the public are not involved in the plan or given an outline of their responsibilities and duties. Other staff members may be inadvertently creating a poor image for the school because they lack an understanding of good community relations techniques. A community relations workshop or other in-service training will help all employees understand their community relations role in the school and provide them with information and methods of relating to the public. An aggressive administrator not only sees to it that employees understand their community relations role and responsibility, but also gives them assistance and direction in carrying out the role.

GENERAL COMMUNITY RELATIONS RESPONSIBILITIES

Regardless of the position held in a school system, all employees have at least three general community relations obligations or responsibilities: do a good job in carrying out daily work, know the school system, and know the community. Prior to being hired, prospective employees should be apprised of these obligations.

Do a Good Job

It is not uncommon for school employees to feel that what they are doing often goes unnoticed. But it is important to consider the number of students who observe what school employees do each day and relate their observations to their parents or friends. Students are quick to notice how school employees are carrying out their daily work, particularly in the case of teachers.

Someone once said that a good school-community relations program begins in the classroom. It might be added that an effective community relations program is also maintained there. If teachers are doing a poor job of teaching, the image of that school in the community will likewise be poor. Teachers have an obligation to do the best job of teaching as possible. Essentially this is what schools are all about, and the public understands this very clearly.

Noninstructional personnel, as members of the educational team, should be aware of the ef-

fect their daily performance has on the image of the school in the community. Students who visit the school office can quickly see if office workers are performing their duties well and efficiently. The bus driver who drives carelessly, the custodian who does not clean the building well, and the cafeteria worker who delays the food line are all known in many homes in the community, and they cause many local citizens not to think well of the school.

Know the School System

Responsible administrators should keep employees informed about the school system by providing them with information or sources of helpful information. Each employee, in turn, should make an effort to learn more about his or her place of employment. Unfortunately, this is not always the case. Either out of apathy or by design, employees make very little effort to learn more about their school district; they do not realize that to many people in the community, they are the only contact with the school. Citizens look to the employees for many answers to questions about the school. When an employee is unable or unwilling to provide information to a citizen about the school district, the image of the school suffers.

Know the Community

The third general obligation all school employees have is to know the community in which they are working. This responsibility falls primarily on teachers. Usually, the noninstructional employees are residents of the community with a reasonable although not necessarily thorough understanding of the local area.

Teachers sometimes obtain positions in a district and make little effort to understand or become knowledgeable about the community. Often they live in another area and feel they have no need to be familiar with the community that supports the school. The days are gone or are numbered when teachers are required to live in the district in which they teach, but this does not excuse them from the responsibility of knowing something about the community and becoming active in it.

SPECIFIC COMMUNITY RELATIONS RESPONSIBILITIES

No community relations program or plan of organization will function successfully until employees know exactly what they are expected to do and understand the limits of their authority. While the general community relations responsibilities usually apply to all employees in all school districts, specific responsibilities may differ between one system and another. Those described here may be tailored to the needs of a particular school system.

Teacher

The teacher is a frontline interpreter of the school system through daily contacts with members of the different publics—particularly the students. In this capacity teachers have a number of specific community relations responsibilities:

Do as good a job of teaching as possible. The backbone of any community relations program is the teaching job done in the classroom.

Work constantly for good relations with pupils, parents, and people in the community. Much of this book is related to working with these three groups. It offers some ideas on working with pupils; outlines the partnership between the parents and the schools; and suggests ways of working for good relations with the community.

Work cooperatively with colleagues. Few school systems can attain or hold the confidence of the community if there is internal discord. Successful schools and teachers have learned that they must live in some degree of harmony if they are to gain the support of the community and maintain educational effectiveness.

Participate in community affairs. It is important that the teacher take an active person-to-person role in the community if the school-community relations program is to be effective. By virtue of background, education, and experiences, he or she should be able to make a contribution to the community.

Work closely with the director of community relations. If a school system employs a director of community relations, he or she, working through principals, can be a great help to the teachers. Usually the director brings to the position a background that enables him or her to see the community relations value of classroom activities which may be overlooked by the teacher. But the director of community relations needs to be informed of the activities the teachers are planning over an extended period of time to make a judgment on their community relations value.

Cooperate in the development of an individual community relations program for a school. Even though a school system may develop a total community relations program, it falls upon each school to develop that part which is unique to the individual building. This possibly calls for a committee of administrators, teachers, parents, and even students to suggest activities that will help the school and the community understand each other better. However, some school principals may choose a method other than a committee to develop a community relations program.

Accept and carry out special assignments in the community relations program. Many teachers feel that community relations are exclusively the responsibility of the principal and the director of community relations. They believe that they have been hired only to teach and not to carry out community relations responsibilities. This is a traditional belief which may stem from the preparation within a teacher training institution. But times have changed and teachers must accept and carry out special assignments in the school's community relations program.

Specialists

Specialists are those professionals in the school whose services in no way reduce class size. Usually included among specialists are subject specialists, counselors, psychologists, home visitors or social workers, librarians, nurses, doctors, and dentists. Many of their community relations responsibilities parallel those of the teachers. Others are unique.

Subject specialists. This group includes the coordinators and staff members who have specialized in a subject area such as music, art, languages, and so forth. Their community relations responsibilities include those of a teacher plus the responsibility of keeping their colleagues and students informed of the activities and developments in their subject field.

Counselors. Like teachers, the guidance counselors work closely with the pupils, the parents, other staff members, and the community. They have a major responsibility in making sure the relationship with these various publics continues to result in better education for the students and continued support of the schools.

School psychologists. Psychologists' relations with the various publics are similar to those of a guidance counselor; likewise, many of the responsibilities are the same. Much of what has been suggested in the way of activities to promote confidence and understanding of the school apply to the school psychologists.

Home visitors or social workers. Many school systems are fortunate to have a home visitor. Often this person is the only contact between the home and the school, a fact that emphasizes the importance of his or her community relations role and personal qualifications.

Librarians. An important responsibility for the success of a school-community relations program falls upon the librarians. They have contacts with students, parents, and the community and work closely with colleagues in making sure that students are provided a good education. What they do in establishing and maintaining good relations with these groups is instrumental in building the image of the school that is conveyed to the community.

Nurses. Many students in the course of the year come in contact with the school nurse. This, of course, means that there are many occasions for direct or indirect contact with home and colleagues. The importance of the nurses in the school-community relations is apparent in the skill with which they perform their duties and the manner in which they work with students, parents, colleagues, and the community.

Doctors and dentists. Often these two professionals, because they are usually part-time employees, don't consider themselves part of the school team. Yet their level of competency in treating students and their contacts with parents and the community are bound to have an effect on the school-community relations program.

In the community, these medical professionals have contacts with colleagues and patients that give them an opportunity to interpret and explain the schools. This means that school administrators have an obligation to provide the school doctors and dentists with helpful information about the schools. Conversely, they should keep the schools informed of information, community attitudes, and opinions toward local education.

Tax Collectors. Schools need to work closely with these folks to keep them informed about the schools. They come face-to-face with many taxpayers who are critical of the schools. Tax collectors who understand the school district and its needs, goals, programs, and procedures can answer many critics. In fact, they can provide citizens with a significant amount of positive information about the schools. But this requires school officials to maintain a structured program to keep tax collectors informed through workshops, meetings, and literature.

Support Personnel

This group of employees typically includes the clerical, maintenance, and cafeteria workers and the school bus drivers. They all have a measurable influence on the school-community relations program, yet they are sometimes overlooked by school officials.

Clerical personnel. In a real sense these employees are on the front line of the school-community relations program. They are often the first contact the parents and the community have with the school. What they say, the tone they convey, and the courtesy they extend all contribute to the attitude and opinions formed by the public about the schools. The sheer number of contacts with the public each week puts clerical workers in an instrumental position of developing good or ill will for the schools. It cannot be stressed enough how important these employees are to the effectiveness of the school-community relations program internally as well as externally.

Maintenance personnel. Opinion of a school is often formed from two impressions—the appearance of a building and the personnel associated with the school. Often overlooked in a community relations program are the maintenance

workers—custodians, groundskeepers, and mechanics. Their influence is felt primarily in the housekeeping and the general appearance of the building and grounds.

If they take pride in what they do and in keeping the building clean and maintained properly, this will reflect favorably on the school. Well-kept buildings and grounds say something to the public about the school system—that tax money is being spent wisely, that management is effective, and that public property is maintained properly.

Bus drivers. In many districts bus drivers, after teachers, comprise the second largest group of school employees. Their contacts are primarily with students, some parents, and with the community. It is with these groups that their primary community relations responsibilities lie.

Cafeteria workers. These employees also hold a strategic position in carrying out a school-community relations program. Many students carry home impressions of the cafeteria that influence parents' attitudes toward the school. An adequate selection of food, a diverse and popular menu, and reasonable prices impress children. Cafeteria workers have the responsibility of being courteous and clean, treating students with respect, and serving them efficiently.

IN-SERVICE TRAINING

Provision for in-service training is a part of a good community relations program. Staff members must possess the knowledge and skills required to meet their responsibilities. Training may be given either through direct instruction or indirectly through a series of devices. The nature of the training will be determined by the experiences of the staff and the demands of the local program.

Direct Training

The more usual and successful types of direct training are as follows:

Orientation programs.   These are designed to acquaint the new staff members with the school system and to help them make a satisfactory adjustment. During this training, their attention is directed to the community relations objectives and activities of the school system and the responsibilities they must meet. A staff member who has gone through a good orientation program is better equipped to interpret the schools and to build wholesome relations with the public.

In-service courses.   These are formal courses taught by competent instructors both from within and from outside the school system. They are used to train personnel for work done in all branches of the system. Courses in radio, television, editing, motion pictures, videos, interviewing, news reporting, opinion polling, and correspondence make it possible for interested staff members to receive technical training and qualify themselves to work with special communication media. Other courses of a more generalized nature may also be organized and offered in connection with the community relations program.

Workshops.   The workshop method of training is regarded as an excellent means for increasing staff efficiency. It is built around problems which grow out of daily experiences, or it may be used for planning purposes. Held during the school year, the summer months, or both, the workshops meet in small groups with consultants to exchange ideas and to pool thinking. Groups may be set up to deal with such matters as home visits, open-house programs, oral and written expression, relations with parents, lay advisory committees, news reporting, and the like.

Clinics.   This word is sometimes applied to short, intensive training programs for experienced personnel in specialized fields of service. For example, a clinic might be held for teachers who are responsible for gathering and reporting news stories. The purpose of the clinic might be to review their work and find out how it could be improved or it might be to propose a new system of reporting and acquaint teachers with the procedures.

Special meetings.   From time to time the staff may be called together for special meetings devoted to community relations. Matters of current interest can be taken up with the entire group and points emphasized which are in need of immediate attention. They are more effective for disseminating and imparting important information than are written communications. The response to these meetings is favorable when good instructional techniques are employed in the presentation of materials.

Preschool conferences.   As the title suggests, they are held before the official opening of school in the fall. Anywhere from three days to two weeks are set aside for the conferences. During this time, the staff can work without interruption on the program for the year. They may be assisted by consultants and resource persons. The results more than justify the time expended.

Study groups.   Study groups are valuable for the intensive analysis of relationship problems and the compilation of significant information. Participation is on a voluntary basis, but those who take part agree to attend scheduled meetings and remain with their group for the prescribed period of time. The work of analyzing relationships and formulating working hypotheses is done under the direction of a trained leader, and no group deals with more than one problem area. The problem areas may include teacher-pupil relations, teacher-parent relations, administration-staff relations, relations with community groups, and alumni relations. Although this type of study group has not been tried by many systems, those that have tried it are enthusiastic about it.

Faculty meetings.   Time can be set aside in regular faculty meetings for in-service training in community relations. The agenda should be planned cooperatively by the staff and administration and restricted to topics in which there is a mutual interest. More will be achieved when subject matter is presented with the aid of films, videos, slides, charts, graphs, printed materials, demonstrations, objects, and panel discussions.

Executive luncheon meetings.   Executives need training just as much as other staff members in the school system. This training can be carried on through a series of monthly luncheon meetings. The conference method of discussion, using carefully prepared material, is effective in dealing with problems that need attention and in presenting new ideas for consideration. Not enough has been done to stimulate the growth of executive personnel in school systems generally.

Indirect Training

Indirect training is accomplished through the use of instructive devices. Some of the devices are the following:

Handbooks.   Two types of handbooks contribute to the training of personnel in service. One supplies information that should be known by staff members in order to discuss the school intelligently with the public. The other outlines the responsibilities of each person in the program and how they should be handled. Both may be revised annually and distributed for ready reference and reading.

Internal publications.   These may take the form of a magazine, bulletin, newsletter, or folder. They are prepared for employees of the school system. Published semimonthly or monthly, they keep readers informed of what is happening in the system and offer many practical suggestions for better community relations. Sometimes they contain a citation column for bestowing recognition on those who have performed outstanding services. An attractive internal publication is indispensable in the training program of a large system.

Films, videos, and slides.   Shown occasionally at faculty and other group meetings, they give meaning and reality to the work in public relations. A school system would do well to produce videos, films, and slides based on the material in handbooks that are distributed to employees; nothing else gives so much life to this material or stamps it more deeply into employees' minds. Systems that cannot afford to make their own videos, films, and slides may borrow or rent appropriate ones from other systems, commercial agencies, and professional organizations.

Case studies.   Staff members derive a great deal of benefit from brief, simple reports of case studies made in the system. Each case study contains a description of a community relations problem and a statement of the method used for solving it. Not only do these reports help staff members learn how to identify their own problems but they also show how to go about the task of working them out successfully. They may be published in house organs or printed separately. An edited collection of case studies makes excellent material for an orientation program and for in-service courses.

Bulletin boards.   Graphic and printed materials can be placed on the bulletin boards in each school and special department of the school system to keep staff members informed and to draw their attention to important ideas and changes in the program.

Exhibits. Portable exhibits offer excellent opportunities to show visually the need for community relations, how the program is organized, the placement of responsibility, the factors that influence public opinion, topics for news stories, printed communication materials, and similar points of interest. They can be circulated for scheduled viewing in all parts of the system.

External publications. Staff members should receive copies of every external publication, including the annual report of the superintendent to the board of educa-

tion. They should know how the schools are being interpreted to people in the community and the nature of the publications distributed. The information contained in these publications is essential to their own work of telling the school story.

Checklists and rating scales. These devices cause staff members to look at themselves and evaluate their own practices. Used sparingly, they can be valuable aids in the training program.[3]

Subscriptions to publications. A number of worthwhile national publications on school-community relations are available at a reasonable price to distribute to employees. The National School Public Relations Association in Arlington, Virginia, publishes many of them.

ENDNOTES

1. *1993 NSPRA Directory,* (Arlington, VA: National School Public Relations Association, 1993).
2. *Evaluating Your School PR Investment* (Arlington: VA: National School Public Relations Association, 1985), pp. 51–54. Reproduced by permission.

3. The National School Public Relations Association, 1501 Lee Hwy., Suite 201, Arlington, VA 22209, has examples of these checklists and rating scales.

6

THE COMMUNICATION PROCESS

In building a school and community relations program, close attention should be given to the communication process. Although some kind of communication takes place in all walks of life, effective communication doesn't just happen. It is the result of carefully planning the kind of information that needs to be disseminated, the particular audience that is to be reached, and the choice of tools that are best fitted for the job. The job itself is that of bringing about understanding, gaining acceptance, and stimulating supportive action for ideas or proposals.

Communication is not just telling or hearing something. In the true sense of the word, it means communion or a mutual sharing of ideas and feelings. It comes from the Latin *communicare,* meaning "to share" or "to make common." In this setting then, communication is the giving and receiving of a share of anything. This is accomplished through the use of language, which may be spoken or written, or the use of symbolism, or variations of sound or light, or some other such mode. Usually, the word *communication* brings to mind the sending or receiving of a letter, a telephone call linking one speaker with one listener, a conversation between friends, the publication of a newspaper, a radio or television broadcast, or a batch of leaflets that are delivered in the mail.

In any event, communication is a cooperative enterprise requiring the mutual interchange of ideas and information, and out of which understanding develops and action is taken. Communication can also be regarded as a tool for drawing people and their viewpoints closer together, and thus facilitating the quality of the relationship they enjoy. Actually, it is, as the sociologist Char-

les Horton Cooley pointed out some years ago, "the mechanism through which human relations exist and develop."

From this point of view, the nature and importance of the communication process in a school-community relations program will be discussed with reference to the elements of communication, communication and persuasion, mass media techniques, and words.

ELEMENTS OF COMMUNICATION

In communication theory, five elements are identified in the transmission of a message. Figure 6.1 identifies them as the source or sender of information, the message form used by the source (encoder), a channel that carries the message, the decoder who perceives and interprets the common language, and a receiver who reacts to the message after conceptualizing it. This simple pattern of message transmission has just as much application to a complex city newspaper which puts messages into print and sends them to thousands of readers as it does to the encoding, sending, and decoding of a letter from one friend to another.

Source of Information

The source of information may be a person or a group of persons who possess certain ideas, feelings, and needs, as well as a reason for wanting to engage in communication. In selecting the source as the starting place for a message, it should be remembered that the source has been influenced by messages received earlier and by perceptions made in the past. In reality, the source is the

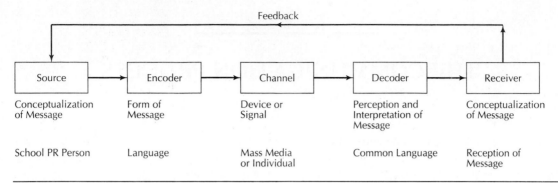

FIGURE 6.1 A common communication model with examples of components.

human brain—a highly developed internal communication mechanism that is able to combine concepts stored there, and so to create ideas, establish purposes for communication, and decide how a message will be transmitted.

The Message Encoder

The information furnished by the source must be put in message form before being sent to a particular person or audience. Here a number of factors come into play. They are important determinants of message effectiveness and may be summed up briefly as follows:

▬ Although language is the principal tool in coding a message, still there are times when a body movement, a facial gesture, an unusual noise, or some other sign will convey just as much meaning to the receiver of the message.

▬ Senders must understand their messages themselves before they can make them understood by their receivers.

▬ To impart information or feelings, the sender and receiver should know not only what the words, phrases, or other signs mean, but both should be able to interpret these elements in the same way.

▬ Unless a message can be decoded easily and accurately, there is a danger that the receiver's attention will shift to something else which appears to offer an equal or greater reward for less effort.

▬ A message is received more readily when it contains one or more cues or suggestions that appeal to the receiver's needs and interests. Such cues or suggestions become an inducement for decoding and accepting the message.

▬ Once the source determines what ideas the message should convey, he or she can decide how to express them in a form that will appeal to the receiver.

▬ The use of symbols in a message makes it possible to compress and simplify complex information. When such symbols as the Red Cross, a school building, or the American flag are used, they stand for concepts that people readily understand and grasp.

▬ Most encoded messages contain a number of parallel messages. When a message is delivered orally, the words, those that are emphasized, the rate of delivery, the pauses, and the facial expressions are all interpreted along with the content of the message.

From this list it is evident that effective encoding calls for a message form that is appropriate for the particular situation, place, and audience.

The Channel

When a message has been coded, the sender must select a channel that will carry it to the person or audience for whom it is intended. The channel may be a word-of-mouth conversation; an oral presentation on radio or television; a written document in the form of a letter or a memorandum; printed matter like a newspaper, a book, a magazine, or a brochure; or a combination of words and pictures through the medium of motion pictures, videotapes, slides with sound tracks, and the like. These are merely some of the more commonly used channels in message transmission.

At the same time, it is essential that the sender know which of these channels are available in the community, how extensively they are used, and how effective each is in reaching various audiences. One channel, for example, might be better than another for message delivery to a foreign-language-speaking segment of the population, while a still different one could be used with good results for keeping professional persons in the community informed about critical school problems.

Channels that are selected for message transmission should be free from distracting elements that discourage audience attention, such as printed pages of a leaflet or brochure in which the type is smudgy and hard to read, or poorly reproduced photographs and line drawings in a photojournalism piece, or static noises that punctuate a radio broadcast. Such distractions terminate communication possibilities almost at once.

The Message Decoder

Assuming that the transmission channel is working satisfactorily, the question then arises of whether or not the decoder is able to decode the message accurately. This means interpreting the sign or the way in which the message is coded. If the message is coded in written English, will the decoder understand the vocabulary? Does his or her background of knowledge and experience enable him or her to comprehend quickly and correctly a reference, for example, to a system of open education, a nongraded curricular arrangement, or a mini-course? Unless the reference kindles the same meaning in the mind of the reader as in the mind of the writer, the attempt at com-

munication may be only partly successful; and it may even be totally unsuccessful.

The matter of interpreting the words of a message is further complicated by the fact that the same words have different meanings for different people. Words have generally two kinds of meaning: (1) a denotative or dictionary meaning that has more or less universal acceptance and (2) a connotative meaning—a meaning that is read into the words because of the reader's background and experience. For example, the word *school* denotes a place where children go for an education under the direction of qualified teachers. To some individuals this may connote a place where many happy hours were spent, whereas to others, it may connote just the opposite, depending on the individual's experiences while attending school.

Sometimes the people who are the decoders will not take the time to review the message carefully unless they feel that it relates to things of interest to them or that their efforts will be rewarded in some way. In view of the many messages that confront one daily, the problem of getting an individual to select and decode those about the local school system is difficult. Suppose, for example, that the letter carrier just delivered a brochure about school taxes for the coming year and also a popular magazine that the resident thoroughly enjoys reading. If the size, title, color, format, and so on of the brochure lack appeal, it will probably be set aside in favor of the magazine. However, if the brochure creates curiosity regarding the tax situation, reinforces the individual's concern over mounting educational costs, or suggests that he or she stands to gain something, the individual may be motivated sufficiently to examine this particular message.

Furthermore, the decoder is more apt to decode a message that calls for the least amount of effort. A six-page brochure on school guidance services that is made up largely of clear photos with clever captions will attract and hold the receiver's attention more than one on the same subject that consists of six pages of small print. This example illustrates what is referred to in communication theory as Schramm's "fraction of selection" theory. The expectation of reward is divided by the effort required. Thus, a person will select a particular communication, in all probability, if it promises more reward or if it seems to require less effort to decode than competing messages.

The Receiver

When the message reaches the receiver, who is usually the decoder, it is expressed in some kind of shorthand—letters, drawings, photographs, tables, sounds, and so on. If this shorthand is something that the receiver has learned in the past, she or he will respond accordingly. His or her responses will indicate the meaning that the shorthand has for him or her. Although these responses are the products of experience, nevertheless they are modified at times by the receiver's physical and mental state. For example, a picture of an attractive tray of desserts will be more appealing to the hungry receiver than to one who has just finished dinner.

Besides translating the shorthand into meaning, receivers' responses will determine what they will do about the message. The action they take may be based on things they have learned in the past. The word *war* in a message, for example, may call forth strong feelings of antagonism against the idea of destroying human life. This type of response may cause people to start encoding a message in reply—one that expresses their reactions. Thus, each person in the communication process may be both an encoder and a decoder. On the other hand, the decoder may regard the message as being unimportant or may decide not to reply to it, with the result that the process stops there. However, most individuals are constantly decoding signs, reading meaning into them, and then sending back their reactions. Graphically, the flow is shown in Figure 6.1.

The return message from the decoder or receiver is known as feedback. It tells the sender or source how his or her message is being interpreted. This occurs almost at once in a face-to-face conversation where verbal response along with body gestures such as nod of the head, facial expression, or eye-focusing show the receiver's responses. In the light of these responses, the encoder or sender may modify future messages.

The feedback situation is somewhat different when messages are carried through mass communication media such as newspapers, television programs, books, or tape recordings. It is true that the recipients of these messages are individuals, but these individuals supply little or no direct feedback, although occasionally they will express reactions through telephone calls or letters to the sender. The type of feedback to the sender is usually in the form of a refusal to do something—subscribers discontinue taking the newspaper, listeners and viewers shift to another station, and consumers stop buying the product. This is an impelling reason why so much consumer research is conducted by business organizations. It is the only way available for finding out what programs are looked at on television, or what homemakers like about a particular product, or how readers are reacting to given advertisements.

COMMUNICATION AND PERSUASION

A primary purpose behind the communication process is trying to change attitudes and opinions through the use of persuasive messages. In school-community relations this purpose is frequently referred to as that of trying to bring about *informed public consent.* The procedures for achieving this involve the preparation and presentation by the school of messages containing information, ideas, or proposals that the public who receives them considers and then decides what action, if any, it is going to take. In a two-way communication flow, the process is reversed with school personnel analyzing and evaluating suggestions and ideas received from people in the community and subsequently deciding what course of action to follow.

The problem of trying to get individuals to learn new ideas and adopt new behaviors through the use of persuasive messages has been the subject of much research. This research has centered on the persuasive stages people go through, the characteristics of the sender, the message, and the receiver, as well as the results. Some of the findings that appear to have practical application in a school-community relations program will be reviewed in the paragraphs that follow.

Persuasive Stages

A number of studies have shown that people are influenced more in decision making by face-to-face contacts than by the impact of the media. This is illustrated in Lionberger's summary of studies of the diffusion process. Such a process addresses the problem of trying to get individuals to learn new ideas and new behaviors through the use of persuasive messages.

The U.S. Department of Agriculture has considerable experience at getting new ideas accepted. It took the department thirteen years to get American farmers to adopt hybrid seed corn in their planting program. From this long experience, agricultural sociologists have found that acceptance of an idea involves five stages:

Awareness. This stage introduces a person to a new idea, practice, or product. Little or nothing is known about it other than general information.

Interest. This is sometimes known as the information stage and is one in which an individual becomes interested in learning more about the idea, practice, or product. He or she will actively seek additional information.

Evaluation. An individual weighs the merits of the idea, product, or practice and attempts to determine if it is good for him or her.

Trial. The person tries the product, idea, or practice a little.

Adoption. Here the individual decides the idea, product, or practice is good enough for full-scale use.

According to Lionberger, these stages do not always follow in discrete steps; nor are they experienced by all people. He notes:

> What these stages do represent is a useful way of describing a relatively continuous sequence of action, events, and influences that intervene between initial knowledge about an idea, product, or practice, and the actual adoption of it.[2]

Important in this example of the diffusion process are the influential factors at each stage. Table 6.1 lists four factors ranked in order of influence for each stage in the U. S. Department of Agriculture's hybrid corn experience. Mass media play the leading role in *awareness* and *interest* stages while friends and neighbors are most influential at the *evaluation, trial,* and *adoption* stages. In the first two stages, information flows one way, but in the last three stages two-way communication is dominant where attitude change starts taking place. It would appear, then, that to hope for the greatest persuasion to take place, a two-way, person-to-person communication process must exist.

In other words, the mass media (in this case, radio, TV, brochures, and printed material) serve only to inform the public and to make people aware of a situation or an idea. When it comes to accepting or rejecting a new idea, people are apt to confer with a neighbor or friend whose judgment they respect. (Chapter 14 gives additional material on the diffusion of information.)

Too often school districts flood the mass media with news releases and public service announcements, thinking they will be enough to persuade citizens to accept a new idea or change in the schools. Yet, they are not aware that if attitude change is to take place, they must develop some additional communication approach to reach citizens on a person-to-person basis. They need to communicate with those people to whom citizens turn to get opinions during the last three stages of the diffusion process. One answer is a key communicator program which is explained in Chapter 8.

TABLE 6.1 Rank Order of Information Sources by Stages in the Adoption Process

Awareness Learns about a new idea or practice	*Interest* Gets more information about it	*Evaluation* Tries it out mentally	*Trial* Uses or tries a little	*Adoption* Accepts it for full-scale and continued use
1. Mass media—radio, TV, newspapers, magazines	1. Mass media	1. Friends and neighbors	1. Friends and neighbors	**Personal experience is the most important factor in continued use of an idea.**
2. Friends and neighbors—mostly other farmers	2. Friends and neighbors	2. Agricultural agencies	2. Agricultural agencies	1. Friends and neighbors
3. Agricultural agencies, extension, vo-ag, etc.	3. Agricultural agencies	3. Dealers and salespeople	3. Dealers and salespeople	2. Agricultural agencies
4. Dealers and salespeople	4. Dealers and salespeople	4. Mass media	4. Mass media	3. Mass media
				4. Dealers and salespeople

Source: Herbert F. Lionberger, *Adoption of New Ideas and Practices* (Ames: The Iowa State University Press, 1960), p. 33. Reproduced with permission.

Confidence in the Source

The persuasiveness of a communication is greater when certain things are known about the communicator. This is usually the case if the sender has gained a reputation for being honest and direct, is a highly respected person among associates, is thought to be well informed on the subject of the message, or shares a common background or set of experiences with his or her listeners.

A message is also likely to receive favorable attention when it is sent by persons in positions of leadership. Such a person could be the president of a school board, a superintendent of schools, or a civic-minded industrialist.

Some additional research findings are interesting with regard to source credibility. For example, a physically attractive source is generally more persuasive than an unattractive source regardless of the sex of the receiver. Furthermore, if receivers see the gender to be similar to themselves in experiences, opinions, and backgrounds, they are more apt to accept the message. Some researchers define source credibility as expertness and claim that it is related more to attitude change than the source's attractiveness or similarity to the intended audience. However, in order for the expertise to be persuasive, Oskamp[3]

claims that special conditions are needed: (1) the area of expertise must be related to the issue or topic being presented and (2) before the message is to be delivered the expertise must be made known to the audience. In general, researchers suggest that people will often accept or reject message conclusions based on source credibility without paying much attention to the supporting arguments.

In certain unusual situations, researchers have discovered an interesting relation between the source credibility and the passage of time. They found that receivers remember the context of a message from a noncredible communicator, think about it, and sometimes later accept the message after they have forgotten where it came from. This phenomenon is known as the *sleeper effect*. In brief, then, the tie between the source of a message and the content of a message is not the same in perception as in memory.

Support of Personal Views

Much research has been done on attitude change when the receiver of a communication is exposed to a message that agrees or disagrees with his or her point of view. Among the more important findings are these:

▬ People tend to read, watch, and listen to communications that are in agreement with their beliefs and interests.

▬ When they receive a message containing a point of view or information that casts doubt on their position, they either disregard or distort the message in order to confirm existing attitudes and opinions. Actually, they only hear or read what they expect to hear or read, not what the message says.

▬ In some instances, exposure to such material leads to restructuring of the message by receivers so that the content agrees with their predisposition or at least so that it is made tolerable. They end up, in other words, perceiving the message as though it reflected their own point of view.

▬ People remember the content of a message that supports what they believe much better than they remember material that is antagonistic to their convictions.

▬ Information and ideas about a subject receive most attention from those who are most interested in it or the ones whose minds are most firmly made up beforehand. Those who have no interest in the subject pay little or no attention to communications regarding it.

▬ When a discussion of an issue reaches the stage of controversy, those taking part in it are apt to ignore additional information unless it happens to agree with their attitudes and convictions. At this point it is usually too late for further information to influence them; in fact, too much information may produce a negative reaction.

▬ In an area where few opinions have been formed, the chances are rather good that a well-devised communication will accomplish its goal. In an area, however, where opinions are fixed and strongly defended, the chance of achieving attitude change is only slight. Where this is the case, it is better to take existing attitudes and try to redirect them slightly.

Benefit to Receiver

Messages can be persuasive when they deal with the receiver's needs or appeal to his or her self-interest. It is only natural to look more sharply at the content of a communication from which one can gain something. A communication could, for example, request that one serve as chairperson of a committee that is highly regarded by members of one group, or it could contain an offer to finance a research project in which one has a strong interest. In much the same way, citizens respond favorably to school communications that explain the services children receive from the tax dollar. Although indirect, this type of benefit makes citizens feel that a worthwhile return is being received from their investment.

Sometimes a message is persuasive because it is received when the individual has a predisposition to change. Suppose, for example, that the receiver has been active in an independent citizen movement to upgrade instruction in the schools and feels that this activity is no longer satisfying. As a result he or she may have become predisposed to change. Then a message is received describing the value of citizen involvement in the formulation of educational policies under the auspices of the board of education. The receiver's new predisposition to change may cause a positive reaction to similar communications rejected on prior occasions.

Group Influences

Research studies have turned up a series of findings about group influence on the receiver's acceptance or rejection of a message. To begin with, a message is more likely to stimulate a favorable response if the content of it relates clearly to group values and beliefs. Group values and beliefs are those established by the family, friends, co-workers, and organizations to which the receiver belongs or would like to belong. On the other hand, if the content is in disagreement with group norms, it will probably be rejected unless it undergoes substantial change. It is difficult to persuade the receiver to believe in something or to do anything that runs counter to the value system of his or her groups.

This raises the question of what individuals receive in return for conforming to the standards and beliefs of a group. Research on this question shows that they get two returns for conformity. First, they identify closer with the group and enhance their acceptance as members, and second, they receive some ready-made interpretations of experience and consequently find it easier to meet the daily pressures of life and its accompanying problems.

It has also been found that receivers cannot be persuaded easily if their acceptance of a message will cause them to lose face among their peers. In speculating on this possibility, the sender should scrutinize all available alternatives before transmitting the message and word it accordingly.

There are other ways in which the individual is influenced by the judgment of other people. For example, an individual who will go along with the position of a speaker when the position appears acceptable to the majority of the audience may be less likely to agree with it when he or she senses a discrepancy between the speaker's position and that of the audience. It has also been observed that an individual responds to appeals in a crowd that he or she would scarcely consider, let alone accept, apart from the group. Thus, it is sometimes possible to convince an individual to accept a point of view in private, even though later he or she will deny it when reacting with a crowd.

Research has also found that opinions individuals have made known to others are more difficult to change than those they hold privately. Also, group discussion and decision making (audience participation) help to overcome resistance to persuasion.

Presentation of Issues

In presenting issues to an audience, the question has come up of which method is more effective to use—a one-sided or a two-sided message. In other words, to present only your position, or to present both yours and the opposite one. Research results indicate the answer varies with the conditions and circumstances under which the presen-

tation takes place. Some of the important findings are listed below and should be regarded as guidelines in school and community relations.

■ Presenting only one side of an argument often causes the audience to feel that it is being talked down to by the speaker. Those who are well informed on the subject and those who think they are resent this type of treatment.

■ If it appears that an audience is unfriendly and skeptical about the integrity of the speaker, as well as rather well informed on some aspects of the subject, the presentation should be carefully balanced and highly objective.

■ When a group is initially exposed to a two-sided communication, such as the pros and cons of constructing a new school building, it is more likely to resist propaganda to which it is subsequently exposed.

■ Persons of low intellect and limited schooling can be influenced by a one-sided message if the content is limited to arguments favoring the communicator's position.

■ Persons with high intellectual ability and good educational backgrounds tend to be more influenced by a two-sided message.

■ When audience members are well informed on an issue, more persuasion is accomplished by reviewing both sides of the matter, but when they are poorly informed, then a one-sided presentation is more effective.

■ A one-sided message is more apt to influence persons who were initially inclined to support the position being advocated, but a two-sided communication is more influential for those who were opposed at the beginning.

■ More attitude change occurs when the desirable features of a proposed change are presented first and the undesirable second.

■ When different communicators present two sides of an issue successively, the side presented first has no real advantage. But when a single communicator presents both sides, the material presented first seems to have more impact on the audience than that presented subsequently.

■ In controversial situations, messages that offer some reasonable conclusion to an issue are more likely to be persuasive than if the audience were left to make up its own mind.

— When conflicting information is important to the audience, failure to divulge such information may be regarded as an indication that the communicator has not looked at the other side carefully enough.

— Research has yielded conflicting findings on the matter of whether the opening or closing of a message should contain the more important content. By starting with the weaker points, an interested audience looks forward to what is coming later. But an apathetic audience is more likely to be aroused when the important points are presented at the beginning.

— Research findings lack agreement on the effectiveness of emotional versus rational appeals. Sometimes messages containing one type of appeal are more persuasive than the other type. Appeal effectiveness of either emotional or rational messages seems to depend on the issue under consideration as well as on the composition of the audience.

Fear-Arousal Messages

Are people persuaded to change their attitudes and behaviors because a message arouses fear and insecurity? Much of the research in fear-arousal messages confirms that as these messages increase from low to moderate levels, attitude and behavior changes increase. However, as the messages progress from a moderate to a stronger level, persuasion is less apt to take place. Apparently strong fear evokes ego defenses that block attitude change.

In some studies it has been found that when an audience is exposed to conflicting messages on the same issue, the use of a strong threat appeal tends to be less persuasive than the use of a minimal one in bringing about attitude change. However, if the communicator wants the audience to remember the threat and nothing else, then a strong appeal may prove to be persuasive.

Therefore, it should be recognized in school and community relations that fear-arousal mes-

sages, either direct or indirect, will not evoke acceptance or help to gain the support required in providing a sound educational program. Messages that help people in the community see reasonable and feasible solutions to educational problems are more effective in gaining support for needed school programs.

Repeating the Message

Advertisers have known for many years that repeating a message through a variety of media helps to achieve persuasion. The principle of repetition applies equally to school-devised messages. For example, in a rapidly growing community in which kindergartens are just starting, it might be necessary to let parents know of their availability and their advantages in early childhood education. By carefully selecting the timing of releases on the subject, a direct mailing of brochures could be made over a three-week period. At the same time, both straight news and feature stories could be prepared for newspapers and spot announcements for radio and television news programs. Both the news stories and the spot announcements could be scheduled three or four days apart over the same three-week period.

Scheduling the announcements about kindergartens in close succession and through different media not only strengthens the impact of the initial exposure to the message but also converges a variety of announcements on the audience from more than one direction. Repetition with variation promotes better message understanding and acceptance.

However, a qualifying note should be emphasized here. Repetition of a message can have an attitude enhancement effect only if the content (stimulus) is positive or neutral. If it is negative, the opposite effect will take place.

Personality and Sex Variables

The personality of the receiver has a dramatic effect on how the message is processed. Research indicates that people with low self-esteem are predisposed to attitude change when exposed to persuasive messages. This is particularly true if the messages are simple and poorly substantiated. Conversely, high self-esteem individuals are more often persuaded with complex, but well-substantiated, messages. Experts in attitude change also indicate that individuals with chronic high levels of anxiety and aggressiveness usually resist persuasion.

As the personality of the receiver has been researched extensively, so too has the effect of gender on the persuasiveness of a message. Although some research has indicated that women are more easily persuaded than men, subsequent research indicates that this opinion is false.

> The stereotype that women are more persuadable than men has bitten the dust. Research by Dr. Alice Eagly, a psychology professor at Purdue University, shows that out of a total of 148 studies of conformity, 76 percent reported no difference between men and women.[4]

Further Findings about Persuasion

Further findings about persuasion in messages that try to effect attitude change and stimulate behavioral action are presented below in summary form.

— There is usually better assurance that an audience will comprehend more clearly the nature of a message when it contains a stated conclusion. However, this concept does not always work successfully. A suspicious audience may view the stated conclusion as a deception, while a sophisticated one may regard it as an insult to their intelligence.

— When a message suggests a pattern of action for the satisfaction of particular needs and interests, the suggested pattern should generally be in agreement with the norms and beliefs of the group to which the receiver belongs.

— In trying to validate the information received in a message, broadly educated people are likely to turn to outstanding authorities, while less well-educated people are likely to turn to their friends and neighbors.

— With reference to matters of taste, individuals who read good books usually listen to good radio programs, whereas those who read light books or none at all listen to light radio programs. This principle of selective exposure applies to a variety of life situations.

— The communicator can influence attitudes or behavior only when the message is accompanied by the possibility of equally valuable changes in the surrounding situation. For example, a parent may pay slight attention to a school leaflet on homework when a child is doing satisfactory work, but the parent may read it carefully when the child's marks drop sharply.

— Attention may be drawn to communications containing important information through the use of "indicators." These are devices that suggest that the message may be valuable to the receiver. Common indicators are boxed stories in newspapers, large headlines over a news story, tones of voice that indicate urgency, sincerity, or fright, colors, and various symbols.

— Face-to-face conversation with a trusted friend who knows a new program from personal experience, let's say in reading instruction, has almost the same influential quality as an actual visit to a school and an observation of the program in operation.

— Effective communication calls for the use of several different communication channels. It has been found that some channels may call the receiver's attention to an issue, others to the alternatives that are open, and still others may convince him or her that a choice is a sound one. And some channels may be useful in helping him or her to carry out a decision.

— Women inspire more confidence than men when they act as spokespersons for government agencies, large corporations, and nonprofit organizations.[5]

— Greater attitude change comes about from running a caption with a news photo than printing a news story alone.[6]

▬ Most people attempt to defend their positions with strong rebuttals. If they want to convince someone that their view is the right one, they should start off by emphasizing points of agreement. Then they should try to get the other person to accept several minor points that lead logically to their major position.[7]

THE MASS MEDIA

Much of the communication that takes place between school personnel and people in the community is through the mass media—printed publications, newspapers, slides, filmstrips, motion pictures, videos, exhibits, radio, and television. These media are commonly thought of as vehicles or means for transmitting identical messages to many individuals at the same time. For instance, several thousand people may read a feature story in the evening newspaper describing a special school program in child care for high-school students. An equal number may see on a television program the floor plans and site arrangements for a proposed school facility. And many may receive a leaflet about mathematics or listen to a speaker give an illustrated lecture on competitive sports and character development.

Unlike a small group of parents discussing a proposed change in the school lunch schedule or members of the parent-teacher association listening to a talk on teen-age health problems, those who constitute a mass communication audience have practically no contact with each other. One person may be looking at a television program on a travelogue through Ontario without knowing whether anyone else in the house next door or on the same street is looking at that program.

However, each person who is independently viewing such a program, reading a news magazine, or hearing a radio broadcast, and so on is connected with various groups in the community, such as family, close friends, fellow workers, members of a lodge, or a church congregation. This fact is important in mass communication because the real impact of messages transmitted by means of mass media is produced through the dissemination of ideas and information by individual receivers in small group situations.

A leaflet on the teaching of spelling in the schools, a news story about the president of the school board, or a television interview with an outstanding teacher may be the subject of conversation over the dinner table, among business associates, or at a social gathering in the neighborhood. What is reported by the individual receiver is then reinterpreted by the group, and the outcome is translated into group opinion and possibly group action. Thus it would seem that an important outcome of mass communication is the influence of the individual receiver in message distribution and opinion development among members of his or her group.

In addition to this, there are other outcomes associated with the use of the mass media. First is that mass communication makes it possible to deliver a message to large numbers of people in a relatively short period. For example, a newspaper story on a proposed annual school budget may be read by a fairly high percentage of citizens in the community the same day it is printed. Moreover, each reader receives the story in identical form, thereby minimizing the element of distortion that often characterizes message distribution on a person-to-person basis. Second, the mass media are most effective in creating awareness on the part of message receivers. The mass media serve as agencies through which information about an innovation, such as a change in the traditional conduct of a school board meeting, is brought to popular attention. Third, research findings consistently indicate that the mass media serve generally as means of reinforcement rather than of change. People select messages that they want to see and hear—messages that confirm preexisting beliefs and attitudes. Fourth, most people who learn about an innovation or an event through one medium, for example, the local newspaper, are also likely to learn it through other channels as well. And fifth, there is evidence that frequent repetition of a message helps it to gain acceptance, providing, however, that it is repeated in various ways. The identical repetition of a communication tends to annoy people and can reduce the chances of its being regarded favorably.

Certain limitations are connected with message transmission through the mass media because of the diverse nature of the audience. In face-to-face communication, the encoder is able to observe the way a communication is being received and to modify it if the receiver's reaction suggests this need. On the other hand, in mass media communication, the sender is dealing with large groups and many classes of people. Thus, if a school pamphlet is published for general distribution in the community, careful attention must be given to its readability; otherwise it may be pitched above the level of reading appeal and understanding of many of the people who receive it. In view of this limitation and the corresponding lack of feedback, it is advisable to appeal more often to important publics rather than to the general public. This means that a subject can be treated differently for different audiences that make up the several special publics of the school. For example, a leaflet on the financial needs of the school district could be written and designed one way for business people in the community, another way for parents of elementary children, and still another way for senior citizens.

It should also be noted that readers, listeners, and viewers have been exposed to thousands of mass media communications and are therefore able to distinguish between those that are attractive in appearance and skillful in design and those that lack these qualities. This exposure to good techniques causes people to demand excellence in all publications and programs without being conscious of their reasons for doing so. Parents may not expect a school newsletter to look like a report distributed by a large corporation to its stockholders, but they expect it to have an attractive flag, good page layout, readable type, interesting illustrations, and timely news. Skill in handling the mass media is no guarantee of establishing communication with all receivers, but it does make it much more likely.

WORDS

Successful communication is tied closely to the way in which words and symbols are employed in messages. Although there is a large body of research studies on this subject, only the more pertinent findings will be reviewed. If used correctly, these findings should improve the meaning and acceptance of school messages intended for various community audiences.

Words are tools for fashioning messages. When used properly they enable the message receiver to interpret accurately the purpose and meaning that the sender had in mind. The achievement of this outcome calls for a thorough knowledge of word usage and its application in communications for specific audiences.

Research indicates that there are several measures of word usage that must be taken into account by message encoders. To begin with, senders cannot tell other people something they themselves do not understand. They must know precisely what they want to say and then make the message easy for the receivers to comprehend. However, in making the message easy to comprehend, senders must be sensitive to the fact that word meaning varies with individuals and environmental conditions. The word *football,* for example, has a different connotation in England than it does in this country. The word *dog* to a canine enthusiast may refer to a friendly, loyal animal, whereas to a person bitten by one the word may represent an unfriendly, vicious animal. In this respect, words can play on an individual's feelings and tap his or her memory as well.

It is likewise necessary to know the meanings of words that are brought into play by self-interest groups. Each group has words and phrases peculiar to the goals the group stands for in American life. Bankers talk about prime interest rates, physicians about preventive medicine, educators about curriculum and instruction, and workers about fringe benefits and union contracts. Knowing the meaning of words that are used by self-interest groups enables the message writer or speaker to select those that will be received favorably and understandably.

The meaning of a word is influenced by the context in which it appears. For example, the word *rare* has a different connotation when it refers to a sense of humor than it has when used to describe a piece of meat. Or take the words *progressive* and *education*. When used separately in a sentence, they are regarded as positive words with acceptable meanings. However, if combined into the phrase *progressive education* they acquire another sense and to some people become negative words that have emotional overtones. In short, the meaning and reaction to a word can be changed by placing it in another context.

The number of syllables used also appears to have some effect on the readability of printed material. It has been found that words with as many as four or five syllables add to reading difficulty. And it is for this reason that reading specialists advocate the substitution of words with fewer syllables whenever possible. The longer the physical length of a word, the less chance there is of its being understood.

Somewhat similar is the pronunciation problem created by the use of words unfamiliar to the reader. Instead of focusing on what a word means in the message, attention is diverted to the question of how to pronounce it. The reader is often required to spend some time analyzing a word before he or she is able to say it correctly. If there are too many unfamiliar words in the message, the pronunciation block may become large enough to destroy the message. However, when there is uncertainty about the status of a word in the mind of the reader, the word can be clarified casually without suggesting that the reader is ignorant. For example, it could be said in a school publication that "we want to *correlate* or *pull closer together* our English and social studies in the middle school program of studies."

The semantic effect of word combinations is something that enters into the study of word usage. Research shows that each word in combination, such as *gregarious person, handsome man,* or *brave boy,* has a modifying effect on the other.

If the words in combination are out of harmony, they tend to cancel each other out, but if they are compatible, a new connotation emerges. Usually, the measured meaning of words in combinations leans toward the adjective instead of the noun.

While much has been written advisedly about the necessity of setting aside technical words and phrases in education and using instead language that is understandable to the layperson, little or nothing has been said about avoiding terms that emphasize disadvantages common to minority groups. For example, school reference is frequently made to underprivileged and culturally deprived children, slum areas, apathetic parents, lack of home motivation, and expectancy based on intelligence quotient. There are, of course, occasions and circumstances when the use of these terms is acceptable, but if their use produces tension or continuous disagreement, then they should be dropped. Often the terms irritate the minority group members, especially those living in extremely modest circumstances and seeking improvements for themselves and their children. The attitude of these minority group members changes when schools no longer speak of their children as "deprived," "depressed," and "disadvantaged," but refer to them rather as having a "likelihood for good intellectual development," "untapped potential," or with "latent abilities." This positive frame of reference not only indicates that the school has a forward look for children but shows that the school wants to instill these expectations in them.

With the women's movement came the awareness of sexist words in written and verbal presentations. This recognition was incorporated in the spirit of a number of federal regulations that went into effect in the 1970s. Educators, therefore, should be aware of the need to substitute such words as *woman* for *lady, chairperson* for *chairman, letter carrier* for *mailman,* and *staffed* for *manned.* These are but a few of the terms needed to purge writing and presentations of sexist words. Publishing companies and newspapers often can provide a comprehensive list of functional, nonsexist terms.

Moreover, the length of sentences as related to reading difficulty is brought out in the research on this subject. Reading becomes harder as the number of complex or compound sentences increases. In contrast, it becomes easier when short, simple sentences with fewer prepositional phrases are used. Moreover, the meaning of short, concise statements is less likely to be distorted and more likely to be accurately reproduced. The significance of short sentences is apparent in readability studies where short sentences are equated with ease of reading.[8]

ENDNOTES

1. Herbert F. Lionberger, *Adoption of New Ideas and Practices* (Ames: Iowa State University Press, 1960), p. 3.

2. Ibid., p. 23.

3. Stuart Oskamp, *Attitudes and Opinions* (Englewood Cliffs, NJ: Prentice-Hall, 1977), p. 183.

4. "An Old Husband's Tale?" *MS* (January 1983), p. 68.

5. "Male-Female Communication," *Communication Briefings* (February 1982), p. 1.

6. "Persuasion," *Communications Briefings* (August 1982), p. 1.

7. Ibid.

8. Frank Grazian, "Try These Formulas to Improve Writing—Bonus Item," *Communication Briefings* (August 1986).

7

COMMUNICATING WITH
INTERNAL PUBLICS

Internal communication has become increasingly important to school boards and administrators as a vital part of comprehensive school-community relations programs. In the past it was not uncommon for school systems, in developing a community relations program, to concern themselves exclusively with ways and means of communicating with their external publics. Rarely did they think of structuring a program of effective two-way communication with their internal publics—the employees and students. This has changed as the age of involvement has spread throughout society, including education.

Internal publics, particularly employees, began to see themselves in a different role, one that called for a more active part in the total planning of the educational program along with their professional and personal welfare; and school systems began to realize that good relations with and among internal publics were a necessary part of good public relations.

WHY INTERNAL COMMUNICATIONS?

School administrators and boards are coming to understand the importance of good internal communications. This awareness has been brought about by the need to gain continued public support of education. School boards and administrators can no longer get that support alone; they must enlist the help of employees, and doing so requires a structured internal communications program.

School districts, then, see three reasons why a good internal communication program is important: (1) a good external communication program

cannot survive without it; (2) constructive ideas will be suggested by employees because someone is listening and informing them; and (3) human needs, such as recognition and a sense of belonging, will be met, thus making employees more productive.

SCHOOL BOARD ACTIONS

In analyzing the causes of good and poor relations within a system, it is advisable to start with the board of education. This body sets the climate of the school system through the exercise of its authority, the conduct of its business, and the relationships it maintains with administrators and staff members.

Board Authority

A local school board is given broad discretionary powers, both the right and the authority under state law to manage the school system; what matters is the manner in which the board of education exercises this authority. If it refuses to listen to the advice of the chief executive officer, shows indifference to the welfare of the employees, usurps the functions of the administrator, rules on matters about which it is ignorant, issues unreasonable orders, makes political appointments, tries to summarily dismiss teachers, listens to parental complaints without consulting principals and teachers, and engages in other undesirable practices, it soon creates unfavorable working conditions and lowers the morale of employees. The result is that the school employees no longer feel a loyalty to the system and do not hesitate to say what they think about the board of education and the policies with which they are forced to comply.

The Conduct of Board Business

The board of education is legally required to conduct its business in regular meetings and in special meetings called from time to time. All meetings are open with the exception of executive sessions. In a number of states the decisions reached in executive session are not binding until voted on in open meeting.

Whether or not a board adheres to the proper conduct of its business exerts a direct influence on public and employee attitudes. A well-organized meeting in which sincere efforts are made to serve the school community will inspire employees with confidence, respect, and trust; a poorly managed, perfunctory, and discordant meeting will leave a residue of discontent.

Relations with the Superintendent

School board relations with the superintendent deserve special consideration in any discussion of internal affairs. In many systems, the board of education is organized into a series of standing committees. Each committee is made responsible for some area of the school program. There may be committees on personnel, buildings and grounds, transportation, finance, public relations, instruction, and welfare. This system is used to expedite board business and divide the amount of work carried by members. However, it has definite weaknesses that should be recognized.

■ The executive officer is required to report to committees instead of taking up problems with the whole board of education.

■ These committees become policy-making bodies because their recommendations are, as a rule, accepted by the board without much question.

■ Members of the board have but slight understanding of the system aside from the specific areas in which they work on committee assignments.

■ The tendency is strong for committees to encroach on the administrative function of the superintendent.

This form of board organization can easily produce unfavorable relations with superintendents and reduce the effectiveness of their leadership in school systems.

Complaints received by board members from teachers, parents, and people in the community are another cause of poor relationships if they are handled incorrectly. Sound administration requires that all complaints be referred to the superintendent of schools and cleared through him or her with members of the staff. If satisfaction is not received by the complaining party, the board can then request the superintendent to report the facts and tell what he or she has done, before any official action is taken. Instead of following this procedure, or one comparable to it, some board members assume responsibility for settling complaints themselves. They not only take over the authority of the superintendent but also undermine his or her prestige in the school and community. The incorrect handling of complaints is a fertile breeding place for discord in the relationship of the board and the superintendent.

The kind of interest that board members show in education problems is another potential area of disagreement between board members and the superintendent. As the professional advisor of the board and the educational leader of the school system, it is up to the superintendent to keep the board informed of current problems and to recommend courses of action for meeting existing needs. Although superintendents do not expect the board to approve all of their recommendations, they do expect that the members will consider suggestions with a fair degree of impartiality. If board members are casual or indifferent about a superintendent's recommendations, or if their decisions are made for personal, business, or political reasons, he or she is left with the alternative of either protesting vigorously or else going along with the board for his or her own security. In the long run, superintendents who play the game for their own security may enjoy smoother relations with the board, but their leadership role in the school system and the community may be forfeited.

Adverse relations may also develop from the kind of methods employed by the superintendents in dealing with boards. For instance, they may withhold vital information to protect themselves or they may initiate important policies without consulting the board beforehand. Some superintendents destroy goodwill by assuming an attitude of intellectual superiority and by insisting on the right to decide all educational policies. A few may try to bring community pressure to get what they want and, failing this, engage in a whispering campaign to defeat members who are up for reelection.

Relations with Staff Personnel

Board relations with staff personnel are carried on mostly through the superintendent. He or she is expected to advise the board on staff problems and to recommend policies. Since members of the board enjoy relatively few contacts with staff personnel, they may not understand or appreciate the viewpoints of their own employees. Without this insight, they are prone to decide matters of policy in terms of finance instead of human value. Staff members are quick to sense the temperament of a board and to feel that it is indifferent to their welfare. Nothing that a board can do is more detrimental to morale than to accentuate finance at the expense of human welfare.

Some observers of education are of the opinion that selfish and foolish behavior on the part of many boards of education has caused militancy among employees. These observers contend that by allowing unsatisfactory working conditions and salaries, some school systems have actually caused their employees to depend on unions. Undoubtedly, if such conditions do exist and if

boards are antagonistic toward their school staffs, the growth of a union can be stimulated.

ADMINISTRATION-EMPLOYEE RELATIONS

Relationships between the board of education and the superintendent of schools have a positive or a negative effect on relationships between the superintendent and the employees. A superintendent who enjoys good relations with the board is more likely to look on his or her job as an opportunity to build a better school system. Employees catch the spirit of the superintendent and welcome the leadership provided. A different reaction takes place when the superintendent is forced to contend with an unpleasant board that is more interested in saving money than in building a good school system.

Primary relations between administration and employees start with the superintendent and flow down a line of authority to the assistant superintendent, directors of special departments, supervisors, and building principals, according to the size of the system. The superintendent is the one who sets the overall pattern of relationships, because of his or her position as chief executive officer. Under proper administrative conditions, success or failure is bound up closely with the willingness of the employees to support the superintendent's policies. In systems where desirable administration-employee relations are found, the superintendent is usually a capable executive who possesses a dynamic and pleasing personality, a deep respect for human values, and an ability to work democratically with people. His or her policies follow a clearly defined philosophy of education and management and include recognition of staff achievements, opportunities for growth in service, staff participation in policy and program development, fair treatment, satisfactory working conditions, and a sincere concern for staff welfare. What a school system has in the way of organization, administrative procedures, instruction, plant, and esprit de corps is due largely to the policies, leadership, courage, and vision of the superintendent.

Except in small school systems, the superintendent must rely on subordinate administrative and supervisory officers to promote desirable staff relations. Poor subordinates, however, may do much to impede his or her leadership and efforts to build a unified school system. They can misinterpret policies and badly manage excellent programs. Their individual struggles for prestige and power may divide staff loyalties and set up competing factions. Unless superintendents have capable and reliable subordinates, they may find themselves heading a mediocre and strife-torn system.

Aside from the superintendent, perhaps the most important administrative officers are the building principals. They are in more intimate contact with the staff than their immediate superiors. Their attitudes and actions determine the way in which many teachers and other school personnel think and feel about the school system.

Human Relations in Improving Employee Relations

The day has long since passed when school administration can be considered as purely a technical skill of developing a budget, constructing and maintaining school plants, assigning teachers, accounting for students, operating school cafeterias, and providing transportation. All these are necessary and vital to the operation of a school or a school system; but another skill, namely, human skill, must be considered in any discussion of good school administration, particularly where internal relations are concerned.

Katz defines human skill as "the executive's ability to work effectively as a group member and to build cooperative effort within the team he or she leads."[1] Running through studies in all areas of administration is a consensus that although technical skills cannot be disregarded, human skills are of far more importance. The relationship that should exist between human and technical skills has been outlined by Chandler:

In effect, the superintendent must be an expert in human relations. He [she] can employ persons with technical skills required in the construction of buildings, in budget making, and in school business areas, but no staff member can relieve the superintendent of his [her] human relations functions.[2]

School administrators, therefore, must focus attention on acquiring skills to deal with human problems. A necessary requirement for an administrator to develop skills in human relations is a positive attitude toward the supreme worth of all individuals. Not only must this attitude be present in the administrators, it must be evident and manifested in their behavior. It is not enough for them to state that they believe in democratic administration and total involvement of their staffs and employees; they must verify this philosophy in their day-to-day relations with their employees by showing their regard for others and by generating goodwill among school employees. Good human relations is a matter of using good common sense in administration, which in turn will generate mutual respect and goodwill.

In a successful school system the spirit of goodwill is a pervasive feeling that emanates from the board of education, the chief school administrator, and members of the administrative and supervisory staff. Educators too often think they are practicing good human relations if they provide their employees with good salaries, comfortable lounges, released time, social functions, free coffee, and reserved parking spaces. Important as these features are in the total picture of good employee relations, if such benefits are provided out of a spirit of paternalism to make the employees more compliant, they will not bring about the desired result of good human relations. Employees must perceive that administrators and supervisors are being sincere and honest with them if goodwill and mutual respect are to develop in a school system.

Administrators must train themselves to be sensitive to the importance of communicating through their own behavior and action. If this behavior belies what they say, they will invariably have difficulty in maintaining good human relations. In taking action or making a decision, administrators must anticipate how their employees will perceive the matter. Take, for example, the superintendent who informed the staff that the budget was to be cut and no additional hiring was to take place. In the meantime, the superintendent, preoccupied with an additional assignment from the board of education, hired an additional secretary. The new workload may have warranted the hiring of an additional person, but the school personnel perceived it differently as they had slashed their own budget and denied themselves services. To them the superintendent's behavior destroyed the sincerity of what had been said and served to reduce chances of improving relations with them.

Ultimately, good human relations will lead to better employee relations because of job satisfaction. A problem in education is that a number of administrators make the assumption that the factors that contribute to job satisfaction also contribute to job dissatisfaction. According to Herzberg[3] these are two separate sets of factors. He includes under satisfiers (motivational needs) such factors as achievement; recognition; work itself; responsibility; advancement; and growth. Under dissatisfiers (hygienic needs) he lists policy and administration; salary; work conditions; interpersonal relations with supervisors, peers, and subordinates; status; security; supervision; and personal life. The hygienic needs relate to the condition of the work while the motivational needs relate to the work itself. In order for the employee to move from the hygienic needs to the motivational needs, where morale and productivity improve, the hygienic needs must be reasonably met.

In relating Herzberg's theory to education, Sergiovanni and Carver note:

> It must be remembered, however, that in general providing of hygienic needs prevents decreases in performance but will not increase performance. The motivation to work beyond what is necessary to meet minimum requirements comes from the satisfier set—achievement and recognition, for

example. According to the theory, these are the motivators. This concept is of fundamental importance, for the theory suggests that it is a mistaken notion to assume that school executives can buy teacher motivation through concessions across the collective-bargaining table or in similar ways. The bargaining process as we presently know it is largely limited to hygienic concerns.[4]

RELATIONS AMONG TEACHERS

Relations among teachers should be evaluated for the effect they have on public opinion. Poor relations have resulted in serious damage to school systems and to the status of professional employees in the community. Teachers have undermined support and respect for the school system by criticizing the work of colleagues to pupils, parents, and the public. Some teachers have openly opposed school policies—as well as newer educational practices and legislative proposals aimed at improving their own welfare—in newspapers. Teachers who engage in these practices are both their own worst enemies and the enemies of the school system. The problems they create must be worked out by administrators who wish to improve and strengthen relations with the community.

The reasons for poor relations among teachers can be traced to a variety of causes. The more typical are lack of administrative direction, instructional practices, unethical conduct, division of responsibility, and formation of cliques.

Lack of Administrative Leadership

Unity among staff personnel is difficult to produce without strong administrative leadership. Lack of such leadership diverts attention from problems of teaching and learning and brings into prominence petty differences and personal irritations common to any group of people. This in turn leads to rivalry, clique formation, destructive criticism, disagreement, and quarreling. These human weaknesses are less significant and destructive in a school system where the administrative leader brings teachers together to share ideas, to identify instructional problems, to pool resources, to define acceptable goals, and to coordinate their services.

Instructional Practices

Instructional practices in any good school should be guided by a definite statement of the philosophy and objectives of teaching. When there is no definite agreement on such philosophy and objectives, friction may develop between teachers and may leave parents confused as to what kind of education their children are receiving. One teacher may believe that children grow best in a democratic institution with as much freedom as they can manage successfully, whereas another teacher may believe that children should be kept under strict control and be told exactly what to do. One teacher may give home assignments as an aid to subject-matter mastery, and another may think that home assignments are unnecessary. One may employ a methodology of recitation, drill, and testing; another may build instruction around problems and projects involving many different types of learning activities. Differences in instructional practices can be a serious cause of poor relations among teachers.

Unethical Conduct

Unethical conduct creates friction among teachers, and examples are numerous. For instance, a teacher may attribute the weaknesses of a class in arithmetic to poor instruction by the previous teacher and make this opinion known to pupils and parents. Or sometimes parents are told that their children do not read well thanks to the methods used by the second-grade teacher, or that their children will pay an educational penalty later on because certain members of the staff are not upholding desirable achievement standards. Teachers who show initiative and imagination, who experiment with newer methods, and who try different curricular arrangements are often ridiculed by colleagues for their efforts. Any teacher who is

the target of unfair criticism and abuse by colleagues is bound to feel resentful.

Malicious gossip and rumor are other forms of unethical conduct that induce strained relations among faculty members. Illustrations are legion of teachers circulating stories and raising clever questions that throw doubt on the moral character of a fellow worker, thus injuring his or her status in the school and community. These unfair practices can disrupt harmony among staff members and cause much unnecessary suffering. Teachers cannot work together efficiently and present a solid front to the public when they are beset by malicious gossip and rumor.

Division of Responsibility

Disturbances often arise over the division of responsibility among teachers. A heavy classroom schedule will be accepted without too much complaint, provided some teachers do not receive fewer classes, smaller sections, and fewer preparations than others. Sponsorship of extracurricular activities may bring vigorous protest from those who are assigned such difficult, time-consuming activities as newspapers, yearbooks, and dramatics, for which no allowance is made in work load. Resentment over unfair division of responsibility becomes acute when there is a reasonable suspicion that favoritism has been shown to some members of the staff. The resentment is directed as much at these members as at the administrative officers who are responsible for staff assignments.

Formation of Cliques

Cliques are small, exclusive groups of individuals who band together for their own interest and protection. They keep to themselves as much as possible. In an individual school, members of the foreign language department may remain apart from their colleagues, feeling that they have little in common with the rest of the faculty. Teachers of mathematics and science may set up their own clique because they regard themselves as being intellectually and socially superior, while teachers of college preparatory students may adopt a corresponding attitude toward those who instruct vocational students. It may be necessary for young teachers to band together in meeting the dominance and abuse of older teachers. Teachers who belong to minority groups are often forced to act as a unit for protection against discrimination.

Cliques thrive mostly in schools where nothing is done to involve the staff in the study of common problems and where administrators remain in the background. The influence of such cliques can be modified when the causes are known and suitable measures worked out for diverting attention to instructional improvements.

RELATIONS WITH
NONINSTRUCTIONAL PERSONNEL

School administrators and boards of education sometimes forget that noninstructional personnel are also frontline interpreters of the school. Custodians, mechanics, secretaries, clerks, bus drivers, cafeteria workers, and maintenance personnel have many contacts in the community with friends and neighbors and through membership in religious, fraternal, and social groups. Their attitudes toward the institution and its personnel are just as important as those of teachers in influencing the public mind. When noninstructional personnel are dissatisfied with their jobs and do not get along well with staff members, the reasons are usually associated with politics, job definition, recognition, and economic welfare.

Politics

In a number of school systems, custodians, mechanics, maintenance workers, clerks, cafeteria workers, and bus drivers are political appointees. They are employed not because of their ability but to pay off political favors. Lacking the qualifications required for understanding and performing their duties effectively, they invite criticism and attack from professional personnel, who have worked for years to establish high standards of selection.

Unfortunately, citizens are not always aware of this condition, and much educational work must be done before they will be ready to clean up boards of education that are dominated by political organizations. Teachers' associations can assist in educating the public to the facts and in demanding that school boards establish definite qualifications for the employment of noninstructional personnel.

Job Definition

Much of the trouble between instructional and noninstructional personnel could be avoided through the technique of job definition so that each individual understands what is expected of him or her. When responsibilities are not well specified, the result is often disagreement over who does what. The janitor claims that the teacher should have children pick up pieces of paper on the floor before they are dismissed. The teacher blames the janitor for leaving the window shades uneven or not arranging seats in proper order. Clerks refuse to duplicate work needed for classroom instruction and object to teachers using office phones during certain hours.

Recognition

Noninstructional staff personnel want acknowledgment and praise for outstanding service just as much as teachers, and they seldom receive any. Instead, they are treated by some teachers as social inferiors and are criticized in front of pupils. Conflicts involving noninstructional personnel would be reduced and almost eliminated if friendly attitudes were shown toward them and they were accorded deserved recognition. Better relations have been promoted in schools where these workers are invited to faculty meetings and serve on staff committees dealing with matters in which they have an interest.

Economic Welfare

In the past the economic welfare of noninstructional personnel has been notoriously poor with respect to salary, sick leave, and retirement. Some improvements have taken place in recent years through collective bargaining, but the condition is still bad in many parts of the country. Their insecurity accounts for a large share of the disloyalty they feel toward the institution and the ill will they hold toward the teaching group whose economic position has undergone steady improvement. As essential workers, they are entitled to higher wages and the protection afforded by sick leave and retirement.

IMPROVEMENT OF STAFF RELATIONS

The improvement of staff relations starts with the board of education. Through its actions in conducting meetings, showing an intelligent concern for instructional problems, extending fair treatment to administrative staff personnel, and maintaining a strict division of labor between policy decision and policy execution, the board of education can inspire confidence and build a real feeling of security that will permeate the entire school system.

Given this condition, the superintendent and those who assist him or her have an excellent opportunity to foster good staff relations and to make progress toward the achievement of educational goals. The extent to which they succeed will depend on their friendliness, understanding, integrity, and skill in working with people.

In a small school system, the superintendent is the person responsible for establishing cooperative relations with and among members of the staff, largely through leadership in everyday affairs that involve close personal relations. As a school system increases in size, opportunities for personal relations between the superintendent and the staff become fewer. It then becomes the function of the superintendent to establish the climate for good relations through personal contact with representatives from various groups in the school system. Along with this, the superintendent must instruct his or her intermediary assistants and supervisory personnel that they are responsible for close personal relationships with each employee under their supervision. Of this group, none is quite so important as the individual principal. Unless he or she seeks to achieve good employee relations, efforts on the part of the superintendent at the district level might be diffused and therefore ineffective.

But more is needed to effect wholesome internal relations between members of the staff and the administration than a spirit of personal leadership by those in charge of a school system. There must be practices and structures that contribute to the development of good relations.

A number of studies of internal communications and staff morale reveal that managers and administrators mistakenly assume they know what each employee wants from his or her job. Managers rate good pay, job security, and promotion and growth at the top; employees put them in the middle of their top ten wants. At the top of employees' lists are interesting work, appreciation of work done, and a feeling of being "in" on things. Table 7.1 details one study.

In another reference to employee needs, five major objectives are listed:

Opportunity—the opportunity to do something significant and important by their own personal standards
Recognition—recognition that they have made the most of the opportunity presented
Belonging—the sense of being part of things
Economic security—the ability to plan ahead with confidence in their relationship with their creditors
Emotional security—the ability to plan ahead with confidence in their relationship with everyone else—superiors, subordinates, associates[5]

It would seem, then, that managers and likewise school administrators tend to communicate from a value perspective that is different from school employees. In reality, what the school ad-

TABLE 7.1 Workers' Wants

What workers say they want	What managers think employees want
1. Interesting work	1. Good pay
2. Appreciation of work done	2. Job security
3. Feeling of being in on things	3. Promotion and growth
4. Job security	4. Good working conditions
5. Good pay	5. Interesting work
6. Promotion and growth	6. Tactful discipline
7. Good working conditions	7. Loyalty to employees
8. Loyalty to employees	8. Appreciation of work done
9. Help with personal problems	9. Help with personal problems
10. Tactful discipline	10. Feeling of being in on things

From a study of an employer-employee "Want List" by George Mason University presented in *Report of the National School Public Relations Association Staff Renewal Committee* (Arlington, VA, 1982), p. 8.

ministrator thinks is important to the employee is not. If morale is to be improved and internal communications accomplished, the school administrator must attempt to understand the needs and wants of employees and communicate from that perspective.

Perhaps, one way of approaching the problem is through a structured internal communications program that encompasses participatory management approaches fostering good employee feedback and involvement. Some components of a functional internal communications program would be one-on-one conferences, a one-three-six workshop, internal advisory committees, recognition of accomplishments, attention to working conditions, involvement of employees in planning, quality circles, shared decision making, staff development programs, preserving teachers' rights, orientation of new employees, informing substitute teachers, hosting intern teachers, and internal publications.

One-on-One Conferences

The purpose of these conferences is to enable the administrator to learn the values and priorities of each employee regarding the job assigned. In addition, the employee learns what the administra-

tor and the school district think is important for the organization.

One technique used is to give the employee a sheet of paper in the conference while the administrator also takes a sheet of paper. The employee is asked to list what is important to him or her to get the job done. Simultaneously, the administrator lists on a sheet of paper what he or she feels the employee considers important to complete assigned duties. They then compare the lists, discuss the differences, and see how the employee's values do or do not mesh with the school's values. The second phase of this process reverses the first phase. The administrator lists what he or she feels is important to get the job done. At the same time, the employee lists on a separate sheet of paper what he or she thinks the administrator considers important to carry out his or her duties. Perceptions are then discussed with a better understanding of each other's values resulting.

A wise administrator will have a conference with each employee. If the employee's values differ greatly from those of the administrator or the school district, the school official must take action to show the employee that he or she will have to adjust the values to come into line with those of the district. This would happen only in extreme cases. Usually, what the employee feels important to get a job done is something that can be effected by the administrator—for example, getting sufficient supplies, being able to post students' work on walls, having a parking space, or proper furniture in a room. Once the administrator understands these values of employees, he or she can communicate messages that address what employees feel is important. Otherwise, employees will tend not to listen to what is communicated.

One-Three-Six Workshops

Another technique to gather feedback from employees emphasizes candidness by employees, yet provides anonymity. All employees of a school district or a school meet in a group. Each employee is asked to list anonymously all his or her likes and concerns about the district or school. Each employee then joins two other employees, and the three combine their lists. Those three, in turn, join another group of three employees, and they too combine their lists. No names appear on any of the lists. The coordinator of the session lists on a flipchart, overhead projector, or board all the likes and concerns. Employees then vote to identify the top ten likes or concerns. The employees can be formed into committees to develop strategies for eliminating the concerns and maintaining the strengths of the school district or school.[6] This One-Three-Six Workshop is a communication approach that gives employees an opportunity to be heard and to feel a part of making their school or school district better.

Internal Advisory Committees

Regardless of the size of the school system, employees want some contact with the chief school administrator other than through the usual administrative channels or over a bargaining table. They want to be able to express their concerns, to have some direct impact on policy development, and to suggest ideas that will improve the overall effectiveness of the school system. Many employees

feel that in order to be heard they must communicate with all levels of administration, particularly the top level. The traditional procedure of communicating through one's immediate superior is viewed by many employees as a deliberate move to keep them silent and under control. And it is often true that a step-by-step procedure of communicating upward through the levels of administration tends to stifle employee initiative and creativity.

Some foresighted school administrators, recognizing the need to communicate with employees and to involve them in the overall planning of the school system, have created a superintendent's advisory committee. The committee is designed not only to hear what members of the internal community have to say but also to inform them of the many activities of the school district. A number of models have proved functional. One is in the form of a general advisory committee with membership from all constituencies of the school system. Another model is that of special advisory committees according to positions—one for the faculty (teachers, counselors, and librarians) and another for classified employees (office workers, transportation personnel, cafeteria workers, and the maintenance force). Normally, if a general advisory committee is organized, there is little need for special advisory committees and vice versa.

The effectiveness of advisory committees depends a great deal on the attitude of superintendents and their ability to orchestrate the whole communication process that develops. If, in creating an advisory committee, their attitude is to talk "at" the representatives and not "with" them, the committee as a one-way communication vehicle will eventually become ineffective. However, the committee can be helpful to the entire educational program if superintendents perceive issues from the viewpoint of an administrator and an employee, if they are sensitive to the importance employees might place on an issue, if they can effect change where change is possible and offer a rationale where change is not possible, and if they keep the committee informed.

Many times a concern of a committee may seem to be insignificant to the superintendent although it is of major concern to the committee. Often it is an item that can be changed or corrected by a simple memo or phone call from the superintendent. For example, to teachers, getting their supplies on a Monday rather than on a Friday may be vital, yet the superintendent may not be aware of such a problem. Furthermore his or her administrative staff may not be aware of the problem either. An advisory committee then may be one of the few ways such an overall problem of the staff can be revealed.

There are times that the superintendent will have to reject the advice of the committee and say "no" to a requested change in procedure. And it should be understood by the committee members that this will happen. In these cases the superintendent should give the rationale for saying "no." Committee members may not agree with this decision, but with an explanation they will understand better how the decision was reached.

Particularly important is the committee's ability to help the superintendent communicate with the other employees. If a new program is being launched, details can be relayed to the committee for further dissemination. The details of the annual budget can be passed along to the employees through the committee as one of a number of ways of keeping the employees informed of the activities of the school system.

Over a period of time the superintendent should be able to begin anticipating sensitive areas among employees from the issues discussed at the advisory committee meetings. In turn, he or she may be able to effect change or develop a communication strategy that can eliminate a possible crisis or confrontation with employees.

Recognition of Accomplishments

Another policy of far-reaching importance in building good relations is that of recognizing the outstanding accomplishments of individuals and groups. All individuals, no matter what kind of work they do, are psychologically so constructed that they must know whether or not their labors are being appreciated by those above them in line of authority. They may not be willing to do their best or to expend extra effort if what they do is taken for granted. Every study of morale among workers in industry has borne out this point, but for some unexplainable reason little has been done about it in the administration of education. And yet it can be accomplished rather easily, with a letter praising an employee, a note of thanks, a pleasant telephone call, or a congratulatory note.

Working Conditions

Continuing attention to the improvement of working conditions represents still another step in the growth of wholesome employee relations. Improvement of working conditions means more than putting a few easy chairs in the faculty rooms. It involves suitable furniture for pupils and teachers, reasonable work programs for non-instructional personnel, and other considerations. It also means school officials should take up these items before a union or an association forces them to do so.

Involvement in Planning

Administrators interested in fostering good internal communications would be wise to involve all employees in the planning processes for the entire school district. It would seem that each employee has enough expertise to benefit the school district by serving on a planning committee or task force—on curriculum, long-range goals, finances, buildings, athletics, or community relations, for example. Employees asked to serve on such planning committees or task forces will feel a sense of belonging and be honored that they are invited to help improve the school district. Their interest in working for the schools should increase once they have a chance to be heard and possibly effect needed changes. Additionally, this upward communication from the employees as a result of serving on planning committees or task forces has another benefit—many new ideas are generated that ultimately will help the instructional program either directly or indirectly.

Aside from involving employees in general district planning, some school officials have found it helpful to involve employees in designing activities for their own positions. Often known as management by objectives or administration by objectives, this type of planning requires the employees to develop goals, objectives, and activities for their own positions. Once these are developed, the employee meets with his or her administrator and negotiates a final plan, usually for a year. This type of planning requires communications between the employee and administrator in order to agree on a plan and to monitor the progress periodically and gives the employee a chance to have a voice in his or her professional activities.

Quality Circles

For many years Japanese industry has been using quality circles. In turn, U.S. industries have also discovered their benefits and have adopted them. And, now, quality circles appear in American education to improve relations among employees and administrators.

Usually a quality circle is composed of seven to ten people who do similar work. They meet voluntarily on a regular basis to identify and analyze sources of problems, to recommend solutions to the administration, and, where possible, to implement solutions. Each group has a leader or facilitator to keep the discussion from digressing from the prescribed agenda. The leaders might be educators from outside the district until facilitators can be trained from among administrators and employees within the school district.

Quality circle meetings have a definite structure to them with an agenda, a conducive meeting place, and limited guidelines for functioning. In many cases the agenda would be determined by the circle ahead of time and would not include such items as pay, insurance, benefits, personalities, or grievances. Likewise, meetings would not interfere with the negotiation process. Meetings are scheduled for conference rooms with the necessary supplies and equipment to enhance productive discussions and analyses of problems.

The quality circle process consists of six major steps: problem identification, problem selection, problem analysis, recommended solutions, management review, and recommendations for implementation.[7]

Important in the quality circle process is the selection of the problems to be addressed. Members develop lists of problems related directly to their jobs which they consider of major importance to carry out their work in an efficient manner. Noncircle members such as other employees and administrators are contacted for problems the circle can discuss. Circle members then compile a list of the problems, put them in some order of priority, and begin to address them.

The circle members are the ones who select the problems to be worked on. No pressure or guidance from outside the circle should be permitted. Once a problem is analyzed and a solution is determined, a formal presentation is made to the appropriate administrator. Acceptance of the recommendation by the administration is a strong motivation for the circle members to address the next problem on their list.

The quality circle process cultivates better internal communications by (1) meeting a basic need of employees, the need for a feeling of belonging, (2) providing for employee feedback of creative ideas and suggestions, (3) encouraging all employees to focus on the primary purpose of helping students learn better, and (4) establishing an environment of communication between the administration and employees.

Shared Decision Making

Some school districts have taken the innovative staff-involvement step of letting some schools run themselves. The principal, the union steward, and elected faculty representatives together make decisions on the total educational program for their school. With this system, known as a School-Based Management/Shared Decision-Making program, each school controls its own budget and focuses on curriculum and program planning, collegial decision making, and strategic planning.

> Decentralization of decision-making has revolutionized many previously rigid policies, programs, and procedures. Each school has begun to reflect the "culture" and specific needs of the community it serves, rather than the broadstroke effect that characterizes many large, impersonal schools and school systems.[8]

The program promotes innovative thinking. And with staff members being involved in operating their schools, they tend to take increased interest in their work and profession.

Staff Development

The administration of a school district communicates with employees more, perhaps, by action than by words. What is done often has more of an impact than what is said. Programs established to benefit employees are important in this respect. One that says to employees "You're important" is a staff development program that helps employees improve professionally.

A staff development program provides employees with professional direction, permits them to attend conferences and workshops in their field, reimburses them for courses taken, and provides salary increments for professional development. Such a program not only makes them better employees but also communicates that the district does care about its employees. Ultimately, this should have a positive effect on the students.

A staff development program, along with other employee communications methods, often can solve problems resulting from employee *"coast-out"* (a term coined by Don Bagin to describe an employee who merely does an adequate job but in a sense rests on his or her oars until retirement, sometimes many years away). Many times the school administration has not provided an atmosphere that recognizes or uses the employee's expertise properly. A staff development program with numerous one-on-one conferences

between administrators and employees will unearth the coast-out syndrome and will tailor programs that will motivate employees to strive for more efficiency. Employees, particularly teachers, who feel a minimum loyalty from the school district, will direct their professional skills outside the schools where recognition and satisfaction are more easily attained; when this happens, motivation is low, and teachers use the minimum energy to provide an adequate result in the classroom.

Many districts overlook the support employees in a staff development program. Maintenance personnel, custodians, office workers, bus drivers, cafeteria workers, and other noninstructional employees are motivated to do a better job when provided a formal program to improve themselves. A staff development program, obviously, will not motivate every employee to improve, but if functioning properly, it will communicate a positive message to all employees that the district wants to help them professionally. Many, if not most, will respond.

Preserving the Right to Teach

Sound administration cannot overlook the importance of giving teachers the right to teach within the limits of defined policies. Teachers are highly sensitive to this right and resent petty interruptions and attempts to force the adoption of narrow ideas by those in authority. Not infrequently misguided boards of education and superintendents of schools permit vested interest groups to dictate course content or to insist on the removal of content that is inimical to their welfare. When teachers are told what or what not to teach, they develop feelings of insecurity and become cynical toward the school system and their role in the education of children and youth for life in a democracy.

Orientation of New Employees

A well-structured orientation program for new employees can be extremely effective in developing good staff relations.[9] Employees new to a school system can become bitter and resentful if they are not properly familiarized with the school or are not told what is expected of them. Successful programs have included a meeting with the district's central office personnel to learn about the characteristics of the system and to be informed of the procedures for pay, hospitalization benefits, purchasing, and housing availability in the area. Afterwards, they meet with the administrators and other employees of their assigned department or building. Often they are assigned a "buddy" from the current staff to be with them during orientation. Generally the "buddy" is from the same department in which the new staff member will be working and therefore can be readily available to help and to answer questions that come up. New employees who are made to feel welcome and are helped in adjusting to their new duties will probably be better employees.

Substitute Teachers

Often overlooked in employee relations programs are substitute teachers. Generally, they are members of the local community who can carry their impressions of the school to their friends and neighbors in the community. Prior to the opening of school, it is wise to meet with all substitute teachers who have registered with the school system. At that time they can be given information on the policies and regulations of a school, a schedule of classes, some facts about enrollments, a map of the room locations, and the procedures to follow if they are reporting for a teaching assignment. If they are called to substitute for a regular teacher, their job is made easier if they are provided with a set of lesson plans, a seating chart, a roll book, and a copy of the books and materials needed for the teaching assignment. Additionally, they should be warmly welcomed into the teachers' dining room for coffee and for meals. Department chairpersons or subject coordinators in high schools and principals or head teachers in elementary schools can be very helpful in welcoming a substitute teacher to the school

and to a teaching assignment. Some systems provide substitute teachers with a publication that outlines what is expected of them and contains helpful hints and suggestions for carrying out their teaching assignments.

Intern Teachers

Many school districts cooperate with colleges and universities in permitting intern teachers to gain classroom experience under the direction of a veteran teacher. Essentially, these temporary teachers are staff members, and they gain many impressions of the district, including the attitude of the employees, during their stay at a school. Careful planning is necessary prior to their coming to ensure that they are familiar with the procedures and policies of the district, that they know what is expected of them, that they are given public notice in their hometown press, and that they become familiar with vital data of the school system.

Internal Publications

A school district can lose face with its employees when they constantly learn about happenings in the district from an outside source, usually through the mass media. Occasionally this is unavoidable. Nevertheless, the superintendent and his or her administrative staff must be continually sensitive to the need of the employees to be kept informed as soon as possible of activities in the district.

Many districts inform their employees through a program of internal publications. One of the most popular publications is that which summarizes the actions of the board of education. Many districts attempt to have a brief write-up of board meetings in the hands of the employees prior to public discussion in the local press or on radio or television. However, in some systems this is impossible since the meeting may be televised or aired on the radio. Still, though, there are many details that can be supplied to the employees, such as the appointment of personnel or the letting of bids. The publication may be simple in design with a colorful masthead. The summary can be photocopied or inexpensively printed.

An employee newsletter or house organ is another popular medium of communicating with employees. The format of internal publications can range from a printed newsletter with photos to a photocopied sheet highlighting general activities of the school system. These publications are written in clear, simple language that avoids educational jargon, as many of the employees are noneducators.

Many school systems that distribute publications externally overlook the importance of distributing the same publication internally, for example, a community newsletter, a pamphlet welcoming new parents, or a calendar of school activities. School employees feel more a part of the educational team if they also receive copies of external publications that the school sends to the community.

Other popular internal publications are curriculum newsletters, a formal publication that notifies employees of vacant positions in the district, a substitute teacher handbook, general information brochures, an internal professional publication that contains articles written by employees, and written summaries of important internal meetings (Figures 7.1, 7.2, and 7.3 are examples of internal publications).

COMMUNICATING DURING NEGOTIATIONS AND STRIKES

Unfortunately, the image the public has of a school district when a strike occurs is not a pleasant one. Much of the image has to do with the messages coming from both sides. Many citizens can't understand how "educated" people can adhere to an emotional rhetoric that points an accusing finger at the other side. Nor can they understand why, in the negotiating process, time is wasted by both sides starting from extreme positions, knowing that ultimately both sides will have to compromise with a moderate position.

"Why," they ask, "couldn't they start with reasonable demands and positions, cut the rhetoric, reduce the emotionalism, and get the children back to school?"

The public image of schools is unfortunate because this is the very public whose confidence in the schools is needed for continued support. That confidence has not been as high as it should have been in recent years, caused in part by strikes; the long, drawn-out negotiations process; poor communications with the public; and poor internal communications.

Mistakenly, many school systems believe that negotiations procedures are confined to a period of haggling over demands laid on the table by both sides. But there is more involved. It is the overall picture of what takes place throughout the year that has a decisive impact on the negotiating sessions.

It must be emphasized that good employee relations are achieved and less severe bargaining sessions experienced when teachers and noninstructional employees are consulted by the board of education and the administration on questions relating to their welfare and their working conditions. Their recommendations may not always be accepted, but this is less important than the right to make their wants known. School employees are willing to go along with a policy or a program when they understand the facts behind it, even though the policy runs contrary to their opinions.

Many of the demands placed on the bargaining table by employees are concerns that employees may have expressed to the administration, and they were ignored as being insignificant. Take, for example, a request by teachers that a desk and a chair be available in each classroom. This furniture had been missing for some time despite the fact that it was requested for three years in a row. The administration felt it was insignificant, didn't have the money for new furniture, and therefore ignored it. Ultimately, the request for the furniture became a demand at the next collective bargaining session. It didn't have to be, and additionally it made the negotiations on other

Rowan College of New Jersey

BOARD BRIEFS

Board Briefs is a summary report of the Board of Trustees' meetings prepared by the College Relations Office. This summary is not intended to be an official transcript of the meeting.

January 6, 1993

At its meeting on Tuesday evening, the Rowan College board of trustees:

• Approved the appointments of adjuncts Wendy Aita and Carol Heines; part-time faculty Francis Sutman; graduate assistant Suzanne Cruice; and a leave of absence for Judith Lancioni;

• Approved a 3 percent salary adjustment, effective July 1, 1992, for the following managerial staff members: Frank Amoresano, Pearl Bartelt, Abbas Bhagat, Judith Burger, Ronald Butcher, David Butters, Eric Clarke, Francis Cloak, Robert Collard, Anna Conway, Claude Damico, Donald Davis, Wade Devlin-Scherer, Christopher Dickerman, Harley Flack, Robert Fleming, George Friebis, Craig Frierson, Donald Gephardt, Nancy Hall, Robert Harris, James Henderson, Wayne Hoffner, David Kapel, Gerald Kennedy, Andrew Kozak, John Kuhlen, Edith Loigman, Francis Looney, James Lovegrove, Thomas Monahan, Gail Mossman, Ross Moriarty, William Murphy, Bruce Paternoster, Gregory Potter, Samuel Raffa Jr., Samuel Raffa Sr., Lawrence Reader, Joyce Rigdon, Denise Rivers, Michael Rose, Linda Ross, Marvin Sills, Thomas Stokes, Marguerite Stubbs, Sandor Szilassy, Philip Tartaglione, Jeffrey Toughill, Philip Tumminia, Peggy Veacock, Richard Wadleigh, Robert Wear, Richard Williams, Elizabeth Wriggins and Robert Zazzali;

• Approved the appointment of Dr. Simon Ostrach as chief consultant, the creation of a national advisory board of distinguished educators, engineers and related professionals, corporate executives and others to assist the board of trustees in determining the feasibility, content, cost, size and other factors relevant to the establishment of an engineering school and the "Process for Developing a School of Engineering" policy;

• Awarded a single prime contract with bidding for construction of the new library to F.W. Vesper Co., Inc. for $13,439,485;

• Awarded a contract without bidding for data processing software services for the student dining cash card system to Griffin Technology for $34,063.36;

• Awarded a contract with bidding for condensate line replacement in the Bole Administration Building to D. Falasca Plumbing, Heating, Cooling Inc. for $26,600;

• Amended a contract with bidding for temporary employment services for temporary employment in the College Store during the first two weeks of the semester with Accu Temporary Services for $25,000;

• Awarded a contract with bidding for 26 microcomputers for Academic Computing to Professional Computer Upgrade for $51,168;

• Awarded a contract with bidding for microcomputer replacement parts for Academic Computing to Professional Computer Upgrade for $13,000;

FIGURE 7.1

FIGURE 7.2 *Super Sub,* a handbook for substitute teachers at Mesa Public Schools in Mesa, Arizona.

items more testy because of the lack of trust by the teachers. Through special or general advisory committees the school administration should be identifying such concerns and meeting them where legitimate. This can reduce the time needed for negotiations.

Experts contend good communication is the key to keeping the school district together during negotiations and strikes. Bad communication can cause confusion and diminish the school system in the eyes of the public, the media, and the employees. It is vital that all three of these publics be kept informed. Public statements should be objective and be made jointly or by either side. They should outline the issues being covered but not the biased position of each side. The statements should be totally factual, free of emotion, and not slanted to make one side or the other look good or bad.

Important, too, is the need for one spokesperson for each side. For the school district that could be the communication specialist, the chief negotiator, or the president of the board of education. Otherwise, if various members of either side make public statements, confusion and inaccuracies result. Experts believe the superintendent should not be the spokesperson because after negotiations or a strike, he or she has to unite the employees and the district to get back to educating children.

Anytime financial figures are presented, particularly in salary increments and percentages of pay increases, they should be given with background information explaining how they were determined. Otherwise both sides may accuse the other side of lying because inaccurate figures are revealed. In reality, often both sides may be accurate, but they are not explaining how they arrived at the final data. For example, the employees may say they are being offered a 6-percent increase, and the school district says the employees are getting a 10-percent increase. They are both correct if they explain how they determined the percentage. The employees are not including a scheduled increment as part of the overall increase and the school district is.

Communication between the school district and its employees is vital during negotiations or a strike. Many districts make weak attempts to communicate internally at such times, feeling the employees' organization or union will provide that service to the employees. School districts must not abdicate this responsibility. Otherwise, the employees may not understand fully the position of the school district on issues.

In communicating with employees school officials should be aware of the provisions of the Taft-Hartley Act of 1947. Section 8(c) of the Labor Management Relations (Taft-Hartley) Act

The Bulletin

Inside this issue:
- Two schools participate in inaugural activities. Page 2.
- WJ, Blair publications named among the best in the nation. Page 8.

February 1, 1993   A weekly newsletter for employees of Montgomery County Public Schools   Vol. 35, No. 22

National spotlight focuses on county

4 seniors among top in national science contest

The selection of four MCPS students—three from Montgomery Blair HS and one from Walt Whitman HS—as finalists in the 52nd annual Westinghouse Science Talent Search last week represented an impressive achievement for the students and an honor for the school system.

MCPS had four of the five finalists in Maryland, placing the state second in the nation in the number of finalists. Only New York had more finalists. The local students accounted for 10 percent of the 40 finalists nationwide in this prestigious competition, which honors students for creative independent research projects.

Montgomery Blair HS had more finalists than any other school in the nation.

The finalists were selected from 300 semifinalists nationwide. MCPS had 10 of the 17 semifinalists in Maryland, which was tied for second in the nation in the number of semifinalists from one state. In total, 1,662 high school seniors in 684 schools entered this year's competition.

Winners will be selected after final judging in Washington, D.C., from March 4 through March 8. Each student will be interviewed by a panel of scientists who will evaluate the student's scientific creativity. Based on the interviews and the students' research, 10 top scholarship winners will be selected. The top winner will receive a $40,000 scholarship, one

student will win $30,000, one will receive $20,000, three will get $15,000 and four will earn $10,000. Each of the other 30 finalists will receive $1,000 scholarships.

The MCPS finalists, their schools and research projects are: Steve Shaw-Tang Chien, Montgomery Blair HS, "Multi-Dimensional Extention of Wythoff's Game" (mathematics); Wei-Hwa Huang, Montgomery Blair HS, "The Peg Solitaire Army" (mathematics); Mian-Lai Liu, Walt Whitman HS, "Regulation of Immunoreactivity in 293 Cells Transfected Mutant Amyloid Precursor Protein (APP)" (biochemistry); and Elizabeth Dexter Mann, Montgomery Blair HS, "Paral-

(continued on page 5)

Voices vs. violence

Winners of 8th-grade poster and 10th-grade essay contests in the Voices vs. Violence campaign receive awards at a Jan. 13 breakfast to launch the campaign, sponsored by the Mental Health Association of Montgomery County. From left, Richard Parker, assistant principal, Quince Orchard HS, award for the most entries; poster contest winner Hennie Yoo, Lee MS; essay winner Lisa Johnson, Springbrook HS; essay runner-up Jaspreet Chowdhary, Paint Branch HS; poster runner-up Melissa Naylor, Lee MS.

Major businesses join in efforts to increase efficiency

Several major national and regional corporations have joined together in a unique partnership to improve the effectiveness of key management functions in MCPS and ensure the efficient and disciplined use of school system resources.

This first-of-a-kind initiative in MCPS, called Corporate Partnership on Managerial Excellence, involves hands-on problem solving and fact finding by company representatives who will be working closely with MCPS employees over the next six

(continued on page 3)

FIGURE 7.3   *The Bulletin,* published for employees of Montgomery County Public Schools in Rockville, Maryland.

relative to employee communications and collective bargaining reads:

> The expressing of any view, argument, or opinion or the dissemination thereof, whether in written, printed, graphic or visual form, shall not constitute or be evidence of an unfair labor practice under any of the provisions of this Act, if such expression contains no threat of reprisal or force or promise of benefit.[10]

Judicial decisions have been recorded since the Act was passed. More instructive than definitive, the decisions essentially say that for an employer to be charged with unfair labor practice for coercive and threatening communications with employees, the "totality of conduct" of the employer toward employees must be judged.

The National School Public Relations Association[11] recommends these communications guidelines with the employees when a strike takes place:

- Be factual, low-key, and nonthreatening.
- Don't editorialize with many subjective observations about the strike.
- When the school district rejects certain demands of the employee union, explain why.
- Be careful not to incriminate all employees because of the action of the leaders.
- List concessions the school district has made.
- Explain the financial implications of the district's offer to the employees.
- Communicate with all employees, not only those planning to strike.

Not to be overlooked is communication with students, particularly at the secondary level. Some educators feel that it is important to communicate with students once a strike occurs. Perhaps it would be wise to communicate prior to the strike. Any communications should be factual, stating issues and the school district's position. Care should be taken not to portray teachers or any other employees as being at fault in a strike. Otherwise, when the strike is over, student respect for the teachers may be difficult to restore.

COMMUNICATING WITH PUPILS

A universal question asked in many homes each evening across the nation is, "What did you learn in school today?" The answer to such a question is important, of course, but perhaps just as important is the emphasis such a question places on the student as a communications link between the school and the home. An impressive number of parents in every community form their judgments of a school system from the comments that are made about it by pupils. They hear the pupils discuss their teachers, talk about homework assignments, express opinions on the value of what they do in classes, evaluate the fairness of rules and regulations, and describe experiences they had with the principal, office secretary, doctor, nurse, cafeteria workers, bus drivers, and other workers employed in the system.

No school can expect to enjoy the confidence and support of parents unless the comments of most pupils are favorable to the system. Much may be done in the name of community relations, but what a school system does may be neutralized if the day-to-day relationship with pupils is unsatisfactory.

The Pupil as an Individual

All pupils from kindergarten through grade twelve, whether they are quiet, docile pupils or discipline problems, want their school to care about them. They want their teachers and principal to convey the feeling to them that they are interested in them as individuals. How well the school fosters an "I-care-for-you" feeling with its students will go a long way in helping the individual develop a healthy attitude toward learning and a positive approach when he or she discusses the school in the community.

Often the organizational nature of the school system tends to foster an impersonal relation between the school and the student. Consider the cool, impersonal characteristic of a student number, a form letter, a locker number, or a computerized report card. Necessary as they may be to the proper functioning of a large school system, these impersonal relationships cannot stand alone as the only recognition of the student. They tend to reduce all students to a common denominator, whereas the students want to be treated as individuals. Needed, then, are programs and teaching methods that raise the pupils' self-image and recognize their human dignity.

Respect for Personality

It has long been an accepted belief in a democracy that respect should be shown for the worth and dignity of the individual. Effective teachers subscribe to this belief because they know that it leaves its mark on the behavior of pupils and satisfies a human need for security. Teachers show this respect by treating serious breaches of conduct in private and by working quietly with pupils who present problems of social adjustment. Honest mistakes made by pupils are acknowledged pleasantly, and suggestions are offered for overcoming these mistakes in the future.

Allowance is provided in the learning process for individual differences, and tasks are assigned that can be handled successfully. In order to encourage continued work, a wise teacher acknowledges a sincere effort on the part of the pupil. Such teachers are not hesitant in helping pupils to understand their own weaknesses and natural limitations, but the help is given without undermining self-confidence or injuring the student's status in the group. Teachers arrange situations and delegate responsibilities from which youngsters gain a sense of importance. The common amenities of social life are practiced, and departures from them are not permitted. Pupils come to feel that they are individuals in their own right and that they are each contributing to the group. Teachers who show respect for personality in these and other ways stimulate better learning and enjoy the cooperation and good will of the learners.

Discipline

The handling of discipline plays a major role in establishing satisfactory or unsatisfactory rela-

tions with pupils. Effective teachers regard good discipline as a condition that is essential to good learning. When pupils become restless, inattentive, and annoying, teachers examine their own practices to find out if they are responsible before they reprimand the pupils. Experience has taught them that most youngsters do not become restless and disturbing in the classroom when activities move along at a brisk pace, when they are being challenged, and when learning is made exciting.

Moreover, competent teachers understand the normal behavior of pupils at different stages of growth and development and make allowance for these in their planning. They are able to prevent situations from arising that would call for disciplinary action. Their knowledge of child growth and development equips them to make distinctions between normal behavior and symptoms of maladjustment and to refer pupils who show these symptoms to trained counselors.

Less competent teachers can make mistakes in disciplinary action, thereby placing a strain on their relations with pupils. One of the mistakes is that of employing punishment freely for slight infractions of rules and failure to meet achievement standards. As examples, they lower academic marks for poor deportment, they prevent participation in extracurricular activities for unfinished homework, they assign copy exercises as a panacea for absence and tardiness, and they detain an entire class for the misdeeds of one or more members. The cumulative effect of their actions is dislike by pupils and criticism by parents.

Pupils want their teachers to be consistent in discipline. They want to know the rules and discuss them for relevancy and purpose. Pupils don't like teachers to make study a punishment by imposing extra work. Pupils also don't respect teachers who lose their temper; these teachers then lose their ability to solve discipline problems in a professional way. On the other hand, pupils respect teachers who admit they are wrong if they have treated a pupil unjustly.

A major disciplinary mistake is the administering of corporal punishment. Although the laws of some states permit a teacher to administer corporal punishment, it is doubtful that the overall result is ever constructive. A few children may show evidence of better behavior because of rough handling, but the facts do not seem to bear this out with the rank and file of pupils. Instead of trying to abide by rules and regulations, those who have been disciplined often regard the violation of rules as a kind of challenge. Instead of feeling friendly and respectful to teachers, they regard them with suspicion. And instead of entering school with a sense of enjoyment and enthusiasm, they resent the time that must be spent there.

In addition to these by-products of corporal punishment, the school becomes an object of damaging publicity whenever a child is allegedly abused or injured, and parents may demand action against the cruelty of a teacher. The newspapers often pick up and give full play to stories of this nature. And interestingly enough, no matter how wrong the pupil may have been in his or her conduct, the chances are that public opinion will be against the teacher. Judicious boards of education and superintendents now prohibit or restrict physical contact with pupils. They know that corporal punishment often impedes the development of wholesome relations with pupils and that it often invites destructive complaints and criticism in the community.

INSTRUCTIONAL PRACTICES

Relations with pupils are changed for better or worse by the instructional practices of the teacher. Among the more crucial features are homework assignments, marking systems, examinations, and guidance procedures.

Homework Assignments

Schools have traditionally followed a policy of giving pupils assignments of homework. A few schools do not believe in homework; nevertheless, those that do believe that the assignments are educationally beneficial to pupils. This policy has been generally accepted by young people and their parents.

Continuing support of the homework policy may be damaged by the introduction of such questionable practices as requiring so much homework that time is taken from children for rest and relaxation, allowing assignments to pile up unevenly, engaging children in dull and worthless copy exercises, failing to explain clearly what is expected, assigning problems that are too difficult for pupils, and committing the sin of not correcting and returning assignments turned in by pupils.

School officials should give high priority to establishing a regulation that requires consistency of assignments by all teachers. A pupil and his or her parents may have difficulty understanding how and why each teacher has a different set of homework rules. Thus, standardized regulations can serve to reduce criticism over the nature and amount of work involved in assignments. If criticism does arise, school officials should check its validity. It may be discovered that teachers are beginning to introduce practices that should be corrected before more serious trouble is encountered.

An intelligent parent who takes an interest in homework knows whether or not assignments are worthwhile and reasonable, and will resent school officials who defend poor practices. One solution would be that of inviting pupils and parents to meet periodically with faculty members and review the whole question. This is an excellent means of preventing problems and of bringing pupil and parents closer to teachers.

Marks and Marking Systems

Marks and marking systems should be included in any examination of instructional practices because of the effect they have on pupil attitudes and feelings toward teachers. So much importance is attached to marks in connection with promotion, graduation, and college admission that it is natural for pupils to be concerned. Because their welfare is tied up in marks and marking systems, pupils want to know how teachers evaluate tests, written work, and special assignments and whether or not their methods are fair and impartial.

Teachers who establish fine interaction with pupils take full advantage of this interest. They devote as much time as necessary to the enumeration and discussion of factors that enter into the evaluation of tests and work submitted by pupils and the explanation of how these factors are weighed in arriving at the judgments expressed in terms of percentage or letter grades. Teachers are receptive to suggestions made by pupils for modifying and improving the marking system, recognizing that pupils will believe more fully in the fairness of the system if they have had a hand in devising it. These teachers recommend that the whole subject of marking be studied by members of the faculty under the direction of the principal. They are convinced from their conversations with pupils and the remarks pupils make that some standardization should prevail among the different teachers in the school. Consistency promotes confidence and faith in the marking system.

Teachers who are concerned about their interaction with pupils try to eliminate the tension and fear that too great a stress on marks inevitably produces. They do not want marks to be regarded as the end products of learning or the principal cause for motivating achievement. Teachers want pupils to look on marks and marking systems as convenient and helpful tools for understanding their own strength and weakness and for guiding their efforts toward self-improvement. It has been their experience that pupil growth and development take place more rapidly when the progress of the learner, rather than the satisfaction of academic standards, is made the point of attention.

Examinations

Examinations are generally accepted by pupils as a necessary part of learning. To them examinations are a challenge that affords them the opportunity to determine how well they are doing in their classwork and where they need to improve. Seldom do pupils object to taking examinations that cover material they have studied. Their atti-

tude toward examinations changes when practices are introduced that they think are unfair. Included among these practices are administering examinations for disciplinary purposes, inconsistency among teachers in methods of scoring, test items foreign to the material studied, too much concern for test results instead of their diagnostic value, and criticism for poor outcomes without attempting to discover the causes.

Guidance

Although the teacher plays a major role in guidance and counseling, the pupil's attitude toward the school often is affected by the guidance specialist. This member of the educational team must ensure that he or she does not convey the feeling that guidance is inquisitiveness, but rather a kind of caring about the pupil. Many times when pupils feel they can no longer communicate with their teachers, they will expect the guidance counselor to be a good listener and one who can get a message to their teachers in their behalf. If a counselor can maintain a human approach from day to day and can provide a tangible link between the students and their school, he or she can then be an answer to many pupil needs.

Pupils are quick to detect the overzealousness of some counselors in getting as many students as possible into college. This is particularly true of the pupil who is not interested in college but rather in career education. Too often entire guidance departments have conveyed a "We-are-only-interested-in-college-bound-students" image. Consequently, many pupils who are not college bound can see very little help coming from such counselors. It is incumbent on guidance departments to extend themselves to the pupil, individually or as a group, rather than to take the position of waiting until pupils walk into the guidance office. Guidance counselors can project a constructive image through orientation programs with entering students and through planned programs of meeting all students in small, informal discussion groups. Counselors can also improve their image by clarifying their role with the instructional staff and by placing equal emphasis on career and college education.

RELATIONS OUTSIDE THE CLASSROOM

Pupils have numerous contacts with instructional and noninstructional personnel outside the classroom. These points of contact should be considered as means of increasing friendliness and cooperation between pupils and members of the staff.

Library

The library is one point of contact where pupils form definite opinions of schools. The nature of their opinions varies with the personality of the individual in charge and the services they receive. A librarian who greets pupils with a smile, chats cheerfully, and tries to understand their needs sets an entirely different tone from one who gives short answers, shows impatience, and demands observance of minor regulations. In some schools the library is associated with the instructional media or instructional resource center in which a number of learning devices are housed, such as video- and audio-tapes, films, records, television studios, and microfilms. This arrangement increases student-librarian contacts and makes the librarian's role even more important.

Medical Centers

The protection of a child's health is now an established part of the school program. School board policies and state laws require that pupils be examined periodically by physicians, nurses, dentists, and other specialists and that they receive first-aid treatment and care for sudden illness.

How medical personnel handle their contacts with pupils and parents is important in building good community relations. Nothing wins praise more quickly than the tactful and efficient administration of medical services and a high degree of personal interest in children needing corrective and remedial attention. Unless medical personnel are sensitive to their legal parameters and their community relations opportunities, they may handle child and parent contacts poorly.

School Office

It is surprising how many times in a school year pupils have occasion to visit the school office. Every time they enter the office they have contacts with staff members. If they receive courteous treatment and their business is handled efficiently, the office stands high in their estimation. However, if the pupils feel, for instance, that secretaries think they are assistant principals, that they do not welcome students, or make them wait unnecessarily to see the principal, pupils' feelings about the office weaken good internal communications.

Cafeteria

School cafeterias exist for the benefit of pupils and the convenience of staff members, not for the accumulation of profits. In this respect, they may be thought of as service agencies having the function of preparing and distributing wholesome meals. The extent to which they fulfill this function determines how they are appraised by pupils. Perhaps no other agency outside the classroom undergoes a more careful scrutiny than does the cafeteria.

It would be beneficial to all concerned if the director of the cafeteria made efforts to communicate with the students, discussing the various aspects of food preparation and explaining why certain food can or cannot be served. Often in establishing communications with students the cafeteria director will uncover helpful suggestions for improving the food service.

Physical Plant

Relations between pupils and custodial personnel who are responsible for the physical conditions of the building and grounds should be examined. Although these men and women who perform

cleaning and maintenance services have no jurisdiction over pupils, they sometimes assume this
authority and treat pupils who disobey their orders with shouts, abusive language, and even
rough handling. Resentment against abusive
treatment may be expressed by marking walls,
plugging lavatory facilities, and scattering paper
on floors. This condition is disruptive of the unity
sought in a school and should be prevented.

Conflict possibilities between pupils and
custodial personnel can be reduced and usually
eliminated if thought is given to the problem. The
solution should start with the employment of individuals who have social intelligence. The limits
of their authority should be defined clearly and
procedures outlined for reporting pupils who violate regulations. Such personnel should be made
to feel a responsibility for the success of the
school and should realize it is their job to earn the
goodwill and respect of pupils.

Transportation

The school bus drivers are in a unique position to
influence pupils' thinking. They do not regard
bus drivers in quite the same way as they do other
members of the staff, and they talk freely in the
driver's presence about the school and the teachers they have in classes. In the course of a year a
driver can learn a great deal about the school and
how pupils appraise it. Competent bus drivers
who regard themselves as members of the staff
can be exceedingly helpful in correcting false
statements of pupils and explaining reasons for
policies and practices pupils do not like. Drivers
are in a special position to listen to their complaints, discuss their problems, and bring out
facts pupils might not consider. Drivers' services
in interpreting the school to pupils and reporting
their attitudes to the principal can be invaluable.

THE PUPIL AND INTERNAL
COMMUNITY RELATIONS

The school itself consists of many internal publics, and the pupils constitute the most important

internal group. As such, pupils should be given a
chance to become involved in the entire internal
educational community by making suggestions
and participating in school planning. This is particularly true in the secondary school, where pupils want to be considered associates and not
subjects of the rest of the educational team.

Until recent years educators traditionally
used a one-way method of communicating with
the students, either from the principal to the student or from the teacher to the student. Announcements were made over the loudspeaker in
homerooms, at assembly programs, by written
memo, or in the classroom through lectures. The
students were to be "seen and not heard." They
were talked "to" and not "with," for in the judgment of many educators, they had very little to
offer by way of suggestions about their school
programs or their school life. Out of such an
environment student activism emerged, and the
traditional method of communicating with students was revealed as lacking effectiveness. In
fact, this one-way method contributed greatly to
the rise of student militancy since students were
neither kept informed nor given answers to legitimate questions, and they were also denied an
opportunity to contribute ideas to the school.

In recent years, however, it has been learned
that one of the most effective methods of communicating with students, particularly at the junior
and senior high-school level, is a two-way structure enabling them to express opinions, make
suggestions, and offer constructive criticism on
various aspects of school. At the same time, they
learn more about school policies and procedures,
staff duties, and responsibilities. Such two-way
communications can be accomplished through
student advisory committees, suggestion boxes,
ombudspersons, student surveys, and student
town meetings.

Student Advisory Committees

Some schools have developed excellent programs
of two-way communications with students at the
secondary level by restructuring the student coun-

cil and perhaps even changing its name to the "Student Advisory Group" or the "Student Advisory Committee." Successful administrators will see to it that all students are eligible for election to the group regardless of grades or discipline problems. Good administrators know that they must structure some type of student advisory group to hear the voices of all students. Here is where the democratic system must work at its best. The principal meets with the students periodically, listens to their suggestions, and grants their wishes when common sense dictates that they should be granted. He or she always explains the reasons for decisions. These committees become a two-way communications process whereby student leaders come to understand the problems of the principal, and the principal comes closer to the student body.

The student advisory committee does have many good ideas and is often helpful to the principal in a time of crisis. Its members can squelch rumors among its constituency and in turn reduce inflammatory rumors in the community. The key to success of this type of communication is the credibility of the principal, who naturally must "tell it like it is" and be truthful with the students.

Student Opinion Surveys

Student advisory committees do provide some amount of feedback from the students. However, a sound internal community relations program also calls for direct information from the students concerning their feelings about the school. One of the most common ways of getting this direct feedback is through a survey or questionnaire.

Some schools have developed a functional student opinion survey for high-school students. It asks student opinions about report card grades, class procedures, extracurricular activities, changes in school plant and procedures, courses, weaknesses, rules and regulations, student government, counseling, teacher attitude, and study halls, among other topics.

When students participate in such a survey, they assume that the results will be shared with

them or some action will be taken by the school to implement suggestions. If the survey is filed away and nothing is done with the information, the school's credibility with students is weakened. A major consideration, therefore, in planning a student survey is the disposition of the findings. Prior to administering the survey, students should be informed that a summary of the results will be shared with them, and valid suggestions will be implemented.

Student Town Meetings

Student town meetings can be in the form of a student assembly in which all students have an opportunity to participate. Such assemblies are similar to the traditional assembly programs except that there is no performer or guest speaker or musical program. Instead, it is the students' town meeting in which teachers and administrators ask for student thoughts, criticisms, and ideas. Some meetings are held after school hours for the entire student body. Or they can be held during school hours in small groups on the grade level or in each classroom.

Suggestion Boxes

Strategically and conspicuously placed suggestion boxes located throughout a school provide another opportunity to obtain student thoughts and reactions. Many of the suggestions might be categorized as humorous or cynical; nevertheless, if one good suggestion is received from every ten submitted, it makes the project worthwhile. The presence of a suggestion box throughout a school has a way of conveying to the students that a school thinks they are part of the educational team.

Ombudsperson

The concept of the ombudsperson has merit in a school if an administrator is committed to developing feedback from students about the school procedures, staff, programs, or facilities. Students can confide in the ombudsperson without fear of recrimination. Often students are reluctant to talk to teachers or counselors for fear they will be reported to the principal or other school officials. The ombudsperson then becomes a communicator, facilitating the circular flow of information between school officials and students. Whoever fills this position must gain the confidence of students to make the system function.

STUDENT UNREST

When student activism erupts into unrest or violence, unfavorable publicity generally results for the school. Citizens begin pointing an accusing finger at the local educational system or begin classifying all students as an unappreciative new generation. When student unrest has reached the point of actual violence, it is usually too late to resolve the crisis immediately. Instead, school officials have to weather the situation until emotions become less charged.

Why Students Rebel

Frustration is the primary reason for most student unhappiness and unrest. Frustration is part of life and cannot be eliminated entirely. Nonetheless, when it pierces the very heart of a student's self-esteem and personal dignity, it should be avoided. Many times teachers and administrators nurture frustration by showing a lack of love or respect for the students as individuals; by applying rigid rules without considering circumstances; by not providing an opportunity for every child to experience success in the classroom; by not permitting students to be heard; by overburdening students with demands beyond their ability; by not providing good channels of communications with school officials and with other student groups; or by not seeking student input at various decision-making levels of the school system, particularly in the junior and senior high schools.

Students are looking for well-defined channels in a school through which their influences can be felt. When there are no such channels or when these are not clearly defined, frustration often sets in, and a protest is not uncommon. The students' protest is an attempt to prove their importance and to say that they want to participate. They want to be heard and to present their ideas and suggestions. Often school officials believe students want to take over the schools. This is not necessarily true. If students are given an opportunity to be heard and to be involved and if the school officials and the staff can convey the idea that they do care about the students, unrest and destructive activism can be minimized.

Channels of Influence

Much of what has been presented in this chapter has been addressed to the idea of providing channels of influence for students. Many of the ideas presented, if implemented, could alleviate or prevent student unrest. However, three additional areas should be covered—biracial committees, student involvement in the community, and student publications—which are helpful in minimizing student unrest.

Biracial Committees. Poor communication among students themselves, ironically, is a source of much student unrest. This can surface as racial conflict or conflict between cliques or "in" groups or "out" groups. Much of the conflict spills into the school from society itself, where ethnic groups have drawn battle lines for years. All students want to be recognized by school officials and by other students. They want to be recognized for what they are, their customs, their ethnic backgrounds, and their culture. As long as student groups within a school cannot relate these cultural and ethnic characteristics to one another or do not have an opportunity to learn about another ethnic group, the chances are great for misunderstanding and for rumors to develop and fester.

When potential abrasive situations are possible among racial groups in a school system, ample time during the day should be provided for students to come together in a meaningful way for solving their problems. A biracial subcommittee of the student government can often serve as a functional group to provide constructive dialogue between two factions and to serve as a logical vehicle to develop meaningful understanding of different customs and cultures. Often these biracial or human relations committees with representatives from each class and each racial group can identify racial problems, suggest solutions, hold forums for all responsible opinions, advise curriculum committees on including the history of various ethnic groups, advise school officials on racial matters, and hold rap sessions between racial groups so that each comes to understand the other better.

Student Involvement in the Community. In many schools, student thirst for action goes beyond the talking and listening stages, particularly when the issues are social and political injustices in society. Students' concern for their fellow humans often takes the form of direct action to alleviate human suffering in the areas of poverty, ignorance, hunger, pollution, housing, or health. They become frustrated when action is not taken; consequently, they may become restless and strike out at the academic establishment because they cannot gain a sense of satisfaction by working for their ideals.

Student interest in solving political and social problems can be a positive force, especially in secondary school. Authorities on student activism claim that one of the best ways of meeting students' thirst for action is for the school to offer meaningful and worthwhile activities for community involvement. Such activities can include many school-coordinated community service programs, such as fund-raising campaigns for less fortunate citizens, suggested proposals to eliminate pollution and to protect the environment, tutoring programs for migrant workers' children, work in hospitals and nursing homes, public opinion surveying, recreation programs in housing projects, voluntary work with welfare agencies, and other activities that show a concern for human welfare and justice.

Not only do community activities channel student unrest toward constructive outlets, but such activities also relate the students' education more directly to social and political problems of concern to them. Furthermore, student concern and involvement in the community often help improve communications among students, between students and teachers and administrators, and between the school and the community. Not to be overlooked is the amount of goodwill generated by such community service. The aid of faculty members and community advisors is often needed to coordinate student involvement in the community.

Additionally, when the classroom is extended beyond the walls of the building, the community becomes a laboratory for learning. Students have an opportunity to brush against reality, develop further sensitivities to social needs and problems, and acquire a deeper sense of civic responsibility. The community by-products of students' study and involvement in the community are increased public confidence in the abilities of these young people, a better understanding of the educational program, and a willingness to support the school system more generously.

Student Publications. Schools have learned that students will make their views known even when the school officials haven't asked for them. If students are not given an opportunity to express themselves in a school paper, particularly in secondary schools, they will often resort to an underground press. Such papers have been nightmares for those administrators who have not provided students with a channel for self-expression. The delicate task of school officials in this matter lies somewhere between permitting absolute freedom of expression, often with vulgar and obscene words, and a totally censored publication which does not represent student thinking. A middle road is needed, giving expression to students' ideas but in words that are acceptable to the community. Students generally will go along with a school ruling against the use of obscene language if they are permitted to state their opinions on school issues as they see them. If the school paper affords students that opportunity, the probabilities are slight for the appearance of an underground paper.

Some believe the number of underground student newspapers will increase as a result of a U.S. Supreme Court decision in 1988. In *Hazelwood School District v. Kuhlmeier* the Court upheld, by a 5 to 3 vote, the right of public high school administrators in Missouri to censor stories from a school-sponsored student newspaper. In the previous fifteen years the Court's decisions had given student-journalists extensive protection under the First Amendment. The Court contended in the Hazelwood case that if a school's decision to censor is "reasonably related to legitimate pedagogical concerns," it is permissible.

Here are some examples given by the Court of what could be censored:

- Publications poorly presented—"Ungrammatical, poorly written, inadequately researched, biased or prejudiced, vulgar or profane, or unsuitable for immature audiences."
- Sensitive topics—"The existence of Santa Claus in an elementary school setting," "Speech that might reasonably be perceived to advocate drug or alcohol use, irresponsible sex, or conduct otherwise inconsistent with the 'shared values of a civilized social order,'" and "The particulars of teenage sexual activity in a high school setting."
- Political subjects—matters that would "associate the school with anything other than neutrality on matters of political controversy."[12]

In another commentary on the decision, Thomas Eveslage notes:

The simplified summary of the Supreme Court's ruling . . . did not particularly surprise or alarm advisers, students or administrators. Many have believed for years that the school has final authority, and publications have operated that way despite lower court decisions limiting that authority.[13]

Some school systems have established a school communications committee that is helpful in setting guidelines of good journalism and in developing a relevant learning experience for students in school publications. The committee is made up of students, faculty members, parents, and citizens from the community, some of whom may be members of the local media or adults with experience in journalism. Such a committee can be helpful as an advisory group to the principal or to a school board if necessary. With the presence of students and laypersons on the committee, dissident students are more apt to accept the committee's recommendations and suggestions as not coming directly from the principal. Such a committee will eliminate the feeling on the part of students that all school publications are under the thumb of the school administration or faculty advisor.

The question arises from time to time whether student publications should be sent home and shared with key people in the community. Parents and taxpayers are able to learn a great deal from these publications about the instructional activities of the students and the nature of the educational program.

Often overlooked in the field of communication are publications of the elementary schools. At intervals during the year thousands of elementary teachers and pupils prepare simple one-to-three-page news sheets that are sent home to parents. These news sheets contain samples of work done in class and describe and explain some of the learning activities carried on with a particular group of pupils. Although greatly underestimated for their value in communicating with parents, checks on readership show that such publications are read thoroughly and are genuinely interesting to most mothers and fathers. Parents find these papers to be clear and convincing evidence of pupil achievement, and quite often these news sheets are passed around to neighbors and friends.

ENDNOTES

1. Robert L. Katz, "Skills of an Effective Administrator," *Harvard Business Review* 33, no. 1 (January-February 1955), p. 34. (Reprinted in *Business Classics: Fifteen Key Concepts for Managerial Success,* President and fellows of Harvard College, 1975, p. 24.)

2. B. J. Chandler, "Working Relationships," *Nation's Schools* 53, no. 1 (January 1954), p. 47.

3. Frederick Herzberg, "One More Time: How Do You Motivate Employees?" *Business Classics: Fifteen Key Concepts for Managerial Success,* President and fellows of Harvard College, 1975, p. 13.

4. Thomas J. Sergiovanni and Fred O. Carver, *The New School Executive, A Theory of Administration,* 2nd ed. (New York: Harper & Row, 1980), p. 104. Also see Thomas J. Sergiovanni, *The Principalship, A Reflective Practice Perspective,* 2nd ed. (Needham Heights, MA: Allyn and Bacon, 1991), pp. 242–243.

5. Executive Reports Corporation, *Breaking the Communications Barrier* (Englewood Cliffs, NJ: Prentice-Hall, 1971), p. 6.

6. For further details see Eileen Breckenridge, "Improving School Climate," *Phi Delta Kappan* 58, no. 4 (December 1976), p. 314.

7. Robert J. Shaw, "Tapping the Riches of Creativity among Working People," *Management Focus* (September-October 1981), p. 27.

8. *Renaissance in Education,* joint publication of Dade County Public Schools and the United Teachers of Dade, Miami, Florida, n.d., p. 3.

9. For additional information see Walter St. John, *The Best Ideas in Employee Communication* (Blackwood, NJ: Communication Briefings, 1987), pp. 9–10.

10. Harry A. Millis and Emily Clark Brown, *From the Wagner Act to Taft-Hartley* (Chicago: The University of Chicago Press, 1965), p. 422.

11. *School Public Relations: The Complete Book* (Arlington, VA: National School Public Relations Association, 1986), p. 173.

12. *Hazelwood School District v. Kuhlmeier, What it says. What it means. Where student journalism goes from here.* Unpublished monograph (Washington: Student Press Law Center, n.d.), pp. 1–3.

13. Thomas Eveslage, "Hazelwood v. Kuhlmeier, A Threat and a Challenge to High School Journalism," *Quill & Scroll* (February-March 1988), p. 9.

8

COMMUNICATING WITH EXTERNAL PUBLICS

Schools that communicate with their external publics in some organized way enhance their chances of getting better public support, minimizing criticism, learning the values and priorities of a community, and receiving many functional ideas that will help them educate students better.

For many schools any designed program of communicating with external publics is very limited or nonexistent. The school officials have not seen the need for an ongoing program. And those who have usually limit it to parents or to some school-related group. This limited approach to community communications can be self-defeating given the limited financial resources available to schools and the growing number of nonparents in many communities.

The communicating process between the schools and external groups should encompass both one-way and two-way communication. Schools should use not only newsletters, news releases, radio and television programs, and brochures but also many person-to-person programs to inform the general public about what's taking place in the schools. Too often educators have relied heavily on one-way communications to get the school story to the community. Often this has served to make citizens aware of some activities in the school without fully understanding them. Person-to-person activities combined with the one-way communications process can help external publics to understand many decisions made by school officials and programs in their schools.

Any program of communication with external publics would include the study of the role of pupils in community relations; teachers' associations and the community; the importance of par-

ent relations; school liaison groups; key communicators; general community groups; public criticism and attacks; and communications during negotiations and a strike.

THE PUPIL AND COMMUNITY RELATIONS

Someone once said facetiously that a school has a good community relations program if it has "a snappy band and a winning football team." There is some truth in such a statement, of course, because it underscores the importance of the pupil in relating an image of the school to the community and the necessity for involving students in the school's community relations program. When students visibly represent the school, the public tends to look on them as personifying the characteristics of the school itself. This is true in a structured setting such as a public event or in a singular setting of a child walking past a house on his or her way to and from school.

In many ways, pupils do more to keep the school in the public eye and win support for it than some of the other things that are done to bring about good community relations. For example, parents will go out of their way to attend a play, read a newspaper account, see an athletic contest, or listen to a concert in which their children have a part. Even people in the community without children in school feel a certain sense of loyalty and pride when individual pupils win academic contests and scholarships or one of the athletic teams enjoys a successful season. Psychologically, some of these people identify themselves with the institution and, as a result, take more interest in the total instructional program.

Whenever parents and friends witness a demonstration, read a student publication, or watch a skilled performance by pupils, they generally express surprise that youngsters can do so well. Their impressions are conveyed by word of mouth to friends and acquaintances in the community. The cumulative effect of favorable reactions in the course of a year may influence, more than is realized, the attitudes and opinions of citizens toward the school and how they vote on financial proposals.

There is not much doubt about the value of pupil activities and accomplishments in cultivating and strengthening relations with the community. It happens, however, that some schools overlook the public relations opportunities connected with such routine events as commencement, plays, musicals, athletic contests, and service projects, while others emphasize the publicity side of these events and lose sight of their educational worth to pupils.

Public Presentations

Although public entertainment by pupils is hardly a function of the school, nevertheless there are sound educational reasons for having pupils present enjoyable and entertaining programs. The mere knowledge that they will appear before the public adds incentive and zest to the work they are doing in school.

At the same time, the institution has an excellent means at its disposal for acquainting adults with different phases of instruction and demonstrating the nature and quality of the result.

Musical Programs.   Aside from athletics, no activity has caught the fancy of the public more than music. In most communities, taxpayers are perfectly willing to have their boards of education start music instruction in the elementary grades and to loan instruments to pupils during these early years. School systems do a great deal to further musical understanding and appreciation through a school band, orchestra, glee club, and

chorus. Although these activities are carried on usually before or after school or during a club period, many schools include them in the regular program of studies.

Opportunities to present the musical accomplishments of pupils are numerous. Musical groups can be scheduled in connection with other events like assemblies, commencement exercises, and dramatic productions. The band can play at athletic contests and take part in civic celebrations. Invitations can be accepted by all musical organizations to appear before interested clubs and societies in the community and to put on radio and television programs when there is no conflict with regular studies.

Of all musical groups, the school marching band has more public visibility than any other group by the very nature of its attractive uniforms and marching music. Its appearance has a head-turning effect on citizens nearby. Care should be taken by band directors to ensure that in public appearances the band appears to be organized and drilled, and has knowledge of what it is supposed to do. The public does not expect to hear professional quality music from a school band, but citizens are quick to recognize a band that has been poorly prepared for a public appearance. Such a negative judgment can be extended by citizens to the entire school.

Dramatic Productions.   Dramatic productions in the form of plays, puppet shows, pageants, and operettas rank high on the list of entertainments that bring people into the school and which are sought by groups in the community. Here again spectators are usually amazed at the versatility and skill displayed by pupils.

Dramatic productions make it possible to involve parents and interested citizens. These individuals can help make costumes, properties, and stage sets. In some instances, they can also take part in programs.

Forensic Activities.   Although forensic activities of pupils lack the appeal of dramatic productions, they do much to place the school in a favorable light before parents and citizens. Debates, dialogues, and addresses demonstrate the ability of pupils to think on their feet, organize material, and express their thoughts in a clear and convincing manner. Greater good is often done by "telling the school story" through the forensic activities of pupils, especially before civic groups, than by any number of speeches by members of the professional staff.

Assembly Programs. Regular and special assembly programs are another avenue for presenting the pupils and educating the public to the affairs of the school. These programs may be built around everyday happenings in class and extracurricular activities or around the observance of special days, weeks, and anniversaries. The programs for these assemblies may be developed by pupils or undertaken jointly with outside groups and organizations. There are always a number of groups and organizations in the community that welcome the chance to share in programs of this character.

Regular assembly programs have appeal for parents, particularly when their own children are participants and the programs deal with topics related to their interests. The opportunity should never be overlooked of inviting prominent citizens to take part in programs. They might administer oaths to incoming student officers, chair a discussion, or speak on a vital subject. Like parents, they will hold the school in higher esteem after experiencing well-organized assembly programs.

Field Trips

Field trips to places of interest in the community are an excellent device for bringing notice to the school and for explaining some aspects of the educational program. A merchant, for example, who takes pupils on a guided tour of his or her store shares an important learning experience with teachers and pupils. When boys and girls ask

questions that indicate their grasp of a subject, their host recognizes the fine work the school is doing.

At the same time the full cooperation of parents should be secured. They like to know when a trip will take place, how pupils will be transported, and the measures adopted for supervising conduct and protecting the safety of pupils. In fact, if invited, some parents often agree to go along on trips with the children and to share in their learning experience.

Athletic Contests

For many citizens the only contact with a school is through its athletic teams. These citizens may know very little about the school's instructional program because the American tradition has been to highlight a school through its athletic teams. This can be seen in the newspaper column inches devoted to sports coverage versus the amount given to other school activities in the local press. Also, it can be seen in the number of people who attend an athletic function, compared with those attending another type of school function. It seems that the American public wants a rather comprehensive athletic program in its schools, particularly in its high schools. When a school attempts to suspend its sports program, public outcry and sentiment practically demand the return of athletics even if it means a rise in taxes.

Adults who view athletic contests often admire the fine precision with which a team makes a play and the resourcefulness shown by its members in the face of stiff competition. They observe the physical stamina of players and the products of character-building experiences, such as cooperation, fair play, and courage. They go away from these contests with many impressions of the school and the contributions it makes to pupils. Unfortunately, attention is sometimes directed away from the educational side of participation in contests by the premium attached to having winning teams. Adults seem more interested in enhancing the reputation of the school and community than in the welfare of pupils. Pressure is brought on boards of education and school officials to replace unsuccessful coaches and to overlook eligibility requirements. No expense is spared to support winners. They are accorded community-wide recognition and treated like idols. Under these circumstances, the public conception of the worth of the educational program is determined by the outcome of contests.

On the other hand, there are some adults, not necessarily win-or-else advocates, who judge the value of the educational program by the appearance of the team, how well it is organized, and whether some planning had taken place before the team appeared before the public. Since athletic teams may be the major image of the school in the community, it is wise for an administrator to ensure that a team is properly coached and organized, that it has presentable uniforms, and that it follows acceptable rules of conduct and fair play.

Commencement

As one of the oldest activities of the school, commencement programs make it possible for pupils to highlight for themselves and their parents the meaning and value of an education. The traditional commencement program of a few remarks by class officers and by the principal, followed by a main speaker, is sometimes replaced by a different type of graduation exercise.

In this ceremony members of the class being honored take over responsibility for most of the program. They may give short talks explaining what they have studied and accomplished in school, introduce honor students, present awards to outstanding classmates, or dramatize in play and pageant form some of their school experiences. During the week of commencement, demonstrations and exhibits of classwork may be arranged for public inspection and an open house held for tours of the building. These exercises are more interesting to parents and visitors, and they also enable them to get a better insight into the school and its products.

Commencement is an appropriate time to invite leading citizens and distinguished graduates to the school. Their names can be printed in the program and they can be honored from the stage.

Work-Study Programs

Work-study programs, often known as *distributive education* or *cooperative education,* provide other opportunities for pupils to represent their school in the community. These programs call for a pupil to attend classes for only part of the day and to work in a job related to his or her courses of study for the rest of the day. These positions may be in business, industry, or law, or in public service fields.

The pupils come in direct contact with members of the community, and the impression they make or the information they pass along about their school, whether good or bad, often will be interpreted as gospel by the public.

The community relations aspect of such programs that can easily be overlooked is the need for the pupil to be properly informed and prepared to represent the school and to be observed and supervised properly by the school. Also, it is wise to take time and give work-study pupils some information and facts about their school district in case questions are asked.

Close cooperation and liaison with employers obviously are needed if the school wishes to place the pupils in the most educationally beneficial positions. Such cooperation is also needed if the employer is to understand that all pupils are not alike. Many employers are inclined to judge the school by the performance of one student. Directors of work-study programs should thoroughly inform the employer of a student's intellectual capacity, academic record, and personality characteristics.

Accomplishments

The reported achievements and successes of pupils and graduates have a receptive audience in any community. People are interested and naturally curious to learn what pupils are accomplishing and how well their preparation fits them for life. If the school wants citizens to value its program and acknowledge the competencies of its staff, it must continually show them what pupils are achieving and acquaint them with the recognition, awards, and honors that have come to its graduates.

Services performed by members of the student council or student advisory committee are a form of achievement in citizenship training that deserves public recognition. Citizens should know, for example, that these youngsters publish a handbook, arrange and conduct commencement programs, act in an advisory capacity to the principal, operate an after-school employment bureau, and do many worthwhile things for the benefit of all pupils in the school. Although these activities in themselves may seem to lack news appeal, they can make excellent stories when treated properly.

Whenever standardized achievement tests are administered in basic subjects, the results should be published and interpreted against the background of the pupil population. Significant comparisons can be made with the norms of previous groups in the system and with state and national averages. Sometimes it is advisable to treat the data by individual schools, grades, and curricular divisions.

Pupils can be featured who receive college scholarships and win awards for outstanding accomplishments. Citizens are more interested than ever before in high-level attainment and the recognition it brings to the school and community. Newspaper editors are aware of this interest and assign a prominent place to stories of outstanding pupil achievement. This publicity can be supplemented by honoring winners at special assemblies, presenting their awards on radio and television, introducing them at service club and civic organization meetings, and by issuing citations to parents for their contributions to the success of these children.

In addition to scholarship and award winners, there are always a number of pupils in every school who have unusual talent and ability.

Some Precautions

Activities through which pupils are presented to the public should be a logical part of the instructional program and should fit in with its educational objectives. Unless this principle is respected, there is always a danger of exploiting pupils for publicity purposes.

This is especially true in districts where an exaggerated sense of importance is attached to the winning of athletic, forensic, dramatic, musical, or journalistic contests. Backed by sentiment in the community, coaches and sponsors will adjust their aims to the training of those pupils who can bring recognition to themselves and the institution.

A somewhat similar issue is raised by the large number of essay and individual prize-winning contests that are sponsored by industries, business firms, and civic organizations. In the interest of furthering their own special purposes, these sponsors would like the school to make their contests a part of the classwork done by pupils. This is an impossibility in view of the large number of contests, let alone the time that would be taken away from other instructional matters. Perhaps the best way of dealing with this issue is to post all legitimate contests for the notice of pupils. Then, if pupils want to enter them, it would be with the understanding that preparation must be done after school hours—and that class preparation will take precedence.

Finally, the school has a moral obligation to see that pupils maintain a desirable balance between participation in public activities and preparation of scheduled studies. Instances are common of how talented pupils have been encouraged to undertake a variety of activities at the expense of their own health and educational progress in order to achieve favorable publicity for the school. This form of exploitation should be avoided.

COMMUNITY RELATIONS ROLE OF TEACHERS' ASSOCIATIONS

Teachers' associations are groups that have an interest in promoting the welfare of the teacher. The basic question is how can they promote the cause of education when there is sometimes a tendency for teacher groups to put their personal interests above the ideals of service for education. The prevailing stress on the economic welfare of the teacher must be brought into proper balance with the equally important concept that members of the profession deserve rewards only to the extent that they work for better schools and the continuous improvement of their own services. As a result, teacher groups must devise and use every means possible for increasing their contributions to the cause of education while keeping the public fully informed of what they are doing.

This means that a teacher group must be aware of and understand its community relations role as a part of the overall school system.

Relations with School Systems

Many local teacher organizations become confused with their community relations role and begin covering areas that are exclusively within the responsibility of the school district. For example, community relations committees of teacher organizations may develop a publicity plan that calls for news releases on topics such as curriculum, budget, transportation, facilities, and libraries. Normally, these are subjects that should be handled by the school district since it has the background information to develop a proper news story.

Generally, the teachers' organization should confine itself to interpreting the organization to the public and developing community relations programs that will help the public better understand the teacher and the profession. If asked, it can help the school district to publicize programs

and students. Conversely, a school district should not assume the role of interpreting the teachers' organization to the public unless asked.

The relationship between an individual teacher organization and a local school system should be made clear to the public, the board of education, the superintendent of schools, and members of the association itself. All parties should be fully cognizant that the association is completely independent of the school system and that it has the same rights and privileges as other groups in the community. No question should be left unanswered regarding the purposes and program of the association and its desire to cooperate with school officials and community groups on all matters related to the education of children and the welfare of teachers. Failure to establish clearly the character and position of the association tends to weaken its professional standing and to invite the assumption of control by school officials.

Good relations with the local school system are important in achieving the objectives of the organization. These objectives can be developed more quickly when the board of education and the superintendent meet periodically with representatives of the association to discuss mutual interests and to explore opportunities for working on common problems.

Relations with the Community

Too often teacher groups become active in a community only when some crisis arises or when there is the need for salary increases. In order for a teacher organization to relate properly with the community, it must have a continuous, systematic program of communicating with the external publics. This, of course, is a leadership function of the officers.

There must be a commitment to effective communications with the public by the officers of the organization. They must see the value of communicating with local citizens if their organization is going to be beneficial to them and to education. Local teacher groups have taken on a more active role than in the past and have become more collective in their actions. Therefore, they have an obligation to interpret this role to the parents and the citizens in a community and to attempt to develop greater understanding of the teaching profession.

More than ever teacher groups must develop a well-planned community relations program if the public is ever to understand the changing teaching profession. All the acceptable methods of communicating with the public should be used: press, radio, television, community involvement, political activity, community surveys, publications, citizen advisory committees, and community opinion leaders. Some suggested community activities are listed in a later part of this chapter.

Community Relations Activities

Every activity of a teachers' group influences the opinions of laypeople about the group and about the profession it represents. This influence may be favorable, unfavorable, or mixed, depending on the manner in which the particular activity is conducted. In a formal sense, however, a community relations program is usually thought of as a collection of activities for interpreting the work of a group or organization and for developing the understanding, goodwill, respect, and support of the public that is desired.

Business Contacts. In the daily business management of a teachers' group, many personal contacts take place among the officers and staff workers and the representatives of various firms, governmental agencies, and special-interest groups, as well as between private citizens and members of the association. The contacts may come about through direct relations or through telephone calls, correspondence, and appearances at outside meetings. Each one is an opportunity for identifying the organization with ideals of service and for passing on information and creating wholesome impressions that form the basis of good public opinion.

Membership Training. The members of a teachers' organization are community relations agents of that association, just as much as the officers and staff workers, and should be trained to meet their responsibilities. This training should be outlined by national and state associations and carried out for the most part by local branches in their own communities. It should include the preparation and study of handbooks and manuals containing information on the work of professional organizations, problems of the teaching profession, current developments in educational thought and practice, and how individual members can contribute to the advancement of the teaching profession. Workshops conducted at state and local levels form another part of the program for achieving wider understanding of professional ideals and services and acquiring sensitivity to community relations opportunities.

Political Action. In the past many teachers' organizations have taken the position that member welfare and the cause of education were better served by the independence of the teacher organization from political connections. As the teachers became militant, they reversed their position and came to appreciate the value of taking intelligent political action on the election of public officials, important social issues, and legislative proposals.

It is reasonable to assume that better qualified individuals can be nominated and placed on school boards, city councils, and state and national legislative offices if teacher organizations take an interest in their appointment or election. Teacher groups should make objective studies of the qualifications and views of candidates and publicly endorse or oppose candidates. Their standing in the community will become stronger if teachers go to the polls and back up these recommendations as testimony to their civic interest and desire to see competent men and women in office.

As a special-interest group, teacher organizations have every right to take sides on important social issues and to make known the views of the teaching profession. This is a part of democratic functioning and a means of creating enlightened public opinion. With some possible exceptions, the various teacher organizations should confine their work to issues affecting child and youth welfare and education. The major work of collecting and presenting information on social issues should be done on the national and state level, with local units serving as key points for distributing much of the material through the personal contacts of members, newspaper releases, and open meetings.

Community Activities. A local teachers' organization carries on good community relations when it takes an interest in the community and performs services that establish it in the minds of people as a fine neighbor and a worthy civic agency. How an association may best express this interest and perform services is determined by local conditions and the attitudes of members. The possibilities for being identified constructively with the life of the community are numerous.

In practically all communities the members of teachers' organizations can lend support and furnish leadership in drives and campaigns that are conducted by such organizations as the Red Cross, Boy Scouts, United Fund, Girl Scouts, and a host of other character-building and philanthropic groups. Full advantage has been taken of civic drives and campaigns by business and industrial firms to associate themselves with the good citizen concept. It is time that teachers' groups took their place alongside these and other community groups in contributing to the public welfare and bringing favorable attention to themselves.

Teachers' organizations should also be represented on civic committees for the study of specific problems affecting the community. Their technical knowledge and skill in a wide range of fields make them valuable members of civic committees.

At the same time, the local teachers' organization should make a detailed study of the purposes and programs of organized groups in the community in order to determine which ones are concerned with educational and human welfare problems. The various community groups should be invited to discuss their programs with members of the local teachers' association, and to learn in turn what the teachers are trying to accomplish. This exchange of information makes it possible to explore opportunities for cooperation and to develop projects in which there is mutual interest.

Special Events and Speakers' Bureau. The sponsoring of special events and services is another means for a teachers' group to earn prestige and acquire recognition in the community. It can set up a bureau and furnish a list of speakers to every group and organization. It can entertain civic groups at luncheons and dinners and acknowledge their contributions as well as those of private citizens to the advancement of public education. It is helpful if a teachers' organization identifies and works with the community power structure, a handful of influential citizens who are usually the key to community understanding and support. The community activities of the local association should also be supplemented at the state and national level by its own national organization.

Publications. Interpretive materials may be presented continually through the publications of teacher organizations. The leading publications for this purpose are the official journals of national and state associations and those of local groups in large communities. These may be supplemented by pamphlets, newsletters, special bulletins, and reprints of articles appearing in professional and lay magazines.

Although printed primarily for the information of their own members and their interpretation to the public, copies of journals and supplementary publications should also be distributed to officers of important state and national groups, certain governmental officials, presidents of boards of education, and the principal libraries throughout the country. The local teacher organizations should be made responsible for selective distribution within their respective communities, including leaders in social and civic life, newspaper editors, radio commentators, and outstanding private citizens. Planned distribution of professional publications can net excellent results in general public understanding, appreciation, and support of the program carried on by educational associations.

Direct Publicity. Although coordination of the local, state, and national organizations is essential to effective planning of publicity programs, the real job of publicizing the teaching profession and the cause of education belongs to the local association. It is closer to the rank and file of the citizenry, and its members enjoy more widespread contacts than are possible by state and national groups. Its publicity should be fitted to local needs and conditions, using the services of the larger associations to full advantage. Increasingly, some local groups have carried on effective publicity through regular space in newspapers and by means of radio broadcasts and television programs, while others have placed reliance on an assortment of publicity devices, such as articles in lay magazines and in house organs of business and industrial firms, window stickers, letter enclosures, paid newspaper advertising, billboards, posters, bumper stickers, calendars, leaflets, exhibits, and slides.

Suggested Activities. In developing a community relations program for the whole year, a teachers' organization should structure it in such a manner that the community is constantly made aware of the existence of the organization. Too often citizens only hear about a teachers' group during negotiations, when money is the primary issue. As a result, the teacher is identified as always wanting more money and is not seen in the overall perspective. Activities should be scheduled to show that the teachers are interested in the welfare of the community and the local citizens. Here are some suggested activities:

— Take full advantage of American Education Week to publicize the teaching profession and education.

— Recognize a "friend of education" in the community at an annual dinner sponsored by the local teachers' organizations.

— Sponsor singing in nursing homes periodically.

— Sponsor benefit activities such as dances, fairs, and dinners to raise money for a worthy community cause.

— Participate in local parades with a float clearly identifying the name of the local teachers' organization.

— Sponsor an exchange teacher program with a foreign city.

— Participate in community projects to clean up the environment and to provide recreational facilities or mobile libraries.

— Provide summer or Saturday tutorial programs.

— Set up window displays and exhibits in the community.

— Develop an activity for senior citizens.

— Establish a scholarship fund for needy students.

IMPORTANCE OF PARENT RELATIONS

The bottom line of any school-community relations program is to help the children learn better. And they learn better if parents are involved. This is Holliday's position, and Henderson verifies it in the thirty research studies she has reviewed for the National Committee for Citizens in Education.[1] Therefore, a good school-community relations program should encompass the concept of a partnership between the school and the parents.

The partnership concept calls for the free and continual exchange of information between parents and teachers and the involvement of parents in school affairs. Exchange of information enables teachers to acquire a knowledge of pupils that they otherwise would be denied. Teachers gain a direct understanding of difficulties experienced by parents, particularized experiences of children, and influences that have been determinants of their behavior. They learn how parents think and act, what their attitudes are toward life, and what they want for their children. And because of this parent relationship, teachers see children differently and are able to deal more intelligently with their needs.

Parents also acquire valuable information from their contacts with teachers, information that is useful in living with their children at home. So often parents are unaware of what their children are like outside the family and how they act with other people. They know relatively little about their children's school experiences and what teachers must contend with in directing their growth. Parents are able to comprehend from analyses of test results, school records, behavior reports, and classwork how much progress their children have made and how much more they could make with help at home. They reach agreements with teachers on plans for attaining common objectives.

A successful partnership involves more than exchanging information with parents and acquainting them with the school. It includes cooperative work on problems that affect children and advance the cause of education. Nothing else produces in parents a better understanding of the school and a deeper sense of responsibility for its progress.

In spite of these outcomes, it is usual for some administrators and teachers to oppose the partnership concept when they should be promoting it. They are, in reality, afraid that parent participation may lead to serious interference with their rights and duties. They do not believe that parents are qualified to decide what education is best for children or to discuss technical matters of curriculum building and instructional procedures. In some cases they are correct in their assumptions. They forget, however, that parents are well qualified to make contributions for the advancement of education. Parents can discuss intelligently with administrators and teachers the purpose of education and many of the specific outcomes they would like for their children. Their knowledge in specialized areas makes them valuable resource persons for committees engaged in curriculum development. They have skills and talents that can be drawn on for the enrichment of curricular and cocurricular activities. Many parents are highly competent in problem-solving procedures and the formulation of policies that reflect the wishes of the people. They can be of inestimable value in helping to chart the course of education while leaving the technical details to professionally trained educators.

Those who argue against the involvement of parents seem to forget that no other group of citizens in the community exerts a stronger influence on public opinion, and that only through a broad sense of favorable opinion can the school expect to make significant progress.

INITIATING CLOSER CONTACTS

Initiating closer contacts with parents in order to break down the barrier to cooperation involves the question of what activities are most appropriate to interest parents in joining the school family. There are numerous ways of starting a school-community relations program that will appeal to parents—a program that will bring parents into the school so they will become acquainted with teachers and learn to take a direct interest in various phases of instruction. *Parent representatives* for each grade level are a commonly accepted means for accomplishing this purpose. Either the principal appoints the parents or they elect their own representatives in each grade to promote good relations with teachers. Periodic meetings are held to discuss schoolwork. The agenda may call for a consideration of pupil difficulties in mathematics, questions of social development, personal habits, or physical health. Discussion topics are decided on by parents, in consultation with teachers; included are items of most concern to both parties. Handled adroitly, this plan can be highly effective in joining parents and teachers together.

Another system, the *invitational visitation* technique, has produced good results in schools that have used it. It is a technique whereby a certain number of parents—usually five or six—are invited by the principal to spend a half-day visiting classes, having lunch, and observing pupil activities in the school. The principal may select parents at random, have parent-teacher associations and community-interest groups name some, and draw other names from a preferred list. A new group of parents is brought in each week for as many weeks as the principal and teachers decide. These visitors are given a mimeographed evaluation sheet and asked to use it for guiding their observations. The evaluation contains such questions as what parents think of the way discipline is handled, whether or not they would change the methods of teaching, and how valuable they consider the learning activities to be. Each of these questions is discussed in conference with the principal and one or two teachers at the close of the visitation. The conference provides an excellent opportunity to clarify observations and to further interpret the work of the school.

A variation on this technique is that of *inviting committees of parents,* from time to time, to meet with the principal and discuss what they like and dislike about the school. The danger inherent in this approach is that the negative side may be overemphasized at the expense of practices deserving commendation. The technique has some merit when parents are asked what they like most about the school and how they think the school could be improved. Concern with improvement is a constructive lead that directs thinking to problems needing solution and offers opportunities for involving and sharing responsibility with parents. Often principals can get constructive leads for improvement by inviting six or eight citizens to lunch or inviting business people to breakfast.

Most parents respond favorably to personal invitations from teachers and pupils asking them to attend some school event. The event may be a room exhibit where they can see their own children's work, a classroom play, an open-house program, a special lecture, a luncheon prepared by pupils, or a discussion on school parties.

The use of *checklists* has also proved helpful in bringing about closer cooperation between parents and teachers. One type that deserves attention covers the joint responsibilities of home and school. Statements are set forth describing what both the school and the home can do to further the growth and development of children. Parents are asked to check those items that apply to their own practices as well as to the school practices and to confer with teachers on the results. This sort of instrument suggests possibilities that parents may never have realized before and lets them know that the school wants to work cooperatively. Another type of checklist represents an inventory of contributions parents can make to the educational program. They are invited to check those items they are willing to contribute, such as speaking to a class about a trip to a foreign country; explaining their occupations; demonstrating a hobby; lending books, pictures, and objects to the school; or serving as aides on field trips taken by children. The information compiled from these checklists enables teachers to enrich the learning process and to involve parents voluntarily in the actual work of the school.

Another good suggestion is for the principal to *write the parents of new pupils* in junior and senior high school inviting them to visit the school at any time and to confer freely with teachers. A similar effort can be made in the elementary schools by brief, friendly phone calls by teachers to parents of new children in their rooms. Letters sent to parents of secondary-school pupils are sometimes accompanied by a bulletin or handbook containing information parents want on marks, attendance, homework, health requirements, college entrance requirements, cafeteria services, extracurricular activities, and expenses.

Besides these means for promoting closer cooperation with parents, many others have been used successfully. Briefly, some of these are:

— Asking parents to be present at physical health examinations of their elementary school children
— Giving teas or coffee "klatsches" for parents of preschool children
— Having night sessions so that parents may attend classes
— Opening the gymnasium and other school facilities to the parents for recreational purposes
— Having a telephone tended in the evening for questions from parents or citizens
— Inviting parents to observe their children in activities related to classwork
— Arranging meetings in the school library for advising parents on books they may wish to purchase for their children
— Asking parents to help with birthday parties and similar events for elementary school students.

PARENT VISITS AND CONFERENCES

Schools move closer to a realization of partnership when they adopt policies providing for parent visits and conferences with teachers as a regular part of the educational program. Such policies establish friendly relations, minimize misunderstanding, and promote lay-professional cooperation.

Parent Visits

The initial problem of motivating parent visits can be surmounted rather easily when the policy is thoroughly publicized and the school takes the initiative in arranging for parents to visit the school. Parents are often reluctant to take it upon themselves to contact the school and ask if they may visit the classrooms. Once parents learn of the open-door policy through the mass media and from parents who have visited the school, their reluctance and shyness give way to natural curiosity. They are interested in seeing how their children behave in the classroom, what the teachers are like and how they handle their pupils, whether or not methods of teaching are much different today, and how their own youngsters compare with others of similar age.

School visits can be very helpful to the teachers in communicating with parents of low socio-economic status. They intensely desire a good education for their children and view it as a way for their children to obtain a better life. In successful visitation programs, it has been found that low-income parents are responsive to bus tours. Many have no available transportation and on such a tour they are more at ease because they are with neighbors and friends. Coupled with the tour could be a simple and direct program including the use of visual aids such as slides, charts, and videos in reporting the work of their children. If possible, it is helpful to include in the program a paraprofessional employed in the school system from their neighborhood. They will be able to identify with this individual, who in turn will facilitate communications between the school and the parents.

An open visitation policy can also be extremely helpful in establishing a liaison with parents of private and parochial school students, as well as with parents who have no children in school. This latter group of parents includes those whose children have completed school or are preschoolers. Often such parents are skeptical of modern public school education because of a lack of knowledge of its purpose, scope, and legal parameters. In point, such parents may not understand the absence of a dress code or the freedom of expression in student publications in a public school. During a visit to the school, a review of court decisions that permit students more latitude in dress and in expression will quickly clarify the school's position for the visiting parents. In a similar way a presentation of the positive aspects of the school, such as the achievements of the students, the variety of courses offered, the resources available to the students, and so forth, can go far to establish good relations with these parents.

Parent Conferences

Because parent conferences have turned out to be a valuable method of clearing up sources of misunderstanding and of interpreting the instructional programs, such conferences have become an accepted practice in many school systems. In some instances they have replaced the report card, and in others they have served as a supplementary or correlated report. Teachers are able to tell their story more accurately, and parents are able to get a more complete picture of their child's progress, including a review of his or her marks, reading-test scores, achievement-test scores, interest inventories, participation in extracurricular activities, and anecdotal records. In addition, the teacher can share with the parents his or her observations of the student's work habits, behavior, attitude toward learning, and relations with others.

There are times when parents come to the school tense and excited after being notified of difficulties involving their children. Conferences under these conditions are naturally strained. It is not uncommon for a parent to become highly emotional and shout unreasonable opinions about the school and make verbal attacks on the teacher. In such cases a wise teacher will not become equally emotional or launch a verbal counterattack. As in any conference situation, the burden of being tactful, courteous, considerate, and truthful must be carried by the teacher. Any manifestation of attitudes to the contrary will only be met with more tension and alienation, which reduce chances for harmony.

Good conference procedure depends on the ability of teachers to listen attentively and understandingly, to sift facts, to determine the nature and limits of any conflict, to correct misunderstandings without engaging in arguments, to use simple language free from ambiguity, jargon, and emotional coloration, and to present clear issues to which thought should be directed. All conferences should end on a constructive note and should culminate, if possible, in a mutual plan of action on behalf of the children. A record should

be made of each conference and filed for future reference.

Sensitive Subjects

Sex education, AIDS, civil rights, abortion, communism, and religion are all touchy subjects and may set off explosive feelings in a community when they are included in the school's curriculum. The degree of sensitivity toward these topics may vary from time to time and from one community to another. Such sensitive subjects can become crises if the community relations aspects of teaching them are not handled properly.

When a school is ready to introduce a controversial topic into its curriculum, the parents and the community should have been prepared. It is wise to invite parents to view the books, films, videos, and other materials the student will use. Parents should know exactly what is going on. This can be handled through general parent meetings, panel discussions, parent conferences, or a parent advisory committee which is involved in every stage of planning of the controversial program.

WRITTEN COMMUNICATIONS

Written communications in the form of printed materials, letters, and samples of pupils' work constitute another means for promoting home contacts and keeping parents informed of their children's progress. In many districts such communications are the only direct link with the home and as such they are a primary factor in shaping parent attitudes toward the school.

Printed Materials

The most common type of printed material for communicating regularly with parents is the report card. It is issued several times a year to inform parents how their children stand in subject achievement.

Advances in educational thought and practice have created dissatisfaction with the traditional report card. Leaders in elementary education believe that a more accurate description should be given of the child's growth and development. They have devised cards that include information on student growth in subject-matter mastery, learning skills, habits, attitudes, and social behaviors. This type of card reflects the philosophy of the elementary school and is more descriptive of a child's total progress.

Like any departure from convention, newer types of report cards and reporting practices are often opposed by parents. These parents do not understand what was wrong with the traditional report card nor why the changes were made. Much of their opposition could have been avoided had the proposed changes been discussed with them in advance or had they been made parties to the work of devising improved methods of reporting.

Another means of written communication used by many schools is the monthly or quarterly newsletter or bulletin mailed to parents of school children and to citizens of the community. The purpose of this publication is to keep parents and citizens informed on such features as instructional practices, outstanding professional activities, lunch menus, fiscal matters, and special problems facing the school system. Though small school systems are reluctant to publish printed newsletters because of criticism from taxpayers on the question of expense, they can nevertheless publish similar information in attractive mimeograph form.

Increasingly, school systems issue annual handbooks for parents to provide a ready reference for answering questions that are commonly asked. Opening usually with a friendly foreword by the superintendent explaining the purposes of the handbook, such publications supply information on the school system, the board of education, entrance requirements, attendance regulations, school hours, procedures for telephoning the school, appointment procedures, emergency school closings, pupil personnel services, transportation, curriculum offerings, taxes, and a directory of the schools in the system. In some

districts, individual schools have their own parent handbooks. Whatever the case may be, these handbooks constitute an important means of communication with the home and the community.

In addition, some schools have established the practice of enclosing leaflets with report cards as a device for helping parents understand specific aspects of the educational program. Because youngsters frequently remove these leaflets from report card envelopes and throw them away, a number of school districts are now sending them by mail. Their value is somewhat doubtful unless they are kept very brief and are easily understood, interesting to read, and timely.

Letters to Parents

Letters and personal notes from teachers can improve relationships between home and school. In the past, too many letters were limited—and still are in some schools—to reports of unsatisfactory work and disciplinary problems of pupils. This one-sided reporting has been balanced in recent years by written communications on things students do well and on contributions they make to the school. For example, if a pupil has done a fine job as a library assistant, a motion picture operator, a stage hand, a receptionist, a hall monitor, a club president, or a committee chairperson, a letter of commendation is sent to parents by the activity sponsor. In the same way, alert classroom teachers note outstanding achievements and significant behavior changes that deserve recognition. Their letters may describe superior classwork, improvements in study habits, acts of courtesy, special talents, and honor roll status. Parents who receive these letters feel pleased and grateful for the information.

Teachers sometimes object to writing favorable notes and letters to parents because of the extra work involved. The idea is more acceptable if an experimental period is established to determine how many notes and letters are written on a weekly average and how these communications are received by parents. Usually, teachers find at the end of the experimental period that the load has not been heavy and that parents are genuinely appreciative of the information they are sent.

Schools often find it necessary to publish form letters for general distribution to parents on such items as opening and closing dates of school, control of contagious disease, new policies and regulations, procedures for emergency school closings, use of plant facilities, bus schedules, and parent-teacher meetings. These form letters are important media for conveying information and creating favorable impressions of the institution. Unless they can be duplicated exceptionally well, they should be printed or typed on an automatic typewriter on regular stationery and blocked out attractively. Close attention should be paid to vocabulary, tone, and simplicity. They should close with a handwritten signature. Good form letters invite better relations with parents.

OPPORTUNITIES FOR PARTICIPATION

The suggestions made thus far for parent involvement tend to establish closer relations between home and school and to set a foundation for parent participation in school affairs. Leadership for parent participation should come from administrators and teachers. In this section a number of successful projects that schools have used to involve parents are described.

Study and Discussion Groups

Study and discussion groups have grown rapidly ever since parents have indicated a desire to become more involved in the schools. Such groups represent an increasingly popular concern for childhood education and a desire on the part of laypersons to know more about the schools their children attend. Organized at times at the request of parents, such groups are known by a variety of titles, including parent-teacher study groups, parent-teacher discussion clubs, grade and homeroom councils, parent study councils, and parent workshops.

Study and discussion group interests fall into two broad classes. One such class is concerned

with policies and practices of school systems and methods by which parents and teachers can work together. Discussion centers on such subjects as report cards, homework, school parties, discipline, health, drugs, pupil adjustment, sex education, dress codes, pupil personnel services, and the teaching of fundamental skill subjects. Occasionally, modern teaching methods are treated in detail for parents who wish to know how to help children correctly with homework.

Curriculum Planning

Work connected with the study and improvement of curriculum at all levels affords rich opportunities for parent participation. Parents can take an active and constructive role in helping the school define the purposes of education, the objectives for specific fields, and courses of study. They have served effectively on faculty committees concerned with the adequacy of the curriculum, revision offerings, and introduction of changes that could not be attempted without their support. They have served as resource persons, because of their specialties, in the preparation of units and have worked with teachers in the selection of materials and equipment for vitalizing the units.

Contributions to Classwork

Parents can make worthwhile contributions to classwork. They can speak on topics about which they possess firsthand information. They can loan rare books, objects, phonograph records, videotapes, historical collections, and motion pictures. They can aid on field trips by serving as chaperones, checking attendance, exercising accident safeguards, and taking part in follow-up activities. They can be members of textbook committees, report card committees, and others dealing with improvement of teaching.

Extracurricular Activities

Parents enjoy taking part in extracurricular activities with children and adolescents. Any number of them possess talent and technical knowledge that can be used advantageously. Some schools call on them to work with teacher sponsors of clubs. Parents are willing to assist pupils and teachers in designing simple costumes for dramatic productions and lending a hand in building stage scenery. They respond freely to invitations to participate in plays, musicals, assembly programs, and athletic games and to act as judges for contests and chaperones for parties and dances.

Room Parents

Parents are either elected to these posts by parents of children in a given grade or room or else they are appointed by officers of the parent-teacher association. Their function is to represent the parents of children in the grade or room, work with the teacher, and serve as a link between the home and the school. In setting up a room parents' organization, it is necessary to have the responsibility of the parents clearly understood. Moreover, the period of service should always be specified.

The responsibilities of the room parent may be to help in developing friendliness among parents of children in the room, encourage parents to attend PTA meetings, assist as a welcomer at open house and other school functions, assist in the cafeteria and on school grounds on special occasions, and help new parents and their children be accepted in the community. The room parent is the special liaison between the particular classroom and the community for that particular year. She or he can render valuable services to the schools and interpret the work of the teacher better than any other one person at the particular time.

Teacher Aides

Some schools use parents as teacher aides, depending on their qualifications and availability. Qualified adults and former teachers frequently substitute for teachers while they attend professional meetings and conferences or when they are out sick. Parents frequently assist in the lunchroom at noontime and help with playground and classroom activities.

SCHOOL LIAISON GROUPS

Four principal types of organizations are found under the social liaison groups classification: (1) parent-teacher or home and school associations, (2) neighborhood associations, (3) advisory groups, and (4) groups of former students.

Parent-Teacher Association

A local parent-teacher association may be described as a voluntary organization whose membership consists of teachers in an individual school or school system and the parents of children who attend the school or school system they support through public taxation. Devoid of legal authority to make policy decisions or to administer educational programs, the primary purpose of this association is that of promoting child and youth welfare in the home, school, and community. Local associations are usually organized around individual building units and separate divisions of the educational system, that is, elementary, junior, and senior high schools. Where junior and senior high schools are housed together or the elementary and secondary programs are in the same building, a single association serves the combined unit.

Typically, the membership of local associations consists of parents, teachers, and administrative and supervisory officials of the individual school and school system. Invitation to membership is also extended by local associations to interested citizens in the community whether or not they have children in school.

City-wide associations are often formed in communities where there are several building units. Each unit sends representatives to a central group whose activities are governed by a constitution and set of bylaws. The same idea has been carried out on a county and regional basis in rural and semirural areas. The larger association speaks for the entire membership on important issues that cut across the school system, and this larger grouping makes it possible to share experiences and develop better programs.

Apart from the direct benefits of parent-teacher cooperation received by children and youth in home, school, and community, several community relations by-products must be considered in looking at the importance of local associations. Good community relations start when parents and teachers come to know one another and to talk about what they want for young people. Through these conversations, parents soon learn to know the school, to understand what teachers are trying to do for children, and to appreciate instructional conditions and problems. At the same time, teachers and administrators are made aware of the needs, interests, and attitudes of people in the community and the responsibility they have for adjusting the school program to local conditions. This is a two-way process and the backbone, in many respects, of a sound program in school and community relations.

There are many types of parent-teacher organizations, each with a name that attempts to indicate its primary purpose for existing. Some educators classify the various types of parent-teacher groups as individual school associations, homeroom and grade councils, mothers' and fathers' clubs, school and parent councils, home and school associations, and parent study clubs.

Neighborhood Associations in Urban Districts

Common in large city school systems are the neighborhood associations. Generally, they operate within definite geographic limits and are keenly interested in education. Additionally they are interested in housing, recreation, and community improvements. They depend on membership dues for income. These groups offer the schools another excellent method of establishing and maintaining good community relations.

Neighborhood associations differ from city to city, and it is difficult to be specific about them.

Nevertheless, there is an eagerness and willingness on the part of neighborhood associations to play a supportive role in the local schools. In return they want the schools to help them to achieve their goals of community improvement. Schools, however, are not always responsive to the invitation to join the associations in improving the community. This is regrettable because schools miss many opportunities for good community relations. It has been shown that school administrators can be helpful to associations by making them more concerned with and involved in the educational decision-making process, inviting members to serve on advisory committees, participating directly in association activities, developing interaction between school personnel and associations, structuring an on-going two-way communication process between the schools and the neighborhood group, and working with universities in providing associations with leadership training.[2]

Citizen Advisory Committees

A further opportunity to bring the public into closer contact with the school and to involve laypersons in the educational program is provided by citizen advisory committees. As the name implies, these committees are composed of laypersons who study educational needs and problems and then advise school authorities on whatever action they believe should be taken.

One reason for school-sponsored advisory committees is the desire of boards of education, sparked by dynamic superintendents, to cooperate as fully as possible with members of the community. The boards realize that the responsibility of long-range planning for better schools is a public one and that the advisory committee is an excellent means for sharing this responsibility. Through this committee they can acquaint a representative body of the citizenry with the conditions and problems of public education, pool information, and work for common goals. Often advisory groups are formed by school boards and superintendents to meet a pressing problem or an emergency for which public support is needed. This is not always the most appropriate time to form an advisory committee. Often when a crisis is on the scene public attitudes have been formed, and the public may view this as a ploy on the part of the board of education to substantiate its position.

Authorities contend that an advisory committee should be formed well in advance of a possible crisis in order to develop credibility with the citizens. But even more important, a citizens committee formed at a noncrisis time can advise a school board on positions that are and are not acceptable to the public. In this way boards can avoid some unnecessary crises. Also, the committee can be helpful in apprising the public of facts and conditions that necessitate a particular decision by a school board.

Selection of Members. Different methods are used and various factors considered in the selection of citizens for membership on school-sponsored advisory committees. Essentially, there are three primary methods of selection: by the board of education, by invitation to community-interest groups, and by asking people in the schools and in the community to suggest names.

Whether one or a combination of methods is employed for selecting members, the advisory committee should be as representative of the community as possible. Representation can best be ensured when population factors are taken into account in drawing up the composition of the committee and when criteria of the individual qualifications of members are determined.

Size. An advisory committee should be large enough to represent the community adequately and small enough to encourage informal, efficient working relations among the members. Size may be affected by the nature of the school district and responsibilities assigned to the committee. Many advisory groups have fewer than five members, but the optimum size appears to fall somewhere between fifteen and twenty-five. Where a large committee is organized to increase citizen partici-

pation, an executive body of ten to fifteen members may be established to plan and coordinate the activities of the several subcommittees into which the advisory group is broken. An intelligent use of subcommittees makes it possible to widen the scope of the advisory committee program and to tap the talents and interests of many citizens. The number of subcommittees depends on the amount of work brought before the advisory group and the number of people who are involved.

Term of Office. The term of office for advisory committee members should be stated in the policy of the board of education.

Officers and Meetings. During the initial meetings of a new advisory group, the president of the board of education should act as chairperson until he or she is satisfied that the members have learned to know one another well enough to elect their own officers. The officers should be a chairperson, vice-chairperson, and secretary, and each should hold office for a period of one year.

Meetings should be held monthly during the school year, and more often if necessary, and should last no longer than two hours. Longer meetings discourage attendance. Special subcommittees may meet more frequently than once a month if they have definite assignments to finish within fixed time limits.

It is not uncommon for school-sponsored advisory committees to include administrators and teachers. These school representatives usually have ex officio status with no voting power. They attend all meetings, provide leadership in planning study projects, keep the board informed of activities and developments, and assist in numerous ways. Unfortunately, school staff members have a tendency to dominate because of their superior knowledge of the school system and to assume more responsibility than they should. An advisory committee is likely to function better when administrators and teachers are not actual members but cooperate in other ways with the committee.

A brief written report should be filed with the school board immediately after the advisory committee has completed a study. A *joint meeting* with the school board should then be held after board members have had an opportunity to review the report. Subsequently, the board's reactions to the report should be sent to the committee along with an expression of appreciation for the work that was done.

Relations with Former Students

One community group that is often overlooked by educators interested in good community relations is the former students of a school. It is surprising how many former pupils accept invitations to attend school functions and events. Many of them are young people whose formal education came to a halt either before or at the time of graduation. Their willingness to return suggests that they feel a sentimental attachment to the school.

Relations with this group should be founded on a continuing interest in the welfare of former pupils as well as a desire to provide useful services, such as the following:

- Sponsoring social affairs for the opportunity they afford to meet faculty and pupils
- Sending congratulatory letters to former pupils
- Mailing an annual inventory card for information concerning their work, marital status, family, and so forth
- Disseminating this information through publication to former pupils
- Issuing periodic newsletters concerning individual graduates
- Providing counseling services for personal problems and vocational placement
- Publishing honors won by former pupils
- Mailing them district publications
- Developing any particular services that seem appropriate in the local situation.

Practically all of the activities listed can be performed without having a formal association. Those who have worked closely with alumni and alumnae groups, however, are convinced that better relationships will be developed if these and other activities are channeled through an organization to which the credit can be given.

KEY COMMUNICATORS

Citizens often do not accept or reject an idea until they talk with residents of the community whose opinion and judgment they respect. These key people or opinion leaders in a community must be identified so that they may be informed about the schools, learn quickly what the community is thinking, and get the public involved in the schools. The concept of "key communicators" is probably not an innovative one for some school officials. Many educators have applied the ideas behind the key communicator approach in their schools. Few, however, have formalized it in the manner suggested here.

Benefits of Key Communicators

Being person-to-person in nature, the program enables the school officials to get the pulse of the community with quick phone calls to key communicators. Likewise, rumors can be quelled when they are sparks. Because key communicators have developed a solid rapport with school officials, they can help the community gain and maintain confidence in the school. And perhaps above all, a positive school story can also be spread. The key communicators, then, serve as gatekeepers of information to and from the community.

Prior to making major decisions, school officials are often interested in the community's feelings toward an issue. Such decisions could include the change of attendance lines, a tax increase, the closing of a school, or the moving of administrators or teachers within a district. Many cases are documented where school officials, insensitive to community feelings, had to reverse a decision when citizens protested vehemently. One way of getting an early pulse of a community on an issue is through the key communicator program.

A major benefit of having a key communicator program is the squelching of rumors. Too often in almost every community rumors get out of hand. In many cases, such rumors, although unfounded, have resulted in severe problems for the school. Rumors about drugs, violence, racial problems, school closings, and the like get started with no foundation. Usually, these rumors could have been quickly ended in their early stages with a key communicator program.

Likewise, through a program with personal contact and phone conversations with school officials, the key communicators come to know them as people rather than distant figureheads. Mutual understanding and trust are developed which key communicators pass along to the community. The image of the school is conveyed as it is rather than as it is perceived by the community.

Newspapers, radio, and television cannot cover many positive activities of schools. By nature, they tend to highlight the negative happenings. By having the key communicators in the schools and by sending them brief newsletters, more activities, including more positive ones, can be made known to local citizens. This is not to say that key communicators shouldn't be given negative news. They should—schools must level with them. Candor ultimately will help in establishing credibility with the group.

Type of Person Who Should Be a Key Communicator

Any person who talks to large numbers of people should be considered for key communicator designation. Persons who are believed and trusted by their audiences should definitely be asked to serve. They need not have the usual power-structure status that educators frequently seek for school help. They are citizens who sit on top of a hypothetical pyramid of communication in a community. Specifically, the key people are barbers, beauticians, bartenders, owners of restaurants, gas station operators, doctors, dentists,

letter carriers, or people to whom citizens turn and ask, "What do you think about . . . ?"

It's important to identify key communicators who will talk to all the different segments of the community. In some communities, it might be difficult to identify key communicators, especially in new developments that have not yet identified their opinion leaders. In that case, any person can be asked to serve as a key communicator to tell the school story and to report rumors. Usually that person will then become an opinion leader.

Starting a Program

If a superintendent decides to begin such a program, ordinarily a list of people would be compiled by various employees independently. A demographic look at the community would be taken to make sure that various groups would have someone on the list. The names from the employees would be reviewed and the key communicators chosen. Usually the same names appear on many lists. Key people can also be identified by the local chamber of commerce, a telephone book, or the county and the city directories.

The superintendent then sends a letter to each person advising that the person has been selected and explaining the purpose of the key communicator program—to help improve schools through better communicators. If the invitation, both written and by phone, comes from the superintendent's office, the affirmative responses will be greater. A personal phone call usually brings from 85 to 95 percent attendance. The secretary's phone call alone usually attracts about 60 to 75 percent attendance, and the letter alone about half the people invited.

Once the list of key communicators is compiled, the superintendent, with a personal phone call, invites six or so different key communicators at a time to lunch in a school cafeteria until all have met with the superintendent. At the lunch or any get-together, the tone is informal. No formal agenda is prepared and the time pressures of all involved are respected. This means that the meeting is held to sixty or seventy-five minutes at the most. The guests should feel free to raise questions or to join a discussion. Often visitors will be seeking information that the superintendent assumed they knew. This is a confidence-building session that allows people to see that the chief executive is a person who cares about children, understands that problems exist, seems to be doing the best possible job to solve them, and is receptive to ideas and encourages questions and suggestions. People are asked to call when they hear a rumor and are told that they will be apprised of information about the schools when a problem, a challenge, or a need exists.

Perhaps once a year the entire group of key communicators will be called together for a meeting (budget or bond issue or test score results consideration). This enables them to see that other people in the community care enough about the school to give time to help communicate.

Size of Membership

The number of key communicators varies from district to district. Some small districts might use only fifteen or twenty. Others may use twenty people for each school. The number can run as high as 250 to 300 in a district with 40,000 residents, but the number is not the key. If, for instance, a person feels slighted and wants to be a member, add him or her. Every person can help in some way. It is unusual that a person who gets involved in the schools in this way does not aid the school's program either directly or indirectly. It should be noted that the key communicator program can be initiated at the building level as well as at the district level.

GENERAL COMMUNITY GROUPS

In order for a school system to meet the educational needs of a community, it must know the community and understand its unique characteristics. A functional way of identifying the educational needs of the community and establishing two-way communications with the citizenry is through organized groups. The number and types of groups generally reflect the attitudes and concerns of the community. If a school district maintains a liaison with community groups, it can pass along the school story to them. In turn, members of the groups will relate the school story to their friends and neighbors. And, conversely, the groups can help the schools by relating the thoughts and opinions of the local citizens.

Many organized groups maintain programs of an educational character. Some are based on principles in harmony with the ideals of public education, and some are not. The problem in community relations is to cultivate the friendship and cooperation of groups who share mutual interests in education and society and to prevent others from exploiting and injuring the schools, without creating community conflicts. In considering relations with organized community groups, consideration will be given to surveying community groups, the types of groups, and pressure groups. Opportunities for cooperation and attempts at exploitation are covered in the following section.

Surveying Groups in Your Own Community

Before an effective community relations program can be organized, a survey of the community groups should be made to accumulate pertinent facts and eliminate guesswork. Through a survey of the organized groups in the school district, a list of community leaders may be obtained. Usually, the local chamber of commerce keeps a complete roster of civic and welfare clubs and youth organizations.

A card file should be set up, listing the name of each organization, its officers, type and number of members, dates of meetings, purpose of organization, how it can work with the schools, special interest in education, and a record of each cooperative activity with the school system.

A list should be compiled of school personnel who are members of different groups and who can serve as liaisons between the school system and the organizations with which they are affiliated. The superintendent can best interpret the educational program to some groups, whereas other members of the staff may work just as effectively in interpreting the school program to members of their own groups.

The schools need to know what people in the community think of the schools and what they expect of them. Everyone has opinions about schools, and being asked to express them is a compliment. It takes only a bit of stimulation and direction to make school personnel fine reporters of thoughts and feelings expressed by members of groups to which they belong.

Community Groups

Although general community groups are not educational in character, many do participate directly or indirectly in the school program. The following classification can be tailored to the local school situation.

Civic.   Among the more prominent civic groups are the American Association of University Women and the service clubs, namely, Lions, Kiwanis, Rotary, Exchange, Jaycees, and Optimist. All of these groups concern themselves with problems of education, health, social welfare, better government, delinquency, and recreation.

Cultural.   Cultural groups are found in the fields of art, music, architecture, horticulture, literature, drama, intercultural education, and race relations. Many are small, self-contained units whose primary purpose is catering to the leisure-time interests of the members.

Economic.   The principal economic groups are labor unions, farm organizations, chambers of commerce, economy leagues, manufacturers' associations, automobile clubs, real estate boards, retail merchants' associations, and others of a specialized character.

Fraternal.   As a rule, fraternal groups are organized to support certain ideals, increase fellowship, and indulge in leisure-time recreational activities. A few have a definite religious interest. Among them are the Masonic Order, Knights of Columbus, Brith Sholom, Knights of Pythias, and a host of lodges bearing the titles of Elk, Moose, Eagles, and Owls.

Governmental.   Local, county, state, and national governments maintain agencies that cut across several areas of human activity. These agencies provide services in health, recreation, law enforcement, safety, family life, child care, housing, and so forth. Many of these services complement those of the school and point up the necessity for cooperative relationships.

Patriotic.   Groups like the American Legion, Sons and Daughters of the American Revolution, Veterans of Foreign Wars, and United Daughters of the Confederacy have extensive programs for the conservation of real and assumed values pertaining to the American way of life. Stress is placed in their programs on the teaching of government, civic responsibility, health, and patriotism.

Political.   Political groups include the major political parties, League of Women Voters, and small organizations having a dominant interest in government. For the most part, caution must be exercised in dealing with political groups. The school is limited in its relations with these groups mostly to granting the use of buildings for public meetings and obtaining information for instructional purposes or political activities and voting practices.

Although the League of Women Voters makes politics a subject of strong interest, it is an independent organization without political affiliation. It tries to educate citizens on the issues they must decide at the polls and the qualifications of candidates for public office.

Professional. The professional groups in law, medicine, dentistry, pharmacy, architecture, and engineering have consistently supported programs for good schools. They take an interest in the educational program and will cooperate with administrators and teachers on matters related to their special fields.

Religious. The religious groups consist of denominations that maintain places of worship in the community and secular organizations engaged in religious work. Their purpose is to promote moral and spiritual values. Because of differences in sectarian doctrine, they are divided on issues relating to public education.

Retired Groups. As the population and life expectancy have increased, the number of organized groups of retired people has grown. Some schools have instituted successful programs where retired citizens are asked to help in schools; they are used in an advisory capacity, especially retired teachers and administrators, and they are given free admission to school activities and adult evening school programs.

Welfare. Numerous welfare agencies, operate in the field of health, recreation, child care, and family life. Because welfare agencies are concerned with the alleviation of human suffering and the improvement of social conditions, their activities bring them into contact with the school.

Youth. Among the organizations having a deep-seated interest in young people are the 4-H Clubs, Future Farmers of America, Young Men's Christian Association, Young Men's Hebrew Association, Young Women's Christian Association, Young Women's Hebrew Association, Boy Scouts and Girl Scouts of America, Junior Red Cross, and the Police Athletic League.

Some operate within the school as a part of the extracurricular activities program, and several are staffed with teachers and administrators who volunteer their services. With a few exceptions, these groups are anxious to work closely with the public schools.

Pressure Groups

Some pressure groups are created to prohibit the school system from taking a planned course of action. When citizens become dissatisfied with the school system and the officials in charge of it, they often form pressure groups. These groups are formed without invitation from the board of education and the superintendent of schools. Usually, they take a name that includes the word *citizens* or *taxpayers,* often combined with the word *concerned,* to inform the public that this is a group that wishes to confront the school system on some issue or issues. These groups place heavy reliance on the publicizing of factual information and the development of supporting opinion to gain acceptance of their recommendations.

Expressions of dissatisfaction that have brought about the formation of pressure groups include the desire to keep taxes down, indignation over a proposed building program, dissatisfaction with the school system's guidance program, concern for a high incidence of dropouts among secondary pupils, opposition to a proposed curriculum, resentment over a prolonged teachers' strike, displeasure with the failure of elementary youngsters to reach norms on standardized tests in reading and spelling, and a great many other issues.

Pressure groups frequently have grown out of meetings called by one or more civic groups for the purpose of discussing means for increasing public concern and interest in the schools. In a number of places the initiative for organizing pressure groups has come from parent-teacher associations. They have taken the initiative because it seemed advisable to have a wider representation of taxpayers involved in the study of a problem and because a broad-base committee would carry more weight with the board of education and the general public.

Other independent groups have sprung into existence when citizens took an interest in a particular educational problem and decided to find out what could be done about it. As examples, a young people's service club became interested in the opinion of the public toward the schools; a veterans' organization became interested in a statistical report concerning juvenile delinquency in the community and felt it should help with the problem; and a neighborhood business association listened to a speaker on school finance matters and decided to investigate the local situation.

Prevalent in many school districts is the pressure group that is extremely small in number, yet is quite vocal, often giving the impression of being larger than it is. This type of group is usually the work of one person who, under the guise of a large organization, continually attempts to make the public look with disfavor on the school system. Such an individual will call for a public meeting, but a very small number, often fewer than ten people, will attend. To continue to have the public think that he or she speaks for a large group of citizens, the mass media are flooded with position papers, news releases, charges, and criticisms against the school district. This is the type of person who gives the organization an emotional title and appears at most school board meetings, contending to represent a group while in fact representing only himself or herself. Often such persons represent what is considered an extreme point of view; they are often sincere, but can be an annoyance to a school system.

In large urban school districts there have been pressure groups advocating administrative decentralization and community control of the schools. This type of control would provide for an elected local school board to function in conjunction with the central board of education. If carried to the fullest, community control means that local representatives would control all aspects of the schools, including personnel, curriculum, textbooks, discipline, testing, and finances. Educational authorities are not in agreement whether or not community control is good for the local schools. The more fundamental question is,

"What leads local citizens to demand community control?" Obviously, the schools are not communicating with, or are not responsive to, the communities they serve. Consequently, local citizens feel compelled to advocate community control as the only way of forcing schools to reflect the wishes of the community and meet the needs of the students.

Handling Group Pressure

One of the best ways of handling group pressure is to detect it before it gets too intense. Often strong feelings can be identified by key communicators and confronted before they spread through the community. Another way of handling group pressure is to have a comprehensive data base of the community and its feelings at all times. Surveys of the local citizens will easily deflate groups that feel their thinking represents the feelings of the entire community. A third way is to get and keep the community involved in the schools. This can be done through citizen advisory groups in such areas as goal setting, sensitive programs, school closings, declining enrollments, and communications with the public. With citizens being involved in the schools and helping with their own expertise, a better understanding of the schools can be transmitted to the community. Group pressure can also be prevented by keeping the public and the employees informed. An informed public tends to support schools provided the school officials make logical and sound educational decisions.

Nonparents

An increasing number of adults in our society have no school-age children. In 1990, according to the U.S. Census Bureau, the number of people aged fifty-five and over exceeded the total national K-12 population. A sizable number of adults with no children in school are senior citizens; however, many are young married couples, career people, singles, and parents of preschoolers. For them, the mass media are the primary source of information about their schools. Studies have shown that nonparents and parents alike are interested in what's being learned in schools, how much it costs, and how the school board functions and makes decisions.[3]

Often the attitude of nonparents is "The number of students in many schools is going down, but the schools keep asking for more money. And to top this, they are graduating kids who can't read and write." This unfavorable attitude is then manifested in the defeat of budgets and bond issues. Some communicators contend that the attitude has been caused in part by the schools' failure to communicate with nonparents or to get them involved in the school in some way.

The implication of the nonparent phenomenon is obvious for schools—they will have to expand their information network. Sending news home with the students will still be vital, but schools will have to structure communications for this special public—to identify nonparents, to develop methods of communicating with them, and to get them involved in schools in some manner. A number of ways exist to identify nonparents' groups in a community. Senior citizens' groups are easily identified because they usually are well known and have a specific building for meetings. The other nonparent groups may be more difficult to locate. Religious congregations can be helpful in that many have organizations for single, widowed, and divorced people. The local chamber of commerce can be helpful, as can some municipal governments.

The nonparents more difficult to locate are those who do not belong to a group. The U.S. Census Bureau can provide demographics, but no names, on the population in a school district. Likewise planning commissions can be of some help, and election records, which can be purchased, provide names of those who voted in school elections. It is up to the schools to contact these voters to determine if they have children in the local schools. People with no children in school or those without children often are attracted to condominiums and garden apartments. These, of course, are easily identified in a community, as are retirement villages or leisure residences.

Schools must use both one-way and two-way methods of communicating with the nonparents. The mass media should be provided with information of interest to them. Students should be kept informed about the schools to pass the word along to their parents and many of their parents' friends who do not have children in school. School newsletters are helpful. Of course, one of the best ways of getting the word to and from the nonparents is the key communicators program.

There are indications that people who have been inside a school within the last year tend to be more favorable toward the schools. Thus, some programs should be developed to get the nonparents into the schools and involved in some way. One of the better programs, entitled "See For Yourself," was created by the Columbus, Ohio, Public Schools. The program, no longer formalized, resulted in many citizens getting currently involved in the schools. When it was started it included making mailing lists of nonparents living near a school, placing classified ads in papers inviting nonparents to the schools, having students write personal invitations to nonparent neighbors, contacting local employers to release employees to visit schools, asking real estate offices to hold staff meetings in the schools, and inviting organizations to tour schools. Among many other activities the "See For Yourself" program invited senior citizens to attend a school event, show their travel slides to a class, volunteer in the library, read to children, and eat lunch at school.

Many districts have answered the nonparent question of "What's in it for me?" by providing learning opportunities for nonparents through community education programs. Lifelong learning is becoming important to many adults, especially older people. They have funded education over their years and now look to the schools to meet some of their learning needs.

To help the older and younger generations communicate better and understand one another, consider intergenerational programs. Bringing together teenagers and older citizens will dispel many myths. Teenagers will not stereotype everyone over sixty-five as slow drivers who have hearing problems. Nor will older citizens categorize all seventeen year olds as reckless drivers who play loud music. School leaders can help effect better understanding by sponsoring programs that bring the groups together.

Larkin suggests that such programs also encourage older voters to support school needs. He also urges the following when communicating with older citizens:

1. Use larger print for letters and publications.
2. Use posed rather than action photos.
3. Don't patronize or treat them like children.
4. Don't stereotype. Many market segments exist among senior citizens; consider the young-old audience, many of whom are vigorous and healthy.
5. Don't consider all senior citizens to be poor; they aren't.
6. Speak loudly, clearly, and slowly when talking to a group of older people.
7. Remember that for every sixty-nine men over 65, there are a hundred women.
8. Encourage discussion; they like to be asked their opinions.[4]

OPPORTUNITIES FOR COOPERATION

It is apparent from the preceding description of types of community groups that many hold interests in common with the school. These groups are part of the school's public, and they offer numerous opportunities for interpreting the needs, programs, and problems of the institution. Their concern and cooperation should be enlisted to such an extent that they assume a responsibility to work for the support and advancement of education in the community.

Policy on Cooperation

Good community relations means that the community is pleased with the educational services that the tax dollar has purchased. Although this statement is simple, the procedure for bringing about this result is complicated—complicated because the school must deal with many segments of the public and satisfy a wide diversity of opinion on education.

As a matter of policy, the local board of education must recognize that the school has an obligation to promote intelligent understanding of what it is doing and win good will from as many groups as possible, regardless of the size of the group or the sex or age of its members. People who belong to community groups are paying the school bills, and they are entitled to know what services the schools offer and why, as well as the problems that confront them.

The local policy on cooperation with groups should provide that every person connected with the school system gets into the act, from the president of the board of education to the worker in the cafeteria. They should get into it by joining organized groups and sharing in their activities, by being invited to assist in the program of the school whenever possible, and by taking full advantage of opportunities for cooperative action related to school and community welfare.

To work successfully with groups, school personnel must know, for example, something of the fears, ambitions, and frustrations of parents in their relationships to the school. They must recognize that childless couples and career women may be heavy taxpayers who represent a sizable segment of the population and that these individuals should not be neglected in enlisting support for the school.

Furthermore school personnel must be aware of the fact that older members of the community can interpret the school only in the light of their own experiences unless they are informed differently. This group seldom understands the impact on schools made by new housing developments, child labor laws, and compulsory school attendance regulations. They cannot fathom the demands of a curriculum expanded to meet individual needs of children or the tremendous cost of education which accompanied these changes.

The policy must be one of interpreting the school program to all groups in the community and inviting their cooperation in the tremendous task of advancing the cause and quality of public education in our democratic society.

Community Involvement

Educators can no longer take the public-be-damned attitude toward the day-to-day operation of schools. No longer can they say, "We know best and we will tell the public how schools should be run." Young parents, older citizens, parents, and organized groups become offended if the school arbitrarily makes decisions that directly affect them. In a sense, they want to become involved and want to know the rationale before school decisions are made.

The idea of involving citizens in schools frightens many educators. This is understandable, but one fact should be kept in mind: in the majority of cases an informed public is more apt to support schools than not to support them. The public can be partly informed through the mass media and special publications, but more important, schools must get citizens involved in their programs in order for educators to understand people's attitudes toward the schools and to learn what the citizens want to know about the schools.

There was a time in education when the local boards and the chief school administrator could reasonably determine what a community expected of its schools. This is no longer true for at least two reasons: first, school systems became larger and more isolated from the community, and second, parents and citizens became better educated and no longer accepted previously established goals and ideals.

Being more interested in education than previous generations, these citizens demand to know more about their schools—how their tax dollar is being spent and what the educational plans of the school system are. They want to become involved in and be part of their schools.

One of the ways of involving the community is in the educational planning of the schools through goal setting. By working on goals, citizens can better understand the role of the school and provide the board of education with an accurate reflection of the community opinion of those goals.

Successful programs involving the community in determining goals emphasize that a total commitment by all involved is a necessity. School board members must believe in the program and back it 100 percent. Likewise, administrators must be committed to it and become active in the goal-setting process.

Generally a program is initiated by the passage of a formal resolution at a school board meeting. It gets off to a better start if the resolution is passed unanimously by the board. In addition to authorizing the program, the board resolution also authorizes any necessary funds and offers the support of the board in providing personnel, facilities, and supplies needed to carry out the program.

Important also is a well-formed plan of action. Initial planning for the program should include the setting of a time frame and the appointment of a project director. The plan of action generally calls for the selection of an advisory committee. The guidelines on selection of members for such a committee have been outlined earlier in this chapter.

A study of successful programs involving the community in determining and ranking goals suggests these additional considerations:

1. Since each district is unique, it should develop a program that will best suit its community.
2. The size of the school district and the amount of participation by citizens should determine whether the goal process should be performed on a districtwide or school-to-school basis.
3. Almost anyone who wants to become involved in the goals process should be accepted.

4. Board members, administrators, and committee members should attend a goals conference, or a consultant should conduct an in-service workshop for them.
5. The whole goal process should be publicized thoroughly throughout the program.
6. Information should be published in different languages if non-English-speaking people live in the community.
7. A structured program for internal and external communication is vital.
8. All points of view should be given an opportunity to be considered throughout the goal-setting process.
9. When the statement of the goals is finalized, the board of education should accept it as soon as possible. If there is a difference between the board and the advisory committee, it should be discussed and resolved.
10. The board of education should publicize and disseminate the agreed-upon goals and formally thank the advisory committee members for their dedication and service.[5]

Attempts at Exploitation

Every effort should be made to take full advantage of the opportunities for cooperation with community groups. Nevertheless administrators and teachers must exercise critical judgment as to the values or dangers inherent in the school's relationships with such groups. Cumulative experience shows that many groups, both intentionally and unintentionally, try to further their own interests in ways that harm pupils, disrupt the operation of the school, and violate its character as an impartial, nonsectarian, classless social institution. Their attempts at exploitation take the form of demands on the time and talent of teachers and pupils, clever commercial propositions, and propaganda materials.

Service Demands.   The school is deluged every year with requests from philanthropic groups and organizations for help in raising funds to support their work. Teachers are expected to explain the work of these organizations and to get contributions from their pupils. Some groups put pressure on boards of education and administrators to have each employee contribute a suggested percentage of his or her salary and to solicit funds door to door after school hours. Seldom do schools and school personnel receive adequate public recognition for what they do.

Even though philanthropic groups perform excellent and needed services, it is questionable whether public schools are justified in giving active support to all these drives and campaigns.

Commercial Activities.   A considerable number of business firms, industrial organizations, and promotional agencies, under a banner of cooperation, attempt to exploit schools by sponsoring contests, demonstrating products, and distributing materials.

Though important, it is doubtful that the educational value of these contests is worth enough to offset their negative features. The problem can be controlled if boards of education adopt policies and establish criteria by which the number of contests are limited and judged in terms of the contribution they make to instruction.

Propaganda Materials.   School people have a grave responsibility to see that pupils receive an education free from bias, half-truths, and propaganda. In meeting this responsibility, they are constantly under pressure from organized groups who wish to use the school for implanting ideas and doctrines in the minds of the young.

These groups have spent millions of dollars on printed and visual materials, supplying them to teachers and pupils without cost or at a small fraction of their actual cost. The materials deal with such topics as free enterprise, local business efforts, manufacturing processes, U.S. ideals and traditions, labor unions, temperance education, international affairs, and civil disobedience. On the surface, these materials may appear to be excellent sources for the enrichment of classroom teaching, but objective examination will disclose the propaganda they contain and the motives behind their publication.

The problem of preventing their use in school is difficult for these reasons: (1) they help to satisfy a need for more instructional materials than boards of education are willing to furnish; (2) they deal with subjects in more thorough and interesting detail than do standard textbooks; and (3) it is sometimes difficult to distinguish between propagandist and nonpropagandist materials. Perhaps one solution lies in the establishment of a national or regional clearinghouse through which all free and inexpensive materials should pass before they are accepted for instructional purposes. Standards could be drawn up that would govern the inclusion of these materials in an annual catalogue.

MEETING CRITICISM AND ATTACKS

The problem of trying to develop wholesome relations with community groups is complicated further by unfair criticism of and attacks on schools. Condemnations of public education made by misinformed citizens and special-interest groups have been responsible for weakening popular confidence in the work of the instructional program and in the competency of professional personnel. Unless checked, these unfair criticisms threaten to destroy some of the fundamental principles underlying the free school system in this country. No longer can boards of education, administrators, and teachers ignore the seriousness of the problem and simply hope that these forces will expend themselves in time. Intelligent measures must be taken to counteract their destructive tendencies and to foster friendly relationships. Solutions for this many-sided problem must start with a definite understanding of what the criticisms and attacks are like and how they may be met.

Role of Criticism in Public Education

Since the nature of criticism is usually unfavorable or faultfinding, there is a tendency to over-

look or suppress it. This is a mistake. For one thing, neglected criticism grows and becomes exaggerated. And on the other hand, some criticism is inevitable and when used wisely can be valuable to a school.

First of all, criticism can be used to measure unrest in the community. A community with low morale will pick on its school. For example, communities suffering from disorganizing influences, such as unemployment, political upheaval, religious bickering, or other negative factors, often will involve the schools in their problems. Obviously, these periods of unrest are a poor time to sponsor bond elections or introduce innovations into the curriculum.

Criticism can also measure interest. When people want to help, they are often interested in the neglected and inadequate aspects of the school system. This type of criticism is well intentioned, though often unenlightened and vague. The critic in this type of situation is also different from other critics.

Critics sometimes tell schools things that other people hesitate to mention. Constant involvement in a situation may produce "blind spots," and educators are as subject to this difficulty as other people. Sometimes only the frankness of a critic can motivate further evaluation and action. Instead of avoiding critics, we should realize that their barbs and frankness can add perspective to the management of a school. As long as there are human beings working in the school system, there is a need for criticism and evaluation. The possibility that mistakes will be subject to public discussion should keep schools dynamic, flexible, and subject to change.

Types of Critics

The art of meeting critics hinges on the capacity to identify the different types of critics. Following are some general categories into which most of them can be classified. It must be remembered that these categories are general and they do overlap. It should also be remembered that a particular critic may be reclassified as times and situations change.

The most bothersome are the *hostile critics.* They suffer from uncontrolled feelings of hostility. Instead of becoming upset or angry with the real cause of their feelings, they "take it out" on the schools. Psychologists call such attacks "misplaced hostility." Earmarks of the hostile critic are fairly uniform but vary in degree. The hostile critics can be identified by the following characteristics:

They are unduly emotional. These critics are not only angry; they are full of other emotions as well. They are irate, highly incensed, and easily insulted.

They are personal in their complaints. Complaints from this type are almost always in terms of personal happenings. They or their children have usually been insulted or neglected. They demand immediate action and punishment of the alleged offender.

They classify people by status. These people appeal to personal privileges. Because they live in a certain neighborhood, or know the mayor or the board member, they feel they should have preferential treatment.

They have a deep sense of right and wrong. For these people there is only one right answer. They usually have the "right" answer before contacting the schools. Their thoughts and actions are rigid and allow for few exceptions.

They are suspicious by nature. Extremists of this type demand investigations. They suspect that the nation is going to the dogs and that there are subversives around every corner. The most radical of them pester police stations and the Federal Bureau of Investigation.

Less dramatic are the *uninformed critics.* However, in terms of numbers and influence, they are important. They, too, have identifiable characteristics.

They are indifferent. These people are usually uninterested in school programs and activities. Their visits to the schools are few. Unless someone talks about schools when they are around, they are not bothered by what is going on in the classroom.

They repeat criticism, not create it. After they hear or read about the schools, they willingly repeat what they have heard or read—it is seldom that this type of critic has firsthand information.

They tend to be negative. Because other interests are more important to them, they are willing to believe criticism. For example, if this criticism substantiates their position about taxes, they are likely to pay attention to what they hear or read.

They accept explanations and facts. Since they are not emotionally or intellectually committed to a point of view, they are responsive to facts and explanations from the schools that make sense to them.

Then there are the *professional critics.* They are self-appointed or work for particular organizations interested in low taxes or some particular brand of education. They are motivated by the desire for fame and feelings of self-righteousness for saving education from "professional" educators. Such critics have some of the following characteristics:

They are intelligent and clever. These people could be of great help to education. It is unwise to underestimate their influence. Their supporters are usually few in number, although their actual strength is difficult to determine because many of them are hidden behind some front organization.

They profess friendship and support of education. This group mingles with school people. Sometimes they are people who left the teaching profession because of various dissatisfactions. They study education and can speak highly of it when it serves their personal purposes.

They sponsor organizations and resolutions. They seek strength and recognition through organized fronts. They have impressive letterheads and do considerable corresponding with newspapers and other groups.

Finally, there is a group who can be considered *enlightened* critics. They are friends of the school but avoid or reject any suggestion that they are rubber stamps for school officials. These critics can be identified as follows:

Friendly. These people have no axes to grind. They know many school people. They are proud of their associations in education.

Educated on school subjects. Facts and information are important to them. They criticize after studying a situation.

Specific. Criticism from this group is usually spelled out in detail. They ask questions more than they give answers. They know what they are talking about and expect to receive specific replies.

What Can Be Accomplished

An opportunity to meet the critic should seldom be refused. Before each meeting, however, the educator needs to have some general idea of what broad goals might be achieved. Ideally, the critic would listen to his or her explanation and be converted, but this is not very likely.

Conversion to one's point of view seems to be a worthwhile goal in community relations, but practically speaking it is too often an impossible one. Conversion implies very often that the other point of view is wrong or valueless. Such an implication is not likely to win friends or influence the critics. This is particularly true for the hostile critics, whose very criticism develops out of insecurity and confusion. The more they are attacked, directly or indirectly, the more they will defend their position.

The school representative will find the creation of *understanding* his or her fundamental goal. Understanding is based on facts and explanations. This type of approach will evoke favorable responses from many, particularly the uninformed critic. It can also make

the professional critics use care in what they have to say. Critics who comprehend what the school is trying to do will usually support a well-organized, purposeful program. They may say that if they were responsible for a program, it would be somewhat different, but these critics usually do not want such responsibility and, providing they understand what is happening in the classroom, would rather just accept the school's programs.

Many hostile critics lack the emotional stability or capacity to understand. In contacts with such individuals, the schools must seek to develop a sense of respect for educators and educational programs, as the best that can be gained in this situation. No matter how prejudiced or upset emotionally a person may be, he or she is capable of recognizing understanding, consideration, and capacity to study a situation. The critic can also realize when an educator is well informed about the situation and has facts to justify his or her conclusions. All this should be accomplished without the hope or expectation of the actual conversion of this type of critic, although hostility can be minimized.

The greatest gain from facing critics is the development of understanding—not necessarily conversion. And sometimes the only practical goal is that of developing respect. If understanding and respect are achieved, there is every reason to believe that better support of the schools will follow.

Facing a Critic

All critics should have at least one interview with a designated school representative. This interview will be one of two types. Either it will involve people who seek out a school representative, or it will involve people who are asked for a conference because of their statements or articles about the school.

When someone asks to speak with a school representative, the representative's main task during the first interview is to listen and to ask questions. He or she should get a detailed description of the complaints and find out what happened, as understood by the complainant, when it happened, and who was involved.

If criticism centers on policy and practices, find out what the person knows about school policies. Seek the source of his or her information. While this questioning is taking place, try to get some insight into his or her motivation. A word of caution is in order: Don't assume the role of district attorney. Remember this person is not on trial. Questions that ask for further enlightenment and specific examples are least likely to offend. It is always helpful if the school official is not sitting behind a desk when talking with a critic. The desk signifies authority which the critic may resent.

It is helpful to know if the critic is speaking for himself or herself, his or her family, his or her neighborhood, or an organized group, or if he or she is there to repeat random comments picked up somewhere. It also helps to know if the criticism is local or part of a national reaction. Is it chronic or the result of a particular situation? Is it hearsay or factual? Getting details about the critic and the criticism in the first interview is more important than giving answers.

Whether or not explanation should be given during the first interview is a matter of judgment. There is considerable satisfaction in receiving immediate answers, and time may be saved. On the other hand, some people call just to complain and are satisfied after doing so. Explanations only upset them further. An advantage of a second interview is that it allows time for feelings to settle and new perspectives to develop. The situation might correct itself in the meantime.

The temptation to defend the schools or their representatives should be avoided while one is listening to complaints. This may be difficult, particularly when the attack seems unjustified. It should be remembered that defense often implies some degree of guilt and that there is no reason to assume such a position. Furthermore, defensiveness sometimes handicaps the school representative in his or her efforts to develop understanding, respect, and support.

The stronger the disagreement, the more important it is that the communication be honest and effective. Don't assume that the other person understands what you say or write. Occasionally ask the critic to check his or her understanding against yours. Likewise, be sure you understand what he or she is trying to communicate. Listen to everything a critic says before you begin to formulate your answer or question.

Preparation should be made for the second interview. Tentative goals should be outlined, and then the appropriate techniques should be chosen. Facts, explanations, and clarifications organized around the criticism should be assembled.

If this second meeting is a personal interview, the critic should be invited to the school office. Home visits are to be discouraged because of the potential distractions in the home. The visitor should first be given an opportunity to revise his or her story or to state a new conclusion. Time, as indicated, may have erased the complaint, or he or she may have been satisfied after telling the story. In such cases, school representatives can thank complainants for their interest in the school and tell them that their interests and services will be useful to the schools in the future.

If the critic is not satisfied, the conference should proceed. The essence of the conference should be communication, so that some form of understanding may be reached. The school representative need no longer assume a passive role.

In presenting the school story, be mindful of the time involved. Long interviews may defeat your purpose. Emphasize your points but avoid repeating them. Assume that the critics are capable of asking for clarification if they don't understand what you are presenting. Remember that in interviews it is necessary to extend to others what you are seeking from them. That is, if you want understanding, show understanding. If you disagree, either at the beginning or at the end, you should still show respect for the critic's point of view. Also remember that the more you disagree, the more important it is to maintain further contact.

Focusing the Answer

Personal attention to a critic calls for answers tailored to his or her particular needs. Clichés and generalized explanations repeated over and over may temporarily satisfy many critics, but they do very little to build genuine understanding and support for the schools. To help focus answers, the following suggestions are offered:

Measure the Cultural and Intellectual Background of Your Critic. It is better to overestimate the critic's intelligence and training than to underestimate them. However, errors in either direction should be avoided. We need to remember that a growing percentage of citizens are college graduates. Although they may not know too much about the professional aspects of education, they are well read and are motivated to learn. This is particularly true of both the uninformed and the enlightened critics.

Evaluate the Emotional Climate When the Complaint Is Made. Hostile critics are not seeking answers—they want to release tensions. Appeals to reason are not likely to succeed, at least in the beginning. Understanding through listening and patience are usually good antidotes to emotion. You can give reasonable answers later.

Make Use of Personal Interests and Needs. People will try to understand what concerns them. Application of this truism will do much to focus your answers. Members of the chamber of commerce, for example, will be more interested in comparative costs, vocational education, and productivity. Members of other groups will be more interested in classroom activities, educational programs, and philosophies. There is no reason to believe, however, that other interests cannot be developed in people or that such interests do not already exist. Eventually, the public can learn to think in terms of school needs.

Include Illustrations and Examples In Your Answers. People tend to think in concrete terms. A person is not likely to think philosophically when playing the role of a critic.

Avoid Side Issues and Exceptions. Admittedly, education is complex and interrelated. However, we are faced with the challenge of giving simple answers. Side issues and exceptions only complicate matters when we are trying to create understanding.

Don't Give the History and Background of Problems Unless Requested. As interesting as the total story is to you, it can't be assumed that other people will want to listen to the details. Keep your focus on the problems or criticisms expressed by the critic.

Avoid Long Answers; They Can Create Hostility and Destroy Interest. The fact that educators have been accused of being "long-winded" should invoke cautiousness.

Avoid Professional Jargon. Even if such terminology is understood, its effectiveness is limited.

Follow-up Work on Critics

Your answer to critics may satisfy them and the case can be considered closed. However, a dynamic community relations program does not stop at this point. Many critics can become friends and supporters of the schools. Criticism should be the beginning of the relationship, not the end. This is particularly true for the uninformed critic and the enlightened critic.

After the final interview, there is need for follow-up work—a phone call, a letter, or a personal visit to ask if everything is still in order. There might also be an opportunity to tell the critics how the school has offered time and effort to resolve their complaints. Let them know their interest in the school is important.

A file of critics' names should be kept. These people can be used on committees. They can be called on to answer questionnaires. Send them invitations to dedications and other special events. And remember that they can serve as barometers of opinion in their particular segment of the community.

Public Meetings

Using public meetings (instead of a personal interview) to face and answer criticism is full of dangers. The emotional impact of mass psychology is constantly present. To be sure, the group might stampede the meeting in favor of the school, but even if this does happen, such support is temporary and not substantial.

The attraction that public meetings hold for crackpots always opens up the possibility of useless talk and wasted time. Unless meetings are carefully organized, there is no way to control these purposeless speakers. If they are controlled, you run the danger of being accused of "railroading" the meeting. Prestige and vanity also become involved in public meetings. Sometimes useless and undesirable commitments are made in public. Because they are made publicly, it becomes more difficult to persuade people to change their evaluations and opinions.

Such meetings can seldom be decision making, and therefore they are likely to be dull and disappointing to some of the audience. This does not mean they are not useful. Public meetings can be constructive if they are called and designed for specific purposes. A meeting organized to clarify issues and impart information can be productive. The basic requirements are good speakers, effective visual aids, and prepared speeches. People can also be brought together for purposes of debate. In such instances, respected and reasonable leaders should be invited to present the issues. Questions from the floor should be written.

Another technique is the small-group discussion method. Issues can be presented in a general meeting and then discussed in small groups by trained leaders. After discussion, summaries are prepared to be given to the whole group and to interested citizens.

In rare instances, where feelings are particularly intense and widespread, meetings can be called just to "blow off steam." When this is done, there should be little attempt to develop understanding or make decisions. About all that can be hoped for is order. This type of meeting may clear the air, but there is also the risk that feelings will become more intense.

Minimizing Criticism

Although criticism cannot be avoided, it can be minimized. Because schools are handy targets for misplaced hostility, a part of a community relations program should be devoted to the development of skills and policies that prevent such attacks. Following are some suggestions for avoiding criticism.

Never Ask for Advice Unless You Are Able To Use It.   There are a number of reasons for this policy. First of all, people usually guard their own opinions. They want approval of them. To be invited to offer an opinion and have it completely rejected creates a defensiveness in a person that often is expressed negatively toward the person who requested it. In the second place, if it is really approval you want, instead of advice, the intelligent person can distinguish the difference. It is an insult for you to use subterfuge to gain his or her approval.

Avoid Telling Half-truths.   Even if the complete story is not entirely favorable, it is better to give all the facts. By doing so, you show the school position is one of strength—a strong program can afford to expose its weaknesses. This policy also avoids the danger of a hostile critic "revealing" something to the community. Such exposes are embarrassing and sometimes even damaging. The public should never be led to feel that the school officials don't trust them. Usually it is better to let all the facts of a situation be available and risk criticism than to try to conceal unfavorable facts, only to have them become known later on. As long as the schools are public, the public will want to know the entire story.

Seek Support in Advance. People criticize for not being told as well as for not understanding. The critic's sting can sometimes be blunted or dispelled by having the school's supporters prepared to face him or her.

Be Consistent. It is usually best to have one person make all important policy announcements. Other statements and clarifications should refer to the official announcement. Written releases always serve as a record in case of misquotations or misunderstandings. A briefing of the employees will help avoid conflicting reports. Besides their public relations value, staff briefings also contribute to good morale.

Anticipate Criticism from Certain Decisions. Educators often make decisions without looking over the horizon to public reaction. Some unpopular decisions must be made, but many poor decisions are made that cause unnecessary criticism.

Teamwork Needed

Although the responsibility of meeting the critic is delegated to particular individuals, the ultimate success of any program depends on the entire personnel of a school or a school district.

Complaints will be made to everyone. Each person who receives a complaint should evaluate and then deal with it if it is something that can be settled immediately and if it is within his or her jurisdiction. Other types of complaints should be referred to the central office. The same principles of understanding and listening are applicable whether you resolve the complaint or refer it. Criticism resolved on the spot should be summarized periodically and reported to the responsible department.

In return, the central office staff should report back to the teacher or person making the referral. If the criticism is received by someone in the central office, it is important for morale and teamwork that any individuals involved be informed. When advisable, the critic should be referred to the individual involved. Occasionally, a summary of this aspect of community relations should be given to the entire staff.

Community relations leaders within the school should constantly advise the staff of positive ways of working with critics and alert them to effective community relations techniques. In other words, effective communication on all levels is the key to teamwork in facing criticism.

COMMUNICATION DURING NEGOTIATIONS AND A STRIKE

There was a time when school districts didn't worry about planning communications during negotiations or a strike. As a result, schools were painted into corners and outmaneuvered by employee groups with well-orchestrated programs of communications. Local citizens received basically one side of the issues and often perceived their elected school officials as being cold-hearted and unreasonable. A school district must have a communications plan with administrative and communication procedures set up weeks or months in advance of negotiations to eliminate confusion and chaos that can result when a crisis occurs.

The importance of a communications plan can be seen in the impact a strike and the subsequent settlement have on a community. Ultimately all citizens will have to finance the settlement, and children's education will be interrupted. Parents, especially working parents, must make arrangements to have their children cared for if classes are cancelled; local services, such as police, traffic, and transportation, have to be rearranged if a strike occurs; and the confidence the community has in its school officials and, ultimately, the support of the schools are at stake.

Handling themselves well during negotiations and a strike will indicate that school officials have integrity, reasonableness, and the leadership qualities to continue with the stewardship of the community's children and tax dollars.

Communication Suggestions

Communications experts have suggested the following thoughts for school districts involved in negotiations and a strike:

- Communications should begin as soon as negotiations begin.
- The school district should refrain from partisan statements and stick to transmitting facts.
- The school district should have one spokesperson, probably the chief negotiator with advice from the communication specialist.
- The objective is a settlement; it is not to make the employees look bad with a propaganda campaign.
- Overreaction by school officials to an employee group's remark can cause the community to respond emotionally by supporting "underdog" employees.
- Public charges and countercharges tend to delay settlements by diverting attention from issues to personalities.
- The communication specialist should be close to the negotiating team but not on it. In this way he or she can learn and understand issues and actions at the bargaining table. Likewise, the specialist can advise the district spokesperson on working with the media, content of public statements, and suggested written materials.

Informing the Media

The primary source of information about negotiations and a strike will often be the news media. Employee organizations, with the help of state and national affiliations, are usually better prepared to use the media to their communication advantage. School districts must combat this with

a well-organized plan that emphasizes facts rather than emotions and recriminations. Chapter 11 provides guidelines on working with the press; newspeople can be helpful during negotiations and a strike.

Informing Parents and the Community

The media are important sources of information for parents and the community during negotiations and a strike. But they should not be considered the only methods of communicating with the external publics. A key communicator program outlined earlier in this chapter can be most effective in getting and keeping the community informed and in learning what the feelings of citizens are toward issues in negotiations and toward the strike. A word of caution is in order—the key communicators program should be established long before a crisis, or those participating in it may think they are being manipulated.

Parents and the community are interested in getting answers[6] to questions like the following:

- "What's it going to cost me?" The financial impact of various proposals should be revealed periodically during negotiations.
- "How will the settlement affect the quality of education?" School districts should be specific when relating the effects on the educational program and use research to strengthen their positions. Likewise if in the judgment of school officials a counter proposal would weaken the quality of the educational program, the opinion must be passed along to the community. But, again, it has more meaning if backed by solid research.
- "Will the schools be in session if a strike occurs?" Parents and the community need to know the details of the schools being open or closed relative to lunches, transportation, early dismissal, and safety.
- "Where can we get up-to-date information about the strike?" The community and parents need an up-to-the-minute source in order to make

plans and carry out day-to-day activities. One of the best methods to provide this service is through a telephone hotline with messages recorded and updated by school officials. Communication experts also recommend that school districts set up a communication center where strike information can be gathered and disseminated.

Communication Plan

A school district should start planning for next year's negotiations as soon as this year's settlement has been completed. A valuable step in such planning is to identify employee wants that can be met prior to negotiations. Many of these are minor wants such as a need for a piece of furniture in a classroom, a parking space, or secretarial help. If ignored, they can be part of major demands at negotiation time.

Wise communication planning includes the following measures:

■ The superintendent should anticipate major demands of employee groups and keep the board of education and the district administrators informed.

■ The chief school administrator, with the help of the communication specialist, should meet with board members and the chief negotiator to plan communication strategies. The specialist should constantly advise school officials on the public relations implications of certain decisions made by them.

■ A workshop should be conducted on the role of board members in negotiations and a strike. Individual board members are under an enormous amount of pressure from citizens either to get the students back in school or not to give away everything to the employees, Many times they are under personal attack with threatening phone calls and letters. Also, board members can often be drawn into a communication war in the media. Board members should be cautioned to refrain from this type of action and to realize that anything they say publicly may be taken as the feeling of the entire board. By law the position of a board can be formalized only at a legal meeting. Boards should act as a unit rather than with many voices during negotiations or a strike.

■ A major part of a communication plan is that section that determines the publics with whom the school district must communicate, the information that should be passed along, when the communication should take place, how the information will be passed along, and who will communicate with various publics. A standard form for developing this part of the communication plan is shown in Figure 8.1.

■ An evaluation of the plan should be conducted to determine what should be retained in future plans, what should be dropped, what could be improved, and what could be added.

Publics	Information	Method	Communicator	When

FIGURE 8.1 A form for developing a communication plan during negotiations and strikes.

ENDNOTES

1. Albert E. Holliday, "In Search of an Answer, What Is School Public Relations?" *Journal of Educational Public Relations* 11, no. 1 (2nd Quarter 1988), p. 7; Anne T. Henderson, *The Evidence Continues to Grow: Parent Involvement Improves Student Achievement* (Columbia, MD: National Committee for Citizens in Education, 1981).

2. Richard D. Hanusey, "A Study of the Influences of Neighborhood Associations on Public Schools of an Urban District as Perceived by Administrators" (Doctoral dissertation, Temple University, Philadelphia, 1973). Also see, Donald M. Austin, "Neighborhood Associations: Characteristics, Structure, and Issue Orientations" (Doctoral dissertation, the University of Oklahoma, 1986).

3. *School Public Relations: The Complete Book* (Arlington, VA: National School Public Relations Association, 1986), p. 57.

4. Francis P. Larkin, "Some Guidelines on Dealing with Senior Citizens," *Communication Briefings* 1, no. 1 (Blackwood, NJ, 1981), p. 8.

5. Richard D. Bagin, "Techniques for Involving Community Ranking and Determining Educational Goals" (Master's thesis, Rowan College of New Jersey, Glassboro, NJ, 1973), p. 29.

6. *School Public Relations: The Complete Book* (Arlington, VA: National School Public Relations Association, 1986), p. 172.

9

COMMUNICATION ABOUT SCHOOL SERVICES AND SPECIAL EVENTS

A significant portion of this text deals with direct and indirect forms of personal contact with the public outside the school. Both of these forms of personal contact arise from meetings, conversations, telephone calls, correspondence, home contacts, observations, and special events. They are important in shaping popular attitudes toward, and opinions of, the institution and its personnel.

It is a reasonable assumption that no school system can expect to develop and maintain desirable relations with people in the community until it studies the nature and location of its contacts. It should have a practical knowledge of where such contacts occur and how they are handled. An attempt should be made to appraise their effectiveness in creating impressions and conveying ideas that develop public understanding, cooperation, and school support.

In this chapter attention will be given to the more significant types of community contacts that influence public opinion, and suggestions will be made on how they should be handled.

CONTACTS WITH THE BOARD OF EDUCATION

What people think and how they feel about a school system are influenced by the board of education. Because of the board's central position, the behavior of members and the nature of their decisions are watched carefully by citizens and school employees. No community relations program will achieve satisfactory results unless the board of education sets a laudable example for the school system to follow.

Board Meetings

School board meetings are occasions when a school district can either put its best foot forward or it can fall flat on its face. By law these board meetings are required to be public meetings, specifically to keep the local citizens informed about their schools. A school board that conducts an informative meeting goes far in carrying out the spirit of the right-to-know status. Those boards that acknowledge the presence of local citizens at a public meeting by affording them an opportunity to address the board will build much trust and public faith in the community. On the other hand, boards that conduct public meetings in a vacuum, by not explaining certain actions to citizens in attendance, serve to build a climate of mistrust with the very folks who can help the schools. Helpful suggestions on what a board should and should not do at a public meeting are contained in the following list.

Some Dos and Don'ts for School Board Meetings

Do

— Distribute agendas containing all the non-confidential material the board members have.

— Start on time. A newspaper reporter or a local citizen may turn into a critic if a meeting is delayed for an unreasonable length of time for no apparent reason.

— Provide adequate seating for guests.

— Have legible nameplates in front of every member.

— Provide a special place for the press, preferably near the board members. Also assign a school representative to sit with the reporters to answer any immediate question. A press table near the board will enable the reporters to cover all details of the meeting. This proximity to board action will minimize inaccurate reporting.

➤ Give citizens an opportunity to address the board.

➤ Explain to the public any action or discussion by the board that may need clarification.

➤ Be discreet with off-the-cuff remarks. With the press present, these remarks may appear verbatim in the next issue of the paper.

➤ Take the opportunity to have some phase of the school district highlighted. It is an ideal occasion to have students talk about studies, teachers explain a new course or program, or a noninstructional person show a video or transparencies on transportation, cafeterias, or maintenance.

Don't

➤ Permit nonresidents to address the board unless the content of their remarks is known ahead of time. It is not uncommon for organized groups to send representatives to board meetings in a number of districts to espouse a cause and unwittingly spread alarm and aggravation.

➤ Permit citizens to speak out at just any point in a meeting. A specific time should be set aside for them to address the board. If this is not adhered to, a school board will have no control over its own meetings.

➤ Interrupt a regular meeting with an executive session. Instead, schedule such sessions before or after the regular meeting.

➤ Become involved in an argument with a citizen at a public meeting. A number of people who address school boards will attempt to use the meeting as a public forum, hoping that they will stir the anger of a school board. A polite "Thank-you" after a citizen's remarks can often eliminate further problems.

➤ Become involved in spending an inordinate amount of time discussing minor items.

Many boards have made great efforts in recognizing citizens at board meetings and in keeping them informed about procedures and about the board members. Many boards distribute a brochure to help citizens at school board meetings. It contains the names of the school board members, information on how to address the board, the time and place of monthly meetings, and the names of the administrators. Such a publication is helpful to the people attending the meeting and shows them that the school district is sincerely interested in communicating with its citizens.

Credibility Gap of Political Boards

Unfortunately a number of politically dominated school boards still remain in the United States. These boards receive their orders from the local political machine and therefore make decisions that benefit the party in power. They pretend to be interested in the welfare of the children, but more often they are interested only in keeping taxes to a minimum so as to make the party in power look "good." Such boards are appointed by the political power structure or are endorsed for election by a dominating political party that may have been in office for decades. In these localities the school system becomes a haven for political patronage appointments with people being appointed to positions on the basis of party affiliation and with little consideration for their professional qualifications or educational competence.

Local citizens place very little trust in school districts with politically dominated boards. A credibility gap constantly exists and becomes greater over the years. The media are usually unfriendly toward such school boards and constantly question their decisions. Whatever the district does, even when its moves are educationally sound, the media are apt to see an ulterior political motive involved. Community groups are reluctant to become actively involved in the schools because of knowledge of the political control in the district. Even a structured community relations program will be ineffective because the taxpayers place little credence in what a politically oriented school district says. Until the political control is removed from a district, it can expect to have a bad image with the public.

Public Information

For boards that are not politically dominated, not enough stress can be laid on the importance of keeping the public informed of board business. In communities where good schools are steadily undergoing improvement, the board of education has shared its problems with the people and educated them to the needs and policies of the system. This has been done by publishing complete and accurate reports of official meetings in local newspapers; by letting the public know what questions must be decided at future meetings; by inviting citizen expression of opinion before policy adoption; by authorizing the superintendent to prepare materials for the information of taxpayers; by having citizens involved in setting goals and evaluating them for a school system; and by doing business in the open. Every board should develop a plan for informing the people of what it stands for and what it does in the interest of children and the community.

RECEIVING SCHOOL VISITORS

Board of education relations with the public are supplemented by face-to-face contacts of school employees with business people, salespeople, job applicants, parents, social workers, and others who have occasion to visit schools and school system offices. These contacts are crucial in the formation of impressions that create public opinion. School employees should be trained to handle these contacts successfully, and the appearances of offices should be considered in terms of the effect these have on school visitors.

Staff Training

All school employees should know how to meet visitors. They should understand the meaning of common courtesy and realize the importance of performing services willingly and efficiently. Periodic in-service community relations workshops should be conducted for all noninstructional staff members.

Office Workers. A thorough and specialized program should be developed for office workers. These individuals are in the front line of community relations. For a visitor to the schools or to a telephone caller they *are* the school. Often what they say or do creates a lasting impression on the public. The following tips are offered to office workers by the National School Public Relations Association:

1. You must assume that there is no such person as an enemy of the public schools. Your premise must be that everyone's views, no matter how haywire they sound to you, are aimed at school improvement. This attitude will help take the wind out of critics' sails.
2. Know your schools. Know everything anyone might normally expect of you—and more. Know all about such data as class size, building problems, school finance facts.
3. Treat every school patron alike, no matter how obnoxious some of them seem to be. Be willing to listen. Most grievances can be dissolved through friendliness and understanding. Your attitude will do much to stimulate a favorable atmosphere.
4. Never give the impression of superiority. Don't "put 'em in their place."
5. Remember that the child comes first.
6. Avoid generalizing, whether at school or away from it.
7. Be loyal to co-workers. A negative comment about one reflects upon all.
8. Don't breach a confidence whether it's about a child, parent, or teacher.
9. But, on the other hand, avoid giving the impression the school has "secrets." While there may be confidential information about an individual, it should be made clear that the public information policy is frank, honest, and forthright.
10. Remind yourself constantly that your telephone voice should be friendly, cheerful, interested, and helpful. Avoid sounding busy. Be a good listener. Avoid arguments. Make it clear that every effort will be made to pro-

vide the requested information as quickly as possible.

11. Be cordial to visitors. It's more than a smile. Show you're concerned with whatever the visitor is inquiring about. Let hotheads get grievances off their chests. Make visitors feel the schools not only welcome their calls but also appreciate their interest.

12. Don't procrastinate or stall. Make every effort to handle complaints and information requests promptly and politely. If delay is unavoidable, make appropriate explanations or apologies. Make every effort to see that appointments are kept.

13. Don't give the impression that you are trying to "cover" for the administrator.

14. Don't presume to answer for the administration or board unless specifically authorized to do so. Then say, "Pat Doe has asked us to explain. . . ."[1]

At any community relations workshop for office workers telephone manners should be highlighted. Usually the telephone company will send a representative to show a film and to demonstrate telephone courtesy and proper manners. More is said on the handling of telephone calls later in this chapter.

As a follow-up to a workshop, a manual for good community relations can be developed for continual review by secretaries and clerical personnel. It should outline exact expressions and procedures to use in answering a telephone. Such topics as being friendly with people, the need for prompt and efficient service, situations calling for patience and tact, meeting requests for information, where to make referrals, and how to be a good listener should be included.

Custodians, Maintenance Workers, and Bus Drivers. Often forgotten in any in-service community relations workshop are the custodians, maintenance personnel, and bus drivers. Yet these individuals can be very instrumental in cre-

ating a positive image with the public. Many times they are the initial contact of citizens with the school system, each in different ways.

In a community relations workshop, custodians and maintenance workers should be reminded of the importance of being helpful and friendly to visitors to a school. They should have a thorough knowledge of the school and the school system in order to give visitors proper directions and to refer them to the person most likely to be helpful. If there is an evening public event, the custodians on duty should be aware of the importance of their own appearance and that of the areas to be used by the visitors.

Bus drivers in a sense take the school physically onto the highways as they move along streets and roads in their conspicuous yellow vehicles. Their manner of driving, hopefully courteous and safe, goes a long way in advancing a school system's community relations program. Occasionally they will meet parents at bus stops. They should be friendly and answer questions as best they can, avoid arguments, and be sensitive to the parents' innate concern for the safety of their children. Periodically, bus drivers should have the opportunity to attend in-service workshops highlighting their community relations responsibilities as members of the school district family. Some school systems issue guidelines for bus drivers.

Cafeteria Workers. Much of the community relations responsibility of the cafeteria workers lies within the school itself, where they come in contact with students, other employees, and administrators. There are occasions, nevertheless, when they come in contact with the community through meals served to the public at special events. Personal appearance, efficient service, and courtesy are paramount at such an event: The impression made goes a long way in conveying a good image of the school.

Moreover, in their contacts with citizens away from the school, cafeteria workers should know where citizens can get the correct answers to questions about the school system. It is the responsibility of the administrators to schedule in-service community relations workshops for these workers to help them carry out their public relations role.

Appearance of Offices

The appearance of school offices contributes to the impressions visitors take back into the community. As much as possible, offices should reflect the spirit of the system and the educational ideals it stands for. All rooms where visitors contact office personnel and wait for appointments should be furnished in good taste, painted in attractive colors with pictures on the walls, and have facilities for making visitors feel at home. Modern businesses have recognized the contribution of properly equipped offices and waiting rooms in winning the goodwill of customers, and they have employed receptionists who are trained to meet visitors. The same technique could be used by school systems at little or no additional cost by placing qualified secretaries or clerks in this position and scheduling other work for them to do at their reception desks.

HANDLING TELEPHONE CALLS AND CORRESPONDENCE

The number of direct personal contacts with school visitors is small compared with the number of contacts made through telephone calls and correspondence. Too often the use of these tools is taken as a matter of fact, and their part in a community relations program is not considered. Nevertheless, telephone calls and correspondence do determine the nature of the impressions people get of a school system.

Telephone Calls

Each time an employee of a school picks up the telephone to answer a call from a parent, to talk with someone in the community, or to inquire about the price of instructional materials, he or she is playing a vital role in the community relations program of the school. The telephone that is taken so much for granted is a powerful influence for good or poor school-community relations.

Parents are naturally interested in their children and should feel that it is proper to pick up the telephone and inquire of a teacher when a question arises about a child's reading, writing, mathematics, or about something that occurred at school.

The handling of telephone calls to or from the home, involving children at school, also requires tact and good judgment. Messages from parents usually can be delivered to the child rather than the child being called to the telephone. Knowing that the child can be contacted if necessary leaves parents satisfied that the school is doing its part and that the child is in good hands.

The telephone is the most personal contact some citizens have with the superintendent and central office staff. Impressions of the type of people in the office begin with the switchboard operator. It is easy to conclude that a school system is well run or poorly run by the greeting "Hello, City Schools" and the conversation during the next few seconds. In a business, this voice can mean a satisfied customer or the loss of a sale. In a school system, it can mean a vote for the schools at the polls or the loss of a friend of education. The telephone manners of the switchboard operator and other personnel should receive careful consideration at all times. A frequent busy signal or long wait can play havoc with a school system's community relations. School systems should call on the telephone company for assistance in developing the best telephone techniques.

Citizens calling the superintendent or other administrative personnel soon learn that the next voice they hear after the switchboard operator is that of a secretary. The use of a secretary to screen calls is accepted in business. Since this practice often adds to the long wait, however, the secretary should be as pleasant as possible. The efficient secretary is one who recognizes the voices of the people who call frequently and greets them in an appropriate, cheerful manner. She or he knows that certain calls are transferred to the administrator—"May I tell Mrs. Jones who is calling?" Some are handled by "May I help you?" and in other cases the number of the calling party is requested so that the call can be returned as soon as possible.

Surprising improvement can be made in telephone manners and techniques when special instruction is given to employees. Simple demonstrations and periodic discussions of the problem are enough to bring about good results. The secret of continued success, however, lies in delegating responsibility to a staff member for supervising telephone service within a single building or for the entire school system.

Voice mail, a new development in telephone communications, was designed to let the caller leave a taped message for an intended party. Gordon Matthews, the inventor of voice mail, contends that it is being misused and is frustrating callers. Organizations are using it instead as a receptionist, forcing callers to work their way through a maze of menus. He contends that a human should direct the initial call.

Schools jeopardize good community relations by misusing voice mail regardless of how much emphasis is placed on the economics of it. Imagine what happens to unhappy parents or citizens calling the school and working their way through a menu of numbers and names. They will go from being unhappy to being completely irate. The schools have conveyed a "We don't care" attitude to them.[2]

It should be added that efficient telephone service begins with the accessibility of the school to people in the community. They should be able to find the telephone number of any building without having to ponder on how it is classified in the telephone directory. Numbers are classified in many communities under remote headings like "city of" and "township of." Since the average person thinks of "schools" when looking up the number, the first step in improving telephone

service is to see that listings fall under the heading of "schools."

School Correspondence

The letter has some advantages over face-to-face relations and over telephone conversations as a form of personal contact. It enables the writer to communicate directly and economically with the other person and to exercise more control over the expression of ideas. These advantages make the letter an effective instrument in community relations, especially if the tone is warm and friendly and if mechanical details are correct.

No letter should be allowed to remain unanswered for several days. Common courtesy demands a prompt reply. Where facts must be gathered and opinions sought that will cause a delay, an interim letter should be written explaining the situation and promising complete information in the near future. In general, letters should be concise and to the point, with thought given to an outline of their contents before they are dictated. If it appears that a letter requires a lengthy reply, a telephone call may make it possible to handle the matter through a personal interview instead.

To tell an effective story, educators must consider the person to whom they are sending the letter. If the recipient of the letter has very little formal education, a detailed letter may be very confusing. However, it is not always possible to know the background of people to whom letters are addressed, and therefore it is always wise to write with clarity and simplicity.

In composing a letter the following factors should be considered:

Tone. The tone of a letter plays a prominent part in influencing the reaction of its reader. It should be warm, friendly, conversational, and, above all, written as though it were spoken directly to the person who reads it.

Stereotyped Phrases. The quality of a letter may be lowered through the use of stereotyped business phrases, which tend to make a letter stiff and formal. Antiquated expressions, such as the following, should be scrupulously avoided: beg to advise, happy to inform you, please be advised, permit me to state, replying to yours, due to the fact that, may I call your attention, wish to acknowledge, kindly advise, beg to assure, regret to inform.

Jargon.   As in every profession, there is a tendency among educators to employ jargon or a technical vocabulary in discussing their problems and to use phrases that are foreign to the thinking of other people. Words and phrases should convey ideas easily and understandably; they should not be barriers to communication. Words and phrases like *rapport, maladjustment, experience unit, heterogeneous grouping, integrated curricular progression, linguistic construction level, quantified standardization,* and *instructional media* defeat the purpose of good letter writing.

Positive and Negative Words.   It is always important to state ideas in a way that evokes positive rather than negative responses. Of the two lists given in Table 9.1, one contains words and phrases that are considered to provoke negative responses, and the other suggests ways of expressing the same ideas to elicit positive reactions. Both lists may prove helpful as a start in checking school correspondence and improving future writing.

The emotional impact of the first letter on page 167 is decidedly negative, and Mr. Smith probably would assume that the writer is offensive, abrupt, and discourteous. The letter also may raise questions in his mind about the board policy and its application.

To improve the letter, the writer should substitute positive or neutral words for the negative words. The result may at best be a neutral letter (see second letter).

Simplicity.   Words and ideas used in letters to the public should be simple and mean essentially the same to most people. A sentence intended for

one of Roosevelt's famous fireside chats in its original form read, "We are planning an all-inclusive society." In the talk the sentence had been rewritten to read, "We are building a society in which no one will be left out." Simple words transformed this sentence to one that practically everyone could understand.

Form Letters.   Form letters, duplicated in large numbers, are economical and at times functional. But, too often these letters are reproduced on cheap paper, laid out poorly, and are difficult to read because of mechanical imperfections. Sometimes their physical features are enough to discourage a person from reading them. Unless mimeographing is done exceptionally well with an electronic stencil, it is better to use xerography or print, multigraph, or multilith the letters even though the cost is slightly higher. The number of form letters should be kept to the barest minimum unless they can be given the appearance of a personal correspondence. Otherwise, they may not be read.

SERVICING COMPLAINTS

Complaints are made about almost every phase of school operation and the educational program. In some respects such complaints are the inevitable and normal outcome of institutional functioning. Coming from private citizens and organized groups, complaints are made to all personnel in a school system, including board members, administrative officials, teachers, and noninstructional staff members. Whether the complaints are justified or not, good community relations require that they be handled systematically and efficiently.

Importance of Complaints

The proper handling of complaints is important for several reasons. Parents and others who complain do so because they have grievances, real or imagined. They want them satisfied. Unless the school welcomes their complaints, extends courteous treatment, and takes positive action within

TABLE 9.1   A List of Positive and Negative Expressions Helpful in Checking
School Correspondence for Improved Writing

Negative Expressions	More Positive Expressions
Must	Should
Lazy	Can do more when she or he tries
Troublemaker	Disturbs class
Uncooperative	Should learn to work with others
Cheats	Depends on others to do his or her work
Stupid	Can do better with help
Never does the right thing	Can learn to do the right thing
Below average	Working at his or her own level
Truant	Absent without permission
Impertinent	Discourteous
Steal	Without permission
Unclean	Poor habits
Dumbbell	Capable of doing better
Doesn't care	Is unmotivated
Calamity	Lost opportunity
Disinterested	Complacent
Expense	Investment
Stubborn	Extremely self-confident
Insolent	Outspoken
Liar	Tendency to stretch the truth
Wastes time	Could make better use of time
Sloppy	Could do neater work
Incurred failure	Failed to meet requirements
Nasty	Difficulty in getting along with others
Time and again	Usually
Dubious	Uncertain
Poor grade of work	Below his or her usual standard
Clumsy	Awkward in movements
Profane	Uses unbecoming language
Selfish	Seldom shares with others
Rude	Inconsiderate of others
Bashful	Reserved
Show-off	Tries to get attention
Will fail him/her	Has a chance of passing, if

reasonable limits, it destroys goodwill and breeds resentment.

Large business firms look on complaints as one of their best sources of public relations information. They keep careful records of all complaints, no matter how trivial they may seem, and review them periodically. This material enables them to get a picture of prevailing attitudes toward company policies and of shifts taking place in public reactions. Of somewhat greater importance, however, is the knowledge these firms acquire of weak spots in their organization and of services that are failing to meet the criteria of good public relations. Research done by the

Mr. John Smith
60 Church Street
Chattanooga, Tennessee

Dear Mr. Smith:

We *cannot* comply with your request of June 10 to assign your child to the Barger School next year. In *rejecting* your request may we call your attention to the fact that children *never* are allowed to attend a school in another school zone since the Board of Education's policy *prohibits unjustifiable* assignments outside a school zone.

Very truly yours,
Jane Jones
Superintendent

Mr. John Smith
60 Church Street
Chattanooga, Tennessee

Dear Mr. Smith:

I always welcome an opportunity to correspond with parents who are sincerely interested in the education of their children. It is with regret, however, that I explain that Mary will not be able to attend the Barger School as requested.

School zones have been established for all elementary and junior high schools in the city. This has been done to help ensure that one school is not crowded while other nearby schools have vacant rooms. Although a child attends the school in the zone where he or she lives, under Board of Education policy, our board has provided ways to adjust the number of classes between zones. However, in your case the Woodmore School, which Mary will attend, has a small number of classes, whereas Barger's class enrollments are the highest in the city.

I believe Mary will enjoy going to school at Woodmore as much as she did at Barger because it also has a fine school spirit and a principal and faculty devoted to children. I hope we can get together to discuss this and other matters of interest at a convenient time.

Sincerely yours,
Jane Jones
Superintendent

Coca-Cola Company and others indicates that when complaints are handled well, people tell others about the treatment they received. They also buy more of the product. When complaints are not handled well, people also tell others and buy less of that product.

There is no real excuse for schools to overlook the value of similar information in strengthening their own policies and practices.

Procedures for Servicing Complaints

School personnel who are called on to handle complaints need to learn the gentle art of listening while people purge themselves of the problems that weigh on them. Anger, fear, or resentment, growing out of a feeling that a child has been mistreated, builds up within the individual until finally release must be provided. An understanding of the effectiveness of a sympathetic and attentive listener under these circumstances is important.

Complaints and criticisms usually should be allowed to flow freely. Experience has taught many superintendents and principals the effectiveness of listening without comment. When the relaxation that follows severe tension under such circumstances is achieved, it is often advisable to say that the matter will be investigated and that the person making the complaint will be called on for assistance at a later date.

When handled in this manner, most complaints seem to lose their intensity. Quite frequently the parent, citizen, or teacher who has demanded to see that justice is done will request that an investigation not be made if it will embarrass the wrong person. The complainant's reason for bringing the matter to the attention of the school official, it is pointed out, has not been to get the person in trouble, but rather to be sure that the official had all the facts. Chapter 8 gives further details on meeting criticism and attacks.

School personnel, especially those in administrative positions, must learn to analyze criticisms and complaints objectively. Unjustified complaints should be handled in a dignified and professional manner. A sincere belief that the schools belong to the people leaves no other course of action.

MEETING EVERYDAY CONTACTS

Every person who is connected with a public school system enjoys innumerable contacts with people in the community after regular working hours and over weekends, holidays, and vacations. Although little attention is paid to the import of these informal contacts for community relations, people get many of their ideas and impressions about a school system from them.

For too many years school boards and superintendents have kept teachers and noninstructional employees in ignorance of the systems that paid their salaries. Believing that teacher and nonteacher interests should be limited to the performance of assigned duties, school officials did nothing to share their problems, to explain administrative organization and operation, or to take teachers and other school employees into their confidence on policy decisions. As a result, few teachers or employees were able to answer questions people asked about their schools. Even today this condition prevails in some schools' and it is a serious obstacle to good community relations.

Boards of education and administrators must recognize that the everyday contacts of employees outside of the school are a part of the community relations program. Ideally, they should see that teachers and nonteachers understand important facts about the system, feel responsible for representing the school in the best manner possible, and keep their disappointments and troubles within the institutional family.

REQUESTS FOR INFORMATION

Expressions such as "Do they think we should know everything?" have been used by school employees following telephone calls requesting information. Instead of being critical, school personnel should consider such a request a challenge and an opportunity. For those school sys-

tems that accept the supplying of information as a normal service function, there are certain techniques of community relations to be observed and implemented. Since many requests will be made by telephone, the basic principles of telephone courtesy discussed previously need to be observed. Procedures also should be established to ensure that such requests do not violate the basic principle that schools operate primarily for the education of children.

Important documents that assist school employees in answering requests for information are a handbook, directory, and school calendar. As a part of their programs the local professional organizations should provide employees with information on all activities affecting schools on the local and state levels. Citizens do not expect school staff members to be walking encyclopedias, but they do have a right to expect that these employees will have readily available certain basic information about the school system. If an employee is unable to supply information requested, he or she should give the name and telephone number of the person who can supply it.

A common dodge used by employees is to explain that the questions do not pertain to the work they are doing, but this cannot be considered an adequate reply for those who really are concerned about community relations. The employee who is asked about the entrance age for first graders should stifle the impulse to say "That doesn't concern me," if for no other reason than that his or her personal prestige may be at stake.

Here are some of the questions people ask. If staff members cannot answer them, both the employees and the administration should be challenged to take steps to correct the situation.

- What guidance services are available at Hardy?
- In what grade does the teaching of science begin?
- Who is the principal of the Trotter School?
- What are the dates of the spring vacation?
- What is the compulsory attendance age?
- How does a child secure a work permit?

The principal in the office and also at home must consider the supplying of information a normal function of his or her position. Questions will range from the types listed above to other questions about the operation of the school or the school system. No matter how modern its buildings or how complete its instructional program, a school system cannot be more effective than its community relations program and its services to the community. Employees who accept the supplying of information as a normal service to the community win respect for the schools and the profession.

PARTICIPATION IN COMMUNITY LIFE

The number of contacts increases and the school and its professional personnel take on new importance when staff members become identified with the social and civic life of the community relations program. Thought must be given to staff preparation and opportunities for participation.

Importance

Four significant gains are made in community relations when staff members become active in the life of the community. First, the attitudes of citizens change as they learn to know the men and women who are responsible for their schools. Second, participation opens opportunities for social and civic leadership and, consequently, higher status in the community. Third, participation enables staff members to discuss the schools with many people. Fourth, evidence supports the hypothesis that citizen concern for education increases as staff personnel become more actively identified with the social and civic life of the community.

Staff Preparation

School personnel who take part in community life should have an insight and understanding of people and institutions if they are to function success-fully either in their capacity as professional employees or as private citizens. They should be familiar with local history, ethnic and religious groups, customs, prejudices, and social restrictions. They ought to know something of the cultural and economic life of the community, its social agencies, form of government, and channels of communication. Awareness of social organization and community leaders is important.

The bulk of this information should be available from the findings of the sociological survey described in an earlier chapter. With this knowledge, staff members are more likely to be tolerant of local customs, to avoid pitfalls and conflict situations, and to follow an intelligent course of action in their relations with the public.

Participation in Community Activities

Teachers and pupils have many opportunities to participate in community life. Every neighborhood and every district present real problems for study and social action. There are hundreds of problems, including traffic hazards, proper methods of handling trash, sewage disposal, garbage, youth recreational needs, fire protection, and clean streets. Public contacts growing out of successful study projects by pupils and teachers develop respect for the school and lay the groundwork for future cooperation.

Similar results have been attained in districts where administrators, teachers, and pupils responded to requests for assistance from agencies and service organizations interested in the education and welfare of children. The following are some of the activities in which the school can participate: surveying community recreational need; locating pupils who would benefit from glasses, special shoes, and diet supplements; organizing little league baseball teams for after-school and vacation periods; participating in forums and public discussions on local problems; increasing public library facilities; and developing summer day camps for young children.

Participation Identifies Local Talent

Another aspect of participation is that of using community resources for instructional purposes. Any number of competent men and women are available to talk with pupils along lines of their special vocational and avocational interests, to lend objects and visual materials high in instructional value, and to share their knowledge and experience with teachers in curriculum study programs. Classes may be taken on field trips to worthwhile places and interviews scheduled with people in positions of leadership. Cooperative work experience and tours of business and industry are means for understanding the economic life of the community and appreciating employment demands. Each time such resources are used, they enrich instruction and create friendship between citizens and representatives of the school.

Participation through Group Membership

Instructional and noninstructional employees should be encouraged to join community groups and organizations. Their own lives become richer by associating with people of different occupational backgrounds and interests and by engaging in activities of a challenging and enjoyable nature. At the same time, they are in an excellent position to interpret the school and to acquire a knowledge of how people react toward its program.

SCHOOL PLANT APPEARANCE

The appearance of the school plant, both outside and inside, has a continuing and cumulative effect on public attitudes toward a school system. An attractive plant, even though the buildings are old and located on sites that fall below modern standards, is generally regarded as an asset to the community and an expression of educational accomplishment. People have a feeling for and a sense of pride in a system that maintains well-kept grounds and buildings. School plant appear-

ance is an important factor to be weighed in planning a community relations program.

Outside Appearance

There is no justifiable reason why new plants cannot be designed attractively and older ones improved in outward appearance. New plants should be designed to harmonize with their surroundings and to create esthetic impressions by mass arrangement of lines and angles, color and texture of building materials, treatment of terrain, and effective landscaping. With older plants, improvements may be achieved by proper maintenance of grounds, excellent building repair, grading of sites, erection of appropriate barriers, renovation of exteriors, and the planting of grass, flowers, shrubs, and trees.

Not to be overlooked are schools that are no longer in use. Until a building has been sold or converted to other use, the district should be conscious of the external appearance of the building and the grounds.

Inside Appearance

The inside appearance of the schools is influenced, for the most part, by furniture, decoration, and housekeeping standards. A building is always more attractive when it is equipped with good quality furniture, attractively arranged, and kept in excellent repair. Broken, scarred, and worn pieces detract from the appearance and strongly imply to the taxpayer a waste of public money.

Tasteful decorations can transform the tone of a school almost overnight. New effects may be produced by repainting walls in pastel colors that are varied throughout the building, by improved lighting, and by near-white ceilings. What appear to be shabby rooms and offices can sometimes be made into pleasant working areas by dressing up windows, hanging good pictures, and replacing furniture.

Housekeeping standards are of primary importance in the maintenance of a clean, sanitary, and attractive building. Nothing detracts more from its appearance than dirty walls, floors, and windows; unclean lavatories and drinking fountains; paint that is peeling; untidy classrooms and offices; or corridors reeking with unpleasant odors from shower rooms, cafeteria, and gymnasium. Good housekeeping requires the full cooperation of pupils and faculty members and a knowledge by custodians of the standards they are expected to uphold. Some administrators believe that custodians take more pride in their work and make a better impression on visitors when they are dressed in attractive but practical uniforms.

SPECIAL PROGRAMS FOR OLDER PEOPLE

Administrators who are sensitive to the importance of community relations cannot overlook the need for establishing special programs catering to the hobbies and secret ambitions of senior citizens. Many persons, after living for years with an unrealized ambition to work with tools, to master the fundamentals of radio and TV repair, or to discover the fascination that Grandma Moses found in art, finally have the time to indulge.

Programs should not be restricted to the evening school as many senior citizens prefer to pursue their hobbies or more formal educational activities during the day. Such programs have the added advantage of placing the adult in close contact with the regular school programs, particularly if carried out in the same or an adjoining building. Alarm over what modern schools are doing to children often changes to public statements of support as these older citizens become personally involved in special programs. Such programs are valuable also because they provide opportunities for these citizens to know teachers and administrators as people and to see firsthand that they are devoted to the education of our youth.

Programs for older adults can be initiated on the proverbial shoestring. The school system furnishes the buildings, facilities, and coordinating personnel, and the program is under way. Instructors are available in the ranks of the adults.

School buildings become an investment that produces increased dividends when they serve all age groups, and bond issues are more meaningful and better supported.

As the miracles of modern medicine continue, the senior citizen will become an increasingly important political and economic force in the community. The voting potential of the increasing number of older adults takes on an added significance when the support of schools is considered.

Gold Card Club

Quite popular with a number of school districts are the Gold Card Clubs for senior citizens. Usually, the member must be a resident of the school district and be sixty-five years of age or older. Each member who registers with the school district is issued a card annually, which entities him or her to free admission to all athletic events, adult school, concerts, plays, and other public school activities.

Often school districts will call on this group to become involved in the schools as speakers, as advisory committee members, and as feedback agents in the community. These fixed-income citizens often desire a feeling of "belonging" with a school system that they have helped to support long after their children have attended school. A Gold Card Club serves to satisfy this need among those over sixty-five and in a small way expresses a thanks for their support of schools over the years.

Some districts have invited these citizens to participate in Thanksgiving and holiday luncheons held in the schools of the district. Transportation is often provided at least one way. Usually, at these luncheons, the superintendent, a board member, and other staff members welcome the retirees and discuss the schools. A number of topics are discussed informally, from the cost of food and educational programs to budget preparation and even taxation.

Opportunities to recognize senior citizens and to provide school experiences for them are limitless, as are the community relations values that result.

OPEN HOUSE

Often held in the fall of the year, an open house is conducted by many schools to invite the community to visit the schools. Although some schools choose to operate in a constant fishbowl atmosphere by allowing visitors to attend classes at any time, many school officials prefer to invite parents and other interested residents to attend a special program once or twice a year. The purposes of an open house are to acquaint citizens with the nature of the school building and its teachers and staff and to help parents understand more fully the work of the school. Such events also provide opportunities for parents to see evidence of pupil accomplishment and lend themselves to building goodwill for the school system.

Open-House Programs

The programs presented by the majority of schools during open house are fairly simple in design. A common type is that of an escorted tour, with pupils and teachers serving as guides. Visitors are taken through the building and shown its facilities, introduced to members of the administration and instructional staffs, told about objects on exhibit and instructional supplies and equipment used in classwork, entertained in various ways, and served light refreshments. Or the program may start with a meeting in the auditorium at which school officials talk about the educational practices of the institution and pupils furnish musical and other forms of entertainment. This part of the program is followed by visits with teachers in classrooms where pupils' work is on display and explanations are made of the curriculum in particular grades and subjects. The program is often rounded out with a social period for further visitation and refreshments. It is typical in secondary schools to have parents follow the class schedule of their children on a shortened-period basis. By going from class to class, parents

meet teachers, see the physical setup of classrooms, receive information on what is taught and what is expected of pupils, and ask questions on points of interest. Refreshments may be served at the close of the evening.

Variations from these program designs include a day during the week for observing classes in action; afternoon teas for parents and teachers; discussion forums on school policies, challenges, and achievements; clinics for parents on problems of child development; student assemblies open to the public; parent-teacher conferences; and faculty meetings open to students and the public.

Preparing Teachers

Open-house programs are most effective when teachers are adequately prepared to meet their responsibilities by attending to the many details that make a favorable impression on the public. Most teachers have little, if any, background to help them deal with the public in an open-house or back-to-school night situation. Since many teacher-preparation institutions do not prepare teachers for dealing with parents, it is the responsibility of the principal and other school officials to prepare them in this area.

Teachers should convey a feeling that implies that they welcome the opportunity to establish a cooperative relationship that would continue throughout the school year. They should be told of the interests parents have regarding what is being done in the classroom.

An effective learning technique is to have experienced teachers conduct back-to-school night practice sessions using roleplaying. This kind of approach will give new teachers the opportunity to get a feel for the kinds of questions and situations to anticipate. Such in-service assistance is appreciated and pays dividends for the entire school family. At such in-service programs, teachers should be refreshed on school policy on the controversial topics that might be introduced by visitors. If all employees are familiar with policies, inconsistencies that breed problems can be avoided. School officials should not assume that giving new teachers a copy of the policy manual suffices in this regard. Emphasizing the controversial policies and providing specific suggestions to handle particularly challenging questions can be of great help. Teachers should be told which facts most parents are usually interested in so that they can include these in their presentation. In fact, teachers might be encouraged to seek feedback from parents to determine which topics to cover in the limited time available. Parents will appreciate the time taken to determine their interests, and teachers will be ensured an interested audience if the topics have been requested.

Teachers should realize that the way they present facts and material at open house might very well be the single factor determining the image that parents have of them. They should present facts in a clear way that leaves no room for ambiguity. They should be encouraged to use simple language that includes no educational jargon. Open house is an opportune time for teachers to communicate a warm concern for students, when they can convey that they want to work closely with parents for the same goal—the best education possible for children. Simply stated, this is a time when teachers and parents can gain a mutual respect that will serve the child well.

Attending to Details

Good public relations requires that school officials spend an appreciable amount of time in planning efforts, to guarantee a smooth-running open house. More and more school administrators are realizing that involving parents, teachers, and students in planning open-house and other special programs means better programs. Parents, teachers, and students contribute sound ideas and suggestions for such events and support them more when they are involved in their operation. The planning committee for open-house programs should be established in plenty of time to ensure that no unrealistic deadlines cause frustration.

The date should be selected so that it does not conflict with other important community events. It should also be chosen with television interests in mind. For example, if a sports event of national interest is scheduled for Monday night, it might be better to schedule open house for another night. A good night to offer such events is the fifth "anything" of the month. Many organizations to which active parents belong hold meetings on the first Tuesday or the third Wednesday of the month. Because no day of the week occurs a fifth time every month, organizations do not meet then. Thus, the school is virtually guaranteed a no-conflict date by choosing such a night for open house. The time should also be carefully determined. Too often school officials check to see what time the event has been held in previous years and reschedule it for that time. Did it work at that hour? Are new circumstances present that would suggest a change? For example, a split shift might necessitate a later start if custodians need time to prepare the building.

Other key considerations must include the following:

Proper Publicity. An open house should justify three news releases in the local newspaper. One release, about two weeks before the event, should, in a paragraph or two, provide the main facts. The second release, about a week before the event, should give additional information and include a quote from the principal. The third release might be a photo of employees and students preparing the school for open house. This might appear the day before the event. The school district newsletter should include information about the event, and area houses of worship might cooperate in listing it in their bulletins. Notices can be placed in stores and other places frequented by parents.

Effective Invitations. Too often parents and other visitors receive invitations that are written in a cold, almost officious, manner. Such writing is hardly conducive to enthusiastic attendance. Some schools, especially in the lower grades, have children prepare the invitation for their parents. The personal touch helps. Teachers can also call parents to invite them to open house. Many school officials report that such calls result in appreciably larger attendance. The calls also serve to show that teachers do care about students and their parents and that school officials can call about something positive. (Most calls from the school are based on negative incidents.) Another effective technique is for individual departments to issue invitations to parents. Parents and other visitors should be given three weeks' notice of the event in an invitation from the school.

Adequate Staff.   An important ingredient for a smoothly functioning open house is the availability of staff to meet any unexpected problems. This means that the administrator must anticipate possible problem areas and assign staff members to handle them. For example, some teachers may face unexpected emergencies, necessitating their missing the open house. Extra professional personnel and a game plan for this possibility must be ready before the problem occurs. Any time a large crowd is expected, some special arrangement should be made to cope with a medical emergency. A nurse should be on duty to handle any such problem. Custodians should be present to handle sudden clean-up problems and to make sure that the building is in presentable condition for the visitors. Maintenance personnel should also be available to overcome heating or lighting problems. Audiovisual specialists should be close by to cope with microphone and projector problems.

Information Areas.   Parents and other visitors are often frustrated when they don't understand the procedure to follow. They are often reluctant to ask questions of teachers and student guides because they don't want to appear uninformed. Information areas in the halls, staffed by students and teachers, enable people to ask all kinds of questions. For instance, parents who have forgotten their children's schedules should be made to feel comfortable about asking for another copy at an information center.

Comfort Considerations.   From the time visitors enter the parking lot to the time they leave it, they are forming an impression of the way the schools are run. By having an organized parking effort and clearly marked signs directing people to the proper entrance, school officials can get visitors off on the right foot. Alerting area police to the crowd expected can be helpful in overall traffic control. If visitors will be wearing coats, provisions should be made for checking them or hanging them as easily as possible. Remember that many of the people will arrive at about the same time and that security is an important consideration. Routes to classrooms should be easily seen and restroom areas should be designated throughout the building. Displays of student work should be placed in key locations in the halls and lobby. However, traffic flow should not be impeded by poorly located displays that attract attention of crowds and make it difficult for visitors to get from one classroom to another in the allotted time.

Feedback Opportunities.   Administrators can learn much from people visiting the schools. All they have to do is ask for information. By providing visitors with easy-to-understand cards that ask for reactions to the open house as well as for comments about other key school questions, school officials can gain opinions that will help them know what some taxpayers are thinking. Ideas to improve the open-house program will also be received.

CLOSING A SCHOOL

Most special events involving a school district are of a positive nature. They highlight some aspect of the educational program, feature an extracurricular activity, or present some facility to the public. Usually one special event that isn't positive is the closing of a school because of declining enrollments.

Naturally, a school district must do extensive planning before closing a school. It can't be done in a vacuum and announced at a public meeting as a *fait accompli*. Such a move will prompt citizens who are highly critical of their school to fight almost to the death to keep their school open. Important in any planning is community involvement. Once a school district senses the possibility that some schools should be closed, a citizens' advisory council should be appointed by the board. The council should have members from throughout the district to give balance to any thinking and to indicate that all sections of the district have a voice in advising the board. Details of forming a citizens' advisory council are given in Chapter 8.

Cooperation between the school district and the council is vital. School officials should provide a comprehensive data base for the advisory council to use in its deliberations. This would include enrollments, new births, new dwelling units, number of graduates, number of schools and available rooms, and any other information and demographics that would help the council make informed suggestions to the school board.

As part of its activities, the advisory council should schedule community hearings to allow for input from various citizens and groups before advising the board on a course of action. These hearings are not discussions or debates but only listening occasions to get various points of view from a community. Council members should not get involved in an argument with commenting citizens. Instead members should seek all points of view without any judgmental comments.

Neither should internal communication be overlooked in closing a school. Some staff members could be part of the citizens' advisory council. Whatever the case, the employees should be kept abreast of developments and where possible should be included in any planning. Principals as always are vital conduits of information to and from employees. Any planning for closing a school should include details for assimilating a staff into other schools.

Once the decision is made as to what school will be closed, the school district should stress the educational as well as the economic gains resulting from the closing. The American Association of School Administrators[3] contends that there are at least seven elements in a communications program during declining enrollments. School districts should:

▬ Be willing to share information and problems about declining enrollments with the community

▬ Develop a demographic profile of past, present, and projected enrollments

▬ Conduct a formal or informal community attitude survey annually to determine community members' reactions to district programs and what they think about various methods of dealing with declining enrollment

▬ Ensure two-way communication through building level and districtwide advisory groups to determine community feelings

▬ Provide opportunities for all citizens to hear and be heard on how problems are dealt with

▬ Have clear policies regarding school closings, staff reduction, and staff transfers

▬ Have in place guidelines or a "yardstick" to measure change and not to appear arbitrary in deciding to close a school when enrollment falls below a certain level.

BUILDING DEDICATIONS

The dedication of a new school building can provide opportunities for good school-community relations. Frequently, however, many such opportunities are overlooked. To help prepare an effective dedication, many of the ideas advanced earlier in this chapter regarding open house can be applied. Yet it must be recognized that the dedication undertaking requires other specific plans. Overall, the dedication of a new building can be a source of community pride and achievement. School officials should make every effort to demonstrate how the building will benefit many people in many ways. For example, if a new gym is to be used by a large number of community groups, representatives of those groups should be invited to the dedication. Newsletters and news releases should point out how many people are expected to benefit from the facility.

The Green Bay, Wisconsin, schools have capitalized on dedication opportunities to show the curriculum to thousands of people who may not otherwise take the time to learn about it. Combining dedication and open house as many districts do, Green Bay incorporated the following ideas in its effort:

▬ The person responsible for school-community relations meets with the staff about three weeks before the dedication to explain the idea behind the emphasis on curriculum. The staff provides giveaway information for visitors, bulletin board information, and display materials. The staff also receives the dedication and open-house brochure in advance.

▬ A mass mailing is sent about two weeks before the event; a copy of the program, a tour guide booklet, and an invitation are included.

▬ Media promotion is begun about a week before the event.

▬ Prior to the official open house and dedication, a special tour and a dinner are held for board members, town officials, and other dignitaries.

▬ The date is planned to avoid conflicts with major athletic events and programs of other community groups.

▬ Staff members are identified with name tags so people know who can answer questions.

▬ Student guides, identified with name tags and bands for easy identification, are stationed at every building entrance.

Preparing the Publications

Underlying the planning should be the thought that whatever the building is, it will benefit children and others in the community in some way. This means that materials prepared for and about the official dedication ceremony should focus on the people the building will serve rather than on the building itself. The publication should applaud the efforts of the people who made the building possible. This includes all taxpayers, who should be shown how the building will contribute to the overall well-being of the community.

Key community figures should be invited to the ceremony. Area media representatives should be given sufficient notice to assign personnel to attend. Often forgotten are board members who played important roles in the initial efforts to make the building possible. Frequently these men and women are no longer board members when the building is dedicated; a good practice is to invite them and recognize them at the dedication ceremony.

Planning for the dedication must be thorough. To forget someone who contributed in a major way is one way to lose a friend for the schools. Checking and doublechecking with people involved at various stages of the building program is necessary to ensure that no one is slighted.

AMERICAN EDUCATION WEEK

American Education Week is a national observance in support of the schools. It was proclaimed in 1921 under the sponsorship of the American Legion and the National Education Association. Later the U.S. Office of Education and the National Congress of Parents and Teachers became sponsors along with the other two organizations.

The most successful observances of American Education Week are planned and carried out cooperatively by the school and community. The leadership is usually taken by the board of education and the superintendent of schools. Parents and representatives of civic groups and organizations are invited to cooperate in planning this celebration. After a year or two, the entire project may be turned over to the community. The school then takes its place on committees the same as any other organization. It is expected, however, to furnish ideas, materials, and clerical assistance and to prepare a substantial portion of the week's program. This is logical in view of the nature of the celebration. The school can meet these requests without dominating the situation or in any way destroying the feeling that the project belongs to the whole community.

Each year the national sponsoring organizations adopt a theme for American Education Week. An example is *Schools—Your Investment in America*. Local groups are urged to foster store window exhibits, posters, a day for visiting schools, movies, newspaper stories, open houses, and museum displays, special printed materials, a proclamation by the mayor, pageants, and similar activities that illustrate the theme. These approaches can deepen public understanding and appreciation of what education has meant to this nation and what it means today.

BUSINESS-INDUSTRY-EDUCATION COOPERATION

More and more, business leaders are recognizing the importance of quality schools. Some school officials call on chief executives to provide financial support for specific school needs. Company executives, on the other hand, look to schools to help prepare solid workers. Some school administrators work closely with company managers to provide adult school classes that meet the training and literacy needs of workers.

Adopt-a-School is a rapidly growing form of business-school partnership. The Adopt-a-School commitment can take a number of directions, but it primarily focuses on ways a company or organization can help a school do a better job of educating students.

Some companies donate used and new equipment. Others provide executives as speakers and paper-readers. All contribute a caring kind of encouragement that communicates a recognition of the school's importance.

Many schools report that a successful community relations venture is Business-Industry-Education Day. Worked out cooperatively, a day is set aside annually or biennially for teachers to visit different business and industrial firms in the community. Either the same or the next year, the school systems return the invitation to business, industrial, and, in some instances, labor representatives. The purpose of this plan is having each become better acquainted with the work of the other through firsthand observation and on-the-spot discussion.

COMMUNITY USE OF SCHOOL FACILITIES

The public schools belong to the public. One effective way to demonstrate this is to make school facilities available to individuals, groups, and organizations when regular classroom demands are over. Community use of the school at night or during vacations goes a long way toward showing some community members what their tax dollars are buying. People who have been in a school building during the year preceding a school finance election tend to support the needs of schools appreciably more than do those residents who have not been in a school building during that time. Allowing people to use the buildings is consistent with the function of the school as a social institution and is clearly a service in the public interest.

Use of Facilities

In an age of more and more leisure time when public education is no longer considered as something limited to people between the ages of five and eighteen, facilities are used by many people in a variety of ways. The senior citizen group may meet in a classroom or a special meeting room. The Catholic Youth Organization may use the basketball courts one night a week, and the Lions Club may choose to conduct business in the school cafeteria once a month.

The cafeteria may be used for special community banquets and dinners; the gymnasium may be tapped by many groups for dances, athletic events, exhibits, and community recreational programs; the auditorium may be used hundreds of times a year for forums, conferences, movies, dramatic productions of community groups, and other entertainment; the industrial arts areas may be used for automobile and furniture repair so that valuable equipment does not stand idle.

The instructional materials center (or library, as most community members will call it) should also be made available to residents on some controlled basis. For recreational reading and for information about business and personal concerns, the school library can serve many people. The homemaking rooms can be used to help interested residents learn about sewing, cooking, canning, and interior decorating, among other things. Office equipment can be called into service for classes to assist those who want to learn typing or to use equipment in the evening or on Saturdays. Science rooms can lend themselves to productive use by lawn enthusiasts wishing to conduct soil tests or by those wishing to pursue hobbies that require these materials and equipment. Music rooms can bring satisfaction to those in the community who belong to choral or other music groups. The athletic fields can serve thousands of residents who would otherwise never consider the public school as being of any service. For example, the local Catholic high school may play three football games on the public high school field, thus showing that some public school tax money is of value to thousands of parents and friends of the Catholic school team. Such decisions must be made with the good of the community and the service provided by the schools as the prime considerations.

Regulations

Community use of school facilities is a major ingredient in a solid school-community relations program. Yet too often plans are incompletely formed to cover the various requests that will be made of a board of education regarding such use. The board, to be thorough, should anticipate all kinds of requests and should establish written policies to cover those requests. The policies should be adequately publicized to prevent friction and to ensure all groups of equal treatment. If the board does not have such policies, whatever decision is made regarding specific requests is likely to be interpreted by some segment of the community as unfair. The board runs the risk of giving the appearance of reacting to personalities and groups on an individual basis if fair policies are not established that can be applied to all requests. Such policies ease the administrative pressures of making facilities available.

The rules should specify when school facilities are available and the purposes for which they may be used. Also spelled out should be the procedure for applying and for securing approval. The fees should be stipulated and the priority of school functions over other events should be clearly outlined. Also imperative is the responsibility factor; those using the facilities must recognize their legal and other responsibilities. If insurance is required for those conducting a large meeting, this stipulation must be in the rules governing facilities use. What will the school district do regarding the facility? What must the organization do? These distinctions must be made in writing to avoid disagreements that could more than negate the goodwill fostered by the use of the facilities.

In establishing the regulations, school officials must consider the overall benefits accruing to the community. Special pressure groups and internal empire builders must not have the final say about use of facilities. The decision must be based on educational facts and philosophy of the schools regarding the community's right to tap the school district's resources. For example, an athletic director who feels that a football field shouldn't be used by the local Midget team because the extra use will mar the turf should of course be heard by school administrators. However, the administrators must weigh the overall community good against the problems caused by such use. School facilities belong to the community, but guidelines for their use must be established.

ADULT EDUCATION

The extension of educational opportunities into adult life is another service the school can perform for the community. Programs can be established—both formal and informal, cultural and practical—that are built around the personal and social desires of adults for self-improvement. Courses can be offered to meet the needs of a wide spectrum of the community served by the school. Basic reading and writing courses will be needed in some communities to help overcome illiteracy. Others in that community may be interested in learning a skill or keeping up with the modern approaches to mathematics being learned by their children.

Determination of Need

An adult education program, to be sufficiently broad and vital, should consist of more than the offerings which school officials believe adults want or should take for their own betterment. It should represent the needs and interests of the adult population as closely as they can be determined. They may be determined with a fair degree of reliability by dividing the adult population in different ways—by age, educational achievement, socioeconomic background, family status, and group affiliation—and then analyzing the needs in each of the divisions. Or a council on adult education may be formed, consisting of men and women drawn from a cross section of the community. This council can be asked to study the problem and to make recommendations for a suitable program of activities. However, better results are possible when both methods, or others equally beneficial, are employed.

An effective way to determine if a course will be popular is to survey those attending adult school to find out whether or not it would attract enough people to be feasible. Effective adult education programs are conducted by administrators who work closely on an ongoing basis with the people being served.

Program Possibilities

Numerous possibilities exist for developing interesting, worthwhile programs suited to the personal and social needs of adults. As examples, creative experiences may be offered in art, music, drama, crafts, and writing. Discussion groups can be held to consider local political challenges, intercultural relations, civic improvements, world affairs, and so forth. Special workshops can be offered to prepare leaders for community service clubs, the school board, and other organizations. Forums and debates on pertinent issues can be held with the school supplying moderators and speakers. Special courses can be conducted for the foreign-born preparing for citizenship. Classes for those who are illiterate can provide a real service, as can courses designed to help people prepare for the high school equivalency examinations. Industrial education offerings can attract large numbers of men and women interested in learning to use equipment to make and repair items. Sewing, cooking, and hobbies are also commonly attractive areas that adult schools can offer. Foreign languages and recreational skills, such as golf and tennis, are being offered by more and more adult education programs as the amount of leisure time increases. Some adult schools, located in communities in which a large segment of the population is college educated, offer programs aimed at improving competency in jobs. Courses in public speaking, making effective presentations, leadership training, and others are common in these instances. Some school districts cooperate with area colleges to offer undergraduate and graduate programs. The program possibilities are limited only by the desires of the people being served.

Community Relations Outcomes

Community adult education programs that meet the needs of large numbers of people are bound to have a favorable influence on public opinion regarding the schools. Those who take part in the programs almost always appreciate the opportunity provided for continuing their education and satisfying other interests. They become acquainted with regular employees who teach many of the classes and, through these relationships, have more confidence in the school system. Moreover, every class taught by a regular employee serves to demonstrate the advancement made in instructional methods and materials over the years. Many are awakened to a deeper realization of the contribution education makes to their own lives and the lives of others, and they become stronger supporters of the school. The public goodwill and understanding thus created is worth much more than the cost of this service alone.

Publicizing Adult School Offerings

For an adult school to be successful, people must know about it and what it has to offer. This means that the administrator responsible for the adult school must be aware of publicity and communications techniques that will attract students. Many of the ideas explained in other chapters can be easily applied to this undertaking. Some specific publicity ideas follow:

▬ Work with an advisory committee to set up courses and to determine a calendar.
▬ Use the local radio station in a variety of ways. Public service announcements, interview shows, and call-ins to talk shows can bring attention to adult-school offerings. Brief news items explaining new courses and registration can be written for radio.
▬ Get the most out of area newspapers. News stories can be written about registration, the courses offered, and the number of people attending. Feature stories can be prepared on people and on unusual results of a class. Classified ads designed for specific audiences can attract some students. Display advertising can be effectively used to list all courses. A tear-out coupon for registration can be used in the ads. Some school districts share the cost of a large ad in an area

daily newspaper to provide general information about adult schools.
▬ Work with the various community groups. Prepare a video to show the groups what adult school has to offer. Ask those attending the presentation to complete forms you distribute asking for course suggestions.
▬ Distribute evaluation forms at the last class. Ask people to suggest other courses and to candidly react to the course completed. Ask permission to quote them in advertising for the next session.
▬ Distribute a brochure that provides complete information about courses, registration, and so forth to all residences served by the school district. If necessary, get professional help to do an effective job.
▬ Publicize the adult school in other school publications.

COMMUNITY EDUCATION

With this country's population growing older, only 25 percent of the people have children in school. If schools are to get continued support, they are going to have to answer the question "What's in it for us?" from those people not having children in schools. One answer is community education.

A concept that has been catching on more each year, community education goes beyond the K–12 years and attempts to provide education, as requested, for many members of the community. It can provide learning in the classroom or in a field setting for those wanting to learn something new, to fill some gaps in old learning, to spend leisure time more constructively, or for those wishing to retrain for a new job because their occupation has become outdated. In this program the schools, working closely with representative community groups, provide the kinds of services that groups request, if such requests are educationally sound.

Interaction and communication between the schools and the public are important ingredients in a community education program. Common, in addition to learning situations, are such activities as surveys, meetings, feedback channels from the public, publications, and citizen involvement in planning courses and projects. Such activities are also common to sound school-community relations programs. Therefore, a functional community education program focusing on citizen needs can be a beneficial part of a total public relations program.

West offers these thoughts on how school public relations benefit from a community education program:

1. Community education brings people together in a host of face-to-face communication activities through neighborhood and city-wide community councils.
2. Community education enhances school public relations through the neighborhood or block survey, which involves and seeks the opinion of large numbers of taxpayers.

3. In the courses and programs offered through community education, a significant level of communication takes place.
4. People continually subscribing to the services of community education and filling the schools are more apt to support these schools than those who rarely visit them and are unaware of their merits.
5. Community education also facilitates communication through frequent use of the media, print and non-print, which, with regularity, keeps the community in touch with the schools.[4]

In a number of schools the director of public relations is also the community educator. The responsibilities are similar, two-way communications and community involvement, and as more and more school districts become involved in community education, the director of public relations appears to assume the responsibilities of the community educator.

ENDNOTES

1. "PR Pointers for Secretaries," *Public Relations Gold Mine* 3 (Arlington, VA: National School Public Relations Association, 1961), pp. 23–24.
2. Don Bagin and Elias Hull, "Does Voice Mail Help Or Hurt Your Bottom Line?" *Bonus Item* (Blackwood, NJ: Communication Briefings, December 1992), p. 1.

3. "Declining Enrollment and Communication," *Journal of Educational Public Relations* 5, no. 3 (March 1982), pp. 19–21.
4. Philip T. West, "Community Education As Public Relations," *Community Education Journal* (April 1981), p. 2.

10

MAKING ORAL PRESENTATIONS

School administrators who possess the best curriculum ideas and are blessed with the shrewdest financial minds and a complete understanding of how children learn often fail to make the contributions they should. Their failure frequently can be traced to their inability to make effective presentations, whether they be to the board of education, the staff, a service organization, or a hostile taxpayers group. One of the best ways to restore confidence in educational leaders is for those leaders to be effective speakers. This chapter offers ideas and background information that should enable school officials to improve their ability to use the spoken word.

Most school administrators have had little more than a basic college speech course as formal training for their many public presentations. Yet the community's impression of the educational leader is based largely on how well that leader presents ideas in small and large groups. Administrators who invest time in improving their ability to speak will benefit doubly. First, their professional reputation will grow because people tend to color evaluations of accomplishments and failures with their subjective reading of people, and that reading is frequently based on having heard the person speak. Second, public support for programs championed by good speakers is generally easier to gain.

This chapter is primarily designed to engender confidence when administrators must make presentations. To do so, the speaker must focus on more than his or her delivery. Also to be considered are the audience, the topic, and the occasion. The speech is more than what the speaker says; it's what the audience makes out of what was said.

BASIC CONSIDERATIONS

Here are some basic considerations that might be helpful when thinking about that next presentation.

Smile. People like to be happy and around others who appear to be happy. Research done at the University of China, Hong Kong, indicates that people who are smiling are judged to be more intelligent than people who aren't. Smiling helps set a tone for the speaker and listeners. It communicates that you are confident, that you have something that's worth sharing to say, and that the audience should relax and enjoy. Smiling shows that you are indeed human and warm— characteristics not attributed to some school leaders by many taxpayers.

Speak to Individuals, Not to All of the Audience. Select a few people before your presentation; get to know them informally so they feel good about your being there. When speaking, direct eye contact at some of these people. Of course it's necessary to maintain eye contact with all of the people in the room (except with a very large audience). Many listeners equate a lack of eye contact with speaker fear. Eye contact implies that you respect members of the audience as individuals and want to share thoughts with them. Eye contact also allows the speaker to read audience reactions and to switch gears if necessary.

Know What You Want the Audience to Do. No speech should be prepared until the speaker has completed the answer to this question: As a result of this presentation, what do I want the audience to do? Perhaps the intent is to encourage them to accept the closing of a school or to vote for higher taxes to provide better curriculum. Perhaps it's merely to inform the audience of test score results or to move them to write letters to legislators. The intent of the speech must be remembered while planning it. Forgetting the reason for the speech is one of the reasons that so many speakers drift from one tangent to another.

Be Sincere. Audiences want speakers to succeed; it makes the meeting more comfortable for everybody. Even if a group disagrees with the speaker's position, the group still appreciates a successful presentation. One of the most important ingredients for a recipe that results in effective presentations is that the speaker exude sincerity. Audiences will forgive almost anything if the speaker communicates genuineness, goodwill, honesty, frankness, and an obvious interest in the topic and the audience's relationship to that topic. When preparing a presentation, emphasize those things that are important to you. Develop a style that's yours—not one that's been copied from another successful speaker. The most important need is that the speaker be comfortable, and that means using techniques, examples, and style that are yours.

Represent the Schools. School speakers must always remember that they are speaking for the school district, not for themselves. Whether the speaker is a superintendent, a principal, business manager or communications director, he or she isn't seen as John or Mary Smith, but as "someone from the school." One of the key goals for all school speakers is to communicate a feeling of confidence to the audience—confidence in the people running the schools. It is not expected that all speakers will have the answers to every concern, but it is expected that speakers will communicate a spirit of "we'll get the answers for you."

Remember too that schools are people. When speaking about school matters, include students in the discussion. Mentioning a building without

relating it to the people in the building seems cold. Many speakers who must capture audiences' attention with topics that are basically cold and dull envy the opportunities of school speakers. When speaking about schools, speakers are talking about two of the audience's prized possessions: their children and their money. Capitalizing on these interests, speakers can interject anecdotes that bring speeches to life.

Eliminate Voice and Diction Distractors. To help overcome seemingly small but important distractors, ask a colleague to take notes while the presentation is being made. Suggest that the colleague signal you if you are too close to or too far from the microphone. Overcome the tendency to sprinkle comments with "ahs," "you knows," and other space-fillers that add nothing but subtract much from the speech. Avoid falling into the monotone trap; without inflection, the speech might as well have been distributed for reading. Also, find a delivery speed that is comfortable for both you and the audience. Research indicates that people can listen four times as fast as most people speak, but don't challenge the research by sounding like a record being played at the wrong speed. It's also a problem to speak too slowly so that listeners have a tendency to think about other things while they wait for you to get to the next word.

Eliminate Irritating Mannerisms. The overall impact that a speaker makes on an audience is more than the sum of the words spoken. A speaker might be guilty of an annoying habit that gets in the way of comfortable communication. It might be scratching his or her head, bending a paper clip, tapping a pencil, or playing with change in a pocket. Another bothersome habit is putting on and removing eyeglasses frequently. Some speakers can remove glasses at the right point for emphasis; most, however, distract audiences with this habit. To know if they are guilty of any negative habits, speakers should have a presentation videotaped and then evaluate it with the assistance of a speech expert. Joining Toast-masters International is another way to benefit from evaluations.

Be Interested in the Audience. Effective speak-ers must know the make-up of the audience. By identifying the background of the audience and zeroing in on their interests, speakers will have taken a giant step toward preparing a successful presentation. If speakers have tailor-made their presentations, both the audience and they will benefit. Just about everyone has attended a disap-pointing speech given by a personality with a national reputation. For some reason, the presen-tation failed to reach the audience. Why? It may have been because the speaker failed to undertake an important part of the presentation—determin-ing his or her audience's interests and back-ground. The speaker, caught up in a pressured schedule, may have delivered the same speech to your group that was given to twenty other audi-ences. Thus, the speech that was well received in Peoria may have bombed in Seattle.

If the speaker has prepared for the audience, interest in that audience will be communicated. And from this interest the speaker's sincerity will come across to the group. Following the sincerity, enthusiasm can be communicated in an almost contagious way. And this results of course in gaining the confidence of the audience—a key stage of speech making. If you will subscribe to the idea of talking with, rather than at, your audi-ence, you will find an automatic improvement in your presentations. Some educators talk to audi-ences of citizens as though addressing a class and as if they were tired of it all.

THE SPEECH

The organization of the speech is often time-con-suming, and because of this too many school officials are guilty of overlooking its importance. A well-organized, enthusiastic talk helps both the speaker and the listener. Audiences are quick to spot an off-the-cuff performance. Every time you

appear before any audience to speak on any school subject, make it worth their time and yours.

Selecting a Topic

A well-organized speech starts with a worthwhile subject. Chances are, most of the time your topic will be selected for you. You may be asked to tell about your school district's computer program, your plan for educating the gifted student, special education for children with disabilities, or any of a dozen aspects of education. Your topic will be largely determined by the audience, the occasion, and your position in the school system.

Often school officials are asked to speak on "education." "Oh, just talk about anything," the program leader will suggest. Or you will simply be asked to talk for a certain length of time. In that case, start immediately with a thorough analysis of the audience and the occasion. Who are these people? How often do they meet? Why this meet-ing? What do they know about their school sys-tem, or what would you like to have them know? What would you like them to do after hearing you? A good basis for speech topics lies in the aims, practices, and accomplishments of the school system.

Putting the Speech Together

After the subject has been chosen and the specific purpose has been identified, the next step is to organize the subject. Estimate how much time it should take to accomplish your specific purpose. Remember that fewer long speeches than short speeches or medium-length speeches are effec-tive in gaining favorable audience reaction. The determination of what constitutes a long, rather than a medium-length, speech is quickly made by the audience. Wise speakers err on the short side, unless the group inviting them instructs them to speak for a specific length of time.

Many speakers next list all of the key ideas regarding the topic. If there are too many for the time allotted, eliminate some. It is better to communicate a few major points well than to ineffectively communicate a larger number of ideas. Many speech experts suggest limiting each speech to five key ideas. After deciding which key points to make, be sure the facts are current. If specific statistics are needed, get them. Someone *in the audience* is liable to be up to date on one phase of your topic; if your data are not current, your other ideas may be rejected. Check periodicals and then make a tentative outline of the speech.

Every speech can be divided into three parts. First you tell them what you're going to tell them, then you tell them, then you tell them what you told them. In other words, every speech has an introduction, a body, and a conclusion. The introduction stage of the speech can take many different forms. Some speakers, feeling that their time is limited, can effectively start their speech by immediately disclosing what they are going to talk about. Some do it in a completely straightforward manner, such as "I am going to talk about. . . ." This approach may not be the most motivating, but it can be adequate depending on the speech and the occasion. Many speakers prefer to use the motivated introduction technique. Speakers should choose the kind of introduction that works best for them and for the audience being considered. A provocative question, an anecdote that is related to the topic, or a story with a local flavor can be effective ways to begin a presentation. One definite way not to start a speech is with an apology. If you aren't prepared, don't admit it. The audience will be able to tell soon enough.

When arranging the body of the speech, consider using a logical, chronological, or problem-solution method. The logical method presents causes and results of an event or situation. The chronological approach simply tells about events in the order they occurred. The problem-solution method provides the history, causes, and effects of a problem, suggests and evaluates solutions, and recommends the best solution. After selecting the order of the speech material, consider two key questions: Are the main messages emphasized? Are ideas presented in a way that lends itself to pacing the presentation?

Remembering the most important points is vital. Speakers may forget an example or two but they will remember the main points if they limit those key messages to five or fewer. If delivering a persuasive speech, don't fall into the trap of spending a long time on the problem and leaving less time for your solutions. Invest most of the time and ammunition in the solution. When putting the final order into the speech, check to see if anecdotes and concrete examples appear every few minutes; if not, you may want to rethink the order of the presentation. Audiences like examples and stories when they relate to the topic; they become involved with the speaker when those examples are being used. Sprinkle such stories throughout the presentation. Speakers who consider themselves poor storytellers shouldn't tell stories for the sake of their humor only; the stories should relate to the topic so they make a point even if the audience doesn't find them humorous.

The conclusion of a speech is designed to do just that—finish it. Too many speeches sputter to a stop, leaving audiences wondering if the speech is over. One good approach to a conclusion is to restate the main purpose of the speech. Summarizing what was said in the discussion stage is another effective and commonly used conclusion. Some speakers can effectively weave in stories that relate to the points being made. A fitting conclusion for these kinds of speakers may be a story or anecdote that makes a final point. Ending with a rhetorical question that prompts discussion among the audience can be effective, too. No matter which approach is taken, the speaker should keep in mind that the conclusion should move the audience to some kind of action.

Deciding How to Present the Speech

At this point the speaker has to decide on the method of presentation. Do you memorize the speech, write it all out and read from manuscript, or use brief outline notes or no notes at all?

Seldom do busy educators have the time to memorize a speech. Nor is this approach necessary. Most educators read from a manuscript or use note cards that highlight major ideas. Because educators attend many conferences where other educators can be seen reading speeches, they frequently opt for this method. Such deliveries are generally boring; it would be better if the speech were copied and given to the audience to read. Some speakers are able to read a speech effectively, especially if they have had the speech prepared by a professional speech writer who knows how to write the spoken rather than the written word.

In preparing a speech script, consider the following guidelines. Indent the first line of each paragraph; your eye will move more easily to that spot. Use upper- and lower-case typewritten letters. Although many speeches have traditionally been typed in all capital letters, they are more difficult to read than upper and lower case, unless the reader is accustomed to them. Double space all copy and insert subtitles throughout the script as reminders of what you're about to read. Keep margins wide enough so that last-minute notes can be added, and have the lines typed in a way that allows reading blocks of copy rather than words or parts of words. Never hyphenate anything at the end of the line even though some lines will be appreciably shorter than others. This makes it easier for the reader to deal with units of thought. Don't staple or place a paper clip on the manuscript while you speak; avoid making it obvious that you're turning pages. Number all pages in the upper right hand corner to salvage what could be a disaster if the pages are dropped. It's also a good idea to give the speech a title; this helps the person introducing you and will also serve as a guideline for media coverage.

Most educators, however, don't have the ability to read a speech well. It is understandable that some speakers prefer a typed text for presentations where many names and titles will be used. Using notes is probably the best compromise for most presentations. The notes provide a physical and psychological crutch, yet allow the speaker to communicate in a more natural way than a manuscript does. Speakers should not attempt to hide note cards; many listeners appreciate the fact that the speaker did some homework. Some presentation experts suggest that speakers avoid using notes whenever possible, explaining that the audience rapport established without notes compensates for the possibility of some facts being forgotten. This approach is considered, of course, only when the speaker has a strong command of the subject.

After deciding whether to use notes or a manuscript, consider the following suggestions.

Use Comfortable Words

A common problem plaguing educators in both the spoken and the written word is educational jargon. The general public abhors the use of educational gobbledygook that quickly alienates listeners. Listeners in most communities will either be turned off or will begin to distrust the speaker who seems to be trying to "put something over on the public."

Educators sometimes seem to be speaking to impress people rather than to communicate with them. If jargon or uncommon words must be used, explain their meaning. But be sure to do it in a way that isn't condescending or patronizing. Listeners cannot agree with you or support your cause if they do not understand you. Watch the audience closely for looks of bewilderment or uncertainty. If you notice the audience isn't with you, back up and go over previous statements until they seem to be understood. Talking to an audience in a simple, uncluttered, easy-to-understand style will enhance your reputation with the audience and with the community. Hiding behind the cloak of jargon and what some consider a "tower of babble" only angers people who cannot understand you. John Molloy, author of *Live for Success,* says, "Jargon is for jerks."[1]

The need to use plain talk is advocated by Rudolf Flesch.[2] A conversational tone, Flesch claims, allows you to incorporate any necessary technical language, to keep the pace fast, and to follow the ordinary rules of grammar. At the same time it will give the listener time to understand what was said. Flesch suggests that speakers should pause more often than usual when speaking before an audience and should use repetition and spread out ideas. Use filler words in speech, such as "that is," "in the first place," "should we say," "another point," and so on. Use plenty of verbs and personal pronouns. Get used to the habit of saying "we," "you," "our," and "us." It's not "their problem" as much as it is "our problem"; try saying "our idea" rather than "my idea." Talk about people; use contractions and, on some occasions, even colloquialisms. Flesch warns against using gobbledygook and cautions against a display of book learning. And he adds, "to reach an audience at a certain level of listening, you not only have to talk the kind of language they will be able to understand without effort, but ordinarily you will have to go one step below that level to make sure your ideas will get across."[3]

Choose Statistics Selectively

Disraeli said, "There are three kinds of liars: plain liars, damned liars, and statisticians." Educators often find themselves forced to accompany information or persuasive talks with statistical evidence. It helps reinforce arguments and often is an excellent persuasive device. Use figures in speeches if necessary, but use them sparingly. Remember the ear cannot record a factual figure the way the eye can, so follow the cue of the radio newscaster. Rather than quote a figure of 8,128 students, for example, simply say, "more than eight thousand students." Give the source of your statistics and make sure your source is reliable, current, and one that is acceptable to your audience.

THE AUDIENCE

Too often speakers prepare talks without considering the listeners. The first question when preparing a speech should be "Who will hear this?" A speech is a social function, and something should happen between the speaker and the audience. A speech should not be evaluated on what it is, but on what it does. To be a successful speaker, the educator should attempt to see things from the viewpoint of the audience. Ask yourself: "How would I feel about listening to this if I were in their places?" To do this well, an analysis of the audience is necessary. An advance picture of the audience will enable you to tailor the presentation to their needs. If advance knowledge of your audience is not practical, you can draw inferences about it as the speech is being given.

General Information Can Be Helpful

Before planning the speech, take a look at certain information about the audience. This information should help you make decisions about the kind of words to use, the types of stories that will be accepted, and other useful items that will lead to a better speech.

It's important for speakers to know the size of the audience. The size has implications for the telling of stories (groups fewer than fifteen are not usually receptive to jokes), the use of a microphone, audience involvement, and so forth. The age of the audience also plays a part in speaker preparation. If the age range is wide, some will understand certain examples but might miss others. The education of the group will determine what level of vocabulary to use and whether it's prudent to have the audience draw its own conclusions. Aim most of the speech at the average knowledge level of the audience.

Perhaps the most important information is the interest level of the audience. Skillful speakers realize that the way to hold an audience is to appeal to them with a "What's in it for me?" approach. Unless people are attending because of some emotional interest, the speaker must overcome mental inertia by pointing out early in the presentation how members of the audience will benefit from the presentation.

One of the most difficult decisions for the educator to make is whether or not to tell an audience all sides of a story. For instance, if the superintendent is speaking to various community groups about the need to close a building, should he or she discuss options to the closing? For many years, school officials declined to discuss alternatives; instead, they presented the one view they felt was best and attempted to gain community acceptance. In today's more educated world, audiences will undoubtedly hear about other solutions to the problem. Therefore, it is prudent to discuss options with the various audiences, being careful, of course, to explain why the speaker's suggested solution is the most feasible.

Even though you have made an excellent presentation, much of what you said will be forgotten. It is common for an audience to forget a large portion of a speech. Studies have shown that a typical educated audience, fairly interested in the topic of the speech, will probably forget about two-thirds of what they heard within one week's time. (A summary at the end of the speech helps improve their memory.) Use a great deal of repetition in your speech. Repeat your main idea at least three different times. Rephrase it somewhat and distribute the repetitions, but keep hammering away to reinforce your specific objective. On this point, tell your listeners specifically, not generally, the exact purpose of your speech and repeat that purpose. Use a slogan or catchword phrase to sum up your objective. It helps listeners remember the speech.

Attitudes of listeners may change while you're speaking. You have to be keenly aware of the audience response during your talk. Keep your eyes on them. The manner in which they sit in their seats, their facial expressions—frowns and smiles, nods, whispers, laughter, and applause—are all important cues to a speaker. This is one of the main arguments for skill in extemporaneous speaking over the manuscript method. It enables the speaker to be relatively free of notes and to be more aware and sensitive to the visible and audible responses of his listeners. Don't be upset by the behavior of isolated members of your group, but lack of attention from the nucleus of your audience can be a danger sign.

One note of caution about audience analysis. You have to be prepared to change your approach while you speak if it seems that your preliminary analysis was wrong. Don't expect your listeners to adapt to your prearranged plan; the speaker is the person who must be flexible enough to adapt to the situation.

The Physical Setting

The physical arrangement, contents, and previous uses of the room in which you speak all exert some influence on the listeners. The larger the audience, the more formal the speech situation tends to become and the more difficult the task of speaking. A platform would help in this case. Some elevation of the speaker tends to enhance prestige and seems to aid the speaker who is using logical persuasion. If you seek an emotional appeal, the closer you stand to your listeners, the better the rapport.

If you are asked to speak to a fairly large audience in a spacious room, ask in advance about the possibility of needing a public-address system. Don't use one unless you feel it is absolutely necessary to be heard at the back of the room. It is easier to move around if you are not confined by a microphone. A good compromise, if a microphone is required, is to use a lavalier mike that permits the speaker to move around comfortably. It is usually necessary to request this microphone in advance. If the speaker values mobility and feels that moving around allows establishing a more informal atmosphere, such a mike should be requested.

If a public-address microphone is necessary, test it in advance—not by blowing into it, but by speaking into it. Keep in mind that the volume that seems adequate in an empty auditorium may not be enough when the room is filled with people. As far as the microphone is concerned, remember it isn't necessary to shout into it. Ask someone to stand in the back of the room and signal you if you are too close to the mike or if you cannot be heard. Don't move your head too abruptly, and stand at least one foot away from the microphone. Keep your hands off the mike or standard, and watch for sudden coughs or laughs that would be amplified by the public-address system. Even when you are using a microphone, talk with your audience as if they numbered only about a dozen people.

THE OCCASION

In addition to the delivery, topic, and audience, the fourth vital part of a speech is the occasion. As a member of the school system staff, you can expect a variety of speaking experiences. More and more school administrators are being asked to speak, not only to school-related organizations but to other community groups as well. Formal addresses are still common for many superintendents. But many school officials are spending large amounts of time in smaller group discussions with parents, other taxpayers, and students. More face-to-face contact is occurring in school-community relations throughout the country. People are interested in the school story, and the way that many want to learn it is directly from school officials. This, of course, means meetings, and educators are expected to speak at these meetings.

Today's administrators might find themselves speaking to the Lions Club one day, the PTA another evening, the teachers' bargaining group the next day, and an assembly of students on the following day. The occasion varies each time, as does the audience. Different occasions demand different kinds of presentations. Some might lend themselves to an informative speech, some might require a speech designed to secure goodwill, and others might be given to promote a particular goal of the schools.

The Informative Speech

The speech that can be driest and dullest, unless much planning is done, is the informative speech. For a good speaker, it can also be the one he or she least likes to deliver. Yet it is a necessary presentation because people do have to be in-formed before they can make decisions about school matters. The purpose of such a speech is simply to have the audience understand the ideas you present. One of the major factors often present when people do not agree with each other is that they do not understand each other. This kind of speech should be confined to facts and expert opinions; it should exclude argument or persuasion. Examples of this type of speech include speeches explaining school finance, reporting on the school's program for the gifted child, informing citizens of reporting methods, explaining the school's testing system, and discussing the educational challenges caused by declining enrollment.

The structure of an informative speech should be clear and uncluttered. Main points should be limited and should be handled one at a time. Specific evidence should be presented; generalizations can be deadly, especially in an informative speech. Illustrations, humor, and anecdotes should be used when helpful, and in this kind of speech they are almost always welcome. Early in the speech the listeners should be told why they need to know about the subject; otherwise, the audience may see no reason to listen.

The Speech to Secure Goodwill

Obviously, every time you speak, you seek goodwill for your school system. On some occasions you will simply be representing the schools and will be given no specific topic; you might be one of a few speakers. In this role the speaker usually attempts to come across in almost an ambassadorial fashion or, as some would consider it, in a public relations manner. The objective is to leave the listener feeling good about your schools. These situations occur at civic rallies, dinners, conventions, and conferences. Frequently there is little time for preparation, so it is a good idea for every speaker to have some basic information handy at all times.

On these occasions, the audience does not expect a lengthy, persuasive speech. The audience does expect the speaker to be pleasant, to seem glad to be with them, and to offer information about the schools that pleases them while informing them. If speakers can build audience confidence in themselves, that confidence will, in many cases, be transferred to the school system. This will reap benefits in community support of school needs. Among the topics appropriate for these speaking occasions would be a brief explanation of some of the newer accomplishments of the schools.

The Promotional Speech

The chief characteristic of the promotional speech is that it attempts to prove something or to influence an attitude. This is a task of persuasion and involves a relationship between belief and action. This speech is given to audiences that may be prospective supporters. Here is where you seek voter support for a budget, a broader curriculum, and other needed improvements.

First, you must make listeners want to do what you propose rather than feel they have to. Here is one sequence to follow in eliciting an audience's enthusiasm. Gain the audience's attention with a controversial statement or a difficult-to-answer question. Then, show the need and stress the importance of that need to the audience. Next, present the solution you think is best. It's important here to present solid evidence in a believable, enthusiastic way. Demonstrate how the solution will solve the problem or meet the need. If examples of the solution's having worked in other schools are available, share them. Anticipate objections by mentioning them and answering them throughout the presentation. Contrast what the schools will be like with your solution as opposed to what they will be like if your solution is not effected; be as specific as possible. Finally, and most importantly, conclude the presentation with a request for action. Make it easy for the audience to overcome inertia by providing forms and pens for them to sign up for a committee or some other activity that might be forgotten if left for tomorrow.

Introducing a Speaker

Chances are you'll be called on to make many introductions of speakers. Your job here is to present the speaker to the audience in a way that makes them want to hear him or her. The speech should be brief and about the speaker, not about yourself. A simple outline for the introductory speech contains these four main points:

The Occasion.   As an introductory mechanism, explain why the speaker is with you. Consider the appropriateness of the speaker or the subject. Connect the speaker with this audience in some way, if possible.

The Speaker's Qualifications.   Tell the audience why the speaker is qualified to speak on this topic. Who is the speaker? What is his or her position? State the speaker's experience and background. Beware of telling listeners how good the speaker is; this puts the speaker on the spot. By the same token, don't allow the program chairperson to extol the virtues of next month's speaker before this speaker has spoken. It is best to outline briefly the speaker's qualifications, highlighting those things that would most appeal to the audience. Don't read the title of every article written or make the introduction like an obituary rundown of everything the speaker has accomplished. This will subtract from the time the speaker has. Introduce some of the warmer facts about the speaker; for example, note that he or she has three children attending public schools or that he or she too got lost on the winding road to the meeting place. Consider using a quote or two from others who have heard the speaker; they can help set a positive tone.

The Speaker's Topic.   Don't make the speech for the speaker; too many introductions end up stealing many of the main points the speaker had planned to make. Mention the appropriateness of the topic and get out of the way. If the speaker has given the speech a title, use it; if not, a concise statement of the topic will suffice.

The Speaker's Name.   Although many people charged with introducing speakers deviate from the approach, many experts agree that the way to introduce a speaker is to save the name for last. The feeling here is that once you've given the speaker's name, the introduction is over. Be sure you pronounce the speaker's name properly. If in doubt, check. Checking isn't embarrassing; mispronouncing the name in an introduction is. Refer to speakers the way they prefer. If the speaker's name is Patricia and she prefers to be called Pat, act accordingly. After you've made the introduction, sit. It's the speaker's show.

Speeches for Special Occasions

School officials in some communities are frequently asked to preside at after-dinner events. It isn't necessary to develop a reputation as a comedian on such occasions. Although plenty of apropos stories are helpful and a keen sense of humor is an asset, remember you are the transition person, not the star performer. Your main responsibility is to keep things moving.

When you are asked to present awards, do so sincerely. Guard against overdoing the adjectives for each award or the value of each will be minimized. Try to be fair in lauding recipients, watching the natural tendency to go overboard for those you know better than others. The composition of a speech for making each award can be fairly simple. First, describe the accomplishments of the person receiving the award; then describe the award.

During a school year, educators are called on to make numerous courtesy talks. You may have to welcome visitors to the school at an assembly program, bid farewell to staff members leaving the system at a social activity, or speak at a community function. The best approach in these situations is usually to express genuine sentiment without going overboard with praise.

Discussions and Conferences

Much of the school official's speaking activity will be in sit-down situations. Small discussion groups, mini-conferences, lunches with small groups of citizens, and coffee get-togethers are demanding a large portion of the educator's time. More and more decision making and problem solving in business and education are being done after the input of groups at discussion-type meetings.

What you do and say as a group discussion leader depends on the circumstances, of course; but certain tips should be helpful. Discussion can be used to solve problems, as an information technique, or simply to create higher motivation among the participants. One of the basic responsibilities of the conference leader is to organize the procedure to prevent the conference from becoming another time-consuming, fruitless meeting. Much time can be saved if the leader and the participants follow a critical, orderly pattern of thinking.

One of the chief duties of the discussion leader is to strive to have the main phases of the problem considered. On top of that, a conference leader should strive to get good general participation from the group members, promote the unity of the group, encourage opinions and solutions, and curb irrelevant contributions.

The educator in a key administrative position is also responsible for calling and running meetings. To increase your chance of conducting a good meeting, Jorgenson, Scheier, and Fautsko[4] say to be on guard against the following:

■ Lack of relevant subject matter. Often the wrong people are invited and feel misused or abused as they dawdle away the time thinking about the important things that are not getting done.

■ Wrong number of people. Ideally problem-solving meetings should contain between seven and twelve people. Fifteen or twenty are too many because the many ideas and the large amount of information generated cannot be processed effectively by that size group.

■ Allowing one person to dominate. When this happens, others withdraw, and sometimes the group leader incorrectly interprets the withdrawal as assent.

▬ Failure to effect change. When meetings regularly produce nothing new, participants understandably start to question their value. Before calling that next meeting, calculate its cost in terms of person hours. Is the meeting necessary, or can the communication take place in a less costly way?

▬ Failure to review previous decisions. Participants forget what was decided at previous meetings; frequently this leads to repeating discussions unnecessarily.

▬ A lack of understanding regarding who promised to do what at the last meeting. An easy solution: Send a copy of all things promised to all who attended as soon as possible after the meeting.

School administrators find themselves engaged more and more with citizen advisory committees, staff conferences, policy-making discussions, informational panels, and other types of group discussion. Here again it is important that you be well organized and prepared. Prior to any such conference, you should carefully prepare your "reflective" agenda. Plan a brief, informal social session beforehand, so that members of the group have the opportunity to get acquainted. This helps promote group unity and gives you some insight into the kind of people you'll be working with. Think in advance of seating arrangements; you may want to seat people in some arrangement that will avoid having some monopolize or others withdraw from participating in the discussion.

To accomplish your desired results through discussion, try to create an informal group atmosphere. Seek to establish a "we" feeling, allow participants the freedom to express themselves, and stress cooperation and critical thinking. The group should be reminded that the responsibility for a decision at a conference rests with the group, not with the leader.

The spirit of a small-group meeting is so important that plans should be made to ensure that the climate is the best one possible. For instance, if the superintendent will be meeting with twenty people from a neighborhood, the person hosting the meeting should provide information about the people attending. A relaxed atmosphere will enable the people to ask questions and get answers in a way that helps build confidence in the school official and in the school. Respect is gained for the educator who admits not knowing the answer to a question but who promises to get back to the person as soon as possible and does. School officials who have not conducted small-group meetings with taxpayers—either in homes or at the school—will be surprised at the wide range of questions. A meeting called to discuss the budget may spend less than one-fifth of the meeting on the topic. People will ask questions that concern them about the schools; remember that this may be the first opportunity that people have had to talk with a school representative in a small-group situation.

Using Overhead Projectors

When presenting for a half hour or more, speakers may want to include some audiovisual materials to provide a change of pace. Probably one of the most effective is the overhead projector, which allows the speaker to draw attention to key points while maintaining eye contact with the audience. It also allows the presenter to write audience suggestions in a way that can be seen by all. Use the proper size letters so all can easily read the materials presented. Place highlights on the screen. Don't imply that the audience should read details along with you.

Research conducted at the University of Pennsylvania indicates that overhead projection can influence the outcome of management meetings. Some of the results of the 1982 study follow:

▬ Overhead projection reduces meeting length by 28 percent.

▬ When two opposing sides of an issue are presented, presenters are perceived in a more favorable light when they use overhead projection.

▬ Presenters using overhead projection are seen as better prepared, more credible, and more interesting than presenters who don't use overheads.

▬ Group consensus is achieved more frequently when overheads are used.

(Additional information on audiovisual materials is offered in Chapter 12.)

ENDNOTES

1. John Molloy, *Live for Success* (New York: William Morrow, 1981).
2. Rudolf Flesch, *The Art of Plain Talk* (New York: Harper, 1946).
3. Ibid., p. 137.
4. James D. Jorgenson, Ivan H. Scheier, and Timothy F. Fautsko, *Solving Problems in Meetings* (Chicago: Nelson-Hall, 1982).

11

WORKING WITH THE PRESS

The press plays a major role in a school-community relations program. This chapter discusses the importance of the press and offers ideas for improving school relationships with newspaper representatives. It provides specific suggestions to enable educators to increase their opportunities for better news coverage of schools, it offers ideas to assist school officials in their everyday dealings with reporters, and it provides schools with information on how to prepare news stories properly.

The important role of the press in the overall school-community relations program must be realized. Studies consistently show that the prime sources of information about the school are students and newspapers, and not always in that order.

As the number of taxpayers with school-age children decreases, newspapers will most likely become an even more important source of information about schools for many people. This view is contested by some who feel that newspapers have played a key role for many years only because school officials were slow to recognize that other, more personal communication techniques were easily available. Still others suggest that much news will be obtained from computers rather than from newspapers as we know them.

Whatever the role will be tomorrow, the newspapers are here today; and the astute administrator will not underestimate the power of the press. Appreciating the power of the press, the administrator then must understand the role of the press in its dealings with the public schools. Educators are often suspicious of newspaper people, fearing that they will hurt the cause of the schools. But newspapers feel they have a responsibility to report on all public institutions, including public schools.

The Cleveland Press expressed it this way:

> The newspaper, if it is to discharge its duty to the schools, must serve them by being their civic "report card." The paper has an obligation to give the public a periodic accounting of what the schools are costing and just what the money is buying. . . . It has a duty to report accurately, objectively, and dramatically on classroom work and other activities within the school in order that the public, responsible for the support and control of its education, can wisely appraise the school's purposes, accomplishments, and needs. Only a thoroughly informed public can determine whether the schools are strong or weak and just what can be done about it.[1]

When accountability demands that educators show where the money is going and when taxpayers want answers on how the schools are being run, the school administrator must be able to work effectively with the press. For if a newspaper is to issue the "report card" referred to by the Cleveland Press, the newspaper people responsible for printing information about the schools must understand what is going on in the schools. Reporters and editors also need more than a surface knowledge of school activities, achievements, and problems.

The newspaper, of course, has a legal right to this kind of information. School districts spend public funds. Thus, newspapers have just as much right to report about the schools as they do about other government agencies. School officials should know the state law on the public's right to know. School administrators who are aware of the reporter's right to information can save themselves and their schools severe embarrassment. Too frequently school officials refuse reporters information that is eventually made public when a court intervenes. More damaging than the harm done to the relationship with the reporter is the mistrust generated by hiding facts.

GUIDELINES

To help education department employees know what reporters have a right to know, one state superintendent of schools issued guidelines. An elaboration of these guidelines as well as other suggestions follow.

Answer Questions Honestly. Any responsible employee of the school is expected to answer questions about those topics concerning his or her position. The educator who appears to be hiding something by attempting to dodge or circumvent an issue only prompts additional investigation by the reporter.

Every school system needs an operating procedure for dealing with the press. If this procedure fails to give reporters the information when they need it, the procedure will undoubtedly come under fire in the press. More than one school district has felt the wrath of both the press and taxpayers when the superintendent was out of town and reporters were informed by all other administrators that "only the superintendent may speak to the press." Such a situation will provoke three reactions: (1) disgust by reporters, (2) concern for their own competence by other administrators, and (3) puzzlement on the part of citizens who wonder why people running the schools aren't allowed to talk to the press.

All employees should know who can speak for the schools when the superintendent isn't available. And the next person in line should be designated in case the "number two" person is unavailable. In fact all employees should understand their role in working with the press. This includes administrators, teachers, and clerical employees. It may be necessary to conduct an in-service program for employees so that all will be comfortable when speaking to reporters. Local reporters will usually cooperate in such a program because it helps them do their job better and more easily.

Respond Promptly. This guideline means knowing and respecting newspaper deadlines. The reporter who is told by an administrator's secretary that he or she "is busy and will call back" will understandably be irate when the return call comes too late to meet that issue's deadline. Getting information on time is a reporter's job; if the administrator recognizes this pressure and assists the reporter, the reporter will appreciate it and will respond favorably.

Deadlines vary from newspaper to newspaper. The thorough administrator should know the deadlines of all area newspapers, weeklies as well as dailies. Weekly newspapers, because sometimes they are printed some distance from the editorial office, might have a deadline two or three days before the paper is on the streets. By knowing the various deadlines, the administrator can be sure to submit information on time and can avoid bothering reporters and editors with unimportant information and social calls at deadline time.

All Reports and Surveys Are Public Property. You may *not* withhold such data when they are requested—even though you believe the reporter is going to use the material to hurt a program. You do not have to release rough drafts, working papers, preliminary figures, or notes, but you may choose to do so.

Don't Pick Your Own Time for Publicity and Refuse to Provide Information until That Time. Some administrators fall into the routine of sending out news releases every Friday because that's the day allocated to that phase of running the school. But news is often timely, and waiting a few days to release it might jeopardize its chance of being printed. Reporters sometimes seek information about a project or innovation before the program coordinator or principal is ready to wrap up the final report. The educator should answer the reporter's questions when the questions are asked. This does not preclude the possibility of preparing a news release when the project is completed and all the information is available.

For example, much ballyhoo usually accompanies the start of an innovative program in schools. Yet few districts do much to indicate progress and problems as the innovation is implemented. Frequently school officials want to wait until the end of the year to chart and report measurable progress. Yet it's natural for the public and reporters to ask for information before the year is over.

It Is Not Necessary to Be Auditor-Accurate with Figures. Reporters dislike hearing the excuse that not all the figures are available. If reporters need to know the expected September enrollment for the August 15 "Back-to-School" issue, they realize that the figures might not be exact. An approximate number will suffice.

Avoid Education Jargon. The educator must constantly guard against using words that noneducators won't understand. This applies to talking with reporters. Most newspapers cannot afford the luxury of a full-time education reporter who might have the background to understand educational terminology. Thus, school officials should explain educational terms when they use them or should substitute words that everyone will understand. "Minimal fenestral areas" might be fine for a group of educators considering the merits of air-conditioned plants. For the public and for the reporter, however, it's better to say "only a few windows." A criticism leveled at educators is that they try to confuse the public with "educationese" and don't talk the language of the layperson. This contributes to a credibility gap between the school official and the public—a gap that breeds distrust.

Educators who want to establish sound, believable relationships with the public and the press will avoid words and expressions that are jargon-laden and will use easy-to-understand words in their writing and speaking. Language

choice should be made to communicate an idea, not to impress people that they have mastered certain polysyllabic words.

Don't Be Afraid to Say "I Don't Know, I'll Call You Back in Ten Minutes." Reporters looking for answers don't expect school officials to have every response every time. It is appreciably better to admit not knowing than to give an inaccurate answer. Remember to get back to a reporter quickly if he or she is fighting a deadline. Don't allow other problems to intervene if information was promised by a certain time.

Never Ask a Reporter to Show the Story Before It Is Published. Just as a reporter is expected to respect expertise in educators, his or her reporting ability must be respected. Asking to see a story before it's published implies to most reporters that they are not trusted to write a sound story. If certain points should be emphasized in the story, emphasize them in the interview. But remember that the reporter's idea of what's important and the educator's concept of what should be played up may differ. The reporter's responsibility is to the public and to the newspaper, not to making the school and a program look good.

Also, don't ask reporters to send a copy of the story after it appears in the newspaper. They have other responsibilities to think about; besides, educators should be buying and reading newspapers regularly. School officials must remember that newspapers are operated by people who are in the newspaper business. Thus, editors and reporters don't expect educators to tell them how to run newspapers, just as school officials don't expect newspeople to tell math teachers how to explain set theory.

A School Official Who Has Talked to a Reporter about a Substantive Item Should Notify His or Her Immediate Superior. The superintendent of schools should be informed immediately if the topic has districtwide implications or is the kind of topic that lends itself to comment from the chief executive officer. If other key personnel don't know about this matter, the story might wind up being a series of statements from various administrators, each one contradicting the other.

Be a Key Member of the Management Team. School representatives responsible for press relations must enjoy the confidence of key school officials. Otherwise they will be ineffective. The school's press relations person must also have access to all information. This means attending all key administrative cabinet meetings, executive sessions of the board, and all major meetings. If this is not the case, the press will consistently bypass the press relations representative, who will be relegated to writing news releases about PTA meetings and class trips.

Be Accurate. Reporters' reputations ride on the accuracy of their stories. If people read something that is incorrect, they will have less confidence in the rest of that reporter's articles. Thus, it's imperative that all information provided to reporters be checked for preciseness. This is especially important in the spelling of names and the placement of decimal points. People dislike seeing their names misspelled in the newspaper and will usually blame the reporter even if the fault lies elsewhere. This does not enhance the school's relationship with the reporter.

Know All Reporters on a First-Name Basis. Probably the most important step that an educator can take to improve school-press relations is to get to know reporters on a first-name basis. When an administrator is just a title and a name, it's fairly easy for reporters to choose letters on the keyboard that can form critical words. Establishing solid rapport with reporters cannot be considered a guarantee that prevents criticism; however, it can be thought of as a way to ensure a fair chance to tell the school's side of the story.

Reporters will respect educators who make an effort to understand them and their job. This might mean leaving the office to meet with reporters at their newspaper office, or getting together for lunch informally. It's always better to

meet a reporter when no pressure exists for information on a negative story. Once reporters know an educator, it will encourage them to call the school for facts rather than looking elsewhere for them. This ensures the opportunity to present the school's side of a story—an important ingredient when a controversial topic is in the headlines.

Make it a point, in planning the publicity program, to discuss with editors what types of stories they are interested in and how the news should be handled. This responsibility should be assumed either by the superintendent or by the person in charge of school publicity.

Know What "Off the Record" Means. Talking to reporters "off the record" means you are offering information for their knowledge but that it is not to be used in the newspaper. This can be extremely risky and can cause all sorts of problems if not properly understood by all parties concerned. Two schools of thought exist in regard to providing off-the-record information to reporters. One school believes that reporters are always reporters and that any information given to them will eventually find its way into the newspaper. Advocates of this position therefore remind school officials that reporters are reporters all the time, not just when carrying a clipboard at a school board meeting.

Others feel that off-the-record information enables reporters to bring a fuller understanding of complex and controversial issues to their reporting, even though such information is not printable. Here is an example of providing off-the-record information:

The president of the United States is scheduled to deliver the commencement address at a high school. For security reasons, only the president of the board, the superintendent of schools, and the district's public relations person know about the commitment. The president wants no advance publicity. At the April board of education meeting, one of the board members suggests that a controversial ultraconservative speaker be invited to deliver the commencement address. The rationale, the board member explains, is that last year's graduation exercises featured an ultraliberal as the speaker.

The board president, without explanation, says it's impossible to invite the suggested speaker. Reporters remember that the superintendent is labeled a liberal. They scurry to phones to call in this controversial story. But the public relations person intervenes, explaining the circumstances and also the need to keep the information about the president out of the papers. The reporters, all six of them, decide to forget the incident happened.

It must be noted that the community relations person had established a reputation of honesty in all dealings with the press and was known on a first-name basis. Remember, too, that if the reporter acquires the same information elsewhere on the record and uses it, there is no violation of confidence.

Be Available when Negative News Occurs.
One of the most consistent criticisms leveled against school officials is their inaccessibility when something that appears to be negative happens in a school. As one reporter put it: "Why are the same administrators who are always available when a student wins some academic recognition suddenly in hiding when a problem occurs?"

The day when board members and taxpayers expect schools to be perfect is over. However, the day of accountability and administrative responsibility has not passed. And school administrators who are expected to provide leadership for a school district cannot abrogate that responsibility when the going gets rough.

No one expects educators to boast about problems that occur. However, attempting to cover up problems that affect an integral part of the school's operations can lead to much larger difficulties. The wise administrator will recognize the problems, propose alternative solutions, and explain why the solution selected is the most appropriate one. By ignoring problems the administrator projects an image that will not build the confidence needed to gain public support.

Know What News Is.
A major complaint of newspaper editors and reporters is that most school officials fail to recognize what news is. This results in two things: (1) important school news is not sent to the papers, and (2) news releases with no news value demand the time of editors. Educators can improve their understanding of what constitutes news by talking with reporters and editors. It's surprising to many school officials how helpful newspeople can be when asked. Also reading the area newspapers can be extremely helpful in determining what news is.

One of the most common errors made by educators is to assume that something is newsworthy just because it is of interest to them. The editor has a different yardstick: How many readers will the item interest? Answering this one question will encourage many stories to be written and will cause others to be rejected.

Furthermore, different papers have different standards. The local weekly, for instance, might use a story about sixth-graders on a class trip to the police station. However, the daily newspaper will usually reject such a story unless there's an unusual twist to it. Why? Because many sixth-grade classes visit police stations.

School officials complain that reporters don't know enough about the schools. Yet few school people understand the workings of a newspaper. To improve school-press relations, school administrators must gain information about how a newspaper operates.

Compile a Directory of Key News Contacts.
Keep a directory of various editors, photographers, and reporters. This directory should include office and home phone numbers and information about their working schedules and special interests. This will allow the school official to contact the proper people as soon as a news story is available.

Give Home Phone Numbers to Media Representatives.
Few things bother a reporter more than having part of a story and not being able to

get in touch with the knowledgeable person for other integral pieces of the story. School officials, especially the person in charge of community relations, should give the press the home phone numbers of school representatives. News releases should also list home phone numbers of the community relations person and key people mentioned in the releases. Then, when reporters rework their story, they can easily contact people for additional information.

THE ROLE OF REPORTERS

For most school officials, the reporters covering the school will be the people from the papers to know best. Understanding the roles and responsibilities of these reporters will assist educators in their relations with the press. Furthermore, good person-to-person relationships with reporters and editors can overcome fear of the press. A few specifics that should help school officials better understand the role of reporters follow:

■ Reporters seldom write headlines. On some small weekly newspapers, the reporter covering a board meeting might write a headline—as well as sell the advertising and do the proofreading. On most papers, however, the reporter writes the story, and someone else writes the headline. This is important to remember. More than one district has marred its relationship with a reporter by assuming that he or she was responsible for a headline that school officials considered negative.

■ Reporters aren't responsible for typographical errors. The detective on the police force was upset with the reporter when the story referred to him as a defective on the police farce. But it wasn't the reporter's fault. The proofreader missed the errors made by the typesetter. School officials must remember this when a tax increase of 2.2 mills is printed as 22 mills, or when 62 percent of the students achieving some success is printed as 6.2 percent.

■ Reporters also aren't the last ones to work on the story. After the reporter submits a story, usu-

ally at least one editor will read it and change it in some way.

Changes are made for a number of reasons. Editors may want to shorten the story to make room for other stories. In so doing, they may delete part of the story you and the reporter thought was important. Don't blame the reporter for this. Editors may want a different beginning (called the lead to the story), because of some other related news event, or simply because they feel that something other than what the reporter wrote first should be the lead. Remember, it is the editor's news judgment that determines what gets in the paper.

Help the Reporter

Reporters, like all of us, enjoy doing their job well. To help reporters do a better job, try these techniques:

■ Distribute a list of key school personnel, their responsibilities, and phone numbers to all reporters. Give basic data about the school, including enrollment, growth, calendar, and other information that reporters might be able to use.

■ If time does not permit preparation of as many stories as desired, periodically distribute a list of story ideas to all reporters. This list should contain ideas for stories, the people to contact, and their phone numbers. Of course the staff listed as contact people should be notified of this so they will be prepared for phone calls.

■ If a good news story that is not school-related is detected, offer it to reporters. They will appreciate the tip. This helps build the necessary rapport sought.

■ Alert reporters to an announcement that will be made soon. If possible, prepare background material that will enable them to do a more thorough job of reporting. For example, if the superintendent is going to announce at the board meeting a $250,000 grant to improve the teaching of reading, reporters will appreciate receiving as much information as possible about who presented the grant, how it was obtained, who will implement it, how pupils will benefit from it, where such an approach was tried before, and so forth.

— Remember the local reporters when news of statewide or national importance occurs. It's easy to forget the reporters on the local weekly and daily newspapers when wire service reporters or national television personalities seek information from you. The schools may have a once-in-a-lifetime opportunity to gain national recognition. Quite naturally, cooperation is required with those who request information about your schools, but remember that the local press must be taken care of. It's the local reporters who will cover the schools tomorrow and the day after tomorrow, and they should expect to receive special consideration when an extremely important story is available.

— Be selective in suggesting stories to reporters. Many newspapers are understaffed; therefore, reporters don't have time to pursue all possible stories. Just as editors dislike receiving news releases that contain little or no news, reporters resent spending time on possible stories that are little more than attempts to publicize personalities. Point out why a possible story merits a reporter's attention. If the reporter's background in education is weak, explain the educational angle that makes the story newsworthy.

— Issue a glossary of educational terms to reporters. Although this does not excuse school staff members from using understandable language, a reporter, armed with the glossary, might frequently avoid errors when reporting education news.

— Send all reporters a copy of the school district newsletter before the newsletter is distributed to the community. In fact, write a news release on one or two key newsletter stories and include the newsletter with the releases. Taxpayers who see the newsletter mentioned in the newspaper might look for it and read the articles referred to in the press.

— Treat all reporters with the same professional respect. Even though some reporters will be more cooperative than others, remember that public schools have a legal responsibility to provide all newspapers with the information that public right-to-know laws demand.

Because a particular school employee dislikes the treatment accorded the schools by a certain paper, he or she has no right to treat that paper's reporters with less than respect. The employee must not withhold public information from that newspaper's representatives and then offer the same information to a friendly reporter with a competing paper. All newspapers covering the schools have the same right to information coming from the schools. However, if a reporter has uncovered a special story that is not being developed by the school, school officials should not bring this information to the attention of competing reporters. This would justifiably anger the reporter who thought he or she had an exclusive story.

— If reporters err in reporting a story, give them a chance to correct the mistake, if indeed it's worth correcting. School officials who immediately go over the reporter's head to an editor will hardly improve their relationship with the reporter. No one likes to be told he or she was wrong by a boss. Thus, bringing the error to the editor will only alienate the reporter. Too many school officials overreact to errors in the press. A demanded retraction might win the battle, but it could very well lessen chances for winning the war.

Perhaps the reporter and school officials can correct an error without a retraction. For example, a story that implied that a better reference check should have been made on a teacher who was just dismissed could be followed a week later with a feature story showing the elaborate personnel procedures used before a candidate is hired.

Keep a file on the stories written by each reporter. If one reporter makes mistake after mistake, and school officials have done all they can to help him or her, the editor should be contacted. At a meeting with the editor, copies of the reporter's stories, with errors pointed out, should be shown to the editor. Doing this, it must be remembered, may prompt the reporter to look for problems in the schools with a previously unknown zeal, if a new reporter is not assigned to cover the schools.

■ If reporters have done an outstanding job, let them know it. Like all people, reporters enjoy praise. Don't hesitate to let their editors know about the quality of a particular story. Don't, however, thank a reporter for a story. Some reporters will interpret a thank you as some sort of sign that they overdid the story in the school's favor. And most reporters value their reputation for objectivity.

■ If a controversial story is breaking and reporters will be calling, prepare a statement that can be quickly given to them. This will do two things: first, it will enable comments to be consistent, and second, it will please reporters because a statement is ready. In fact, one of the most effective contributions to school-press relations is anticipation of what news is. By anticipating, educators can prepare positions and statements, clearly giving the impression that school officials are organized and know what they are doing.

Common Errors

Educators constantly admit their respect for the press, and yet they often treat the press with great disrespect. This leads to misunderstanding and frequently causes crises in the schools in their relationship with the papers, as well as with the community.

Good press relations suffer when such common errors as the following are made by school people:

■ Threatening, denouncing, and bringing pressure on the editor to print or withhold a story. Nothing produces friction faster and is resented more deeply by the editor.

■ Complaining when the facts of a story are reported incorrectly, when headlines give the wrong impression, or when individuals are misquoted. The remedy lies rather in friendly discussion, accurate copy, and sometimes an objective statement in the section on letters to the editor.

■ Refusing to release timely information to the press or pretending to be unacquainted with the details of a story. Such action creates suspicion and reflects unfavorably on the institution. The story will be published anyway without the cooperation of the school and the benefit of complete background material.

■ Sending out too many releases that do not have news value. Editors are pressed for time; they cannot waste it reviewing copy that belongs in the wastebasket.

■ Complaining if stories do not get published. It must be remembered that news selection is a function of the editor. They work under space limitations and publish whatever they believe will appeal most to readers.

■ Becoming emotional with reporters and editors over the publication of unfavorable news stories. School people must learn to accept the good and the bad in the normal flow of publicity.

■ Being drawn into controversies on a personal basis when the school is criticized or attacked in a news story. No board member or school official has the right to speak for the system unless authorized to do so.

■ Creating the impression that educators know more about reader interests than either the reporter or the editor. The persistence of this attitude is certain to antagonize the reporter and the editor.

■ Failing to invite the press to special school affairs that should be reported in the paper; or, having invited the press, failing to show the courtesy and hospitality that are expected.

■ Causing reporters to sit in the waiting room for a long time for an interview with a school official. If an interview must be delayed, word should be sent at once to the reporter. They have deadlines to meet and cannot afford to lose time under these circumstances.

THE PRESS AND SCHOOL BOARD MEETINGS

School boards and school administrators must be accountable for the way public funds are being spent. One of the ways to be accountable is through the press, and the relationships between school officials and reporters often determine the kind of coverage local newspapers provide.

Too many board members and administrators consider reporters as a necessary evil that must be tolerated. Often this attitude is communicated to reporters who are attempting to do their job. Some school officials give the impression to reporters that they are allowed at board meetings only through the courtesy of the board rather than as a right of our democratic government. Board members and school officials rightly feel that they are performing a community service as they work for better schools. Reporters, too, feel they are rendering a community service—one that informs readers of how public funds are being spent.

Before anyone becomes a board member or a school administrator, he or she should be aware of some key points in the school-press relationship. If these points are not learned from orientation meetings or from educational preparation, someone in the district should assume the responsibility for educating school officials before the initial board meeting.

Before the Board Meeting

The superintendent should prepare for board members a succinct summary of each important item on the agenda. This summary should be delivered to board members long enough before the public meeting to allow them to familiarize themselves with the main topics to be discussed. It should include a statement of the problem, possible solutions to the problem, and the superintendent's recommended solution. Inasmuch as board members are usually busy people, succinctness is appreciated. A more thorough, in-depth presentation of facts and background material should also be included in the materials presented to the board.

Before the board meeting, reporters will appreciate the chance to meet with the superintendent, the board president, or the school communications specialist. If the board meeting is held at night, the meeting with reporters might be held in the afternoon. At this meeting, the agenda could be discussed and resolutions given to reporters. Prepared statements and background materials could be distributed.

For example, if a grant is to be announced at the meeting, provide reporters with plenty of background information, such as the following: Where is the money coming from? Who will be responsible for implementing the program? Has it been tried elsewhere? When will it start? Who can provide additional information? All of this information will permit reporters to write thorough stories instead of hurried, incomplete stories pressured by deadlines and the unavailability of key personnel at midnight following the meeting.

One important reminder: Have someone contact all reporters if some board action is inconsistent with what was discussed in the afternoon session. Failing to do this can cause much embarrassment.

At the Meeting

Make reporters feel comfortable. Provide a press table somewhere near the action. Give reporters a copy of the agenda, and share with them copies of just about all materials board members have copies of. Only a few items might be considered confidential. With a copy of the agenda, reporters will be able to follow the actions of the board intelligently instead of groping for facts in a frustrated fashion.

Nothing alienates the press and the public more than executive sessions of the board. Reporters' adrenalin flows at the mention of an executive session. If they think the board is trying to block the public's right to know about public business, they will move into high gear to ferret out the behind-the-scenes undertakings. Secret meetings, and that's what the public considers executive sessions, will guarantee a bad press. Avoid them as much as possible, especially on the same night of the regular public meeting. Be sure you respect public meeting laws.

School officials with excellent press relations might consider inviting the press to attend an executive session on an off-the-record basis. This can do two things: first, it will communicate clearly that the board is not discussing in private something that should be public; and second, it will indicate to reporters that you trust them and want to cooperate with them. To attempt this, school officials must enjoy a sound relationship with the press.

Schedule something of educational interest at each meeting. The press will love you for it. Too many meetings have required the reporters' presence for four or five long hours, and the only story has been about a dull subject such as who received the fuel bid or about flooring for a new building.

Every meeting should include a brief report on some phase of the school curriculum. The educator making the presentation should limit the report to a half hour and should have copies of pertinent materials for the press. Reporters will usually write a story on the innovation or progress taking place in the schools because the story has news merit.

During the meeting, the communications specialist or someone appointed as the board's press representative should be available to provide needed materials and to answer questions. Each board member should be clearly identified. This will eliminate the possibility of a quote being attributed to the wrong person.

Taping board meetings sometimes helps school officials and audience members choose their words more carefully. It also reminds everyone that everything said at a public meeting is public information. Nothing is off the record at a public meeting. After the meeting, school officials should be available to the press to respond to questions. Radio stations may want to record a brief news spot early in the morning. Someone from the schools should work with the stations on this.

THE NEWS CONFERENCE

The news conference, when properly prepared, can be an effective vehicle to communicate an important news event to the press. Improperly handled, it can backfire, causing immeasurable harm to the relationship between schools and the press. The most obvious consideration when deciding to hold a news conference is whether the reason is sufficiently newsworthy to justify taking reporters' valuable time. A news conference that results in little or no solid news for reporters prompts justifiable criticism and ensures sparse attendance at the next conference.

Planning the Conference

Once it's decided to call a news conference, notify all newspapers. If time permits, notify them with a memo; a phone call follow-up serves as a friendly reminder. The conference should be scheduled for a time that is convenient for the press. This means knowing deadlines of the various papers and planning the conference at a time when editors can spare a reporter. Although most schools will hold such conferences infrequently, conference times should be carefully planned to give equal time breaks to the various papers. This kind of fairness is respected by all concerned, even though some reporters and editors will try to get the break all the time. They are merely doing their job, attempting to do what's best for their employer, but they will respect fairness.

News conferences must be held at a time when the news has time value. However, if the luxury of time is available, a good day to hold a news conference is a day when other news may not be occurring in great quantity. For example, the fifth anything of a month would usually be an excellent day for a news conference. Few town governing bodies meet on the fifth Monday or Tuesday of the month. Thus, little other news is forthcoming, allowing more room for news from the schools.

An often overlooked phase of preparation is anticipating the kinds of questions that will be posed by alert reporters. Someone in the school district, preferably the person responsible for press relations, should play devil's advocate. This necessitates asking the kinds of controversial questions that reporters will pose. School officials who are not ready to field tough questions should not announce news conferences. An invitation to a news conference is an invitation to probe all areas related to the topic of the conference.

At the Conference

Distribute a kit of information and materials to all reporters who attend. This is a time-saving idea that also ensures that key statements are received accurately. If a new superintendent is being appointed, the kit should include a photo plus a biography and some of his or her statements on key educational issues in the community.

At the conference, the key person should be surrounded by knowledgeable assistants who will be able to provide specifics as needed. For example, the superintendent should be able to call on an assistant superintendent to explain an important curricular change if the news conference will include discussion of curriculum in a new school.

Reporters should feel comfortable at the conference, knowing that extra pencils, paper, and other materials are provided. Reporters pressured by a deadline should know where phones are and that the phones will be available to them. They should always be given the full names—check out spelling, of course—of conference participants. Phone numbers, both at school and at home, should also be provided. Participants should be alerted to the possibility that reporters might call later with questions.

After the Conference

Someone should be responsible for obtaining additional facts requested by reporters. This person should be known by the reporters, who should have no reluctance about calling him or her at a later date.

Reporters who couldn't attend should be able to obtain a kit and the basic information distributed at the conference. Most reporters feel, however, that information elicited by a probing

question from a reporter privately after the conference should not be made available to those not attending.

DRAFTING A NEWS RELATIONS PLAN

A detailed plan of action is necessary for an effective news relations program. This means more than assigning someone the responsibility of "getting some stories in the newspapers." An effective program should incorporate the following questions as it develops a direction for its operation: What do people want to know about the schools? How can we find out what's happening in our schools? How can we ensure that our news gets to the media? What do we want to happen as a result of our news relations program?

Answering these questions will prompt educators to look seriously at the content of news releases. It will necessitate the development of a news gathering system that brings news to school officials who can disseminate it. It will stir ways to prepare materials that the media will use, and it will demand a periodic evaluation of the news release program.

WHAT PEOPLE WANT TO KNOW ABOUT THE SCHOOLS

If one of the objectives of the news relations program is to generate public support for school needs, it is necessary to determine which topics taxpayers perceive as important. Thus, if the people are concerned with guidance and discipline, news releases about educational trips of administrators will do little to effect the desired support.

Determining what people want to know about the schools is vital before other phases of the news relations program can be developed. Chapter 3 explained a number of methods for obtaining feedback on school issues, and these can be implemented to find out possible news topics that should be considered.

Interest in what parents and other taxpayers want to know about the schools began as early as 1929. Farley, studying 5,600 people in 13 cities, determined that parents are primarily concerned with pupil progress, achievement, instructional methods, and courses of study.[2]

Since then, many studies have been reported, showing that parents are primarily interested in curriculum and that other taxpayers care most about discipline and costs.

It is more important to know what taxpayers in your community want to know than to know what other taxpayers in other locations in another era cared about, however. Once school officials have determined the interests of the community, a planned program to provide information on those topics can be undertaken.

FOREIGN-LANGUAGE NEWSPAPERS

In addition to preparing materials for English-speaking audiences, school officials in some schools must be cognizant of groups that do not speak and understand English. To serve these groups, some school districts take advantage of foreign-language newspapers. Working closely with editors of these newspapers, school officials prepare articles in time for translation. Or, in some cases, they use a staff member to provide the translation for the newspapers. Urban areas, especially, may be faced with the communications challenge of a Spanish-speaking and a Chinese-speaking audience that would not be served by the usual communications channels. It is the wise educator who provides information for these groups in their language. This might mean extra effort for school administrators, but the effort extended should reap the reward of better overall support for the schools. Some newspapers feature one column written in a language of interest to a large segment of the readership. School officials should seek such columns and capitalize on their availability.

Some schools offer newsletters written in two languages or print part of each newsletter with articles written in a second language. Such efforts clearly communicate that school officials care about the people served. It is important that the person responsible for the non-English portion know the language and its nuances well.

NEWS TOPICS IN YOUR SCHOOLS

Reporters who cover schools can tell of school officials who said they had no news when called. Other reporters will tell of visits to schools that elicited an "I know we have no news stories here, but you're welcome to look around" comment. Usually the reporters leave with enough ideas for stories to keep busier than they want to be.

The difference between the reporters and most school officials in this case is a simple one: The reporter recognizes news, and the school official doesn't.

School news may be defined as information that is of interest to the public. It may be information that people wish to know about the school as well as information they *should* know in order to judge intelligently the value of the institution and its work.

Since school news must compete daily with material from hundreds of other sources for newspaper space, it must be newsworthy. Newsworthiness means that the information contains elements that make it readable—news that the press will accept and the public will read.

Occasionally an educator will be disappointed when a news release about a school play fails to be printed in the area daily newspaper. This disappointment sometimes leads to a negative attitude toward the newspaper that culminates in a do nothing approach as far as preparing other stories. The daily newspaper, meanwhile, would probably appreciate receiving well-written articles on school topics readers would like to read.

Timeliness Is Important

Be sure the average reader won't have a "so-what" reaction to any story submitted. To avoid such a reaction, you should analyze why particular articles in the newspaper seem to interest readers.

First of all, to be of news value, the story should be timely. Daily newspapers, especially, want stories as they happen. Something that happened yesterday might not be news for tomorrow's daily. Thus, it's imperative that someone in the schools know how to alert the press when the stories are still fresh. A news release sent on February 14 about a "recent" Thanksgiving party held by a class will be rejected rapidly. Worse, it will indicate to newspaper people that the school is ignorant of what news is.

The local weekly newspaper may not have stringent standards for timeliness. Shopper specials, which feature advertisements rather than timely news, may also accept articles that miss the daily newspapers' standards for timeliness.

If it is possible to relate a news item about the school to something of national or general interest, the timeliness factor can be enhanced. For instance, high-school students studying political parties and elections would be of more interest around election time than at any other time. A story about the study of a particular foreign language might be especially timely if the U.S. president is presently visiting a country that speaks that language.

If It's Unusual, It's News

Frequently a news story is news simply because it is unusual. Readers want to know about stories that occur for the first time or that have an angle or circumstance that makes them something out of the ordinary. For example, a class of students giving their teacher a report card and evaluating the kind of teaching done would be an unusual enough twist for an effective story. If done on the same day that students received their own report cards, the feature could lend itself to all kinds of interesting quotes. After attracting the editor's attention (and the readers' attention too) with the unusualness of the story, the educator could explain how the report is part of an overall program to encourage teachers to determine how students perceive their teaching. It might be explained that

feedback from students in specific areas will encourage teachers to continue certain practices and to modify others.

If It's Local, It Could Be News

Readers are concerned about what's happening in their community. A murder in a distant city seldom attracts and holds the interest of the average reader. However, one attack in a reader's neighborhood stirs reader concern. Thus, a school's initiating a computerized busing schedule could be news in the local newspaper even though the story has appeared hundreds of times in other communities. Statewide test scores showing the achievements of fourth-grade students may be of limited interest to readers. Yet, the same kinds of scores for the local school system would prompt appreciable reader interest.

Finding ways to give a local angle for a national story can increase the number of stories used by an area newspaper. For example, if a national association of English teachers passes a resolution advocating a certain approach to teaching writing, the school district can release a statement from the English department chairperson giving the district's views on the resolution. Because the statement is coming from someone in the community, it possesses the local flavor editors are seeking.

The concept of local news can be carried to the extreme in the local weekly newspaper or in the area shopper newspaper. This kind of publication usually depends on advertising as its primary service to readers, and news content commands a minimum of attention. Therefore, it is easier to place local stories with little solid news value in such papers. For instance, a list of students who went on a field trip might be printed in the shopper or another weekly. Obviously the daily newspapers responsible for a larger area of coverage do not have space for such material. Local weekly newspapers can also be effectively used for internal morale purposes. Teachers or other staff members seeing their name in any newspaper must feel that the administration likes the undertaking written about.

Names Make News

The cliché "names make news" is not always true. Yet an important person can make a story significant. Thus, a superintendent's issuing a statement about reading in the schools takes on more importance than a similar statement made by someone with less responsibility. If a representative of the state education agency visits the school and praises a new program in career education, this would be newsworthy. The fact that the visitor possesses a state title makes his or her name and statements of some importance to local newspapers.

Every quote in a news story, of course, must be attributed to someone. It is not acceptable, for example, to include the following statement in a news release: "The Sharpkirk Schools are without a doubt the best in the country." Such a statement must be made by someone. If it is not attributed, it will be discarded by most newspapers.

The more important the person making the statement, the better the chance of the statement's appearing in newspapers. Names almost always make news in local weekly newspapers. A list of students named to the honor roll or a group of pupils who went on a field trip will usually be printed by the small weekly newspaper even though the larger daily newspapers don't have room. When preparing such a list, double check to be sure that names are spelled properly. Everyone enjoys seeing his or her name in the newspaper—especially if it's spelled right (and providing it is good news, not bad). Also, check thoroughly to ensure that all students who should be on the list do appear on it.

Innovation Is News

Anything being initiated in the schools could be newsworthy. If it's being done in a way that differs from the way it was done when most of the readers attended school, the topic could rate newspaper consideration. When preparing a news release about an innovation, the educator should look for those bits of information that will appeal to the largest number of readers. This guideline, of course, should be applied to all newswriting.

A new approach to teaching science, a new way to correct tests, a novel approach to gym class, or the use of a common teaching device in a different way can all be considered innovations, and as such, they merit news consideration. Obvious questions will be posed by readers when an innovation is announced. The educator must keep these in mind when explaining the introduction of an innovation. For example: How much does it cost? Has it been used elsewhere, and if so, was it effective? How will it help students learn better? Who decided to adopt the innovation? How will it be evaluated? This last question is one that has gained prominence since accountability became a vital part of education.

Evaluation Is News

As accountability continues to gain importance in education, evaluation must claim appreciably more attention in overall communications and public relations efforts. Evaluation means tests or some measures that can be applied to determine if certain approaches or materials are working. Some schools have been making results of standardized tests known to the public for years. Other school administrators cringe at the suggestion of such score-sharing with the public. Despite the numerous arguments of those opposed to making evaluations known to the public, the trend is toward disclosure.

The releasing of evaluation information requires a large amount of homework by the school administrator who is inexperienced in this area. Releasing such data without sufficient explanation can severely harm the school's relationship with the community and with the press. Most reporters and most laypersons simply do not understand the terminology used by educators in the field of testing. However, those same reporters and readers are intently interested in what the tests or other evaluations show about their schools. The help of a guidance or testing expert can ensure a fuller explanation. Yet, this is not enough. Just as important is the involvement of someone who understands the kinds of questions that reporters and laypersons will ask. By anticipating these questions, the educator can prepare a news release or an in-depth series that provides information that people want to read.

Most readers will not enjoy statistic after statistic. More important would be an explanation of what the statistics mean or what the options are. For example, when evaluations are being published, school officials can use the opportunity to focus on programs and materials that are needed to improve a certain phase of instruction. If the educator doesn't offer possible solutions to obvious problems, laypersons will conclude that the educator lacks the answer. It is better to take the offensive in this situation rather than to react defensively later to the inevitable criticisms.

Controversy Is News

Educators generally overreact to school news that is controversial or negative. Yet, people enjoy reading about controversy; and if readers want it, newspapers will print it. School officials can use this knowledge to their benefit by preparing news articles about the schools that show both sides of a story. This kind of news release is quickly accepted by editors and is well read by taxpayers. It shows that educators do consider more than one approach to solving a problem. A good example of showing alternatives that could be controversial would be the possible ways to close schools in response to falling enrollment. By explaining the various strengths and weaknesses of each possibility in some detail, school officials can demonstrate that various solutions have been considered.

Money Is News

An increase in school taxes is always news because it involves the money of many taxpayers.

Thus, newspapers will constantly seek information about school undertakings that seem to cost more money than others. Reporters have been trained to seek specifics regarding the new school budget or a proposed referendum for a new building. Educators who give the impression of trying to dodge legitimate questions from reporters in these areas will suffer a credibility problem. Thus, it's imperative that school officials prepare elaborate explanations of budget requests for reporters.

If possible, translate dollars into programs. For example, if two new speech therapists are being requested in a budget, explain in a news release that the two therapists will enable X children to improve their speech habits. Explain specifically what two new people, if approved, will do to improve the overall educational offerings of the school system. And after the therapists have been on the job for a while, don't forget about them. Issue a news release showing what the extra $50,000 in the budget has produced in terms of learning. Taxpayers like to see what their money has bought.

When dealing with money items, remember that the average taxpayer has little knowledge of the school budget. Most people assume that the segment of the budget used for instruction pays only for teachers. They do not realize that instructional materials and other items are included in this portion of the budget. Also misunderstood in some schools is the board secretary, who handles key school board responsibilities. Yet many taxpayers balk at the salary because they think the secretary is someone who takes dictation and types.

New Positions Are News

Every time a new position is established, a lengthy explanation of the rationale for establishing it should be provided in a news release. How will this position help students? Why couldn't the responsibility be assumed by someone now on the staff? What kinds of specific responsibilities will the person have? Do similar positions exist in comparable school systems? How will the position improve education in the school system?

When every tax dollar counts, school officials must be ready to justify the creation of a new position. The most effective way is to show, before the person is appointed to the position, how the job will enable the schools to do certain things better. This should be done before it appears as if the administration is on the defensive.

Anticipation of Consequences Is News

A good reporter reacts to a news story by anticipating what will happen as a result of the event triggering that story. School officials too can provide interesting news by attempting to determine what the consequences of a news story about education will be.

For example, a grant being announced to help children with reading problems is news in itself. A follow-up story might feature what is anticipated with the acquiring of the grant. How many children will be affected? What kind of improvement can be hoped for? Will the grant money indirectly assist other programs, or will it be limited to the children specified in the grant?

Another effective approach is to anticipate local consequences of national news about education. For instance, if the president plans to veto a bill providing funds for children of employees working at certain federal government locations, district officials should anticipate local consequences and provide that information to the press.

School administrators should read weekly and monthly publications that provide news on nationwide education. This enables school administrators to keep up with new trends in education, to anticipate problems, and to write knowledgeably for education releases.

TYPES OF STORIES

Newspaper stories are usually divided into two types: the hard (or straight) news story and the feature story. Columns, photographic stories, editorials, letters to the editor, and fillers are other important ways to get school information in newspapers.

The News Story

The hard (or straight) news story is a straightforward account of a happening. It presents the facts in an objective way, and the style is impersonal, direct, and uncolored. It answers the standard questions of *who, what, why, when,* and *where* about an event or happening. Some stories require inclusion of the *how* to complete the story. Details of the story are arranged in decreasing order of importance. This is done because editors seldom have enough space to run the entire story as presented. Frequently stories must be shortened, and the easiest way is to omit the last paragraph or the last two or three. This points out the necessity of placing the most important facts early in the story.

The straight news story can be of different types. It can be an advance story, which tells as much as possible about an upcoming event. It can be a cover story, which relates in detail what took place at the event. This usually is reported the same day the event took place or on the day after. The follow-up story could report reactions of those attending the event and ideas they have implemented as a result of having attended the event.

The Feature Story

The feature story presents factual information, but does so in an interesting and lively way, frequently with a human interest touch. Although the feature story is considered more difficult to write than the hard news story, the feature does allow the writer to be more creative. It also permits emotional content and perspective to be included in the story. Built around some unique aspect of an event or a personality, it is designed to evoke a smile or laugh, to appeal to the imagination, or to stir the emotions of the reader. The supply of feature stories in any school is limited only by the number of people and ideas available. Some topics for feature stories might be a day in the life of a teacher, the first day of school for a kindergarten child, the role of the school secretary, reactions of first-graders to their trip to an orchard, a pen-pal relationship of students with students in a foreign country, unusual projects undertaken by science class students, views of eighth-graders regarding career education, or a comparison of today's sophomores with those of twenty years ago as seen by teachers who taught both groups. The list is endless. Figure 11.1 shows a sample feature article.

The Special Column

The newspaper column is an often overlooked vehicle for communicating school news. The column can be used in two ways: either by providing information to newspaper columnists or by school personnel writing a regular column. Local weekly newspapers will often welcome a column written by the superintendent. Such a column allows opinion and provides a constant opportunity to inform readers about topics of the superintendent's choosing. Newspaper columnists are always looking for topics. They constantly face deadlines and always appreciate having the embryo of a story idea. Every columnist faces days when the ideas are scarce, and a call from a school official suggesting a column topic would be greatly appreciated on such a day. To enhance the chance of making the suggestion one that results in a column, the educator should read all area or local columnists' writings to recognize the kinds of stories that might appeal to each writer.

The Photographic Story

This is a visual era, as evidenced by films, television, and photojournalism. Thus, a good photograph commands the attention of editor and reader alike. The photographic story consistently attracts large readership. Even the reader who spends little time with the newspaper usually notices photographs and their captions. Readership surveys consistently show that people like to look at pictures and prefer them to the printed word. People apparently feel that they can grasp the meaning of a photo more quickly than the meaning of a story, and they feel that what they see is more truthful than what they read.

Editors want pictures that will meet their papers' requirements. Although requirements differ somewhat on minor features, there is fairly general agreement on the major points. First of all, a picture must be photographically sound. It cannot be too dark, too light, misty, or blurred. The details must stand out clearly against a background that is appropriate for a particular story. Second, the composition must be good. Good composition is an arrangement of persons and objects that catches the eye and draws attention to the focal point of the picture. Third, the content of the picture must be important. Content is judged with reference to the people involved and their prominence regarding reader interest. Content is also judged with reference to news value. The picture may be something that is timely—for example, a demolition crew tearing down old houses to make way for a new school. It may show something people want to see—perhaps a senior high-school student being awarded a national prize for an outstanding science effort. Whatever the picture shows, it must be news for the newspapers to use it.

Photos should show action. Children are ideal subjects for pictures, and they are constantly doing things that make attractive pictures. Posed pictures should be avoided, as should pictures with a large number of people in them. Subjects in a picture should look natural, and the pictures should be representative of what's happening in the school. Stilted, posed pictures can contribute to a communications credibility problem that every educator must overcome. Most photographers suggest that more than five people in a picture makes the picture generally unappealing. Three people would be better, and one or two would be preferred in most circumstances. For instance, a shot of the entire school orchestra in

---

'FUN AND EXCITING'

A New Approach to School Menus

LINCOLN, Neb. (UPI)—Can the nation's youth be taught to eat the right kinds of food?

The Nebraska Education Department says yes.

But not by having them stand up in class and read from those old health books that spell out the "basic four" food groups and all the vitamins and minerals each group contains.

"Reading about Sally getting up and eating eggs for breakfast in a 20-year-old health book just isn't going to cut it anymore," said Ray Steinert.

Since last January, the department has been experimenting with an approach to nutrition education that has been found highly promising. It is nearing the general use phase in Nebraska.

"The entire nation is looking at it," Steinert said.

The experiment is being financed by the U.S. Department of Agriculture which, Steinert noted, has long been interested in nutrition for children. Steinert heads the USDA's school lunch division in Nebraska.

Based on the notion that kids generally just don't eat right, the USDA, through the years, has tried to remedy the situation, at least in the school lunchroom.

The USDA not only establishes its "Type A" lunchroom menu but also determines how much of each food is to be served each youngster, and then provides some commodities for preparing the lunches.

But Steinert said serving nutritious foods and getting youngsters to eat them were two different things. Such foods as broccoli and even apricots wound up in the garbage can.

The new approach to teaching nutrition in the classroom begins by throwing away the health books. Mrs. Glenda Uhrmacher, project director, said they really afforded little more than oral reading and memorization practice anyway.

The new idea is to make food "fun and exciting," she added.

An initial list of 30 highly nutritious foods was put together and served in lunchrooms with particular emphasis on foods discarded.

Mrs. Uhrmacher said it was found out early that many were thrown away not because youngsters had developed a real dislike for them but because the children "had a tendency to be afraid of new foods."

FIGURE 11.1 Example of a feature story. Reprinted by permission of United Press International.

action would be unappealing and unusable as far as most editors are concerned. However, a close-up of one orchestra member or of a small section of the orchestra might be effective.

When taking pictures for newspapers, try to take pictures when students are not aware of it. If the subjects are aware, direct them not to stare at the camera. One major "must" for taking school pictures: Be sure children appear in all of them. Judges for a national school publications contest were appalled at the large number of school pictures that failed to include a child. The picture should also focus on one central point, avoiding the tempting idea of including two or three ideas in one photo. Backgrounds for pictures should be simple, not "busy." The background, unless it is

an integral part of the story, should not be so distracting that it detracts from the intent of the photo.

A collection of action shots can, with a small amount of copy, provide an excellent photofeature. Usually the newspaper will take the photos if given the story idea. If the newspaper has assigned a photographer to a school story, someone at the school should have the responsibility of meeting the photographer and working with the staff involved in the picture. The photographer is usually on a tight time schedule. Helping him or her get to the photo location and assisting with name spellings and other information will establish the kind of relationship that every school official would like.

In addition to photofeature stories, educators can use photos to illustrate hard news and feature stories. When writing captions for such photos, remember that the photo and caption will sometimes be used without the accompanying copy. Thus, include the basic news information in a succinct caption. Schools have learned that it pays to maintain a file from which pictures can be pulled at a moment's notice. They keep on hand photos of school officials, teachers, student leaders, new buildings, laboratories, and action photos. A file can be built with the cooperation of the photo staff of school publications. Frequently an editor of a local paper will select a story with an accompanying photo, even if the photo is simply a head and shoulder shot of an official, over a competing story that may be a bit better. Why? Because the photo helps break up the page of copy, and is therefore more attractive to readers.

When sending photos to newspapers, find out the particular paper's requirements. Do they only accept black-and-white prints? What size do they prefer? Will they process your film if you send it to them? Will they use self-developing film? Some newspapers have rigid rules for the action in the pictures they will run. For example, some newspapers will never run a picture of a gavel being passed or people shaking hands. Know these restrictions before preparing pictures that might be rejected. Further, when mailing photos, be sure they arrive the way editors like them. This means no paper clips and no heavy writing on the backs of the photos. Use a grease pencil if you want to write on the back of the photo. Better yet, attach (with paper cement) a double-spaced caption that identifies what's going on, without marring the photo. Photos should be protected in the envelope by cardboard to prevent their being damaged in handling. Handstamp instructions should be placed on the envelope. If a different picture is being sent to each paper, say so. Chances of the picture's being used are greater if the editor knows it won't appear in another paper.

Editorials

The editorial is a type of story in which opinions are expressed by the newspaper on public questions. On most large daily newspapers, editorials are written without the input of local educators. However, reporters' opinions are sometimes sought, and if the reporters have good rapport with educators, solid, helpful information can be provided to the editorial writers. In some instances, editorial writers will contact local education leaders for information before writing education editorials. The public's right to know about school issues, bond issues, career education, reading methods, accountability, test scores, student militancy, and teacher rights makes all these good subjects for editorials. Like all writers who face daily deadlines, editorial writers occasionally experience days when ideas come slowly. An occasional suggestion from an educator, with accompanying accurate information, would usually be accepted and used.

The weekly newspaper, unlike the large daily, will usually gratefully accept editorial ideas. Some newspapers, in fact, will go so far as to run editorials on education topics written by local school officials. It is incumbent on school officials, in this case, to be accurate at all times to protect the reputation of the newspaper and the school.

Letters to the Editor

Letters to the editor are views expressed by readers on questions of current interest, published by newspapers under such titles as "Voices of the People," "What People Think," and "Letters to the Editor." These letters rank high in reader interest. Letters to the editor have several uses in the school's newspaper publicity campaign. One use is to evaluate school interests of some people in the community. Although not necessarily representative of the community's thinking, letters to the editor do indicate how some people feel about certain school officials.

Letters to the editor also provide an excellent opportunity for expressing appreciation for services rendered to the school. Municipal officials who speak to classes on government, parents who help in a study of school building needs, or civic groups who cooperate in a scholarship program can be publicly thanked in this fashion. The general public can be thanked by school officials for attendance at school functions or for participation in some special school undertaking. The administrator will find that it pays to write a letter now and then commending the newspaper for fine coverage of significant school events and happenings.

Occasionally a school official may wish to correct an error in the newspaper or respond to criticism with a letter to the editor. This decision, however, must be made on the individual merits of each case. Most school public relations practitioners agree that a verbal battle in the letter-to-the-editor-section seldom increases public confidence in educators. If the chief school administrator, for example, challenges a critic, the general public will usually side with the underdog against the public official. There are times, however, when a letter to the editor is in order. An example would be if a citizen's letter to the editor accused a drama coach of pocketing funds from student plays. If such an accusation were false, the administrator should explain the disposition of the money in a letter to the editor. Under no circumstances, however, should school officials take up serious criticisms or attempt to meet destructive attacks through letters to the editor. There are better ways to solve such problems without running the risk of engaging in open conflict that does little more than stir animosity and sell newspapers.

Filler

A seldom used but effective means of telling the school story is through the use of filler. Filler consists of brief statements that newspapers employ to fill columns when their stories are slightly short. Instead of a blank space appearing, the newspaper will insert a filler. Usually fillers are purchased from news services and are used with little or no thought to their content. In fact, filler selections are ordinarily made by their length rather than by what they have to say. Filler items, as prepared by the news services, are usually of little or no interest to local readers. For example, the fillers might note an increase in gin consumption in the United States in the past year.

Most local newspapers would be pleased to receive and use filler prepared by the local schools. Filler items should be brief, double-spaced, ranging from two to six typewritten lines. They should contain a headline that would fit in one column of the local newspaper in the point size used by that newspaper for such items. The content can include just about any information about the schools, local or national. Of course local items are preferred by the newspapers. However, sometimes national items can be used with a local tie-in. Filler of this nature tends to keep the schools in the news and also serves as a plus for internal public relations. Many of the ideas submitted for news stories do not merit a news release, yet they can be used for filler.

Here is an example of a filler that a school system could use.

Books Increase

A larger enrollment required more textbooks in the Blankville Schools. This year some 52,000 texts are being used by 8,400 students.

(Computers used by some newspapers make the filler concept obsolete. Check with editors to see if they still use filler.)

NEWS SOURCES

News is found everywhere in the school system. There is never a scarcity of it. For every story published, a dozen more could be written containing important information. A checklist, like the following, indicates sources from which stories may be drawn. If the checklist is developed with the aid of professional reporters, it will be richer in ideas and practical suggestions, besides having the further value of familiarizing the reporters with the makeup and operation of the school system. Referring to the checklist leads to better copy and broader coverage.

Checklist of News Sources

Administrative Activities
  Board meetings
  Board actions
  Board members
  Board elections
  Board officers
  Speaking engagements
  Programs under consideration
  Addresses made
  Recognition received
  New administrators
  Surveys conducted
  Changes in organization
Choosing which school to attend
  Cost of education
  Record systems
  School budget
  Decline in number of employees
  Interviews with board members
  Interviews with administrators
  School calendar
  Slogans adopted
  Research studies
  Educational needs
  Long-range challenges
  Attendance at conferences
  Participation in community projects
Classroom Activities
  Field trips and excursions
  Methods of teaching
  Curriculum study
  Curriculum changes
  Testing program
  Results of testing
  Special study projects
  Exhibits
  Demonstrations

New instructional materials
Textbook selection
Library references
New equipment
Trends in teaching practices
Promotion policies
New techniques and devices
Work of supervisors
Homework policies
Evaluating pupil progress
Parent participation
Provision for handicapped children
Guidance suggestions
Course offerings
Educational objectives
Humorous incidents
Unusual happenings
Success stories of individual children
Character development
Community Activities
  Services to community
  Use of community resources
  Citizen participation in school program
  Special lay committees
  School-community projects
  Staff participation in community affairs
  Cooperation with community groups
  Community surveys and opinion polls
Activities of Graduates
  Business success
  Special awards and honors
  Reunions
  Acts of valor
  Success in college
  Contributions to school
  Alumni programs
  Marriages and births
  Opinions on school questions
  Citizenship activities
  Participation in community affairs
  Services to community
  Vocational outlook
  Work after school
Staff Activities
  Scholarships, awards, and special honors
  New members
  Exchange teachers
  Summer activities
  Acts of bravery

Leaves of absence
Professional interests
Avocational interests
Weddings
Births in family
In-service education
Attendance at conferences
Activities in community
Retirement
Visiting educators
Rewards of teaching
Special talents
Offices in professional organizations
Books and articles written
Promotions
· Biographical material
Deaths
Speeches
Donations to charity
Parent Activities
   Parent-teacher association programs
   Services to the school
   Conferences with parents
   Participation in school
   Special parent projects
   Parent publications
   Officers of parent-teacher association
   Attendance at educational conferences
Plant Activities
   New building construction
   New building financing
   New building locations
   Sale of a building
   Features of new buildings
   Community use of buildings
   Special recreation programs for adults
   Building maintenance
   New installations
   Dedicatory exercises
   Safety measures
   Renovations and extensions
Pupil Activities
   Academic achievement
   Career education
   Scholarships, awards, and special honors
   Hobby interests
   Success in special fields
   Outstanding talent
   School clubs

Musical programs
Athletic events
Various contests
Assembly programs
Student council
Pageants and festivals
Good deeds and acts of valor
Attendance
Graduation exercises
Special projects
Opening of school
Donations to charity
Speeches
Special Activities
   Open house programs
   Observances—birthdays, holidays,
     special weeks
   Operation of cafeteria
   History of school
   Demonstrations and exhibits
   School bus service
   Visits by celebrities
   Guidance facilities
   Drives and campaigns
   Outstanding graduate selects teacher who
     influenced life
   Research projects
   Health measures
   Teaching homebound pupils
   School camp

Useful suggestions may be obtained from the checklist for creating news. By creating news is meant the actual bringing about of an incident or event that has news value. Sometimes this is called manufactured news. Newspapers manufacture news quite commonly in an effort to supply their readers with interesting, informative, and legitimate stories. For instance, an editor might manufacture a story by polling a number of parents on the question of whether or not teenagers have too much freedom. After the story is published, it might be used as a basis for an editorial, and the editorial might prompt, in turn, a flood of letters to the editor.

Schools have many opportunities for creating their own news. An activity might be initiated because it has news interest, or a scheduled event handled differently to increase its news value. As examples, an assembly to honor outstanding graduates would have more news interest if a large number of graduates were in the audience. In celebrating the fiftieth birthday of the school, the news value would be higher if responsibility for the celebration was shared with community leaders. Perhaps the parent-teacher association is about to donate a new piece of equipment for testing the hearing of pupils. By making the presentation a public affair, with a prominent hearing specialist present, the story would receive more favorable attention.

NEWS ORGANIZATIONS

No matter whether a school system is large or small, some form of organization is necessary to provide news. In larger systems, news responsibility is usually divided between a communications director and the individual principals. The person responsible for communications or community relations may be known by a variety of titles. Among them are assistant superintendent in charge of communications and coordinator (or director) of community relations, public information, or public relations. The person responsible for handling communications is generally charged with news originating from the board of education or central administration. In addition, this person provides leadership for other departments and personnel, helping them understand what news is and how to get it to the media.

The communications person also arranges interviews with key school personnel and builds rapport with reporters and editors. To help identify news stories, he or she usually develops a news collecting network; to do this, each principal appoints someone in the building to work with the communications person. Frequently this person is a teacher. In some school systems, the principal sends the information or news release to local media with a copy to the public relations director. In other systems, all news is sent to the public relations person, who then filters it or embellishes it before sending it to the media. This process is commonly used in most school districts. To encourage teachers and other employees to suggest news, easy-to-use forms are placed near staff mailboxes (see Figure 11.2) and the "it's just as easy as a phone call" approach is used. This approach ensures coverage of all schools in the system, immediate reports of stories that break, and the professional treatment of releases.

If the director of community relations is employed on a part-time basis, then he or she may find it expedient to turn the material from building representatives over to a high-school English or journalism class, especially in cases where news is compiled weekly for a school page in the local newspaper. Members of the class edit the material and write releases under the guidance of the teacher, who is often the person in charge of community relations. Copy is checked for news content and style of presentation, and the better stories are selected for publication. Important news from administrative offices is taken care of by the director of community relations.

It is common in small districts for the superintendent or supervising principal to serve as the news representative for the school system. Success in publicizing and interpreting the educational program depends on a sense for news, the ability to write interesting copy, and the time

---

NEWS REPORTING FORM

Name of school _____ Date _____
Who _____
What _____
Why _____
When _____
Where _____
How _____
Picture possibilities _____ _____
Remarks _____
Reporter _____ Phone _____

FIGURE 11.2 Form for news reporting.

invested in the work. Generally, too few heads of school systems know how to gather and report the news, and most such officials are overburdened with other administrative duties. When this situation prevails, various other news-gathering possibilities should be considered. Among these would be appointing an interested teacher to the position of publicity director with an allowance made in the instructional load, for the extra time involved plus extra compensation for the additional responsibility. Although this arrangement was successfully used for quite a few years, it has been used less and less recently. The reluctance stems from the problem faced when the teachers negotiate and sometimes strike. When this happens, the teacher serving as part-time public relations coordinator is placed in an almost impossible position.

Another possibility would be appointing a retired community resident who has journalistic or photography skills. Such people will usually be glad to help the schools and will be happy about having some part-time work. Salary can be negotiated on an individual basis. College students majoring in journalism or graduate students working in related fields may be looking for part-time employment and would usually be agreeable to specific writing assignments. The possibility also exists of tapping the talent of graduate school interns with ability in this field. It is sometimes possible to develop a relationship with area colleges and universities that will enable a district to establish a graduate-assistantlike relationship with a student. Such a student might work twenty hours a week for the school district in return for tuition and some compensation.

However the news-gathering network is established, it is essential that all employees know that the person seeking news is doing so for the superintendent. A teacher, for instance, who is viewed as a colleague by other teachers and clerical staff and administrators might experience difficulty extracting needed information when seen as wearing the hat of the teacher only. The superintendent must communicate clearly to all concerned that the publicity person is acting on his or her behalf and information that this individual requests is in essence being requested by the superintendent.

Inasmuch as most educators don't know how to recognize news, and most of them lack confidence in their ability to write a news release, high priority should be given to an in-service program on these topics. Reporters from area newspapers will usually be glad to participate in such a program. In fact, an effective approach to an in-service undertaking would be for groups of educators to prepare news releases after hearing reporters talk about what news is and how to write it. At the end of the day the staff will have improved its skills in the news area, and the reporters will have some stories to take to their newspapers as a result of these efforts. The person in charge of the news-gathering effort can then conduct workshops or seminars for the building representatives to help them improve their contributions to the overall news effort. He or she can also encourage them to take graduate courses that will be helpful in this field and alert them to workshops and seminars conducted on local and national levels.

As the news-gathering setup is established, it should be clear who is responsible for what. Too many good releases were never printed because they lost their time-value while awaiting approval from two or three administrators who were out of town. If the person in charge of news releases is clearly a capable individual with maturity of judgment, he or she should be able to clear all releases without approval of others. This maturity of judgment would necessitate checking with the proper administrator(s) when controversial items or questions of policy are involved. The chief administrator should choose the press relations person carefully because this individual will be dealing with important information that can enhance or mar the reputation of the schools.

The person's responsibility with the media must be made clear. If the trust level is high, the person should speak for the superintendent in some situations and should attend executive sessions of the board. Only when the communications person has the complete picture is it possible to provide the kind of communications leadership needed. If the communications director is seen as simply a news release writer without access to the superintendent, reporters will bypass his or her office and go directly to the chief executive officer, often requiring the superintendent's valuable time when the information could have been provided by the public information officer.

A sound technique to encourage more people to prepare news releases or to submit ideas for releases is to show that the releases are being printed. A photocopy of each story published should be sent to the individuals involved in the story, as well as to key administrators. This demonstrates that the releases are really being used. This is necessary because often those involved in the stories will not have read the articles because they don't buy the particular papers that ran the story.

GETTING THE NEWS TO THE PRESS

Various ways exist to get news stories to the press. Included are the news release, the fact sheet, the news memo, and the news conference. The last method, the news conference, has already been considered. Of the other methods, the news release is the most common approach to getting news stories in the papers.

If you want to send news releases to a variety of sources nationally, consider using newswire services. You send the release to the service, which sends it by way of computer to the media outlets desired.

Two services are Business Wire, 235 Montgomery St., San Francisco, CA, and PR Newswire, 1515 Broadway, New York, NY.

Preparing News Releases

Editors assign more space to school news when releases conform to press standards. The standards take into consideration style of writing, quality of writing, and the mechanical makeup of the copy. Many editors will confess that they use

some stories that are not as good in content as some they reject. Why? Simply because those accepted were received in a style that enabled them to be used with a minimum of editing. This is especially true with small weekly newspapers and understaffed daily newspapers where rewrite time is a scarce commodity. Editors are busy people who receive a large number of news releases daily. Seldom do they have time to read every release from start to finish. Thus, the first rule for writing an effective news release is to put the key news in the first paragraph. This will attract readers and will also gain the attention of the editor.

Most newspaper articles, especially hard news stories, are written in what is called the inverted pyramid style (see Figure 11.3). The most important elements of the story are told in the first or "lead" paragraph, with each succeeding paragraph being somewhat less important than the one before it. The story has no climax or conclusion. Stories are written in this style because many readers read only the headline and the lead. Also, as noted previously, this style allows the editor to cut the story at any point and know that the least important paragraphs are being lost.

The lead paragraph usually answers some of the following: who, what, where, when, why, and how. However, not all of these questions can always be covered in a lead. A common error of the novice is to try to cram all of this information in one sentence, which becomes a marathon challenge to any reader. Most good leads are written in fewer than thirty words; in fact, most readers prefer leads of twenty words or fewer. In writing

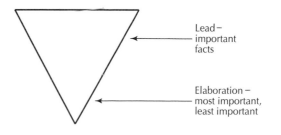

FIGURE 11.3 The inverted pyramid style.

a hard news lead, emphasis is usually placed on a single fact or aspect of the story that is likely to have the strongest reader appeal. In feature stories, the lead varies with the writer and the nature of the material. In either type, the lead can make or break a story, no matter what information follows it. The writing of a concise, forceful lead is an art that requires a sound sense of news and much practice. One way to sharpen leadwriting ability is to read good newspapers and focus on their leads. Here are two leads that present facts concisely:

A new reading program designed to upgrade reading achievement of Blankville's students was announced last night by Superintendent of Schools Harvey Jones.

Enough spaghetti to stretch from Chicago to Green Bay was served in Blankville's school cafeterias yesterday.

The second example could be an unusual lead for a story about the school lunch program. Students might have been involved in determining how much spaghetti was served and how long the spaghetti would stretch if laid end to end. Having attracted the editor's (and reader's) attention, the educator could continue the story to elaborate on the school lunch offerings and the nutritional aspects of the program. Contrast this lead with those routinely submitted by most schools, such as this one:

During the first fiscal quarter of this school year, there were a large number of Type A lunches served to students in both the elementary and secondary schools of Blankville, according to Superintendent of Schools Harvey Jones and Food Services Director William Smith.

The reaction of most readers would justifiably be: Who cares? It might be fine to explain how many such lunches were served, what the Type A lunch is, and why it is nutritionally sound to provide such lunches. But this information should come later in the story, and it should be written in an interesting way.

Here are additional examples of effective leads.

Local high-school students will meet with the mayor at 11 A.M., Monday, in the Council chambers to plan a workshop on city government.

This lead is considered a conventional one, giving, the basic who, what, when, where, why information. While this lead has been traditionally acceptable, the newspaper would make for monotonous reading if every lead were presented in the same style. Variety is necessary for the newspaper; it's also vital for the success of the person writing news releases.

What do high-school students know about their government?

The question lead can be effective, especially when it involves the reader. Some readers will find themselves answering the question. This entices them to read more to see if their answers agree with those presented in the story. Other readers will continue reading after the lead to learn the answer to the problem.

"We want to know where our tax money will be going so we're meeting with the mayor," said James Buren, president of Blankville High School's Student Council.

The quote lead makes the story come alive from the beginning. It seems to add a dimension to the story. In fact, using quotes throughout news releases, when appropriate, provides a certain liveliness that encourages readers to continue reading.

High-school students may be turned on most by rock groups—but they're also interested in their city government.

The contrast lead, which can be effectively used with feature stories especially, provides a change of thought that may entice the reader to read a story he or she would otherwise ignore.

Whether the lead features one news element or another depends on the nature of the story. For example, if the governor declared that school building costs must be cut, the who element would be emphasized because of the governor's prominence. If a similar statement came from a school board member, the stress might well be placed on the effects of the proposed cuts for local taxpayers.

The lead is followed by the body of the story. The body consists of one or more paragraphs explaining the facts. The details are arranged in order of importance, thus making chronological treatment seldom feasible. Paragraphs should not be too long because they become awesome for the reader's eye when put in one column in the newspaper. One typewritten line could well become as many as three lines of type in the newspaper column. Thus the typewritten paragraph of ten lines necessitates the editor's getting the pencil out simply to save the appearance of the paper. Too many long paragraphs make the paper too grey in appearance. It is not necessary to worry about smooth transitions when writing hard news. It is more important to limit the paragraphs to five or six typewritten lines. For a change of pace, there is nothing wrong with a one-sentence paragraph. Many effective leads are just that—a one-sentence paragraph.

Quality of Writing

Newspapers want copy in clear, concise, simple language. Editors do not want to sift through the pompous writing of the educator who is trying to impress rather than trying to communicate. Here are some tips to help school officials who are preparing news releases. Much of this information can be applied to letter writing and writing for school publications.

Use Familiar Words That Are Easily Understood by Readers. Using comfortable words indicates that educators understand their audience and are writing for them. The use of long words for short ones tends to make the release more difficult to read. For example, use *total* instead of *aggregate*. When *use* fits, use it instead of *utilize*. One of the enemies of clear writing is the persistent use of words with more than three syllables.

Avoid Jargon. Educators generally use too many "in-words" that only other educators are comfortable reading and speaking. Be alert to educational terminology and explain it if it's used. Although educators will understand *modular scheduling, accountability, team teaching,* and *percentile,* the average reader will resent these terms being sprinkled in written material aimed at laypeople.

Use Short, Simple Sentences for the Most Part. Although sentences should vary in length and kind, most sentences should be of the subject-verb-object kind. This allows the main thought to be communicated without phrases and clauses getting in the way. Most journalists say it another way: Limit each sentence to one idea. A key roadblock to easy reading is the long sentence. A series of long sentences makes the reader work too hard to get the writer's message. And in an era with so many competing messages, the writer who wants to be read must communicate as effectively as possible.

Use Action Verbs As Much As Possible. Check releases for the overuse of the verb *is* and other forms of *to be.* Substitute stronger verbs that communicate action and a sense of movement when possible. Too many educators insist on writing in the passive voice. When overdone, this communicates a stodgy stiffness and encourages readers to look elsewhere for interesting reading. Editors will change passive voice writing to active in most cases. For example, don't write: "The bill was received by the superintendent and payment on it was made by the Board." Instead, say: "The superintendent received the bill, and the Board paid it."

Identify People When Their Names Are Used.
Give full names, not just last names. If a staff member has a certain responsibility that relates to the story, give the title and responsibility. Too many educators take this a step further and insist on giving early in a story credit to all who worked on an undertaking. Readers are seldom concerned with the names and titles of the people who helped develop a program as much as they care about what the program offers, how it will be implemented, and how much it will cost. Give credit, certainly, but later in the story.

Personalize the Message.   Whenever it is possible to involve the reader in a story, do so. Relating an article to an experience the reader had is an effective way to make a story warmer. For example, an announcement of the expansion of guidance services might start with reference to school services that were missing thirty years ago but are now offered. Or a new approach to teaching mathematics might be introduced with a lead that involves the reader. For example: "Remember when you memorized how many rods are in an acre or bushels in a peck?" The reader will usually be stirred by such a lead and will continue to read. The article could then explain why such memorization has been discarded and what kind of new approach has been substituted.

Avoid Adjectives That Are Someone's Judgments or Opinions, Unless of Course, They Appear on a Quote That Is Attributed to That Someone.   A statement in a release that lauds the school's "excellent" science program should only be made if the person calling it excellent is identified. Using such adjectives marks the school official as a novice in news release writing; the good editor will cross them out.

MECHANICS OF THE NEWS RELEASE

Newspaper editors use a style sheet or style book to prepare their copy. This guideline allows reporters to be consistent in writing certain words. For example, some newspapers spell out the word *street* when it appears as part of an address; other newspapers prefer to abbreviate the word. Knowing the style of the newspapers can enable school officials to prepare copy the way editors want it—a definite advantage in the overall news release program. Although newspapers differ somewhat on technical requirements for abbreviation, capitalization, punctuation, and spelling, most agree on the following standards for written news releases:

— The story should be prepared on white or light paper, $8\frac{1}{2}$-by-11 inches in size.
— The releases should be typed, double or triple spaced, on one side of the paper only.
— The date that the story is being sent and the date it is to be released should appear at the top of the page.
— The name of the person sending the release, the person to contact for more information, and the school name and address and telephone numbers should appear at the top of the first page. The home telephone number of the press relations person should be included.
— Copy should begin about one-third of the way down the page so that enough space is available for the editor to write in a headline. The editor might also use this space to write comments for the staff to follow up on the story.
— Limit the release to one or two pages unless unusual circumstances are present.

The Fact Sheet

In addition to the news release, news can be presented to newspapers in the form of a fact sheet. This technique is effective if the newspaper has sufficient staff to spend the time to convert the facts to a story. Ordinarily the small weekly newspaper will not appreciate the fact sheet because staff time to write the story is scarce.

A check with editors will enable school officials to determine if the fact sheet idea is workable. If the person responsible for getting news to the press has little time to prepare such information, the fact sheet could allow him or her to provide more news information in a shorter time. Fact sheet forms can be available in key locations in all schools. They would be completed by staff members and sent to the school news official,

who would make necessary changes and forward them to the press.

The Phone Call

Often overlooked by school officials as a way to get news in the papers is the phone call. Perhaps school officials feel more secure with a copy of the release in front of them, or perhaps they just never considered the phone call. Whatever the reason, many good stories have been lost because

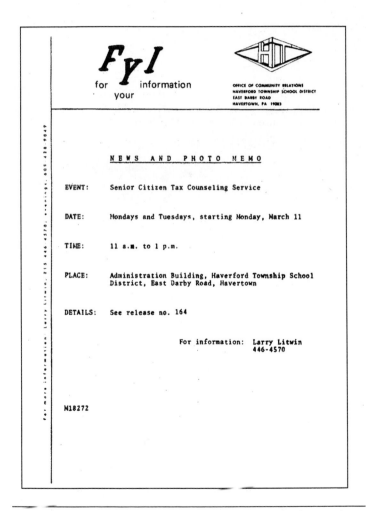

FIGURE 11.4   A news and photo memo from Haverford Township School District, Havertown, Pennsylvania.

educators failed to get the information to the press on time.

A phone call giving key statements made at a public meeting usually will prompt a story in the newspaper. The same comments submitted two days later are stale. In fact, this kind of rapid reporting provides much additional coverage in daily newspapers that don't have enough reporters to attend all meetings.

News and Photo Memos

Some schools have so many news possibilities that the publicity person cannot write all the suggested stories or even find time to prepare fact sheets. The answer, at least for the larger newspapers and occasionally for the smaller ones, is a news memo. The memo simply tells about an event or happening that should lend itself to news coverage. The name and phone number of the person to contact are given, as well as the date, time, and place of the event. Feature story ideas can be distributed this way too. So can possible photo situations that assignment editors might want to consider. Figure 11.4 shows a sample news and photo memo.

ENDNOTES

1. Gloria Dapper, *Public Relations for Educators* (New York: The Macmillan Company, 1964), pp. 25–26.

2. Belmont Mercer Farley, "What to Tell People about the Public Schools" (New York: Bureau of Publications, Teachers College, Columbia University, 1929), p. 1.

12

RADIO, TELEVISION, AND AUDIOVISUAL AIDS

Like public schools, radio and television stations have a responsibility to the public. The Federal Communications Commission is responsible for licensing them—a procedure that occurs periodically. Most local stations like to consider themselves community-minded. This should encourage schools along with other public agencies to use the stations as a means of disseminating public information.

Although most studies indicate that newspapers and students are the main sources of information about schools, some school districts have found that a local radio or television station is the prime vehicle for communicating school information to area residents. Even in places where stations cover large geographical areas, encompassing many school districts, schools can occasionally capitalize on the availability of public service time to communicate a key message.

In addition to radio and television, slides, films, and displays can play important roles in a school's communication efforts. A slide presentation, a film with impact, and an attention-capturing exhibit can contribute effectively to a school-community relations program. All have one trait in common—they require a certain amount of expertise to put over their messages.

Because of this requirement, some school officials hesitate to use these audiovisual media. Yet the impact of such efforts can be well worth the investment of time and money. Many audiences not reached by written communications may appreciate a message carried by an exhibit or a film. The potential impact of well-devised and attractively prepared audiovisual aids is still to be felt as a way for schools to create stronger citizen interest in education.

USING RADIO

Most local radio stations consider themselves community-minded. And there are a large number of such stations, most of which would be more than cooperative with school officials who want to tell some of the school story on radio. The Communication Act of 1934 clearly states that radio stations are licensed to serve as a public convenience or as a public necessity.

Radio stations play a vital role in the overall distribution of news. Because of the immediacy of radio, opportunities abound for providing almost instant information as well as for dispelling rumors and correcting misinformation. Radio is a mobile medium, allowing people to listen while working, driving, or relaxing. Messages can sometimes be communicated to people listening to the radio who would otherwise miss the message. People who would not take the time to read a newsletter or story in the newspaper or come to a meeting might very well receive a radio message. Thus, it is important for school officials to know how to take advantage of radio opportunities.

Broadcasts may serve any one of a number of school purposes, such as those that follow:

▬ To educate the public more fully on the work of the school
▬ To introduce new policies and practices
▬ To invite community cooperation in school improvements

▬ To awaken community interest and concern for public education
▬ To explain the need for more financial support
▬ To assist the classroom teacher in instruction.

Radio is one of the most selective of the mass media in that stations seldom aim their programming at the total available listening audience. Their orientation is toward the saturation of specific audience groups—teenagers, young adults, blacks, farmers, the news hungry, the religion-oriented, and that popular group broadcasters term "middle-of-the-roaders."

Because schools frequently strive to be different things to different people, selective use of the appropriate message on the appropriate station at the right time can produce significant results. Thus, school officials should be aware of the various stations serving the school district's listening audience that can best be reached by each station. By directing specific announcements or information at a particular station, educators might communicate with a large number of those people for whom the message was intended. For example, a 60-second announcement encouraging high-school dropouts to return to school would probably be most effective on the stations aiming at the high-school audience. Yet, an announcement that senior citizens can obtain a school district golden age card for use at school events might be better directed at a station that aims for the older audience.

A 1982 study showed that 39 percent of Americans eighteen and older spent more time listening to radio than using other media. In fact, for the affluent, for college graduates, and for working mothers, radio was the most used medium.[1]

Advantages of Radio for Schools

Radio, in contrast to television, has smaller, more defined audiences and appreciably lower production costs. It is therefore practical for school purposes. Some advantages for using radio as a channel for school communication include:

It's immediate. If children must be sent home because the heating system went awry, radio can inform many people quickly.

It's comfortable. Large numbers of people will listen to school news if it is interestingly presented. Radio permits listeners to learn about the schools while allowing them to do other things simultaneously.

It's quick. Most stations limit the time they give to any one topic on the news. Thus, providing information for the radio usually means capsulizing only the main points of the story.

It's easy. Most radio stations are extremely cooperative, and radio personnel will often work to help school officials learn how to prepare materials for radio.

It's focused. Narrowly defined audiences can be reached with radio, making it more likely a specific message will reach a particular audience.

It's captive. Some audience members are confined to a limited space, such as those in cars, making it easier to reach them.

Knowing How to Use Area Stations

A district planning to use radio should start by conducting a survey of stations heard by local audiences. School officials, while driving back and forth to work, can determine the needed information. They should listen for the basic format of stations—paying particular attention to message length, editorial biases, target audiences, and depth of news coverage. Listening during "drive time" ensures school officials that they are hearing stations at their best since radio is most popular during Monday through Friday rush hours. By gaining this kind of information about each station, school officials will be better able to prepare messages for specific stations.

Public service announcements carried on radio must be on behalf of nonprofit organizations, but no time can be donated to fund-raising functions such as lotteries or bingo parties.

Despite the many demands made on stations' time by public service agencies, most stations claim that they could use more programs from schools. One study of Philadelphia area stations found that 90 percent of the stations desired more school programs if the programs were interesting and timely.[2]

Types of Programs

Radio stations offer a wide range of opportunities for schools, including the following:

Spot announcements. Short 10-, 20-, 30-, and 60-second announcements can be information-giving or can be appeals for support for special school undertakings. They can be succinct interviews with various staff members, or they can be a series of quick comments from students and staff members about a topic of general concern. The shorter the show (or spot), the better the chance of its being used.

Newscasts. Stories to be used in newscasts must have solid news value. In preparing such material for radio, remember that only a short time (perhaps 20 seconds) will be given to the story.

Infomercials. Regularly scheduled short announcements, or "factoids," can develop a regular audience for education oriented information.

Questions of the day. A teaser question on a topic of interest can be presented to the audience as part of another announcement or program. The answer would be offered later in the program or at the end of the spot announcement.

Sports programs. Local stations will sometimes broadcast football, basketball, or other games.

Music programs. There is public interest in school bands, choruses, and other musical groups. Special shows are sometimes taped, especially during the holiday season. If properly informed, local stations might consider taping a brief segment of a musical presentation to use in their regular programming.

Discussion programs. A good panel show on a topic of general interest can be attrac-

tive to stations. Roundtables and debates, if properly planned, can be fast paced and interesting. Topics and participants must be carefully selected.

Dramatic programs and documentaries. Student-produced dramatic productions and special, in-depth programs that probe strengths and weaknesses of a specific school topic can serve the community and show that the schools are providing service to a public other than those actually attending the schools.

Talk and interview shows. Here more than ever the topics and guests must be chosen with great care. A deadly speaker whose monotone lulls listeners to sleep—or chases them to another station—hardly encourages station personnel to air similar shows. Teachers and their new approaches in the classrooms are often overlooked for interview shows. Yet they can be extremely informative and stimulating guests, especially inasmuch as many listeners are concerned with what's new or different in the classroom.

Stations responding to a survey said they air the following programs, in addition to the spot announcements and broadcasts mentioned above.

School Forum. A 30-minute weekly program hosted by the district's school-community relations director. This show features a different school each week.

Learning Is for Living. A 5-minute program about curricula and activities in the school district.

School Scene. A 30-minute program prepared by and featuring high-school students.

Ask the Superintendent. A 30-minute weekly call-in show that allows listeners to pose questions for the superintendent of schools.

School Wrap-Up. A weekly 5- to 15-minute show that offers school news and a brief interview of someone in the school district who made news that week.

School Rap-Up. A weekly panel show that offers students and others an opportunity to discuss and debate key educational issues, usually from 15 to 30 minutes.

School Today.   A 5-minute show that can be used in prime time to discuss current school issues. Most shows can be taped but the opportunity exists to present a live show. This can be effective in an emergency.

The program's format may be adaptable to the needs of the school districts. Other programming ideas might include art, music, and drama, as well as health and science. Health programs produced by students that cover AIDS and other topics of current interest have the potential to draw large, sustaining audiences. General topics that could be covered on a radio program would include drug information, budget information, a review of school board action, rumor information, and answers to questions that people are asking about the schools.

A common complaint of radio personnel is the poor choice of speakers made by school officials. Too often the school spokesperson for a radio show is an administrator with an impressive title, but with a monotonous voice and dull vocabulary that are guaranteed to lose listeners. If it is imperative that such a speaker be on the air, someone with radio expertise should develop a format conducive to the best possible presentation of the speaker's strengths.

Radio stations appreciate receiving good programs prepared by the schools. They suggest, though, that schools use professional or semiprofessional equipment. (Many radio stations will be glad to cooperate in making the station's equipment available for taping and will often help with microphone and taping techniques.) It is also vital that programs be timed accurately. If a school-produced show is supposed to run for 28 minutes, it should run for precisely that time. Any deviation could cause problems for the station.

In one study, a third of the stations reported that lack of cooperation from the schools was the biggest problem faced in school programming. Apathy on the part of school officials, lack of organization, inconsistent availability of program material, and a general misunderstanding of radio were listed as main concerns of radio personnel dealing with educators.[3] Two-thirds of the stations suggested the schools contact and work with a station's manager or program director. As is the case with newspaper reporters, the school's relations with the radio stations can best be enhanced when a school official knows and works with station personnel on a first-name, mutual-respect basis.

Establishing a sound relationship should lead to suggestions for programs that will be aired. Most small stations are insufficiently staffed to produce a large number of public service programs. Thus, programs produced and prepared by the schools save the station money and manpower in addition to giving the community a program that should be of local interest.

Working with the Radio Station

There are many ways in which school-community relations and radio news can be handled together. All are based on the assumption that most radio stations do not have extensive individual news operations. News departments need a constant flow of material, but they need it packaged as much as possible.

Beginning with a late-breaking hard news story, most radio news directors will be happy to take copy down in longhand or tape copy over the phone. The copy, whether read by the community relations person or played into the phone from a recorded tape, must be ready for radio use—15 to 30 seconds reading time—when it is called in. Some radio stations run program blocks, usually 15 to 30 minutes, of soft news or background stories. These programs will use 2- or 3-minute tapes that can be prepared in advance and mailed to the appropriate contact person at the station.

A general rule of thumb would be to avoid a commitment to a long, regular program unless there is a great deal happening in the district. Thirty minutes a week can turn out to be a very long time. However, if a district produces a program of this type, it can be taped at the station and do double duty as the basis for feature stories for the print media. Other radio possibilities might involve shorter, student-prepared reports and use of half-time program slots on stations airing the school sports events to publicize other aspects of school life.

A 30-minute call-in show where a school administrator answers questions from the radio audience can be a positive communications opportunity—or liability. The ability of the school officials to handle difficult questions will determine the effectiveness of such an approach.

Here are some additional recommendations set forth by the National Association of Broadcasters in its copyright publication, *If You Want Air Time:*

1. All types of programming, from 90-minute spectaculars to brief spot announcements, require planning and cooperation with the radio station(s). Teamwork is the key to success in any project.
2. Accept suggestions and constructive criticism. You will be working with experts in a field that is probably foreign to you.
3. Know your limitations. A half-hour interview program might seem ideal for your purpose, but spot announcements, if well produced, can be more effective than a long program which is inadequately prepared.
4. Persons who work for radio stations are usually pressed for time. Do not drop in on them unannounced. Telephone first and set up an appointment.
5. Be on time for a live program or a taping. The clock waits for no one.
6. Submit all program copy and ideas to the program director or station manager as far in advance as possible. Ten days would not be too soon.
7. When writing for radio, use simple, descriptive words that form pictures, give dimension, and add color. Radio reaches only the ear—the listener must be able to sketch in his or her own mind the picture you are trying to create.

8. Make sure all spot announcements are accurately timed. Ten-second spots usually contain 25 words; 30-second spots contain about 75 words; 60-second spots usually contain 150 words.
9. When preparing for a live broadcast or a taping session, accept instructions for proper microphone technique—distance from microphone, voice projection, and how to avoid extraneous noises (paper rustling, chair squeaking, etc.) during the production.
10. After your production has been broadcast, send a letter to station personnel showing your appreciation for their help. This practice will strengthen your relationship with the station and will increase your chances of getting air time in the future.
11. Let the station know of any reactions you receive about your production. The station tries to serve its community and, therefore, is vitally interested in the responses to the programming it broadcasts.[4]

Preparing the Spot Announcement

Getting radio time when a large number of people are listening is of course difficult. The time used most for airing school shows is Sunday between 6 P.M. and midnight. Although few stations (in most surveys, about 10 percent) carry school programs that run longer than 30 minutes, about half the stations broadcast short features or shows of up to 5 minutes. About nine of every ten report carrying spot announcements. The message is clear: the shorter the program, the better the chance of its being aired.

Here are two 30-second radio spots prepared by Kansas City (Kansas) public schools and by Project Public Information, a federally funded project that developed sample school communication materials. These samples would be excellent in some communities but could backfire in others. They are the kinds of spots that would be used by radio stations, however, and they obviously are inexpensive to prepare. It is usually possible to locate someone in a school district, either an employee or a nonemployee, who has radio experience and a good speaking voice. If this is not the case, the local radio station will often cooperate in preparing the spots.

SPOT 1

This is John Wherry for the Kansas City, Kansas, Public Schools.

In observance of American Education Week, here is a quick quiz to tell you how well you are meeting your school responsibilities.

Three questions:

1. Do you know the name of your child's teacher?
2. Do you know the principal's name?
3. Do you know where the school is?

Three "Yes" answers are fine; only one or two mean you may be short-changing your child by not showing enough interest in his education. It's open-house time. Go and get acquainted with your school and teachers.[5]

SPOT 2

Music:—:05

Voice (male):—So, I voted against the school revenue bill. These educators, they think we need more classrooms, teachers, textbooks. Look, I'm not against more money for education, but I just got hit with a thousand-dollar assessment at my country club.

Announcer with tag over music.—If you want the best possible education for your children, you have to help. Know more about your school system. Don't be an adult dropout. This message was brought to you by your state department of education, Project Public Information, and this station.[6]

WRITING FOR RADIO

If time permits, write separate releases for the electronic media. Here are some guidelines for radio news releases. They are basically the same as those for newspapers. However, it must be remembered that radio news is geared toward the ear rather than the eye.

- Write simple spoken English.
- Try to keep one thought to a sentence.
- Try to use the present or present perfect tense.
- Avoid using the word *today*. This will permit news editors to date the story to meet their individual needs.
- Do not use synonyms. Synonyms can confuse the listener.
- Do not use pronouns. Repeat proper names.
- Avoid direct quotes—paraphrasing is safer.
- Always find a way of repeating a location. Repeating the location toward the end of a story is important for the listener.
- Keep adjectives to a minimum. Adjectives tend to clutter speech and obscure the main line of the story.
- Use verbs—do not drop verbs. Listeners need verbs.
- Do not use appositions. Many appositions are not natural to speech. Appositions usually confuse listeners because they cannot see the necessary punctuation.
- Do not start sentences with a prepositional phrase or a participial phrase.
- Give attribution at the beginning of a sentence, not at the end.
- Pinpoint the location. If a release is written to be aired in the same town as the subject of the release, precede the location with "Here in Blanksville...." (Example: "The principal of Wilson High School, here in Blanksville....")
- Avoid the first person. Use "first person" only if you, the writer, really mean "you." For instance—when speaking of the school district—do not use "we" or "our." Simply say, "The Blanksville School District."
- Be conversational. Do not try to be too formal. Choose words that are concise, precise, and grammatically correct.
- Be specific. Do not use vague language or imagery.
- Every release should focus on only one topic or subject. Additional topics should be covered in later releases.
- Use strong action verbs to help the listener visualize the story.

WORKING WITH RADIO PERSONNEL

Here are some general recommendations for dealing with radio stations:

▬ Try to establish a regular contact at a radio station. This will help create rapport and reinforce credibility.

▬ Once a relationship with a radio station is established, prepare *evergreen* short features that may be used at any time, and *sidebars* that support a more important story. They provide a continuing source of program material and help from professional working relationships with local radio stations.

▬ Mail releases ten days prior to an event. Research shows about one-third of the releases received in the mail arrive after the fact because of the uncertainties of the postal system. And, if a release arrives too early, it can be forgotten.

▬ Make releases one page. It's difficult for any newsperson to go through five or six pages of rather dry material looking for the real story buried somewhere in the release.

▬ Type all copy double- or triple-spaced on 8½-by-11 inch paper, using only one side. Start the release one-third of the way down and leave larger margins than usual. This is done so that writers and editors can make notes directly on the release.

▬ Prepare sharp, legible copies. And run off enough releases so that you can provide extra copies if they are needed.

▬ Prepare a news and photo memo when someone of importance or prominence is mentioned in the release. Radio stations can use these memos as biographical sketches and reminders of an upcoming event. News and photo memos should let stations know in a thumbnail whether the person is worth a trip to the school for an interview. If the name is difficult to pronounce, provide a phonetic spelling. These memos should be typed on colored paper so that they stand out.

▬ Team up. The more that schools and organizations become involved in a new project, the more weight a station will assign to it, although many stations will go with the good one-school story, too.

▬ A sense of timing is important. Do not schedule school events on election day, for example, because station personnel are busy and will probably not cover them.

▬ When you visit a station, do not ask for a particular person. Just give your release to the news editor. If you ask for a particular person who is off for a few days, your story may not make it on the air because no one opens the other person's mail.

TELEVISION OPPORTUNITIES

Technological Advances

Miniaturization and improved technology led to the development of video equipment that is smaller, less expensive, more versatile, and easier to use. These changes revolutionized video production, not only making it easier, faster, and more economical for professional television stations to produce news shows, but also making it possible for individuals, community groups and schools to produce quality videos to deliver their messages.

Electronic field production (EFP) and *electronic news gathering (ENG)* techniques are single camera field production processes that use *small format* color equipment (8mm, ½-inch and ¾-inch tape formats) to film, videotape, and edit stories.

A combination camera-videotape recorder, or *camcorder,* is a single unit that integrates the camera and recorder into one lightweight, portable unit. This allows the camera operator greater freedom of movement without need for a cable connection to the videotape recorder.

8mm and Hi8mm video systems offer the smallest video-cassettes available. The small (¼ inch) size of the tape allows the cameras to be small, lightweight, and portable.

Hi8mm videotape player/recorders can be used with professional editing equipment to produce broadcast quality videotape productions.

Prior to development of these new technologies, broadcast standards were *large format* (1-inch and 2-inch videotape), requiring expensive, cumbersome recording and editing equipment. The new generation of small format video equipment makes it possible to produce video of equal or higher quality than the former 2-inch standard and to shoot footage economically and efficiently outside of a television studio.

Field production techniques are easily learned and allow schools to create professional quality videotapes produced from virtually any field location. They may be used for school presentations or as news stories in the form of video news releases.

Television, an extension of radio, is more than the addition of sight to sound. Because people can see the news and other events in action, the impact is greater. TV offers an extension of the radio report and is supplemented with visuals, thus adding credibility to the reporting of the event. In-depth news is obtained from newspapers, and the background information is offered by a number of news magazines. TV stations fall into four categories: commercial VHF, commercial UHF, educational VHF, and educational UHF. Another television opportunity in many areas is cable or community antenna television.

Television is flexible enough to permit the treatment of any subject in a dramatic and convincing fashion. Schools now use TV to supplement classroom teaching. And teachers can evaluate themselves by using videotape. Because videotape can be used repeatedly, if stored properly, schools may have unlimited use of unique lectures, demonstrations, sports events, and programs taped from commercial or educational TV. And, videotape can be erased and used again.

The use of videotape has increased the emphasis placed on in-school viewing and adult education. Schools are finding it within their budgetary means to equip each classroom with a TV monitor so that particular programs can be piped in directly. This is done much like a language laboratory. For example, a teacher who wants to use a particular tape or series of tapes pushes the correct sequence of buttons that triggers the programs desired. The tapes are played from a master control unit in the school. The more sophisticated units feed any number of schools from a central point in the district via a cable.

Television can be used to present news using a video news release the same way radio uses a written news release. A short story, or *package,* is videotaped, edited, and submitted. The video news release focuses on a single topic and tells a brief story.

As in commercial radio, commercial TV stations give a percentage of their broadcasting schedule to public affairs programs. School-sponsored programs usually fall into this category. Such programs can establish a more direct and almost personal relationship with residents. Local viewers can be shown what a modern school is like and how it functions. Or, viewers can be shown why a district needs more money to build, expand, or remodel current facilities.

School telecasts may serve schools in much the same way that radio broadcasts do. A program dealing with problems of the schools is almost as effective in stimulating thought, discussion, and action as a forceful speaker, panel, or roundtable, held in a school auditorium before a live audience. Information received through a visualized broadcast is understood better and retained longer than information received through annual reports, newsletters, newspaper articles, and other forms of printed matter.

It is generally felt that there is less likelihood of facts being misinterpreted when people can see what they are hearing; that conceptions about the school undergo desired change with the presentation of telecast programs; that more low-income families are reached through TV than through any other medium; that exposure to TV programs makes people more conscious of the school and what it is doing; and that educational, cultural, and informational opportunities offered by television are appreciated by adults.[7]

For the most part, the same kinds of programs that are aired on radio may be aired on TV. In fact, a number of programs are interchangeable. Spot announcements, sports and music programs, discussion and panel shows, and interviews and news releases can serve double duty. Once these spots are produced for TV, the voice tracks can often be extracted from videotape or film and dubbed onto audiotape for use on radio.

GETTING TELEVISION TIME

How do schools get air time on television? Just as they do on radio, by calling the program or public affairs director and setting up an appointment. If a small station does not have a director coordinating public service programming, the general manager will usually be helpful. Generally, the basic strategies listed for radio apply to TV.

UHF stations in many markets and the increasing numbers of cable television franchises have given schools their best opportunity of getting their public affairs programming broadcast. For one thing, advertising rates on VHF stations are generally higher because more people watch VHF channels than UHF. Because VHF stations usually sell more commercial advertising, they have less time available for public affairs programming, especially during the popular evening hours. Many VHF stations make public service time available late at night and on weekends. Therefore UHF stations often offer better time periods for schools to present their messages.

If a school is producing something longer than a spot announcement, publicity should be given to it so that residents are aware that it is to be carried on a local TV station. And, if there are spot announcements that are being aired, they should be placed on as many stations as possible. An overall campaign is advocated, with the school producing spot announcements, ranging from 10 to 60 seconds, and extracting from the voice track. By using videotape, the same announcements can be placed throughout a market on all TV stations accepting them, and the audio portion can be offered to all of the radio stations at the same time. Before preparing copies for television, check with local stations to learn their requirements for tape size and format.

Schools could offer local newspapers the same message in the form of a display ad and ask the newspaper to donate available space. The entire campaign should be reinforced with news releases.

Using Educational Stations

Television stations devoted exclusively to educational programs are called education stations and are licensed as such. A license to operate an educational TV station may be held by an educational or cultural institution or by a group of local citizens organized to televise programs in the public interest. A station assigned to one of the 250 reserved channels must function on a nonprofit basis and make its facilities available to public schools, colleges, universities, parent-teacher groups, museums, and other educational agencies.

Capitalizing on CATV Systems

Community antenna television (CATV) systems operate by picking up television signals and amplifying and distributing them by cable to subscribers' television receivers for a fee.

Not all CATV systems originate local programming. However, most CATV systems, in addition to supplying subscribers with the signals of broadcast television stations, also have the capability of providing programming of their own origination. This is called *cablecasting.*

Schools can take advantage of this opportunity to air their programs. However, they must keep in mind that they are reaching a limited audience, only those residents subscribing to the cable. And, only a portion of those subscribers will forgo a popular TV program to watch a school-produced program.

Any program prepared for commercial or educational stations can be carried by CATV systems. CATV is also a good route to take for airing live programs such as board meetings, in-school (classroom demonstrations, assemblies, or theatrical productions) programs, and sports events.

The cost of producing CATV-originated programs is usually less than most programs produced for commercial VHF or UHF stations.

PLANNING FOR EFFECTIVE TELEVISION

As cable opportunities present themselves, school officials should be ready. Many public relations firms invest much time preparing clients for television appearances.

Here's a collection of tips offered by one of them:

1. Seek training before the interview. It will take away fear of equipment.
2. Coach yourself on how to answer a question in 30 seconds.
3. Blend your manners and dress with your message. Your message shouldn't outclass your dress and vice versa.
4. Gain credibility for an unpopular message by admitting the problem. Then talk about it in nonthreatening terms.
5. Be conversational. After taking a voice level test, use that speaking voice during the interview.
6. Be early. Have all materials with you. Take along an assistant or media specialist for last-minute checks and confidence building.[8]

Once a school has its foot in the door of a television station, it should live up to the arrangements that are made. This means keeping appointments, being on time for rehearsals, controlling the conduct of pupils, submitting advance copies of scripts when they are due, furnishing necessary props, and generally respecting the wishes of the station.

Practical suggestions for planning school programs are offered in "If You Want Air Time," available from the National Association of Broadcasters, 1771 N Street, N.W., Washington, D.C. 20036. The Philadelphia School District has developed the following list of suggestions, "Principles in Production Techniques":

1. Simplicity is essential to successful productions. A message can be highlighted and the best camera work done when backgrounds are plain, the number of participants small, and movement from set to set is minimized.
2. A small number of participants facilitates camera work, permits close-ups, and avoids confusion. Close-ups enable the viewer to get a better look at the activity or demonstration being presented, while wide-angle shots reduce objects and people on the television screen to a size that is indistinct.
3. Printed materials and charts should be avoided unless they are large enough to be read easily.
4. Detailed scripts are not necessary for television programs. A prepared rundown sheet may be used instead. The rundown sheet should indicate the various people and items to be shown, the order of presentation, and the physical location of persons and items on the set. It should also state the time allocated to each segment of the story.
5. Interesting content, with a change of pace, helps to produce a good program. Good material is ruined if the pace is too slow or the action does not move fast enough. Smooth transitions enliven the pace of a production.
6. It is not necessary to put makeup on children, but women look better with a medium shade of pancake and dark lipstick, while men need pancake to cover their beards, even after shaving.
7. Contrast in colors is important on black and white television. Pastel colors, for example, look alike, and colored maps can be seen better when they are copied in black and white.
8. The integration of pertinent film material adds scope and variety to a program. Short bits of commercial film can be rented for small fees and used at appropriate points with or without recorded sound.

The National Association of Broadcasters makes a number of suggestions to any organization planning to use TV to communicate its message:

1. Check with the program or public affairs director on slides, films, videotapes and photographs that can be used to help communicate a message. Make sure the text (copy) that is written to accompany visual aids fits with the

slide, film, tape, or photo being shown. Time all copy at a slightly slower pace for TV than for radio. Standard announcements for TV run 10-seconds (about 20 words), 20-seconds (40 words) and 60-seconds (125 words).

2. Provide one slide or photograph for each 10-second spot.
3. Keep in mind that slides are preferable in most cases to photographs. They can be made professionally at a minimum cost. When photographs are used, matte or dull-surfaced prints are preferable since glossy prints reflect studio lights.
4. Ask that visuals be returned immediately after use. Otherwise, they may be discarded.[9]

Personal Appearance

When school representatives go on the air, they will want to look and sound their best. TV personnel will give participants helpful suggestions and appreciate cooperation. The National Association of Broadcasters suggests that personal appearance is vital to the success of any presentation.

Wear suits or dresses of soft, medium colors. Avoid sharply contrasting patterns and colors.

Keep jewelry simple and uncluttered. Pearls and dull-finished metals reflect less light than sparkling and highly polished jewelry.

Men may require a little powder on a bald head, or if the skin is exceptionally oily. Pancake makeup is advisable for a heavy beard or shadows around the eyes. (Station personnel can be of help in suggesting the correct brand and shade of makeup to be used.)

Women are advised to avoid heavy makeup and overuse of lipstick.

Glasses may be worn. On live or taped telecasts, studio personnel will arrange lighting to avoid glare.

Cooperate with the director and floor managers during the appearance. They may find it necessary to give hand signals during the show to control the speed of the presentation. Before the program goes on the air, ask the director questions about the show.

Nearly everyone has preprogram jitters. To relax throat muscles and nerves, it is suggested that participants yawn or stretch their body as they would if they were tired.

When on the air, avoid unnecessary movements or gestures. They immediately attract the attention of the viewer and distract from what is being said and done.

Move more slowly than normal—quick hand and body movements are difficult for the camera to follow.

It is suggested that persons being interviewed look, listen, and speak to the person conducting the interview. However, if a participant has something to say to the viewing audience, he or she should look directly at the camera with the red light on it.

Imagine a good friend is in place of the TV camera. Participants are urged to talk in ordinary conversational tones, with all the enthusiasm and sincerity that they have for the subject. [*Authors' additional suggestions*—Maintain eye contact. Avoid sudden eye movement. Look directly into the camera.]

Participants should not worry about the role they are playing. They are appearing on the program not as an actor or actress but rather as interesting persons in their own right.

Participants should resist the temptation to look at themselves on the TV monitor in the studio; this is distracting to the viewer.

Above all, be on time. In producing a TV program, many things must be accomplished in a short period of time and each minute is usually carefully planned.[10]

Preparing a Television Talk

The National Association of Broadcasters offers the following suggestions on how to prepare a talk for television:

Begin by picking a theme, a central purpose for your presentation—one with which you are familiar, and one in which you believe. You want to create confidence; to carry conviction. But be sure you select a subject which can be fully explained and exploited in the time allotted.

You must create interest at the start. What you say and do in the first two minutes will determine the size of the audience you retain throughout the talk. But avoid a highly dramatic opening unless you intend to maintain the pace throughout the program. Develop your theme logically, point by point. And carefully plan illustrations of your theme. Don't just tell your audience what you intend to do; show them—with charts, still pictures, films, or tapes.

The ending of your talk is just as important as the opening. Don't leave your audience dangling. Reach some definite conclusions—ones that will provoke immediate thought and discussion among the viewing audience.[11]

Suggestions are also offered on how to deliver a talk on TV:

1. Avoid giving the impression that you are reading your talk. Much of the effectiveness of your message will be lost if your eyes are glued continually to the script. There are several ways in which you can deliver the talk convincingly:

    a. Many stations and all television networks have mechanical prompting devices that are used daily by scores of professionals who appear before the cameras. The advantages are obvious; you can look into the camera, with your text continually before you, and thus attain a desirable informality.

    b. You can memorize your written talk. But this presents certain difficulties, including the time involved.

    c. You can type topic headings on small cards to be held in your hand or placed inconspicuously on the table. By glancing at the topic headings, you can develop each point in a conversational manner—being careful to stay with the ideas in your prepared speech. Also remember that your eyes should meet the eyes of the audience and not be cast downward constantly in appraisal of your notes.

2. If you feel that you must read your talk from a manuscript, hold your script in your outstretched hand, then drop your eyes to the script, keeping your head erect.

3. Action can be added by moving about—from the desk or table where you are seated to the charts, pictures, or chalkboard used to illustrate your message. When you do move, move slowly. In rising from a chair, give the camera time to follow you.

4. Usually, a boom microphone will be used—one which hangs above your head out of camera range. The boom operator will keep your voice in range, but your cooperation is necessary. If you rise quickly from your chair, you are apt to hit your head. If you sit down too fast for the boom operator to follow your action, your voice will fade before the mike is back in range.

5. If a table mike is used, speak clearly and directly into the microphone. Be careful not to rattle papers or pound the table. Even the tapping of your foot will be picked up by this sensitive instrument. A lavalier mike that can be easily clipped to a lapel provides flexibility.

6. Whether seated or standing, remember at all times to talk directly to the viewer. Keep in mind that the audience is inside the camera. On each camera is a small red light which is illuminated when that camera is on the air. If you are looking at one camera and the light goes off, drop your eyes briefly, to your notes if you are using them, and then look up at the other camera. This makes the transition less obvious than if you turn your head directly from one camera to the other.

7. Of course there are exceptions. If you are on a panel or interview type telecast, you should not concentrate on the camera to the point of ignoring your fellow participants. Look, listen, and speak to the person talking to you, unless you wish to address the TV audience directly.

8. The floor director will aid you through hand signals in keeping up with the cameras. He or she will give the signals close to the camera so that you can see them easily without looking away from the lens.[12]

After the Show

Once the television production has been completed, remember your own good public relations. Send letters of thanks to station personnel expressing appreciation for their help. Such expressions strengthen relationships and enhance the chances of getting public service time in the future. Also, let the station know about reactions received by the school. Most TV and radio stations are vitally interested in the response participants receive after a program is aired.

Schools could go a step further. A good starting point for a continuing relationship with local radio and TV stations is to ask them to provide speakers for upcoming classes or meetings. More and more stations are encouraging their staff members to speak to community groups and would welcome the invitation.

SCHOOL EXHIBITS

Included in the communications efforts of a school are school exhibits. Various kinds of exhibits can serve a multitude of purposes; all can demonstrate some phase of the school system operation that would be of interest to a segment of the public. A properly planned exhibit can command the attention of large numbers of people who might be attracted to few other communications devices used by the schools. Because exhibits require a minimum of effort on the part of viewers, they frequently allow key messages to be comfortably communicated.

In-School Exhibits

The in-school exhibit is the most commonly used display effort of schools. Most of the time, the classroom exhibit claims more time, space, and effort than any others in the school. The purpose of a classroom exhibit is to show students, parents, teachers, staff members, and visitors what children are studying and accomplishing. Such exhibits are placed on walls, tables, windowsills, and other easily accessible areas. Used effectively as instructional aids, these exhibits should be updated frequently to recapture students' interest and capture the attention of outsiders. An out-of-date notice or a bulletin board with fall-colored leaves in the spring indicates carelessness and poor attitude.

Parents, especially, enjoy seeing their children's work, particularly in the elementary grades. Care must be taken to ensure that the exhibits communicate the major point the teacher wants to share with parents. Every effort must be made to check the display for accuracy. People are quick to judge educators on the basis of their spelling and grammar; therefore, a thorough proofreading of each word on the exhibit is imperative.

The corridor exhibit is an effective vehicle to acquaint visitors with student undertakings and accomplishments. These exhibits should be changed every three or four weeks or as new information and ideas are available. Some of the most important displays should be placed near the main entrance so every visitor will notice them and leave with at least one additional bit of information about the schools.

The all-school exhibit offers the best opportunity for publicizing and interpreting the educational program. Usually an annual event, the undertaking features display materials from all grades or subject-matter departments of the schools. Such an exhibit can be limited to one instructional area, such as homemaking, science, language arts, or health. Modern teaching methods, instructional materials, and individual and class projects can be explained by students and teachers at these exhibits. If a facility is available, this kind of exhibit can be combined with a presentation of a physical education group or a series of songs by the glee club, for example. The all-school exhibit is one of the best means available to bring people into schools.

The systemwide exhibit brings together materials from various schools in the district. Located at a convenient central place, this exhibit usually focuses on one subject or on a specific level of education. Some schools use creativity as a theme to demonstrate ideas presented by students. Others choose to have "science fairs" that permit students to work on a project for a class and to display that project to the public. It is of course necessary to communicate clearly the guidelines for such exhibits or fairs, especially if awards are made for outstanding projects. Many well-meaning parents have become involved in helping their children prepare exhibits, causing consternation on the part of other parents and children who chose to play the game by the rules they understood.

Out-of-School Exhibits

Bringing the public into contact with the works of schools is a desirable outcome of a school-community relations program. One way to take advantage of numerous opportunities in this regard is to use the out-of-school exhibit. The topics covered or the ideas to be communicated are limitless. The only guideline is whether or not the project will help people to understand the schools better. A little imagination combined with models, specimens, photographs, and technical devices can make such exhibits both interesting and informative.

There are many different places in the community where the exhibits may be shown. A local store is a suitable and often-used location. The exhibit may be arranged either in a section of the store or else in the show windows where it can be seen from the street. Another location is the county fair, which schools in rural and semirural areas may use to acquaint the public with their work. In addition, exhibits may be shown in public libraries, hotel and bank lobbies, and government buildings.

Shopping malls are becoming more widely used for school exhibits. Public relations directors for the malls are constantly seeking unusual attractions, and an exhibit prepared by the school can be a positive attraction for both the mall and the school. Some schools have capitalized on the mall opportunity to conduct a class, using modern techniques and equipment.

The portable exhibit can be put to much use in the course of a year. Many companies offer professional-looking display materials that can be easily transported. They can be placed in banks, office buildings, shopping malls, libraries, and other locations. An exhibit can be built around just about any school subject, challenge, or need. This kind of exhibit can provide an excellent backdrop

for a presentation made by a speaker from a school. It can be a sound investment in the overall school-community relations program because it may be borrowed by various community organizations, clubs, and business organizations to help them better consider a school problem or need.

Preparing the Exhibit

No matter what kind of exhibit is used to provide the public with information, the results are better when there is careful planning. Too often exhibits give the appearance of little planning and less knowledge of effective communication techniques. If an exhibit is to prompt community reaction to a school effort, it must be done in a first-class manner. This means that certain basic questions must be properly answered if the exhibit is to evoke positive reactions. Some of these questions follow.

Who Is Responsible for the Exhibit? Too often committees get in the way of decision making. The exhibit planned by a committee can be excellent if it is clearly understood that one person has the final responsibility for it. With deadline pressures to face and materials to prepare, one person must be charged with getting the job done.

What Is the Best Date and Place for the Exhibit? Although this seems like an obvious question, it is sometimes more important than planners think. For example, a one-day exhibit could flop if scheduled on the same day as another crowd-drawing event. Thus, a check with community organizations to clear the date is a wise step in the planning. How long will the exhibit last? Will people be available to staff it if needed? Will the exhibit best be used in conjunction with some other event like American Education Week or would it be better used by itself? Are there available times at key locations that would be worth waiting for rather than accepting a second-best place?

Who Is the Audience? To whom should the exhibit appeal? This is a key ingredient in planning the exhibit. In fact, it is often the vital question that is forgotten as different groups or individuals attempt to guarantee that their interests are protected. The audience consideration must override all other planning topics if the exhibit is to be successful. Some specific areas needing careful planning are the level of the language, the complexity of the message, and the ease of viewing. Unless these are determined with the audience, rather than the school officials, in mind, the exhibit could be totally ineffective.

What Is the Purpose and Theme?

One of the early decisions to be made when planning the exhibit is its purpose. Often overlooked, the purpose is the basis for other decisions, including the topics covered and the materials needed. Perhaps the most important question to ask when determining the purpose is: What do we want people who see the exhibit to go away thinking? Answering this question permits planners to simplify the exhibit, especially if they can agree on one purpose. Communicating one idea is appreciably easier and can be much more effective than confusing the audience with a series of messages containing disjointed facts. Exhibits should focus on a single concept. Each message should support the central theme using both words and pictures to tell the story. Emphasis on visual rather than written material makes it easier for viewers to retain the message. Avoid excessive detail. Try to create a single, bold message that will be easily remembered.

What Should the Content Be?

Exhibits should focus on a single concept. Each message should support the central theme using both words and pictures to tell the story. Emphasis on visual rather than written material makes it easier for viewers to retain the message. Avoid excessive detail. Try to create a single, bold message that will be easily remembered. To help decide which items to use, the following questions might be asked: Does the item fit the purpose and theme of the exhibit? How well will the item be received by the audience? Is it simple and concrete enough to be easily understood? Does it lend itself well to the exhibit form of communication? In selecting content, choose those items that visualize facts, ideas, and illustrations in a way that is interesting to follow and that leaves vivid impressions.

What Display Techniques Should Be Used?

The effective use of display devices and techniques allows materials to be presented in ways that stimulate interest and convey a message clearly and convincingly. Display panels are a common source of message-sending in exhibits. A good rule of thumb to avoid clutter and confusion is to limit one message to a panel. For the best appearance, a panel should usually have its widest margin at the bottom, a smaller margin at the top, and its smallest margins at the sides. Tables are often used to hold brochures and other publications to be distributed to the public. But it must be remembered that the angle afforded the eye by the table is not a very good one for the display of materials. Used with panel displays, the tables can be effective, however. Worth considering as an alternative to a table is a rack, which allows better display of publications and is also more inviting to the audience.

A display of items for any exhibit unit should be arranged so that the items "talk" to viewers and leave them with a feeling that they have gained something worthwhile. This effect will not be produced unless the items are presented in an orderly design that is pleasing to see and easy to understand. There must be an obvious relationship of the parts to the whole and plenty of open space between them. The setting in which items are placed makes a difference in the dramatic impact they make on the viewer. For example, an object might be shown to best advantage if placed on a pedestal, in a shadow box, or with a spotlight trained on it.

Display arrangements must capture the attention of spectators and entice them to be interested in the content. This can be done in many ways, including such things as decorations that carry out the theme of the exhibit, a judicious use of color, contrasts in values, diagonal lines and triangles that suggest motion, broken and continuous lines pointing to a center of interest, a well-placed row of objects, or an object in motion. Displays "talk" more directly to the viewer when they are built around a center of interest. A center of interest is a point to which attention is directed by the arrangement of the materials. The eyes may be guided to this point by a clever caption placed in a suitable position, a cutout figure looking in a given direction, a limited use of converging bright-colored ribbons or a set of objects on graduated pedestals.

How Should Printed Matter Be Prepared?
Once again the key to success is to prepare written messages as if you were the audience. This will help not only in choosing the proper words but also in discovering where to place title cards, placards, and explanatory statements. Printed explanations should be succinct and appealing. A common mistake is to attempt in-depth explanations when a surface statement should suffice. Type size plays a major role in conveying the message, especially for those passersby who do not actively become involved in the exhibit. Remember that some people will walk by the exhibit; for this audience at least one thematic message in very large type should be displayed at eye level.

How Should an Exhibit Be Managed?
The thoughts and feelings people take from a school exhibit are influenced to a great extent by the way it is managed. A physical layout which allows freedom of movement and time to look at displays without being hurried is important, as are courteous treatment, attractive displays, and the opportunity to talk with school representatives. Visitors appreciate attention shown to their needs—well-placed directional signs and arrows, cloakroom facilities, rest stations, and guides to answer questions and escort them through the building. People who represent the school should be knowledgeable about the topics covered in the exhibit. If they are not, they should be told how to refer people to other representatives or to available materials.

Should Audience Participation Be Planned?
Involvement is a common ingredient of successful efforts in many facets of school-community relations. When possible, building audience involvement into the plans of an exhibit is a major step toward success. However, audience participation must be well planned or it could backfire if people get in each other's way or if they fail to understand the kind of participation requested. Some attempts at involvement could cause less confident people to avoid the exhibit altogether. Thus, whatever is used should be relatively simple. The audience may take part in an exhibit by pushing a button to see a picture or illuminate a series of panels; pushing a button to start some mechanism in motion; turning a knob to change from one photograph to another; listening with earphones to a brief narrative; taking a short quiz and comparing answers with the correct ones on a computer; or answering a brief questionnaire about attitudes toward the schools.

What About Publicity?
An exhibit falls short of its goal unless it is seen by a large number of people. Good publicity is the best means available to ensure the presence of a large number of people. All too often, however, school officials tend to underestimate rather than overestimate the amount of publicity needed, especially with exhibits intended for nonparent audiences. Besides securing a sizable audience, good publicity brings the school to the attention of citizens and taxpayers who seldom attend an educational affair, and it acquaints them more fully with the work of the institution. Accordingly, every piece of publicity should carry repeated explanations of what the exhibit covers and the reasons for holding it. This means, further, that several different avenues of publicity should be employed in order to reach as many members as possible of selected audiences.

In addition to newspaper publicity, radio and television spot announcements can be made just before the opening of the exhibit, announcements can be read at parent-teacher association meetings, and notices can be sent to clubs and civic associations in the form of invitations. School children can be instructed to write cards and letters to parents and friends telling about the exhibit and the days and hours that it will be open for their inspection. These and other publicity ideas found in other chapters will enhance the possibility of attracting a large number of people to the exhibit.

FILMSTRIPS AND SLIDES

To create understanding and stimulate constructive action in certain kinds of school situations, slides and filmstrips are invaluable. More than publications and other written materials, they can demonstrate problem situations and achievements in a school district. People can recognize children on the screen, they can see the buildings they pass daily, and they can appreciate problems when they see specific situations with which they can relate. When slides or filmstrips are accompanied by interesting commentary, the chances are even better that viewers will gain much from the presentation.

Good audiovisual presentations bring numerous invitations from community groups that want to see them. Program chairpersons seeking locally important topics are usually glad to have a school representative show the presentation at meetings. People generally prefer to see something rather than merely hear about it; graphs, charts, and tables, as well as other information, are understood with a minimum of effort when presented on the screen rather than as part of a totally oral presentation. Moreover, audiovisual materials contribute to accurate recall for a longer time than do speeches.

Much can be accomplished with slides and filmstrips that bring actual conditions, good or bad, to the attention of people in the community. Showing favorable conditions and practices helps to develop a strong sense of local pride in the system; showing unfavorable conditions and limitations awakens interest and stimulates the

desire to effect essential changes and improvements. These outcomes are especially true when the frame of reference for any audiovisual production is the welfare of children and society.

It should be emphasized that audiovisual productions are not a substitute for other materials and procedures that have been effective in telling the school story. Instead, they should be used in many instances to complement other media when there is need for clarifying and strengthening information and ideas that have been presented to the public.

One of the prime reasons for using slides is their flexibility. Slides allow the educator to prepare a basic presentation, and then adapt this to a particular need or audience. Thus, from a nucleus of a basic slide show prepared for new residents, school officials might also build special presentations for teacher candidates on a distant campus or for new school board members. Although they lack the flexibility of slides, filmstrips are better to use when quantities of the presentation are needed. A filmstrip can be made from slides provided by the school.

Applying Basic Principles

A picture story to be told through slides or filmstrips should be specific and limited to things not requiring motion for complete understanding. A story of broader scope involving motion as an essential factor can be told more effectively through the production and use of a movie film or videotape. However, no matter what medium is chosen, careful and detailed planning should be completed before beginning actual production.

The subject matter of a production should be selected and treated with the particular target audience in mind. It should be kept as free as possible of extraneous and unrelated materials, and it should not be developed too rapidly for the inexperienced to follow the concepts presented. Productions concentrating on a single idea or activity are much more effective than those attempting coverage of too broad an area with numerous minute details. Crowding too much into the production will inevitably decrease its effectiveness.

The slide or filmstrip should not be used for propaganda or to build up personalities, but should always depict the school story with complete candor, truth, and accuracy. It should allow citizens of the community to increase their knowledge, improve their understanding, and heighten their appreciation of what the schools are doing for children and society. Any attempt to conceal or misrepresent a school condition or situation would create suspicion and mistrust in the community.

Although it is recognized that local production of slides and filmstrips cannot always be maintained on a basis of strictly professional quality, all productions can reasonably be expected to meet the requirements of good photography. Certainly narration, dialogue, or commentary, whether recorded or given in person, should be in a clearly audible voice and in plain, lucid English.

Preparing the Presentation

Knowing which pictures to show and to whom to show them is one of the prime considerations in planning a slide show or a filmstrip. Once the basic purpose has been identified, work can begin on the outline, listing scenes in a logical sequence. Production costs for slides and filmstrips are relatively minimal. Slides are made using color transparent film and can be developed through a local camera shop. When taking photos, remember that film is relatively inexpensive. One or two extra shots are worth taking to ensure having all of the needed photos. Although it is occasionally necessary to pose certain photos to communicate a specific idea, most photos should be unposed to convey a true-to-life image.

Some school officials prefer to write the script first and later take photos consistent with the script. Others feel more comfortable working with an outline until the photos have been taken, after which a script is written and (usually) recorded. It must be remembered that the script

should be lively and interesting to hold the audience's attention. Educators must avoid the tendency to use the language appropriate only for colleagues or for a publication. A practical idea that works for some people is to record the script originally, and then to improve it from the transcribed copy. This approach usually encourages people to use words that laypeople will understand—an important consideration for any communication effort. Titles for slide presentations can be photographed from printed or handlettered copy. New software programs for microcomputers can help produce the titles. A menu board can also be used for this purpose. Some graphic arts firms prepare professional title slides fairly inexpensively.

Presenting the Material

Audience reaction to visual materials is affected by the methods of presentation. People want pictures that are in focus and that can be seen easily. This means having quality equipment available. Few situations are as embarrassing as the audiovisual show cancelled because of equipment failure. The audience assumes that educators know how to use the equipment; therefore, it is imperative that back-up equipment be available. Some presentations never take place because of the lack of an extension cord. Slides should be numbered at the top to maintain the correct sequence and to avoid the possibility of being inserted into the projector upside down.

An effective technique for some kinds of material is the use of multiple projectors. Especially useful when statistical data and detailed facts are being presented, the multiple projector technique allows one screen to show an entire budget statement while another or others display details of the budget. This technique can also be used as an attention-getter, but it requires additional technical expertise.

Whether to record the script or to have a school official speak while slides are shown is a decision that many educators do not agree on. Probably the best approach is to incorporate the best of both possibilities by recording the message so it is available, but omitting the tape when a speaker is desired. Recording the message ensures that the key points will be made in the proper order each time. Inflections for emphasis can be controlled and the quality of the presentation is consistent—even if the scheduled speaker is unable to appear. For the proper timing of slide and tape, automatic sequencing equipment is available at relatively low cost. It is wise to tape the message on both a cassette and a reel recorder and make both available to school officials in case only one type of recorder is available at a particular time. Just as an extra bulb should be provided for equipment requiring a bulb, so too should extra batteries be an integral part of the cassette recorder.

Although the recorded narrative offers many advantages, it does not replace the enthusiasm and sincerity of a school official explaining the slide presentation in person. This usually inspires greater audience confidence and encourages people to ask questions. The community relations value of having a school representative present is an added positive factor.

On the negative side of providing live narration is the possibility that the speaker will embellish many parts of the script and extend the show long past its planned length. Shows longer than 15 to 17 minutes will outlive their welcome. About 12 minutes is ideal, followed by a question-and-answer session. The goal is to leave the audience wanting more, not preferring less.

MOVIES AND VIDEOTAPES

The school-made movie or videotape production is an effective audiovisual device for furnishing information to the public. It permits the showing of actual conditions and practices and effectively captures motion—something that slides cannot do. The material, if properly presented, can be easily understood and assimilated, and a substantial number of ideas can be presented in a relatively short time. Movies and videotapes, playing an important role in the community relations pro-

gram, can be used to acquaint people with innovations, accomplishments, and challenges. They can bring the classroom to people who do not come to the classroom to see what modern educational techniques encompass. They can be used to anticipate needed changes and can develop a sense of pride among taxpayers. As with all communication attempts, movies and videotapes must show the schools as they are. Focusing only on problems and negative situations or showing only positive situations can cause critics to accuse school officials of intentionally misrepresenting the facts. A balanced picture of the schools should be shown.

Guiding Principles

The production of school movies and videotapes should be based on a set of guiding principles that are consistent with the underlying concepts of the community relations program and the standards of good production. Every movie and videotape should:

- Carry out a definite objective
- Fit the type of audience or audiences for whom it is intended
- Depict school conditions with truth and accuracy
- Avoid "selling" personalities or spreading propaganda
- Meet the requirements of excellent photography
- Tell a well-organized story
- Cover only one general idea or subject
- Explain the content in understandable English
- Be financed with public funds.

Producing Films and Videotapes

No production is any better than the planning behind it. One of the initial decisions must be whether or not to employ a professional producer. Among the advantages of hiring a professional is that overall excellent quality is just about guaranteed. However, the cost is sometimes prohibitive.

Some schools, tapping the expertise of community volunteers and staff members, make productions on a low budget. Although the quality is seldom as good as that done by professionals, the involvement of residents and employees sometimes overcomes the quality difference. Some schools that offer courses in film or television production are calling on students and teachers to get hands-on experience by making productions that school officials can use for community relations purposes. In some instances, school districts receive consulting help from instructors at area colleges.

Underlying every audiovisual presentation should be a focus on students. Without them there is no need for schools and this should be remembered when planning a production. An empty classroom corridor can be sterile; add students enthusiastically going to their next class and education comes alive. The superintendent behind a desk talking "at" viewers for several minutes can turn off the most interested audience. But a superintendent narrating student action or talking with a group of parents can show vitality in the administration.

An important part of the production is the editing, one of the crucial steps requiring a professional. School officials should be sure that the purpose of the film or videotape is considered at every step of its production. Often personal and political considerations impede progress as individuals and groups place their interests before the good of the school system. The editor must know who is responsible for overcoming such problems.

Students and others usually enjoy seeing themselves in audiovisual productions of the schools. Yet, for the protection of the district, it is wise to acquire a written release from parents of students. Pointing out that the student has been chosen to appear in the production is a sound public relations policy. It is especially important to secure such releases for students who are identified as having a learning problem or who may be depicted in a way that could be construed as negative by parents and friends. Even if the depiction is legally defensible, the time consumed by a lawsuit or the general ill will generated makes it advisable to prevent such possibilities by acquiring a release.

Be alert to other potential problems, too, such as shop students without eye protection, food service workers without hair nets, or athletic participants not wearing head protection.

Using the Films

Numerous outlets exist in the community for showing school-made movies and videotapes. Advantage may be taken of parent-teacher association meetings to tell the education story. Productions may be shown in connection with open-house programs, graduation exercises, anniversary celebrations, and special events attended by the public. American Education Week is a natural occasion for free distribution of films to local movie theaters and TV stations. Notices may be sent to a selected list of clubs, organizations, and civic groups stating that films and videotapes are available and telling how they may be obtained from school authorities. Another more recent use of films and videotapes about schools has been to show the schools in action to visiting accrediting agencies.

After people have seen a school film, it is a practical idea to ask them for their reactions. Brief questionnaires can be distributed, allowing people to complete them anonymously and place them in a container on the way out. Responses will allow school officials to understand how well the productions are being received and will provide suggestions for changes.

OTHER AUDIOVISUAL AIDS

The tape recorder, the overhead projector, charts, and other audiovisual aids can also play important roles in various presentations to the public. The videotape recorder presents many opportunities for community relations undertakings. Videotape equipment allows teachers to show students in action when parents visit. It allows administrators to share some major school events with visitors, and it generally opens up as many possibilities for community relations as the creative educator can apply.

Using audiovisual equipment can add a change of pace to a presentation. It can also get in the way of an otherwise effective presentation if not properly done. Here are some ideas to remember when employing audiovisual materials.

Use computer software programs for video graphics generators. Inexpensive hardware may be added internally to personal computers to allow the computer to interface with a videotape recorder. Character generation software programs can be used to create titles, credits, and graphics to edit onto the final videotape to produce professional appearing broadcasts.

Character generation software programs enable computers to inexpensively function as television character generators to produce a full range of styles, sizes, and colors of letters and graphics which can be stored in the computer and repeatedly used. Drawing and paint programs allow the computer to alter line and color components of television images.

A digitizing unit can be used with a video camera to input camera generated images into the computer. They can then be manipulated with inexpensive software programs and edited to produce creative effects that originated in the camera for inclusion in the final videotape.

Make charts large enough. Test the size by looking at them from the back of the room before the presentation. Make lines broad and heavy and use color for emphasis.

Restrict the details. Stick to the essentials on each chart. Remember, the audience can read only ten to twenty words without losing the speaker's train of thought.

Talk to the audience, not to the chart. Inexperienced speakers tend to address the visual aid rather than the listeners. Learn to point to the proper point on the visual aid while looking at the audience.

Use a chart only when you need it. Keep charts out of sight until you need them and remove them when you are finished with them. Erase points written on a chalkboard when that part of the presentation is over.

Stand beside the illustrative material. Don't stand between the chart and the audience. If listeners are seated close to you, stand at least three to four feet to the side of the chart. Using a pointer simplifies the process.

Use a large enough screen. The standard small screen, 39 by 48 inches, may be too small if anyone is seated more than twenty-eight feet away.

Have the room adequately dark. For graphs this is not necessary, but if you plan to show films or slides, test the room for disturbing light leaks ahead of time. Test your projector or visual equipment in advance.

Pay special attention to making yourself heard and understood. You can rely only on your voice when the room is dark. Talk clearly, and with more force than normal especially if you are at the rear of the room operating the projector. Make sure that the whir of the projector doesn't drown you out.

(See Chapter 10 for additional information on using overhead projectors.)

ENDNOTES

1. Radio Advertising Bureau, New York, 1982.
2. Ralph Burgio and Larry Litwin, "A Study of the Use of Commercial Radio for School Public Relations" (Master's thesis, Glassboro State College, 1972).
3. Ibid.

4. *If You Want Air Time* (Washington, DC: National Association of Broadcasters, 1969).

5. Kansas City, Kansas, Public Schools, n.d.

6. Project Public Information, n.d.

7. *So You're Going on TV* (Washington: National Association of Broadcasters, 1971), pp. 6–7.

8. Joseph Conway, Ruder, Finn, and Rotman: New York, quoted in *Communication Briefings,* 1982.

9. Memo, n.d.

10. *If You Want Air Time,* pp. 8–11.

11. Campaigning on TV (Washington, DC: National Association of Broadcasters, 1966), pp. 2–4.

12. Ibid.

13

PREPARING PRINTED MATERIALS

More and more school districts are preparing publications each year as part of their overall communications efforts. Administrators have learned from research and from the success of business and industrial organizations that planned, informative, and attractive publications are important tools for conveying information to various audiences.

School publications can be aimed at specific audiences, such as employees or prospective teachers, or can be prepared for a general audience, such as all taxpayers. Most school officials consider publications to be vital components of the communications program. It is imperative to remember, however, that publications and other written endeavors compose only one part of the total effort.

The proper use of publications will serve school officials well because the publications can communicate detailed ideas to large numbers of people at a minimum cost with relative ease of production. Some school districts prepare consistently excellent publications that serve their purposes well and garner national awards. A large number of schools, however, distribute publications that are ineffective, unattractive, and basically a waste of time and money. This chapter suggests techniques and ideas that should enable school officials to prepare effective publications that are read, understood, and appreciated.

OBJECTIVES AND SCHOOL PUBLICATIONS

The initial step in planning any school publication is to decide exactly what its objective(s) should be. Too many school officials undertake publishing a newsletter or an annual report simply because "all other districts are doing it." Such a rationale frequently leads to a lack of direction. Publications that exist without goals are seldom effective. Thus, the first step in developing a publication should be a written statement of purpose. Such a statement determines how the publication will be developed, to whom it will be distributed, and how its effectiveness will be evaluated.

One of the major objectives of publications prepared for staff personnel is to establish communication that is not possible through personal contact. Employees want to know what is going on where they work; thus, a major objective of internal publications is to improve employee morale.

Internal publications also can keep the staff informed about educational policies, practices, and problems; they can explain reasons for particular courses of action; and can encourage all employees to submit constructive ideas to improve the schools. If properly prepared, internal publications can contribute appreciably to employees' understanding their role as interpreters of the school system. Such publications should not be aimed specifically at the teachers, but at all staff members.

The major objectives of publications addressed to students are to increase their understanding of educational opportunities and problems and to communicate that informed students are an important part of the school operation. Such publications demonstrate that school officials are concerned about providing information to an important audience. Too often administrators forget students when planning a total publication program.

The major objectives of publications prepared for parents are to cultivate a partnership between school and home, to increase parents' knowledge and understanding of the educational program, to increase parent participation in school affairs, and to educate parents about specific school problems.

Among the major objectives of publications addressed to special community groups and to the general public are keeping citizens informed of the policies, practices, and needs of the school system and cultivating a sense of partnership in advancing the cause of public education. Such publications can also serve to increase lay participation in the school system, show what the tax dollar buys, report on educational progress, dispel misconceptions, and neutralize harmful propaganda. Publications aimed at the community can thank individuals and groups for contributions to the schools and can show how the schools contribute to the community. They can explain problems and possible solutions; they can pave the way for important changes in education practice and can help inform government officials, sometimes leading to gaining their support.

After establishing the general objectives of school publications, it is important to be specific about objectives in subsequent issues. What is the purpose of this issue? What do school officials expect people to do after reading the publication? If the publication is an evening class brochure, readers might be expected to seek a registration form and enroll. If the publication is a bond-issue brochure, people might be expected to volunteer to aid a building campaign or to vote yes in a referendum. Keep a specific purpose in mind for each publication.

KNOWING THE AUDIENCE

One of the first considerations of any communications attempt is a simple one: Know the audience. Too often school publications appear to be written for the school board or for school administrators rather than for the intended audience. It is difficult to prepare one publication that will meet the needs of all audiences; realizing this is a sound beginning.

A good place to start in aiming at a specific audience is to determine, from a content standpoint, what the audience already knows about the schools. A common error is to assume that readers know almost as much as the school officials. This assumption, especially when coupled with a writing style that features educational gobbledygook, frustrates and discourages readers. Educators frequently use terminology that only they understand, forgetting that most people are not responsive to the jargon of the educator. Terms such as natatorium, learning stations, and stanines may be common to the educator but to the layperson they are not familiar and are apt to breed doubt about school officials' ability to communicate and about administrators' sincerity in wanting people to know what the schools are doing.

Use Comfortable Words

In addition to using educational terminology, educators are frequently guilty of writing words that are not understood by average readers. Before preparing a publication aimed at the public, school officials should determine the reading level of that public and write at that level. An easy way to determine the reading level is to apply a readability formula. One of the best such formulas is the Gunning-Mueller Fog Index,[1] which considers average sentence length and the number of words with three or more syllables. For ease of reading, sentence length should seldom be more than seventeen to twenty words, and the two-syllable word is clearly preferred to the five-syllable word. One mark of an educated person is the ability to communicate at a level that a specific audience will understand.

Determine Reader Interest

Before starting a new publication, an attempt should be made to determine the interests of those who will be expected to read it. For instance, a teacher-recruitment brochure should apply research findings in this area and include such information as the proximity of graduate schools, cost-of-living data, and the specific opportunities and challenges that make the district what it is. A newsletter earmarked for the community should meet the interests of that community. Particular interests should be determined before the newsletter is started and rechecked periodically. Again, this guarantees that the publication will communicate with the audience. A publications committee of students, staff, and the public could be helpful in determining reader interest. It may be decided occasionally that no existing publications are natural vehicles for the particular information that is to be communicated, and that another communication technique or a new publication will be necessary. This decision must, of course, be dictated by the needs of the audience and available funds.

CHOOSING CONTENT

Publications that are attractive and well written will gain the attention of potential readers, but the content must be solid as well. Too many school publications dwell on awards and recognition received by the schools and too few include information on problems that the schools are facing, with possible solutions. If content is constantly about the achievements of the district with no mention of problems, people will dismiss the publication for what it is: A puff piece to laud school officials either directly or indirectly. Such a policy could justifiably cause taxpayers to question the wisdom of using tax money to support the publication.

Content should focus on people, not on buildings and programs. Students' learning, teachers' teaching, and people involved in the education process can bring content alive. Emphasis should be placed on what people in the schools are doing.

Instead of an article on the cost of the new speech program, show the new speech therapist in action. Indicate how many students will be helped in how many ways by the therapist's presence. Of course money is important and people want to know how their tax dollars are being used. But show them in a way that communicates more than just figures.

Content must be balanced. Again, what is included in a publication depends on reader interest and the long-range objectives of school officials. Some suggestions for content include classroom innovations, building plans, community relations ideas, problems of students and how they are being met, and follow-up information on previously publicized innovative programs.

If the audience is concerned about a topic, that topic should be treated in the publication. A careful watch must be kept on overplaying one topic because of the personal preference of the editor or an administrator. Many school publications go overboard on cocurricular activities, such as sports and drama undertakings. Although these are important parts of the schools' offerings, they should not be emphasized merely because coaches and advisors cooperate in providing information.

People are interested in reading about those things that are different than when they attended school. This means that publications should explain new materials, teaching approaches, use of buildings, and new administrative and special services.

DETERMINING WHO SHOULD WRITE THE PUBLICATIONS

The writing should be done by people who know how to put facts and ideas into simple, readable language that attracts attention and holds interest. Usually, there are one or two staff members in most school systems who have a flair for writing and can learn to produce readable copy. They cannot be expected to do this work along with regular responsibilities; good writing takes time, and allowance for it should be made in the daily schedule.

If it is necessary to go outside the school system, a local editor or commercial publicist can be engaged from time to time to write the texts of important publications.

The tendency in larger districts is to hire an experienced writer, who is placed on the staff of the superintendent, or to hire a director of community relations who is competent to supervise the entire publications program.

KNOWING HOW TO PRINT IT

Generally, school officials go to extremes regarding printing decisions; they either communicate that the publication is inexpensive by presenting an overall dull, one-color newsletter that attracts few readers or present an extravagant full-color brochure on glossy paper that is certain to cause concern among taxpayers. Inexpensive publications need not be dull; attractiveness should not be equated with expensiveness. Some districts, in an attempt to communicate that publications are inexpensive, prepare them on a mimeograph machine. With today's sophisticated electronic stencil equipment, photographs and line drawings can be reproduced by the mimeograph process. It is not always true, however, that the mimeograph process is less expensive than offset printing or the photocopy process.

School districts should investigate the various costs and the flexibility of available reproduction processes. In the long run, the lowest-cost desktop publishing equipment may be less expensive than the most sophisticated mimeograph equipment for certain applications.

DETERMINING PRINTING PRIORITIES

If the district does buy printing equipment and decides to print most of its forms, as well as newsletters and other publications, it is imperative that someone be given the responsibility for establishing priorities for use of the equipment. Many school officials have caused employees at all levels much grief by making printing decisions that seemed based on personal relationships rather than on printing needs. Guidelines should be communicated and forms prepared to ensure that the person doing the printing is capable and understands the printing needs. If someone is not empowered to make deadline decisions on printing, graduation programs may be wet from ink that didn't have time to dry, newsletters may be distributed on March 30 telling about an event planned for March 25, and report cards may be delayed for a week because the printer didn't realize the importance of the deadline.

GETTING EXPERT ASSISTANCE

The best guarantee for using the most efficient method for each printing job is to have someone on the staff who knows the field. This might be a school communication specialist or a former editor or a printer who knows printing. This person will be able to advise when the school's equipment is not suitable for a particular job in terms of time and money. This person could also advise when two colors are better than one and could recommend many ways to improve the overall impact of a publication. If the staff does not include such a person, it would be a wise investment to tap a consultant to take a look at the district's printing and publications. With a bit of professional help, districts can avoid oft-repeated errors and increase readership.

Using Students to Print School Publications

Some school districts try to save money by having students who are taking courses in printing use their class time to print school publications. Many printing teachers resent this, claiming that such demands interfere with the natural teaching process. If the quality is good, if the teaching schedule permits, and if students can meet deadlines, using this approach can save money and aid in the teaching process. It adds a touch of educational reality and budget-consciousness to a school publication to add "printed by students in our printing course."

It should be remembered that school publications are sometimes the only sources of impressions that people have about the school. If printed sloppily, they can communicate an ineffective administration.

Having Publications Printed by an Outside Printer

Most school districts use outside printers to print some of their publications; many use them for all publications. In either situation, school administrators can save time and money by adhering to some basic principles.

— Get at least two quotes on every printing job. Some legal requirements will dictate that formal bids be received on printing above a certain cost. Be sure someone on the staff knows enough about printing to write specifications that all printers will understand.

— If some printers are guilty of missing deadlines, insert a penalty clause. If the schools have met all the deadlines for submitting copy and reading proofs, then the printer must produce the job on time or suffer a penalty for every day of lateness. This is often a small percentage of the cost of the job.

— Realize that not all typesetters and printers are experts when it comes to layout and design, legibility of typefaces, and other important areas. Some printers do have experts available for these areas; most do not. Thus, giving the copy to the printers with no specific directions and asking them to return the printed publication could guarantee mediocrity at best, especially if the printers are extremely busy.

— Keep a copy of all material submitted. Printers seldom lose copy, but it has happened. The time and cost of making a copy are little when compared with the difficulty associated with having to redo the material.

— Make a copy of the corrected proofs that are returned to the printer. If the printer forgets to make a requested change and 10,000 copies of a newsletter are printed with a spelling error, the school will have clear proof that the error was the printer's.

— Realize that changes made at the proof stages (after the typesetter or the printer has set the type) are expensive. Too often someone in the administration decides to rephrase a statement merely because it flows a little better and insists on the change being introduced to the publication at the proof stage. This means that the copy must be reset, which changes the page layout and can alter the entire publication. Corrections of course should be made at this point; wholesale changes should not—unless the district can afford large bills for alterations.

— Be honest with printers. Occasions will arise when they are under tremendous pressures for other jobs and the school's job is not needed immediately. If school officials cooperate with printers in these instances, printers will reciprocate by helping in deadline situations caused by some unexpected but pressing problem.

SAVING MONEY ON PRINTING COSTS

Every school official should be interested in ways to save money on any phase of the school operation. Printing, in many districts, is a major expense. To save money on some printing efforts, school officials should consider the ideas listed below.

Prepare Camera-Ready Copy

Preparing the material just as it is to be printed can save an appreciable amount of money. Such materials, called *mechanical art* or *mechanicals,* are complete in all or most all of their parts, with all elements carefully and cleanly pasted down in final position. Because such materials are ready for the printer to place into a copy camera to make printing negatives, they are called *camera-ready mechanicals.*

To prepare such mechanicals well, the school must have some basic equipment. Depending on the size of the district, the number of publications it produces, and the academic program, districts may choose to move in one of two directions.

Desktop Publishing

Until the 1990s, if the volume of work justified the investment, a district could have bought a complete professional typesetting system. The advantages included the ability to produce high-quality, camera-ready typography. However, today, a computer provides both high-quality typesetting *and* layout capabilities.

This process is called *desktop publishing.* The term, coined in 1985, refers to systems that include the computer equipment, called *hardware* and the operating programs, called *software.* They bring together the text, graphics, and other elements of a publication on a computer screen and prepare camera-ready mechanicals. While traditional layout involves use of scissors, X-acto knives, waxers, T-squares, right angles, cropping Ls, and so on, desktop layout is done on a computer that contains all these tools.

The Macintosh computer by Apple and the IBM PC (Personal Computer) or its compatibles seem to be the two main choices in the desktop publishing world. A laser printer (at least 300 dots per inch [dpi]) is essential if in-house mechanicals will be prepared for low-cost publications. For better quality, up to 2,540 dpi is required, which means a more expensive laser printer.

If publishing needs are great but cost of this advanced equipment is out of reach for a district, a service bureau can be used. A service bureau is an independent business that provides help in layout, graphics, and production. Along with the computer and printer, a scanner is also useful. A scanner copies a photograph, line art, or text and transfers it to a page layout on a computer. Service bureaus also provide scanning.

Operating programs, called software, include word processing programs, desktop publishing programs, art programs, and numerous others. These must be purchased based on the needs of

the district. Three versatile publishing programs for both the Macintosh and the IBM are Pagemaker, QuarkXpress, and Ventura. If publishing needs are not great and cost is a factor, a word processing program alone may be more affordable. The typeset copy (on computer disk) can then be taken to a service bureau for layout and scanned images.

Desktop publishing allows the communicator to be in control—to set the copy; designate type fonts, leading, and line widths; and do layout. Refining and correcting can be done instantly. Placement of objects and text is accurate. The screen shows exactly what will print out on paper, a feature called WYSIWYG (pronounced wizzy-wig) or "What You See Is What You Get." Experimentation costs nothing but time.

Traditional Layout

If budgetary or other constraints limit capital equipment purchases, a school communication professional can still produce good-quality camera-ready mechanicals. To do this well, the school must have some basic equipment, most of which can be used for other purposes as well as for printing. One key requirement is a typewriter that uses a carbon or a special ribbon for sharp reproduction. Flexibility can be realized if a typewriter that has multiple elements or "golf balls" is available. This allows using different types for headlines and emphasis.

For darker blacks and larger headlines, the school could have the printer set headlines at a fairly low cost or could use rub-on, carbon transfer letters, foto-type, or other relatively inexpensive headline materials. It must also be remembered that someone on the staff must take the time to prepare the camera-ready pages; while the saving is substantial, the cost of that employee's time must be considered.

Generic drawings and illustrations, called clip art, can be purchased inexpensively and can help add interest to type-heavy pages. It can be purchased from companies that specialize in preparing this type of art, and can sometimes be obtained free. Yearbook companies will provide some clip art, and local newspapers throw out clip art at certain times of the year when new material is received. Ask the newspaper advertising manager to save it for the schools. Kits, such as those prepared by the National Education Association for American Education Week, often contain clip art that can be simply placed on publications for camera-ready use. Another source of clip art designed especially for schools is the Educational Communications Center, P.O. Box 657, Camp Hill, Pennsylvania 17011. Many of these sources also provide clip art on computer disks.

Be careful that the clip art represents the community and the student body. If your students are black, white, and brown, your clip art should be too.

Use Bendays or Tints for a Second-Color impact

Schools too often opt for a second color in their printing when they could get almost the same effect by using a screen or tint block. If the ink being used is black, use various shades of gray to break up the page. (These shades are called Bendays or tints.) Bendays can be used by schools in their in-house printing too. Art supply houses can supply materials for screens that are easy to use. Using screens of course saves the extra cost of a second color. Desktop programs allow the user to designate a percentage of screen for a text block (100 percent = solid). A common percentage chosen is 20 percent. If type within the screened area is the same color as the screen, use boldface type.

Edit Effectively

A major portion of the cost of any printing job is the composition (typesetting). This means that fewer words to set will cost less money. Schools could save a decent sum yearly by editing copy better. It is not uncommon for a good editor to condense what was originally a 48-page annual

report to a 28-page report without losing any of the important information. To make this idea work, however, the chief school officer must place confidence in a skilled editor so that the ego-involvement of the authors of the various articles is not permitted to overcome the sound judgment of a professional communicator.

Plan to Avoid Tight Deadlines

Anticipating printing needs is another way to save money. Printers that bid on printing that requires such a tight deadline that they must pay overtime to meet the time-pressured date will necessarily charge more than when they can schedule the work in their regular workday. If working primarily with one printer, provide forms and other materials that have no time strictures so that they can be done at the printer's convenience.

Avoid Elaborate Designs and Bleeding

Unless the school has an artist who volunteers artwork services, elaborate designs may necessitate the printer's placing a graphics specialist on the job. This means more dollars. Be sure that the design in some way enhances the message and is not merely design for the sake of design. Artwork can get in the way of the message rather than helping to communicate it. This is where a professional in the field of publications is needed. Suggestions can more than pay for the fee by encouraging school officials to communicate the most for the least cost.

For example, bleeding is running the artwork, photo, or color off the edge of the page. Research indicates that the readership rate is increased only slightly by bleeding. Yet the cost may increase sufficiently to cause school officials to reject the concept of bleeding almost all the time. Bleeding requires a larger sheet of paper to be used because the color or photo must run to the edge. The only way to do this is to print on a larger-size paper and cut it. Bleeding may be cost efficient if your finished brochure size can be slightly smaller than standard.

Use Standard-Size Paper

Before allowing the creative mind of the art department chairperson to order an unusual-size paper for some special report, check on its cost. Frequently the decision will be to return to a standard-size paper. Occasionally some special effect will be desired, perhaps justifying the additional cost of an unusual size. Check with the printer before specifying a size; he or she may advise that by changing the size slightly, much money can be saved.

Avoid Dating Publications

The astute educator can save money by planning publications to avoid obsolescence. For example, the teacher-recruitment brochure that includes salaries as part of the permanent brochure is outdated by next year when the new salary schedule is announced. One way to overcome this is to print inserts to enclose in the brochure each year. The colors and layout concepts of the original brochure are carried through to the insert. Another approach is to include a pocket in the brochure that allows up-to-date, changing information to be inserted.

Get the Most Out of Each Expensive Printing Item

Some schools publicize the cost of printing each publication. This is sound in that it mandates that educators consider the benefits of the publication against the costs incurred. This cost-consciousness can lead to using an expensive printing item for more than one purpose. For instance, a full-color cover originally used for a teacher-recruitment brochure might also be used for the cover of an annual report.

A logo originally designed for a newsletter can be used on all publications and stationery. An effective logo can communicate the spirit of the school district and serve to identify the publication as coming from the schools.

When designing a logo, be sure to judge how it will look in actual use. Often, a logo, conceived for an annual report cover, looks brilliant displayed on an artist's poster board. But if it is also to be reduced to letterhead or business-card size, the type may become illegible or the lines on the artwork too close together.

Once chosen, a logo may be applied to thousands of items that will carry the district's name over a period of years. A poorly designed logo may haunt a district for a decade or more. It is often worthwhile to engage a graphic designer to aid in the creation and proper application of a new logo. Some school district logos are shown in Figure 13.1.

FIGURE 13.1   School district logos.

Don't Insist That Right Margins Be Justified

For some reason, most educators insist that the right margins of their publications be even (justified). Although this may not require additional labor if the publication is typeset or produced with desktop publishing, justifying margins on a typewriter is very time-consuming. Secretaries must spend extra hours typing the copy a second and third time. Not only is this unnecessary; it may get in the way of easy reading. Usually the size of the typewriter type is fairly large and the columns are fairly narrow. As a result, many words have to be hyphenated, interfering with easy reading. What little research exists on this topic indicates that unjustified right margins are probably *easier* to read than justified margins for average or below-average readers. Findings seem to indicate that the even spacing between words makes text easier to read. The left margin, however, should always be even.

Use Photos Intelligently

Is there an extra charge for using photographs? Are the school's photos good enough to justify any additional charge? Check with the printer. Too many photos offer poor contrast and little action, thus detracting from the publication. It is better to omit poor-quality photos that do not enhance the publication. This will save money and improve the publication.

DESIGNING AND LAYING OUT THE PUBLICATION

Why do readers pick up one publication and toss another in the wastebasket? Reasons differ from reader to reader, but one of the most common reasons is the layout and design of the publication. Some publications simply look inviting; others do not. School officials responsible for preparing publications would do well to pay attention to attractive and inviting design; not to is to waste money. The cost of printing is about the same, the time invested varies little, and the dis-

tribution costs are constant—whether or not the publication is read. And one way to increase the chance of its being read is to make it attractive to the eye in the quick first glance that potential readers give today's mail. Remember that the school publication is competing with other publications, most of which have been paid for. This means that readers feel some responsibility to read some of the publications. The school's publications, on the other hand, arrive free and must capture the reader's attention.

Some editors have the knack of putting together effective publications, and others don't know where to start. The differences in quality are vast. What do some editors know that others don't? What are the ingredients for effective layout and design? The ideas listed below offer suggestions for preparing publications that will be visually appealing.

Prepare Every Publication for Three Kinds of Readers

If school district officials conducted a study of the way readers look at school publications, they would probably be able to group them into three categories: those who casually glance at the publication as they separate the mail; those who spend two or three minutes looking at the publication; and those who read most or all of the articles in the publication. The educator who prepares each publication for all three kinds of readers gets the most out of every printing dollar spent.

The 30-second reader, the one who flips pages not really looking for anything, should have messages especially designed to catch the eye. This is easy to do; therefore, it is surprising that so few school districts employ this approach. One of the most eye-catching methods that also serves as a copy-breaking device is the bold one-sentence or one-phrase statement that teases the reader to read the article from which it is taken. Called a blurb, this device also provides the opportunity for school officials to communicate a few key points to just about everyone who picks up the publication. Inasmuch as the segment of the audience that spends less than a minute on a school publication is relatively large in most districts, it makes sense to include blurbs.

The 30-second reader needs eye-catching messages

For the audience segment that spends about three minutes on a school newsletter, headlines that inform are vital. So are photo captions that provide basic information. These should be written with the assumption that the accompanying story will not be read. For these readers too it is important that the first sentence of every story contain vital elements of the news that the editor deems readers should have. This first sentence should also entice readers to continue reading.

The final segment of the readership audience is the group that will read most of the stories most of the time. However, in most school districts, this segment is the smallest of the three groups.

Use White Space Effectively

School officials are justifiably concerned about getting as much as possible for every tax dollar spent. The public is demanding this more and more. Yet educators who are not knowledgeable in the field of school publications can misapply this concern. For instance, some administrators and board members might feel that every page should be filled as much as possible. They believe that "white space" implies that there isn't enough information to fill up the publication. Yet the publication that has no or very little white space is read less than a publication that uses white space functionally. White space provides contrast as well as a resting point for the readers' eyes.

Break Up Large Blocks of Text

Because all school officials are money conscious, the *dollar-bill test* is a good one to use to determine if the publication is violating one of the basic rules of layout and design. The idea works like this: Place a dollar bill anywhere on a page of the publication at any angle. It should always be touching something other than copy (text). This means that a subhead or a headline or a photo or clip art or a blurb should touch the dollar bill at all times. If this is not the case, the page should be redesigned to avoid the long blocks of type that will undoubtedly cause some would-be readers to reject the page because it looks like too much to read. In addition to the use of blurbs and subheads after every fifth or sixth paragraph, editors can apply other copy-breaking devices, such as an occasional box around an article, a Benday or tint, or boldface type over tint blocks for easy legibility. Bullets or numbers can also be used to break up a long list. A head-and-shoulder shot of a speaker can be inserted in a story to break up a steady stream of words.

A good technique is to collect publications that are appealing. By analyzing them, most editors can come up with ideas that have worked for other people and apply them to their own publications.

Attempt to Maintain a Balanced Page

Theories abound regarding the best approach to maintaining balance on a page of a newsletter. The professional editor knows all about this vital phase of layout and design; the beginner should realize primarily that each page must seem pleasing to the audience. It must not be top- or bottom-heavy. This means that not too much visual weight should be located on one section of the page. For example, the logo and nameplate and two photos should not all be at the top of the page with all copy on the bottom two-thirds.

Consider a Standard Design for Certain Publications

Publications issued periodically may lend themselves to a standard design that can be used time after time with minor variations. A four-page community newsletter or a one-page internal newsletter, for example, may use the same basic format each time. This of course saves the editor time. Such a standard design immediately identifies the source of the publication and guarantees that just about any editor with basic layout knowledge can implement the design concept effectively.

Since such standardized designs for important publications may be used over a period of years, it may be a worthwhile investment to consult a graphic artist to establish a workable yet flexible design that an editor can follow easily.

Determine Which Stories Deserve Emphasis

A common error is to give all stories equal emphasis. Perhaps for internal morale purposes, school officials sometimes demand that each story be of approximately the same length. This only confuses readers; understandably, they wonder what the educators consider important. The editor must decide, after consultation with the superintendent, what is the most important news for each issue. Then the design and layout must be determined to communicate the importance of certain information.

Consider the Relationship Between Facing Pages

When preparing any publication with more than two pages, always plan the relationship of facing pages. If the two pages treat the same subject matter, show that they go together. A few ways to do this would be to run a line over the top of the two pages; to extend a headline over the two pages; and to use the same size type and column width and the same margins on the two pages. The layouts of the two pages also need to be balanced. Consider the page elements as they relate to each other on both pages: photos, heads, boxes, and tints.

Use Color Wisely

The beginning editor usually errs by using too much color. The judicious use of color can enhance a publication and attract additional readers. The misuse of color in an ostentatious and gaudy fashion can turn off readers and add expense. When competing with top commercial magazines for attention, school publications can easily spend a lot of money. Perhaps it is better to offer quality one-color publications than to sprinkle color throughout. If in doubt, consult an expert. When choosing colors, do so intelligently, not merely on a personal preference basis. Consider the psychology of colors. For example, a controversial topic might best be handled with a cooling green as a second color. A brochure explaining the school budget should not be printed in red ink. To attract attention in piles of mail, some schools use a light-colored paper like yellow, green, beige, or blue with black ink.

Using a special color ink is worth considering—asking the printer to mix a black with blue or green will produce a highly legible color that is distinctive. It is still considered one color and will not increase costs with most printers; some will charge a minimal amount for this accommodation.

Some printers run certain colors on certain days, so it would be most cost-efficient to meet the deadline for that "color" day. Another savings is to "piggyback" on another job. If the printer is already printing a black and green job, he can run another job in the same run before changing inks. This works well if the publication has flexibility in color choice.

Don't Print over Illustrations

Every once in a while, a creative person decides to inject a touch of cleverness in a publication by printing copy over an illustration. Usually this backfires. One school district produced a holiday message in red ink over a green tree. Someone thought it was a new idea; most recipients of the publication lost some respect for the publication because the message was almost impossible to read. Black or dark type over an illustration will usually be readable if the illustration is screened very lightly in the background (5-15 percent, depending on the color). This is a graphic device that should be used sparingly.

Choose Ink and Paper Carefully

People are accustomed to reading body type (the text) in black ink. Research indicates that black ink on yellow or white paper is extremely legible. For some reason educators occasionally print publications in green or red ink. Some editors, wishing to vary the impact of the publication by changing a color of ink each issue, print photos in that color. Basically it is not pleasing to see blue or green people. The professional who knows colors can effectively deviate from the standard combinations; the amateur who does this usually misses in an attempt to offer an innovative-looking publication.

Most printers can be helpful when it comes to selecting colors for ink and the proper paper for the publication. Schools usually want to avoid the impression of spending too much money for expensive paper. The printer can assist in this regard. Choose paper with a dull or glossy finish but avoid the high-gloss sheets. Contrast between ink and paper is important, so do not select an ink that is close to the color of the paper. An off-white or cream-color paper can give a rich look and still provide desired contrast.

The opacity and weight of the paper are important, too. Will the reader see the ink showing through from the other side of the paper? If a publication is to be mailed, will the difference between 60-pound and 70-pound paper necessitate adding postage for each mailing? Will the publication be read once and discarded or will it be kept for frequent use? The answers to these questions should help dictate the kind of stock used. The cost of the paper is another necessary consideration. The printer may be able to guide school officials to a less expensive paper that will serve as well as the one originally selected.

GETTING THE MOST OUT OF TYPOGRAPHY

Typography plays a vital role in the overall impact of the publication. An integral component of the layout and design, typography—sometimes in a subtle way—helps determine whether or not people will read a particular article and whether or not they will remember what they read.

Despite its importance, typography is often overlooked when a publication is put together. More often than not, the printer's judgment is accepted. And frequently printers have little background in typography research and legibility studies. The following suggestions are offered to help educators make the best use of type.

Pick a Body Type That Is Easy to Read

If using a printer for the publication, check to see what typefaces (also called fonts) the typesetter has for body type. Adopt one and use it for most of the body type in all publications. Desktop publishing programs offer several fonts, and inexperienced desktop publishers are tempted to use them all. Vary the size, but stick to one basic type to avoid a circus-like appearance caused by mixing a number of types for text. Each typeface has its characteristics. Some are traditional; others are more modern. Some are excellent for headlines but poor for body type. One consideration should outweigh all others when picking a body type: Is it easy to read?

Much modern advertising features *sans serif* typefaces. These are typefaces with no finish strokes or feet on the letters. Yet research indicates that certain *serif* typefaces are more legible and material read in such type is retained longer. Cheltenham and Century are two serif typefaces that offer maximum legibility. Cheltenham communicates honesty and reliability—certainly desirable characteristics for a school publication. Century offers clarity and elegance—again desirable traits. Most readers obviously will not affix these characteristics to typefaces but the editor should know about them. Some other typefaces generally accepted as being highly legible are Times Roman, Baskerville, Bodoni, Casion, and Optima. Readable headline typefaces include Helvetica, Avant Garde, and Optima, usually set in bold.

Avoid Script, Italic, and Bold Type for Body Copy

Script type is difficult to read. Yet some school administrators use it because it is available on typewriters with interchangeable type fonts. Some argue that it seems more personalized because of the way the letters are formed. This may be true, but typeface decisions must be based on legibility, and script is one of the least legible types available. Italic type is also among the less legible typestyles. It should be used sparingly, occasionally to emphasize a point or for a blurb. It should not be used for large blocks of copy. Boldface type should also be used sparingly, for emphasis or for headlines.

Use Upper- and Lower-Case Type for Body Copy. The most legible type, in terms of capital and small letters, is that which we are accustomed to reading. This means the kind of type in which this paragraph is set. Capital letters are used for the first letter of each sentence and for proper nouns, and lower-case letters are used for the remainder of the words. Research indicates that this is the most legible combination. It is also one that readers find comfortable. Occasionally educators use all capital letters for a publication; they are unaware that this slows the reader and takes almost half again as much space as standard upper- and lower-case type.

Headlines are also more readable in upper-case and lower-case letters. One popular style for heads is the first word and any proper nouns capitalized, with the other words lower-case. This is especially useful when the head is written in subject-verb format.

Use a Sensible Column Width. Many school newsletters and other school publications make a negative first impression on potential readers by using only one column of type across most of an $8\frac{1}{2}$-by-11-inch page. This is too wide a column for the eye to follow without a considerable amount of work. And most people won't work that hard to get information about schools. The problem is easily solved. If the paper size is $8\frac{1}{2}$-by-11, use two columns, or one column no wider than 5 inches. Use the remainder of the page width for mini-headlines or use the white space functionally. An easy rule to follow is to limit column width to twice the point size of the font in picas (6 picas = 1 inch). For example, for 11 point type, the width should be no more than 22 picas, or $3\frac{2}{3}$ inches.

Use a Type Size That Is Easy to Read. The same people who insist on using no white space and cramming information on every available square inch of paper delight in using a type size that allows the most words on a page. This is done at the expense of those who have difficulty reading small type, and generally alienates readers. Type smaller than 8 points should never be used in the school publication. In fact, most typography experts suggest that 10-point or 11-point type be used for body copy. (There are 72 points to the inch.) Allow at least two points of leading between lines. Leading, or line spacing, is the space between the lines of type. The greater the width of the column, the more leading needed.

Specify Type to the Printer. When dealing with printers, be specific regarding your instructions on typefaces to be used. They will want to know the name of the typeface and its point size, as well as the weight of the typeface—whether you want light, medium, or bold. (Other more refined gradations are available, but most school officials will do well to know that gradations exist and that a medium weight is usually the one to use except for emphasis or over Bendays or tints, when a boldface type is recommended.) Tell the printer how wide to set the columns and how much leading to use. (If in doubt, ask.) If certain paragraphs are to be indented, communicate that too. The printer will usually provide a list of symbols that are used to designate these various type instructions.

Consider Horizontal Layout Rather Than Vertical. A large number of school newsletters use the vertical layout concept. Issue after issue, they employ the three-column format on an $8\frac{1}{2}$-by-

11-page with each column running the full length of the page. The length of the column has a tendency to turn off some readers. To obviate this problem, the horizontal layout can be used; it allows more typographic versatility without overpowering readers with long columns of type. (Samples of vertical and horizontal layout are offered in Figures 13.2 and 13.3.)

USING PHOTOS TO ENHANCE PUBLICATIONS

A photograph should be used in a school publication to communicate a message, not merely to break up copy or because "all the other schools use them." Photos serve two purposes: they give a bit of information to the hasty reader, and they attract readers to a story. Also, more attitude changes occur with a story and an accompanying picture than with the story alone. Too many editors of school publications are guilty of using sterile, posed, nonaction photos of poor quality; readers must thus conclude that no one in the schools knows anything about how to take a good photo. If the quality of available photos is bad, why advertise the fact by using them? Unless a poor-contrast photo shows some historic event of major news significance, forget it. Such photos detract from the overall first impression of the publication.

Head-and-shoulder shots, though not imaginative, can add to the overall layout of a page and can identify people with whom citizens will be dealing. Action shots are best, and because kids are what schools are all about, school publications should contain shots of students in learning situations. Too many publications use such photos as the superintendent behind a desk or feature the front of a new building (with no students) or a four-member teacher committee posing for the camera.

Some other tips regarding photos for school publications:

- Use large photos; small ones are noticed less and forgotten more quickly.

- Take a close-up shot if possible. If not, crop extraneous background material to focus on the action. You can use two L-shaped pieces of cardboard to help you frame the picture.

- Have the action in the picture point toward the story; if the action is going the wrong way and if no type appears in the photo, ask the printer to flop the photo.

- Place a related photo near its story, preferably *above* it. (Research says stories get higher readership with a related photo nearby as opposed to an unrelated photo placed nearby.)

- Always include a caption, preferably below the photo. Write captions with care; readers' attitudes toward the people in the picture can be altered by the caption.

- Use black and white photos. They reproduce the most clearly. If you use color film, allow enough time for processing and for converting to black and white. Usually conversion takes a few days, and every lab does not handle it. The printer can transform a color photo into black and white for your publication. Printing full color in your publication is usually too costly for most schools.

- Make sure the photos for general or national publication show something unusual about your school—for instance, a teacher-recruitment brochure showing a teacher and a child at a chalkboard tells nothing about the uniqueness of your schools.

- To prepare for the printer, mount each photo on a piece of $8\frac{1}{2}$ x 11 paper, using tape along two opposite edges. Label with the name of the job, top of photo, and person(s) in photo. Type captions on a separate piece of paper and designate the typeface, size of type, and the width.

DISTRIBUTING PUBLICATIONS

A school publication, no matter how well written and designed, does little good unless it is properly distributed. Making the right publication available to the right audience requires planning and implementation.

WESD
WRAP SHEET

A newsletter for District employees - December 1992

Washington District Centennial Books On Sale Now

The District's history book <u>Promise & Progress: One Hundred Years of Commitment</u> is now available for purchase and would make a great stocking stuffer this Christmas! Price is just $3.00 for the 150 page book which includes historical photographs. The history book was authored by Arthur M. Lee, a member of the Centennial History Committee that began this project almost 2 years ago. He was assisted by many current and former District employees and students.

Arizona Public Service generously donated the typesetting and printing of the book which has made it possible for us to offer it at this low price. All money raised from sales of the history book will go to the Northwest Valley Business and Education Alliance which will use the funds to provide scholarships and teacher minigrants.

Contact the Community Relations Office at 2606 to order your copies today.

District Office Blood Drive

As many of you know, Pam Santesteban's husband Tom will be going into University Hospital in Tucson in late December. In an effort to show support to Pam and her family, we are sponsoring a replenishment blood drive at the District Office on Dec. Any blood donated will be credited to Tom and help offset expenses of his hospital stay. The drive will be held Monday, Dec. 14 from 9:00 a.m. - 3:30 p.m. in the parking lot behind the IMC. Call Robin at 2641 or Kathy at 2687 if you would like to donate blood.

Coming in January - A Smoke and Tobacco Free Environment

On April 23, 1992, the Washington Elementary School District Governing Board adopted a new policy. The policy, which bans smoking and the use of tobacco, will affect people in all district buildings, on all district property and in all district vehicles. Signs will be posted throughout these areas.

The reasons for banning all smoking and tobacco are stated in the District policy as follows, "The

Governing Board accepts its responsibility for, and is dedicated to, providing a healthy, comfortable and educationally productive environment for students, staff members and visitors. The Surgeon General of the United States and all reputable medical authorities have concluded that: smoking and other uses of tobacco are causes of illness; secondary smoke is a cause of disease, including lung cancer, in healthy nonsmokers; and the simple separation of smokers and nonsmokers within the same air space may reduce, but does not eliminate, the exposure of nonsmokers to environmental tobacco smoke."

Please be aware that this new policy will take effect on January 4, 1993.

Cholla Middle School promotes peace with "Peace Pole"

World peace took center stage Nov. 17 at Cholla Middle School when students, staff and club members of the Sun City 79ers Lions and Lionesses permanently planted an 8-foot "peace pole" just outside the school office. The planting of the peace pole was part of a series of events designed to

FIGURE 13.2   An example of vertical layout from the Washington School District in Phoenix, Arizona.

The Bulletin

Inside this issue:
■ New banking arrangement expected to save money. Page 2.
■ Coaches sought for high school sports. Page 4.

February 8, 1993   A weekly newsletter for employees of Montgomery County Public Schools   Vol. 35, No. 23

Strathmore ES fifth graders listen intently as Supreme Court Associate Justice Antonin Scalia discusses the U.S. legal system, current issues and his own experiences in his rise to the nation's highest court. The students met with Scalia and toured the court as part of a school/business partnership, coordinated by principal intern Judy Brubaker, with a Rockville law firm.

Fifth graders have 'once-in-a-lifetime' visit with Scalia

More than 100 students from Strathmore ES visited the U.S. Supreme Court and met with Associate Justice Antonin Scalia on Tuesday, Jan. 26.

The visit was the result of Strathmore's school/business partnership with the Rockville law firm of Venable, Baetjer and Howard.

Scalia discussed the U.S. legal system, current issues and his own experiences in a 40-minute meeting with 103 fifth graders from the school. The students also toured the Supreme Court, saw a film on the court's history and operation and visited its museum.

"The children had a once-in-a-lifetime opportunity to converse with a Supreme Court justice, to ask questions and to gain a firsthand view of the court's operations from Justice Scalia," says Judy Brubaker, principal

(continued on page 2)

Sherwood HS English teacher wins state award

In a poster on the wall of Virginia Lockhart's classroom, Garfield the cat exhorts students, "People who can read, should." Recently, the Sherwood HS teacher was honored for her many efforts to ensure that students take Garfield's advice.

Lockhart, an English teacher and reading specialist, was among three Maryland teachers to receive a Teacher of the Year for 1992 award from the Maryland Council of Teach-

ers of English Language Arts.

"It was really a pleasant surprise for this English language arts group to consider a reading specialist for recognition," she says.

Since joining the Sherwood staff in 1981, Lockhart has initiated various activities and programs to encourage students to improve—and use—their reading skills. In addition to courses for students who need to strengthen basic reading skills, she established

"Academic Reading," a one-semester elective that helps students prepare for the verbal portion of the Scholastic Achievement Test and teaches effective reading skills for college.

Her students write periodic book reports, from which she selects comments for Book Talk, a column she compiles for the school's PTSA newsletter to encourage reading among both students and parents.

(continued on page 4)

FIGURE 13.3   An example of horizontal layout from the Montgomery Country (Maryland) Public Schools.

The first group to receive any publication—even those aimed at the general public or at teachers to be recruited—should be the internal audience. Distribution should be made internally first so that employees will be able to discuss topics in the publication intelligently with friends and neighbors.

The obvious approach to distributing the publications is not always the best one. For example, many schools send newsletters home with students, and assume naively that parents are receiving the publications. Studies have shown that after about fifth grade, very few students give the publications to parents.

Newsletters from a school principal directed exclusively at parents serve a purpose. The information ordinarily concerns students, parents, and the school staff; therefore, it is imperative that it be received by parents. Some principals announce in a newsletter mailed home early in the school year that newsletters will be sent home with the students on certain dates. This is followed up by a short article in the local newspaper announcing the availability of the newsletter.

The most effective vehicle is of course the mail. In an era when the public demands better communication from the school, the expense of a newsletter sent to parents is not only justified but a necessity if the home and school are to work together effectively.

Districtwide newsletters should be made available to all residents. Too often school officials send newsletters of a general nature only to parents of students, and include nonparents only before a school finance election. Quite understandably, many taxpayers resent this incomplete "we'll communicate only when we need you" approach. Newsletters should be mailed to all households, taking advantage of the school's nonprofit status to use the lowest possible nonprofit rates. Sound rapport with local postal authorities will serve school officials well, especially when the deadline for information is close at hand. Nonprofit mail does not guarantee delivery by any particular date. If an occasional time-pressure problem exists regarding a publication,

cooperation from postal employees may be needed even more than usual.

The best time for your mailings should be determined with the cooperation of the local postal authorities, who can advise about such things as holiday mail and days when large area firms mail bills and advertisements. If possible, avoid times of the year when reader interest would be down because of preholiday planning or vacations.

Schools use different ways to decide on a mailing list for their publications. Some hire mailing firms to send the publications to all people on their list in the geographic area served by the school district. Others prepare their own list, working from tax roles, voter registration, and public utility customer lists. No approach is foolproof; each is time-consuming to keep up to date. The time and effort expended by school employees must be weighed against the cost of employing an outside firm to handle the mailing.

Public schools, as agencies of state, county, or municipal governments, qualify to mail nonprofit mailings using simplified addresses. Instead of applying a specified name and address, have imprinted Postal Customer Local, Residential Customer Local, or Business Customer Local. The post office will deliver a copy to, respectively, all addresses, all homes, or all businesses. There is no additional charge for this service, though the post office requires that mailers prepare their mailings in a particular way. Discuss the procedure with the local postal authority or customer service representative.

Another technique to explore is inserting your publication into a local daily or weekly newspaper. Depending on how well read the paper is, your newsletter may get wide distribution. it will also be read at the same time the recipient chooses to sit down and read the paper.

In addition to mailing the community newsletter, school officials should place copies in stores and other places commonly frequented by area residents. Placing copies in offices and shops where people must wait for services, such as laundromats and doctors' offices, is a practical technique.

An effective idea is to prepare a news release on the main story in the community newsletter. Released to the media on the day the newsletters are expected to arrive in homes, the story can whet the appetite of potential readers of the publication. For some reason employees have been found to read school publications more after the area press has accorded them recognition by using a story or two from them.

Some publications can be made available through the cooperation of area groups. Real estate agents, for instance, would be pleased to have a general publication about the schools to distribute to potential or new residents. Welcome Wagon personnel could easily distribute the same kind of publication. So could the local Chamber of Commerce, the Jaycees, and other service organizations. In fact, a list of presidents of the various organizations in town might be used to mail publications that do not go to the general public. Also be sure to place copies in all local libraries.

EVALUATING SCHOOL PUBLICATIONS

Just about every editor of every publication at some stage asks: Is anybody reading our publication? The school administrator who is responsible for publications should evaluate them to determine if anyone is reading them; the evaluation results should be the catalyst for improving the publications.

Various ways exist to determine whether or not people are reading publications; among them are questionnaires, interviews, and focus panels. The questionnaire can be included as a readership study in the publication itself. To encourage readers to return the questionnaire, make it an easy tear-off form that takes no more than a few minutes to complete. Even with this approach, a very small percentage of the readers will return the questionnaire—and it is not appropriate to conclude that the nonresponding public shares the views of those who responded. The telephone

survey and the in-person interview can provide data on which to base publication decisions. These methods can be more representative than the tear-off survey.

An editor can learn much from inviting a number of people receiving the publication to discuss it in a small group called a focus panel. Four groups of five or six people can help the editor see strengths and weaknesses as perceived by these groups. Out of these discussions will come recommendations for improvement. This kind of feedback is imperative. Publications can win national awards for their excellence, but if the intended audience is not reading the publications, changes must be made.

Another way to improve publications is to have them evaluated by publications experts who have no vested interests to protect. Often school publications reflect the thinking and biases of a couple of school officials who control the content and the design. Outsiders who know the publication business can suggest improvements. If the intent of the school publications is to inform as many people as possible, investing a small consultant fee in improving the publication will, in the long run, reduce the cost per article read.

Another way to have school publications evaluated is to enlist the service of an association or company that offers a critique service. Three sources for evaluation information are the National School Public Relations Association, 1501 Lee Highway, Arlington, Virginia, 22209; the Education Press Association, Rowan College of New Jersey, Glassboro, NJ 08028; and Communication Briefings, 700 Black Horse Pike, Suite 110, Blackwood, NJ 08012.

DECIDING WHICH PUBLICATIONS TO PRINT

Many school districts annually struggle over decisions regarding which publications to print. Most school officials agree that a newsletter aimed at the general community is imperative. With the ever-increasing demand for accountability and public involvement in public education, this kind of newsletter appears to be a "must" for any school administration that recognizes its responsibility to communicate. Also on the "must" list of most administrators is an internal publication that keeps employees informed of activities and plans. Some districts combine this with a report of school board action. Annual reports, publications for parents, and other special-topic publications must be considered by the district that is concerned with a total publications undertaking. For an example see Figure 13.4.

Many pages in this chapter have dealt with the community newsletter. Suffice it to say here that such a publication can be a major plus for the communications effort. So too can an effective internal publication that dispels rumors and presents the facts.

Many schools now provide a wrap-up of board of education meetings to employees. If distributed the morning after the board meeting and if information is accurately and fairly presented, this publication can help improve employee morale. Everyone likes to know what is going on where one works. Some schools also send a board wrap-up to parents via their children. Parents like to know what is going on, and reading board briefs gives them a sense of inclusion.

Welcome to the School Board Meeting

This type of publication can be beneficial in many ways. It can identify board members and provide biographical information for the audience. It can explain the procedure to be used by those who wish to address the board. By offering such a publication, the board communicates that the same rules apply to all groups and individuals. The inexpensive publication can include some basic facts about the schools presented in succinct fashion. One board's publication is shown in Figure 13.5.

Teacher-Recruitment Brochures

With the supply of teachers dwindling in certain disciplines, districts are preparing teacher-

recruitment brochures. Some direct the brochures to a special kind of teacher or to teachers in subjects, such as math and science, where shortages exist. The brochure should provide information that tells the candidate specifically about the school or whets his or her appetite enough for further inquiry. The Bensalem schools (Cornwells Heights, Pennsylvania) appealed to teachers with the creative brochure shown in Figure 13.6.

Parent Publications

More effort should be put into preparing publications that help parents understand their role in the educational process. School officials and other educators and parents constantly talk about the need for cooperation between home and the school if the child is to receive the best possible education. Yet most schools do little to help the relationship with their publications. Some schools distribute materials that explain to parents what a child should learn in a particular grade. Many schools offer a kindergarten brochure that helps parents as their child takes that first giant step to school. Contact state or national education association or board association groups to find out what brochures they offer. A district can adapt a brochure to its needs or use it as is. Available are topics like "helping your child with homework," "TV and your child," and many others. These publications show that school administrators recognize the contributions that parents make to the education process.

Special-Topic Publications

More and more districts are distributing publications on specific topics. Some focus on one topic in their regularly scheduled newsletter. One issue might offer an in-depth treatment of art in the schools; the next issue might focus on reading. It is usually more effective to include content of broad appeal, however, so there is something for almost every reader. Schools, especially those

Staff Bulletin
of the Tacoma Public Schools, Tacoma, Washington

January 22, 1993   Vol. 26, No. 11

Re-keying buildings begins this month

Next week, the Scheduled Maintenance and Repair Team (SMART) will begin re-keying all school buildings. The team will begin changing the locks at Baker Middle School, and Wainwright and Jefferson elementary schools. The team will work through the summer to complete all buildings before the start of school this fall.

According to Buildings and Grounds Director John Helmlinger, "Most principals welcome this program because they are concerned about the security of their buildings."

In the past, Helmlinger said, there has not been a key control program in place. Employees have made duplicate copies of keys, retirees have kept keys and staff members have transferred without returning building keys. In an effort to control key usage, principals will provide a list of staff members who need after-hour access to buildings on a regular basis. All other staff members can acquire keys for specific periods of time by checking-out keys when needed.

Additionally, the new keys cannot be duplicated. Helmlinger said, "No key shop has these particular blanks — we got them directly from the manufacturer. There will be a responsibility to having a key from now on."

Principals have been given published maintenance schedules, which include timelines for re-keying each building.

Board discusses replacement for Matsusaka

The board of directors met in open session Wednesday to interview finalists for a board vacancy created by the resignation of Gene Matsusaka. Matsusaka resigned from the Tacoma Board of Directors when he was elected to the State Board of Education. *Staff Bulletin* went to press before the board meeting Wednesday evening and before the name of the chosen candidate was anounced. The new board member must be selected by the end of this month or a new member will be selected by the educational service district.

Hotline provides up-to-date facts

The Tacoma Public Schools' Legislative Information Line is updated three times each week. Call 596-2666 to hear the latest legislative information pertaining to education.

Lagos meeting Feb. 5

Pauline Yamashita, Assistant Superintendent for the American International School, will host a meeting for staff interested in teaching at the International School of Lagos.

Interested staff, particularly those who completed applications in December, should plan to attend the Feb. 5 meeting from 4 to 6 p.m. in the fourth floor board room at Central.

For more information contact Dan Barkley's office, 596-1253.

Work on new curriculum progressing quickly, high school health approved

The new curriculum has been approved, and new materials are ordered for high school health. High school science curriculum committees have been meeting rigorously since the beginning of the year, and the science curriculum for many areas has been drafted, Terry Edwards, curriculum alignment administrator, told the school board last week.

The middle school science/health/environmental education committee is looking at an integrated approach to these subjects. Work on scope and sequence for the new math curriculum should start in the spring, and the first draft of the new physical education curriculum for elementary, middle and high school has been written.

This is the progress in each area:

High school health
• Curriculum and instructional materials have been approved by the board,
• materials have been ordered, and
• implementation of the new curriculum will begin in February.

High school science
• Curriculum has been drafted for earth science 1 & 2; biology 1 & 2; chemistry 1, 2, & 3; honors chemistry 1 & 2; physics 1 & 2; and astronomy;
• vocational approval for applied biology and chemistry and principals of technology;
• curriculum development for applied science/general science to begin in early February;
• evaluation of elective science pro-

(Continued on page 3)

FIGURE 13.4   An internal publication from the Tacoma (Washington) Public School District.

Welcome

TO A MEETING

OF THE

BOARD OF SCHOOL DIRECTORS

CHELTENHAM

TOWNSHIP

SCHOOLS

ELKINS PARK, PA.

FIGURE 13.5 An effective invitation to the public from Cheltenham Township Schools, Elkins Park, Pennsylvania.

with their own printing facilities, can publish brief reports on special issues and topics. The Brooklyn, New York, schools distributed an excellent brochure on vandalism to encourage parents to help quell the outbreak of costly destruction of property. Other schools have prepared special publications for parents on topics such as drugs, test results, and the contribution that volunteers can make to the schools. Some schools have prepared publications for substitute teachers, bus drivers, volunteers, and cafeteria workers. Others have distributed special publications aimed at helping parents (and teachers) get the most out of parent-teacher conferences.

The Happy-Gram

Although low in cost and easy to use, Happy-Grams forge links between home and school. Happy-Grams can come in any form: a letter, a postcard, a note. Teachers write a short message telling the parents that the child did something positive. Some schools then mail them home, while others let the child take them home. For many parents, especially those who experienced little success in school, the Happy-Gram can be the first positive note from the school.

"I Have an Idea to Help the Schools" Form

The Haverford Township, Pennsylvania, schools have adopted a total communication package of inexpensive materials to foster two-way communications. Among the materials are forms to facilitate communication between the community and the school. One of the forms, placed in key locations around the community, encourages people to submit ideas to improve the schools. Another form encourages questions about the schools. These forms are inexpensive and can be photocopied. As part of a total publications package, they can be effective. (See Figure 13.7a and b.)

The Annual Report

Before publishing an expensive annual report, school officials should ask the question: What is the purpose of the annual report? Could that purpose be served in a less expensive way? Frequently school districts publish annual reports only because they always have or because other area school districts are producing them. If an annual report is required by law, it can often be done in a way that inexpensively provides the information mandated. Too often school officials rationalize a legal requirement into a full-blown publicity piece for the district. In many cases the money spent on elaborate annual reports could be more wisely invested in a large number of smaller publications.

If an annual report is published, it should contain not only accomplishments of the past

BE A SUCCESS IN BENSALEM

Ben Franklin was
(and all he did was fly a kite)

SCHOOL DISTRICT OF BENSALEM TOWNSHIP ● CORNWELLS HEIGHTS ● BUCKS COUNTY ● PENNSYLVANIA

FIGURE 13.6   The cover of a teacher-recruitment brochure from Cornwells Heights, Pennsylvania.

year and comparisons and contrasts with previous years, but also challenges and problems yet to be solved. Including these topics will ensure more credibility for the publication. Some school districts also effectively use the annual report format for a general publication that provides information for real estate agents, new residents, candidates for positions with the schools, and for community groups that wish to discuss the schools. Also, remember to keep the focus on children.

I HAVE A QUESTION . . .
about our Haverford Township Schools.

NAME _____

ADDRESS _____

Here's an idea . . .
to improve our Haverford Township Schools

NAME _____

ADDRESS _____

FIGURE 13.7a and b   An excellent technique for soliciting public opinion used by Haverford Township Schools, Havertown, Pennsylvania.

The School Calendar

A publication that is gaining more popularity each year is the school calendar. School districts are preparing the calendar and making it available in a variety of ways. Some are distributed free to all parents; some go to all households; some are sold to a parents' organization which then sells the calendar for a small fee; others use advertising as a means of support. The calendar should be attractive enough to grace a kitchen wall for the year. It should run for 12 months and should feature children. Part of the space for each day can be filled with scheduled school activities; another part can be left blank for family messages. The calendar can include general information about the schools such as absentee procedures, inclement weather announcements and phone numbers of key personnel. (See Figure 13.8.)

THE ROLE OF STUDENT PUBLICATIONS

For many years student publications—newspapers, yearbooks, and the like—were considered another arm of the school administration. The purpose of the publications, in many cases, was to show the schools in a favorable light. This has changed appreciably as students have demanded and the courts have backed their right to print material critical of the administration and to use words that some administrators find objectionable. It is imperative that school officials select teacher-advisers wisely because the sage adviser can prevent many community relations problems by establishing student respect for journalistic expertise. Too frequently advisers with no background in journalism are appointed to these potentially explosive positions. Students, sensing that a teacher has little knowledge in the field, challenge his or her leadership and decisions. Chaos and community relations problems usually result, causing innumerable headaches for the administrators.

Before the school year starts, it is prudent for the student editors of the various publications, the teacher-advisers and the school board attorney to get together to discuss the legal issues affecting

FIGURE 13.8 A sample of the cover for a school calendar from Easthampton Township School, Easthampton, New Jersey.

the student publications. If everyone knows the rules and if written guidelines are developed before controversial issues emerge, cool heads can prevail to solve problems through anticipation. Time spent planning can bring immeasurable benefits regarding student publications. When no plans are made and a volatile issue erupts, all the school's officials suffer in some way or another as the community divides on various sides of the issue.

Davenport, Iowa, school administrators approved the following policy statement concerning publications of senior high-school students. The policy was adopted by its board of education.

> The high school publications are vital and necessary tools of education to be utilized in teaching students the purposes and functions of mass media in a democratic society. It is essential that students who participate as editors and staff members be offered the opportunity to gain educational and realistic experiences in the concepts of the provisions of the *First Amendment to the Constitution* which asserts the freedoms of the press and speech.
>
> In order to achieve such experiences, students will be offered opportunities to inform, to entertain, to investigate, to interpret, and to evaluate— all being accepted, responsible functions of the traditional democratic press. Through the open forum function of editorial pages, all students and

other interested persons will have the opportunity to express their attitudes and views. The criteria for the inclusion of a story or any other material in the publication will be those of accepted, responsible journalism, including restraint by the student journalists and the advisers in such matters as libel, privacy, contempt, obscenity, and copyright. It is recognized that a school publication should be prepared and published by students rather than professionally compensated journalists and that it thus becomes necessary to provide the students with a journalism adviser who has professional journalism training and experience and whose duties include: teaching and implementing accepted, responsible journalism; teaching students the mechanical procedures in publishing a media product; supervising the financial duties of the staffs; advising and counseling students in the implementation of the criteria for the inclusion of stories and other material in the publication.

In summary, it is recognized (1) that students will be afforded experiences in exercising concepts of freedom of the press, (2) that they should be free of external forces which seek to restrict these freedoms, and (3) that they be provided with a professionally trained adviser to teach, advise, and counsel them in the achievement of accepted, responsible journalistic performance. The student-journalists must recognize their responsibility to provide a forum for all diverse opinion, to serve the interests and needs of the reading public, and to provide news and commentary that is accurate, fair, objective, and honest.

Newssheets and Newspapers

Thousands of elementary teachers and pupils prepare simple one- to four-page newssheets that are sent home to parents at intervals during the year. Usually photocopied, they contain samples of work done in class and describe and explain some of the learning activities carried on with a particular group of pupils.

Students can serve as reporters. Many schools are using children's computer publishing programs to produce these types of newssheets. Even young children can produce an attractive newspaper with these programs.

These publications are greatly underestimated for their value in communicating with parents. Checks on readership show that they are read thoroughly and are genuinely interesting to most mothers and fathers, who find them to be clear and convincing evidence of pupil achievement. Quite often these newssheets are passed around to neighbors and friends when something related to their own children is reported.

Practically all junior and senior high schools publish a student newspaper weekly, semimonthly, or monthly. Some newspaper staffs are now doing their own layout and design on a desktop publishing program. Most student newspapers are printed rather than photocopied. Compare a printer's capabilities and cost to your school's capabilities and cost before deciding. Aside from the educational experiences received by pupils on the newspaper staff, a well-organized and carefully prepared paper gives an accurate reflection of the daily life of the school. Its stories deal with courses of study, methods of teaching, programs, special opportunities, accomplishments, and shortcomings of the institution.

All members of the administrative and instructional staff should recognize that parents, merchants, professional persons, and other workers in the community—as well as students—read the school newspaper. Copies are taken home by pupils and mailed, in some school systems, to selected adults, including the editors of local commercial newspapers. Surveys indicate that from 45 to 75 percent of the parents read the school newspaper when it is brought home by their children and that it is reviewed with interest by others who receive it.

ENDNOTES

1. A registered trademark of Gunning-Mueller Clear Writing Institute, Inc., 736 El Rodeo Rd., Santa Barbara, CA 93110.

14

CONDUCTING CAMPAIGNS

Gaining community acceptance of an idea—whether it is a budget, referendum, or curriculum change—requires an organized plan of action. The alert administrator realizes that such community acceptance is contingent on trust and understanding—two ingredients that must be developed over a period of time.

Too often educational leaders equate community support with a specific hard-hitting, short-lived campaign designed to produce votes or some other tangible stamp of approval. When the campaign is over, they sometimes revert to considering effective communications as something to be implemented the next time a specific need arises. Although this approach met with limited success in some schools, today's better educated taxpayer demands that communication efforts be conducted on a year-round basis. Less than this prompts justifiable criticism from taxpayers that school officials tell them what they want them to know only when they need approval of an idea. For example, the school district that distributes one newsletter a year—right before budget time—fosters a skeptical attitude on the part of the taxpayers.

This chapter provides information about the ways a community accepts a new idea. It suggests guidelines for introducing innovations and also offers research findings on finance elections. It includes specific suggestions and campaign plans for gaining support for school finance issues.

HOW A COMMUNITY ACCEPTS A NEW IDEA

Although every community possesses its individuality, research findings indicate that, in most cases, a new idea is accepted or rejected in basically the same fashion from community to community. Thus, it is imperative that school officials realize the various steps that take place along the way to community acceptance. Although researchers differ on the number of specific stages in the acceptance or rejection of a new idea, many agree that five stages exist. These are often referred to as the *awareness stage,* the *information stage,* the *evaluation stage,* the *trial stage,* and the *decision* (adoption or rejection) *stage.* Beal has conducted numerous studies in the areas of diffusion of information, communication of innovations, and acceptance of new ideas.[1] He points out that face-to-face communication is the key at the all-important evaluation stage.

It is generally recognized that one-way communications play an important role in the early stages of the adoption process. Newspapers, radio, television, newsletters, and other such communications efforts are vital at the awareness and information stages. Thus, school officials should capitalize on the availability of these media outlets in presenting information to the public. They should also prepare newsletters explaining how the particular innovation or finance issue will benefit the people to be affected by it. But these efforts, though important, must not be considered the end of the endeavor to gain acceptance of the idea.

As noted by Beal and others, it is the evaluation stage that presents the case for face-to-face communication.[2] When people are considering the merits of an innovation or a bond issue, they want the opportunity to ask questions or to determine how others feel about the issue. The school administrator, armed with this knowledge, must prepare a campaign that incorporates a large number of opportunities for people to learn about the proposal in a face-to-face, two-way communications setting. This means utilizing ideas like the small-group meeting, speeches (with questions and answers) to service groups, and citizens' advisory groups.

Rogers and Shoemaker, in an attempt to use research findings and to be consistent with the learning process, with theories of attitude change, and with general ideas about decision making, developed a model of the innovation-decision process.

The model is presented in four stages:

1. *Knowledge.* The individual is exposed to the innovation's existence and gains some understanding of how it functions.
2. *Persuasion.* The individual forms a favorable or unfavorable attitude toward the innovation.
3. *Decision.* The individual engages in activities which lead to a choice to adopt or reject the innovation.
4. *Confirmation.* The individual seeks reinforcement for the innovation decision . . . , but may . . . reverse the previous decision if exposed to conflicting messages about the innovation.[3]

As with the five-stage process, the early stage (knowledge) is dependent on mass media and more cosmopolitan sources for the information. Later stages, however, draw on friends and neighbors for discussion and opinion-sharing, confirming the importance once again of face-to-face communication. Whether considered the confirmation stage or the early phases of the program after adoption, the period after gaining community acceptance is an important one that is often overlooked. It is commonly known that people who buy a new car suddenly notice that many others drive the same brand. People who purchase a particular item observe advertisements for that item appreciably more after they buy the item than they did before they bought it. Put simply, people want to confirm that their decision was the correct one. This confirmation stage, then, is one that should be capitalized on by school officials. For example, after a budget calling for two new speech therapists is approved,

stories about the therapists' accomplishments with children should appear in newspapers and the district's newsletter. A pilot program using the open-school approach should be reported upon to show how the program is working, even if no hard data are available until the end of the year. People often resent being bombarded with information about a needed change and then being told little about the change after it is implemented.

THE CHANGE AGENT

To effect change in a community or to establish a climate conducive to community approval of an innovation, the schools must identify and use a *change agent.* This person must be given the responsibility for conducting the campaign. When schools neglect to charge any one person with the leadership role in a campaign, floundering inaction, conflicts, and confusion result. Often it is assumed that the superintendent, by nature of the position, should be the change agent. This is not always the case. At times the change agent should be someone other than the superintendent, especially if the superintendent has recently suffered a loss in credibility because of some controversial issue. Public confidence in the person selected as the change agent is a necessary ingredient for any successful campaign. The public has been losing confidence in the schools for a number of years.

This has been documented since 1969 by the Gallup Poll of Public Attitudes Toward Education, published annually in the *Phi Delta Kappan.* Since 1974, Gallup has asked the public to give the schools a grade of A, B, C, D, or F. In 1992 the schools earned high marks (A or B) from 40 percent of the respondents down from 48 percent in 1974. At the same time those assigning Ds or Fs increased from 11 percent in 1974 to 17 percent in 1992.

It is vital that schools find spokespersons who are believable. This is especially important when the schools want the public to vote for a levy or accept an innovation. The selection of the right change agents might be aided by the following seven roles of the change agent as identified by Rogers and Shoemaker:

1. *Develops need for change.* A change agent is often initially required to help clients become aware of the need to alter their behavior. . . . In order to initiate the change process the change agent points out new alternatives to existing problems, dramatizes these problems, and convinces clients that they are capable of confronting these problems. Change agents not only assess clients' needs at this stage but also help to create these needs in a consultive and persuasive manner.

2. *Establishes a change relationship.* Once a need for change is created, change agents must develop rapport with their clients. They may enhance their relationship with their clients by creating an impression of credibility, trustworthiness, and empathy with their needs and problems. Clients must accept a change agent before they will accept the innovations he or she promotes.

3. *Diagnoses the problem.* Change agents are responsible for analyzing clients' problem situations to determine why existing alternatives do not meet their needs. In arriving at diagnostic conclusions, change agents must view the situation empathetically from the clients' perspective, not their own.

4. *Creates intent to change in the client.* After change agents explore various avenues of action that clients might take to achieve their goals, they should encourage an intent to change, a motive to innovate. But the change must be client-centered, rather than change for change's sake. Here the role of change agents is to motivate.

5. *Translates intent into action.* Change agents seek to influence clients' behavior in accordance with recommendations that are based on the clients' needs. In essence change agents work to promote compliance with the programs they advocate. This means more than simply agreement or intent; it means action or behavioral change.

6. *Stabilizes change and prevents discontinuances.* Change agents may effectively stabilize new behavior by directing reinforcing messages to those clients who have adopted, thus

"freezing" the new behavior. This assistance frequently is given when the client is at the trial-decision or confirmation function in the innovation-decision process.

7. *Achieves a terminal relationship.* The end goal for change agents is development of self-renewing behavior on the part of clients. . . . Change agents must seek to shift clients from a position of reliance on the change agent to reliance on themselves.[4]

The delicate nature of the responsibilities of change agents, as given above, demands that persons assuming that role be able to get along with all kinds of people. They must possess the confidence of the school board as well as the public. They must be recognized as straight-shooters who can listen as well as speak. They must possess the courage to tell their superiors when they think that public opinion will defeat an almost sacrosanct issue or innovation of the board or administration. To be effective, change agents must have constant access to all information regarding the campaign. Nothing must be hidden from them. If they offer incomplete or incorrect information to the public, their reputation could be marred, leading to a lack of confidence. If this happens, school officials should consider naming a new change agent.

HOW PEOPLE ACCEPT CHANGE

Not everyone accepts an innovation at the same time. People bring different backgrounds and attitudes to the introduction of an innovation. Therefore, they react differently to the efforts of a change agent or school system when information is presented. Educators who want to acquire community support for an idea should be cognizant of the different categories that people fall into as far as their rate of adoption is concerned. A person's innovativeness is generally recognized as the criterion by which one is categorized as an early or late adopter of a new idea. Many researchers use five categories to identify rates of adoption. The categories are innovators, early adopters, early majority, late majority, and laggards.

Innovators

Usually the first 2.5 percent of the people who adopt an innovation are eager to try new ideas. They communicate with other innovators who may live great distances from them. They usually possess more technical knowledge than later adopters and are often employed in high-risk occupations. Innovators frequently have a better financial base than others, allowing them to fail with an innovation and still remain comfortable. The innovator seeks new ventures; he or she is willing to take risks.

The school wishing to gain early support for a new idea should tap the innovators. Usually almost immediate acceptance of the innovation will be forthcoming simply because it is a change from what has been done before. Educators must remember though that innovators do not provide the kind of communication leadership that will encourage large numbers of people to accept the idea.

Early Adopters

Usually considered the next 13.5 percent to adopt a new idea, the early adopters differ from the innovators in that they communicate more with other people in the community. In fact, this group could be considered the most important one to reach because it is looked to by others for opinions regarding the proposed change or finance issue. Early adopters are frequently active in community service groups or are part of the informal power structure of the community. Such people may not appear on the formal power-structure charts but they are sought by many others in the community when decisions are to be made regarding the schools. Such people might be found among barbers, beauticians, bartenders, retired school employees, or in just about any occupation. These are people who talk to many other people, people to whom others come for advice regarding new ideas. They are respected for their judgment and will seldom accept an innovation as rapidly as the 2.5 percent innovator group.

School officials who identify the early adopters in the community are one step ahead in their campaign. By knowing who these people are, the educator can be sure to provide them with sufficient information early enough to ensure that they will disseminate it to others in the community. Early adopters, because of their position of importance among peers, should be placed on a list of key communicators and should be given appreciable information about the schools during the year. This builds confidence in school officials— a confidence that will serve educators well when they present facts to the group before community acceptance is needed for a new proposal.

Early Majority

Representing about the next 34 percent to adopt a new idea, this group provides the necessary numbers for a majority. People in this group are usually joiners—people who belong to various organizations but seldom hold office. This group follows the lead of the early adopters but is reluctant to accept a new idea too quickly. Because they often belong to many of the same organizations as the early adopters, it is possible to communicate with them through these groups. Again, this points out the sageness of working with the early adopters in the community, for they will in most cases communicate with the early majority.

Late Majority and Laggards

Making up 34 percent of the population, the late majority is skeptical and usually adopts an innovation only after social pressures are applied. Laggards, representing 16 percent of the population, are the last to adopt an innovation. Dependent on the past, they are not receptive to change or those who advocate change.

INTRODUCING AN INNOVATION

School officials planning to introduce innovations to the educational program should consider the communications and public relations phase of the undertaking with great care. The best innovation, if improperly introduced and implemented, can backfire. If people feel that school officials are not divulging all pertinent facts, they will develop a distrust that can breed all sorts of problems for administrators. Today's parents and taxpayers are better educated than their parents were; thus, they bring some knowledge to the education process. And that knowledge can indeed be a dangerous thing if not properly augmented with necessary facts about new programs. People fear the unknown, and if they realize they aren't being told enough about a new program, they will eventually criticize it, causing school officials to react defensively.

As with all communications efforts, the first question to be asked before introducing the innovation is: Who is the audience? The first audience to be considered is the internal one—teachers and other employees. Community residents expect those who work in the school to know what's going on there. In addition, morale suffers if employees are not among the first to know about innovations. The next key audience to be considered must be parents of students involved in the change. These are the people who will challenge the change if they do not understand it. Some administrators precipitate problems by assuming that the time it takes to communicate could be better used for immediately pressing tasks. This kind of error leads to problems of time-consuming magnitude—problems that could have been easily avoided with solid communication attempts.

SCHOOL FINANCE ELECTIONS

Despite court cases and appreciable discussion of school financing, many schools are still faced with the challenge of gaining voter support at the polls. And this challenge has been growing greater each year. As the number of people with school-age children dwindles, school officials can no longer count on parents of school children to carry the elections.

As competition grows larger for limited tax dollars (roads, bridges, health care, and the like)

the challenge of gaining voter approval becomes greater.

It is recognized that many schools are faced with gaining support for annual budgets, an increasingly difficult task as teacher salaries increase and the cost of other services and materials continues to rise. Some school systems need poll support to increase taxes in order to maintain the level of educational efforts; others want to improve their programs. In either case, the requirement is the same—getting enough votes for approval. Although the remainder of this chapter focuses primarily on bond issues, many ideas offered are easily adaptable to budget elections.

A look at the past can be helpful before planning campaigns. In fact, many school officials for some reason have been working with incorrect information regarding plans for bond issue campaigns. The research findings presented below should provide background for a campaign. Perhaps more important for the school official is a look at the history of similar elections in the school district. Because of the turnover of board members and administrators, those planning a campaign sometimes forget the importance of an advisory committee or the date of the election or some other specific that could affect the vote outcome.

WHAT THE RESEARCH SAYS

Studies have shown that voters' resistance to bond issues is based on many variables. These are not consistent from school system to school system or from state to state. Some factors in campaigns vary considerably. It is incumbent on school officials to consider local factors before making decisions on these items. Two factors in this category are the month in which elections are held and the length of the campaign period. Some school communications experts proclaim that October is a good month for bond elections. And it may be in some areas. The rationale that students have recently returned to school and parents therefore are receptive to school needs is a sound one. Yet an examination of some 8,000 pages of research on finance elections and voters indicated no one month as better than another for such elections.[5] The length of the campaign also had little to do with the success or failure of the elections. As noted elsewhere, the effective campaign is one that embodies the concept of year-round, two-way communication.

Most important for school officials working on a campaign are those factors that research indicates lead consistently to a favorable vote. They follow.

Support of the Municipal Government. Too many school officials forget about the people responsible for governing the town—until they need them. Every educator should remember that elected or appointed town officials have a large following of people. A liaison that encourages an ongoing exchange of information and ideas between school officials and their government counterparts must be conducive to a better overall relationship. Such communication minimizes conflicts and ensures that both groups will not, for example, publicly announce their desire to use the same site for different purposes. Although some educators still adhere to a "politics and education don't mix" theory, most school officials recognize the need to work with municipal officials and certainly are cognizant of the basic requirement of keeping them informed. A sound idea is to encourage the board of education to appoint one member as liaison to the municipal governing body. The town council can reciprocate, thus making a commitment to better communication between the two groups. If the municipal government opposes a bond issue, either publicly or quietly, the school faces a severe challenge to winning the election.

Demonstrated Need for Additional Classroom Space. People tend to vote for classrooms more than they vote for other building needs, such as administration centers or cafeterias. Thus, it is imperative that school officials clearly communicate the need for classroom space. This, of course, must be done honestly because any attempt to

make the situation appear worse than it is could backfire and damage the district's credibility. If classrooms are crowded, show photographs that prove it. Don't, however, add a few extra students for impact. Students will tell parents, and parents will justifiably resent such attempts. Most people see schools when students are not there; hence, it is difficult for them to realize the problems caused by overcrowding. The educator must demonstrate how the additional building will overcome the crowded classroom problems and how it will help students learn better. Statistics, if not overdone, can be helpful, especially if the capacity of the building has been exceeded. Student complaints about how learning is hindered could be useful in a campaign.

Promise of Additional Curriculum. How does the new building fit in the overall educational plan of the school system? This question, asked by some sophisticated, well-educated parents, is sometimes answered less than adequately by school officials who develop a plan for numbers of students without giving sufficient thought to the educational program and how it would be facilitated by the proposed building. If the building will make new opportunities available in career education or will allow additional individualized instruction, people should be told so. If more students will have more chances to learn more things better, this should be said.

Increasing Student Population. For too many years, it was fairly easy to explain the need for new buildings. As the number of school-age children became larger, the need for more school buildings was accepted. As the demographics of the country changed and declining enrollment became the norm, those communities with new developments and increasing enrollment faced a new challenge. For example, a formerly rural area might have become the latest suburb with the rapid growth that such change brings. Voters will need to be convinced that their community is different from most others. Asking for the help of service organizations to conduct a school population projection might be a sound strategy in this situation. The added credibility that such involvement gives a campaign is well worth the time invested.

Dissemination of Information through All Media.   Using every available newspaper, radio station, and television possibility, the campaign director will be one step toward success. Although the face-to-face phase of the communications effort has the greatest impact in changing attitudes, the media can be important at the information and awareness stages of accepting a new idea or voting for a bond issue. The best job can be done if a sound relationship has been established with representatives of the media before the bond issue need is imminent.

A Large Percentage of Parents in the Population.   Although parents of public school students are not to be counted automatically in the yes column, enough studies have been made to indicate that more such parents vote for bond issues than do the remainder of the population. Parents should be kept informed about the school's accomplishments and needs on a year-round basis. They should be encouraged to visit the schools and to participate in school activities when possible. Involvement of this nature is conducive to people feeling that the schools are indeed theirs. This can usually be translated into positive votes.

Citizens' Advisory Participation.   Research frequently shows that school systems that have involved a representative group of citizens on a committee to help gain support for a bond issue have met with more success than those that have failed to stress citizen involvement. The role played by citizens in the bond issue undertaking must be an active one if overall citizen support is to be expected. The advisory committee should function at the study-of-needs stage of the bond issue. In other words, the group should help determine the system's needs and study alternatives before working for any recommended solution to

meet the needs. This kind of involvement builds citizen trust in the schools.

Consistent factors leading to an unfavorable vote are opposition from any organized group, controversial placement of buildings, a large percentage of parochial school students, lack of public use of school facilities, and a large percentage of people on fixed incomes.

Opposition from Any Organized Group.   When people organize to defeat a bond issue, school officials face an increased challenge. Thus, it is incumbent on educators to find out why people oppose the bond issue. Does the group offer reasonable alternatives that school officials have failed to investigate? Have any members of this group been asked to participate on the advisory group investigating the district's building needs? Does the group have specific concerns that could be overcome with additional information provided by school officials?

The well-planned campaign will consider the role of the opposition and take steps to minimize its impact. For instance, a group gaining publicity might imply that it represents a large number of taxpayers. An investigation might divulge that the group numbers six members—an important fact for reporters and other voters to know. The opposition thrives on public meetings. Such forums present an opportunity for publicity because public meetings are usually covered by the press, which seeks controversial statements. Thus, if public meetings must be held, school officials should be sure that proponents of the building make presentations to offset the thrusts of the opposition.

Controversial Placement of Buildings.   If voters feel that a building site has been improperly chosen in terms of location, cost, accessibility, or some other factor, the vote will suffer. People, especially those whose children will attend the school in question, want to feel that the site selected is the best possible one for their children. Accordingly, it is imperative that the rationale for the site selection be presented to voters with a full

explanation of the positive considerations that might otherwise be overlooked.

Large Percentage of Parents of Nonpublic School Students. Parents who send their students to a nonpublic school often vote against public school bond issues, feeling that the new building will do nothing for their children. If the proposed building does offer opportunities for parochial school children to benefit, these should be explained to the parochial school leaders and parents. For example, if a new gymnasium could be used by the Catholic Youth Organization for basketball games, this point should be publicized. If the science facilities might be used on a shared-time basis with the local Catholic high school, thus saving the Catholic school money, this too should be made known. It is, of course, important for public school officials to develop solid rapport with private school officials before their support is solicited. This means working with officials on such items as calendars, in-service programs, scheduling of key events, and other mutually important topics.

Lack of Public Use of School Facilities. The movement toward community education emphasizes the desire of many people to tap school resources more than is commonly done. Inasmuch as the public schools belong to the public, school officials should encourage community use of school facilities. As more people benefit directly from the buildings, they will undoubtedly feel more a part of the school system. Such a feeling should engender additional positive votes.

Large Percentage of People on Fixed Incomes. People living on fixed incomes frequently experience difficulty paying school taxes. It is not surprising therefore that they are often a voting bloc that helps prevent passage of bond issues. Attempts to change the minds of such voters seldom succeed because the fixed income is difficult to stretch and because older taxpayers infrequently reap direct benefit from the schools. Although issuing a Golden Age card to senior citizens does

little to change their vote on school finance elections, the idea is a sound one. Such cards enable older people to attend sports events, school plays, and other activities free. They also entitle cardholders to free attendance at adult school classes. This approach demonstrates that the school has not forgotten those taxpayers who have been supporting them for a long period. Another effective approach to help relationships with senior citizens is to involve them in some way in schools—as aides, guest speakers, or in some other fashion. A senior citizen on the school board sometimes works in favor of the schools' obtaining support from the senior citizen group. The board should consider publicly supporting tax breaks for senior citizens.

Carter's studies of school bond elections offer the most detailed analyses of voter behavior in school finance elections. In his most comprehensive study of the topic, Carter conducted 3,400 interviews of voters from four large California Cities.[6] Carter concluded that the most significant single factor determining voter support was the degree of participation in school affairs. Most school-related activities, it was found, were directed at students' parents, thus presuming nonparents had no apparent interest in schools.

Carter also found that positive voters tended to get information on the bond issue from face-to-face contact with school officials and through written communications from the school system. The same findings were reported in studies of three New Jersey municipalities.[7] Positive voters received information from face-to-face communication from knowledgeable people and negative voters relied on newspapers or other one-way communication vehicles.

PLANNING THE CAMPAIGN

As noted earlier, the research done on bond issue support can be helpful. But more helpful is the time that school officials invest in researching their own community before starting a campaign. For example, a study of past bond issues might show that three bond issues have passed with the help of advisory committees and that two bond issues without advisory committees failed. In some systems with rapid turnover of school officials, this fact may not have been remembered. A good starting place for planning the campaign is a thorough look at facts from previous campaigns.

Surveying the building needs of a school district can require from several months to a year. Some school officials undertake this responsibility themselves; others choose to employ consultants for this purpose. It should be remembered that many taxpayers are concerned about buildings they consider monuments to school officials. One governor chastised educators for building palaces that are monuments to architects and engineers. If one elected official criticizes another in this manner, certainly taxpayers have their doubts about some of the buildings proposed by school boards. One way to alleviate this concern is to include a cross section of citizens in any group studying the building needs of the district. The use of a consultant sometimes helps obviate taxpayer doubts about school officials asking for more than is needed.

In addition to surveying building needs, the administration should assemble all data pertinent to the problem before any public announcement of an election is made. Included among the data will be the following:

— A complete report on how funds from the most recent bond issue have been or are being spent, including lists of completed projects, current projects, and proposed projects. The report should also include such facts as square-foot costs and the number of children for whom the projects have provided housing.
— An analysis of enrollment trends over the past several years.
— An analysis of current enrollments by grades to determine future classroom requirements in the upper grades.
— A census of preschool children by attendance areas. Members of advisory groups, parent-teacher associations, or other service groups are usually willing to conduct the necessary surveys to provide this information.

— An enrollment projection for the next five years, including data about proposed housing and apartment developments.

Most of these facts are newsworthy, and the superintendent will want to take advantage of every opportunity to inform parents and the general public. The media are usually receptive to stories about enrollment, school building programs, and community surveys. A continuous program of information about these topics will prepare the public for announcements regarding additional building needs.

DETERMINING THE PROPOSAL

As soon as these preliminary steps have been taken, the superintendent and staff should begin developing the specific proposal for meeting the building needs of the district. Every alternative should be examined—including community education, twelve-month schools, additions to existing buildings, split sessions, and whatever else any member of the community might propose. By looking at all possible solutions in depth, school officials can anticipate the arguments of opponents of any proposed program. It is of course helpful in gaining community approval if members of all segments of the community are involved in the vital stages of studying the alternatives. Included in this committee should be parents, other taxpayers, students, teachers, and other staff members.

Once a proposal has been determined, a careful check should be made with state authorities to determine the proper procedures to follow to ensure that the bond proposal is presented in a legally correct way. Such thoroughness negates the possibility of embarrassment caused when a proposal must be postponed or changed because of the intercession of a state official.

ESTABLISHING A PHILOSOPHY

Some school officials adopt a "win at all costs" philosophy for their campaigns. Others select a "tell the people the facts and whatever they do will be the proper result" approach. Some educational leaders feel strongly that it is their responsibility to gain public support for bond issues if, indeed, buildings are required to maintain education at a predetermined level. Others feel that the schools should reflect the will of the community, and therefore there should be little more than factual presentation to woo community votes. Each superintendent and board must decide which approach is better for their needs. This decision will affect other decisions, such as the naming of the campaign director.

NAMING A CAMPAIGN DIRECTOR

Leadership is an extremely important ingredient often overlooked in a campaign. Too often the responsibility is delegated to administrators who face numerous other time-consuming responsibilities. Somehow they are supposed to find the time to exert the needed efforts to guide the campaign and still perform all their other duties. If administrators assume the leadership role for the campaign, they must receive assistance with other duties. If no such help is available, the superintendent must apprise the campaign director of priorities so the administrator will know how to budget time.

Campaign directors must possess the ability to feel comfortable as change agents. They must be able to get along with all kinds of people and possess organizational ability. It is helpful if they have had experience dealing with the mass media and if they know how to meet deadlines. Occasionally a noneducator can serve as campaign director. If this person has served on a committee studying the district's building needs, commands respect of the community, and has the time and ability to lead the campaign, he or she should be considered. Of course this means that the person's relationship with school officials would have to be clearly communicated to all employees. If such a person were not given proper cooperation by the staff, enthusiasm would wane and leadership efforts could be minimized.

TIMING OF THE CAMPAIGN

Well-planned campaigns usually have three distinct phases. The first, which can begin a year to a few months before the election, should include a careful survey of the building needs. It should include a detailed plan for the campaign itself and should identify community leaders who will assist in campaign efforts. This phase should also pinpoint the various audiences to be reached during the campaign. This phase can also include voter registration.

The second phase of the campaign should be a period of community education concerning the building needs of the schools. Newspaper articles, presentations to community organizations, public meetings, and distribution of materials to parents and other taxpayers are activities to be carried out during this phase. This informational program must be implemented far enough before the election to allow community discussion of the needs and to provide answers prompted by the information disseminated. During this period, much face-to-face communication should occur.

Phase three of the campaign usually takes place from a month to two weeks before the election. Bumper stickers are distributed, house-to-house canvasses are conducted, brochures are mailed, and advertisements are placed in the media. A feeling of reaching the campaign climax must be experienced by campaign workers just before the vote takes place. A campaign hastily patched together with little organization and insufficient time to establish any momentum seldom succeeds. On the other hand, a too-long campaign in which campaign workers and the public lose interest before election day can backfire, especially if opponents mount an offensive during the last few days. Knowing the climate of a community can be helpful in planning the campaign length.

FINANCING THE CAMPAIGN

In many states school districts are prohibited by law from spending public funds on campaigns.

Although many states allow schools to provide information explaining the needs of the schools and the advantages of the proposed building, schools nevertheless are often prohibited from urging a yes vote by using school money. Yet campaigns cost money. It is necessary, therefore, to solicit money from business people, service groups, PTAs, advisory groups, and other organizations which support the need for a new building. This is often best accomplished by the citizens' advisory group that is working on the campaign. Two sources sometimes forgotten but used by some districts are architects and contractors who have much to gain from the passing of a bond issue. At times these groups will provide public relations help for a campaign. A budget should be determined to pay for advertising, brochures, billboards, consultant help if needed, and the cost of surveys. In some districts volunteer help can be obtained from talented members of the community. For example, a polling firm executive might donate his or her talent or facilities to feel the community's pulse a month before the election. A public relations firm president with children in the schools might offer his or her expertise to prepare a brochure. People are sometimes flattered to be asked to help. Often, they become a friend of the school and bring their friends to the polls, certainly a desirable by-product of their involvement.

CITIZENS' ADVISORY COMMITTEE

As noted earlier, the existence of an advisory committee enhances the district's chances of winning the election. The committee is most effective if it, or another similar committee, has studied the needs of the district and has been involved in the recommendation of the proposed building. People believe their friends and neighbors in most cases; thus, it is important to involve as many people as possible in the campaign. When people become involved, they feel more committed to the schools and will remember to vote and encourage others to join them at the polls. Too many advisory committees are merely window dressing; they look good on paper but seldom become involved in working on the campaign. Taxpayers become suspicious of the reason for such a committee's existence. One school district successfully used the involvement technique to its fullest—numbering 10,000 persons on the Good Schools Committee working for bond issue passage.[8]

Most school systems, however, will benefit from a committee of active members numbering from 25 to 100. An effort should be made to include members from as many "interest" groups as possible. Parent-teacher associations, the League of Women Voters, the American Association of University Women, labor unions, veterans' groups, service clubs, the Jaycees, the Chamber of Commerce, religious leaders, taxpayers' associations, business people, realtors, mass media representatives, members of the school staff, and students should be represented. Every effort should be made to include representation from all socioeconomic and racial groups in the community. If the group is handpicked by school board members and includes only friends, the committee could justifiably be considered a "rubber stamp" for the board.

The school superintendent or the board of education, independently or together, usually invites citizens to serve on the advisory committee. The group should be organized before final decisions are made concerning the amount of the bond issue and the date of the election. The organization should take place from three to six months before the election. Any proposal submitted to the citizens' committee should be tentative, subject to change on the recommendation of its members.

Presented below are suggested steps on organizing and working with a citizens' advisory committee. These suggestions represent a synthesis of the opinions expressed by many school administrators in literature dealing with this subject.

◼ As soon as a definite proposal for a school bond election is announced, preferably at a meeting of the board of education, an open invitation should be extended to all citizens who may be interested in serving on a citizens' advisory committee.

▬ The school administration should then prepare a letter, signed by the president of the board of education or the superintendent of schools, to be sent to every known organization in the district, inviting each one to send a representative to the organizational meeting of the citizens' advisory committee. It should be explained, however, that committee members are to serve as individuals, not as representatives of the groups.

▬ Letters of invitation should also be sent to other persons who may have influence in the community or who would be able to make worthwhile contributions to the work of the committee.

▬ At the first meeting, members of the board of education and the administrative staff should present the current and anticipated building needs of the district, the proposal for meeting these needs, and the estimated cost of such projects. A detailed report covering these points should be distributed to everyone in attendance. This report should also be mailed to groups not represented at this first meeting.

▬ At least two subcommittees should be chosen at this meeting—the first to make an intensive study of the proposal and to prepare a report for presentation at the next meeting, and the second to prepare a report on committee organization. This second subcommittee could nominate a general chairperson and suggest other needed subcommittees and their chairpersons at the next meeting. The administration should offer all help necessary for these subcommittees to carry out their assignments.

▬ After allowing enough time for a thorough study of the proposal, a second meeting of the citizens' advisory committee should be called. In the meantime, follow-up letters will have been sent to all groups not represented at the first meeting. These organizations will be urged to be represented at the second meeting.

▬ The first order of business at the second meeting should be the presentation of the report from the first subcommittee. This should be in considerable detail, and any modifications in the original proposal should be thoroughly explained. Following discussion, the citizens' committee should vote on the proposal. If the vote is overwhelmingly favorable, the committee can proceed to organize as a working committee to assist in planning and conducting the campaign. If any appreciable number of people oppose the issue, the committee should be asked to continue its study of the problem. Anyone unwilling to accept the recommendation of the subcommittee should be asked to serve on this study group.

Other subcommittees usually formed to assist in carrying out specific tasks of a bond campaign are those on finance, endorsements, speakers, printed materials, newspaper publicity, and radio and television publicity. Ordinarily, a steering committee is also selected to coordinate campaign activities.

REGISTRATION OF VOTERS

One of the key undertakings of a citizens' advisory group should be voter registration. If the advisory group exists to help gain voter approval, selectivity in registration should be practiced. It is especially important to make sure that parents of school-age children and preschool children are registered, for these parents are more likely than others to support the bond issue. It is not commonly realized that many people don't know whether or not they are registered to vote in school elections. Because some states do not require voters to decide on school buildings, people moving to states that require such voting may not know that being registered for "regular" elections makes them eligible for school elections. As many as 15 percent of the people in some communities have been found to think that some additional registration was necessary; therefore, they failed to vote even though they favored the bond issue.

The advisory committee can obtain up-to-date registration lists and check them against school rolls to determine which parents need to register. A letter from the PTA president or from the advisory group might be a solid first step to encourage parents to register. A follow-up phone call or visit providing facts about the ease of registration could be step two. PTA members might survey the community to identify preschool children and help encourage their parents to register. This investment of time provides the schools with a larger list of yes votes—a valuable list for action around election time.

OTHER CAMPAIGN PARTICIPANTS

Certain individuals and groups play important roles in school bond elections. Among these are board members, school administrators, teachers, students, and parent-teacher associations.

Members of the Board of Education

The board of education, of course, is responsible for officially determining the amount of the school bond issue and for authorizing the holding of an election. Its responsibility does not end at this point, however. Board members are also responsible for doing everything in their power to assure that a vigorous campaign is waged. They should be involved at every step. They should assist the superintendent, the school staff, and the citizens' advisory committee in planning the campaign; they should volunteer their services to the speakers' bureau and other committees that can benefit from their talents. The board should constantly strive to build a climate of confidence and trust by conducting most business at public meetings with a minimum number of executive meetings. Board members should remember that their friends and neighbors can learn from them what the needs of the schools are. Some studies indicate that board members' neighbors fail to vote in school finance elections because they lack sufficient information about the finance issue; their board member friend never discussed the subject with them.

School Administrators

All school administrators have made friends in the community and have an even larger number of people who respect their opinions as educators. They should be totally aware of the bond issue facts before they are made public, and all employees should be extended this courtesy. This is good for morale, and it helps the campaign effort as this information is disseminated to other people who assume that the employees know what they are talking about. Principals enjoy a special position with the neighborhoods they serve. They should establish a communications network with parents and others in the immediate community. This network might include a weekly lunch with a different group of six or eight people. It might include an informal newsletter or an occasional principal's forum held to encourage feedback and discussion with parents and others. Whatever the communications channels are, they should be employed to inform people about the bond issue.

Teachers

The role to be played by teachers in school finance elections is still a topic for discussion among school officials. Yet, many leaders of teachers' associations agree that teachers can play an integral role in gaining public support for the budget or bond issue. Teachers' salaries command a large portion of the school budget; therefore, many school officials feel it makes sense for the teachers' association to campaign for the passage of the budget. Others argue that ostentatious efforts by teachers might backfire if taxpayers interpret such efforts as self-serving. A national teachers' group suggests that it is not a question of whether or not teachers should participate in a school tax campaign, but in what way.

Understandably, teachers would like to be part of the planning group that determines what the building will be like. Frequently they can suggest changes that will make the building more functional and also save taxpayers money. In any event, teachers who participate in planning the building can be expected to support its need more than those who play a spectator role. Teachers' associations can be of appreciable assistance during the campaign. Some associations have members who possess expertise in bond issue campaigns and also have access to excellent bond issue materials prepared by state and national teacher associations. The school officials who minimize the role to be played by teachers do the campaign a major disservice.

Students

When most educators consider the role of students in finance campaigns, they think of the ways students can help sell the building needs to the community. This is a difficult area, at best. Using students to sell school needs, unless the students, themselves, organize, can provoke negative reactions from taxpayers. It is generally felt that students should not be used to distribute campaign literature or to make posters in art classes, for example. A contribution often made by students without any prodding takes place at public hearings. Often students will testify at public hearings about the need for more space, citing specifics that only they can fully realize.

Too many schools neglect an important educational responsibility in respect to students and their understanding of school finance elections. Somewhere, in every curriculum, an opportunity should be included for students to understand how public schools are supported. This is especially important now that eighteen-year-olds can vote, but instruction should be provided long before students reach this age. Every high school graduate should know how local schools are financed. High-school students who are eighteen should be encouraged to register. Most young voters pay no property taxes, and therefore do not feel the increased taxes mandated by a positive vote on election day. Election results indicate that most eighteen-year-olds vote for school finance needs.

Parent-Teacher Associations

Strong support for school bond proposals is likely to come from parent-teacher association members. For this reason, school administrators should enlist their help early and seek their aid at every stage of the campaign. Following is a list of suggested ways to use the aid of parent-teacher association members:

— Invite every parent-teacher association unit within the district to be represented on the citizens' advisory committee.
— Arrange through the district council to have meetings of all units. Administrators, board of education members, and district council officers should plan the programs for these meetings.
— Invite the parent-teacher association to assist in carrying on the registration campaign.
— Invite the parent-teacher association to make periodic surveys in all attendance areas of the school district to determine the number of preschool children in each area.
— Ask the parent-teacher association to help in preparing campaign materials, assembling speakers' kits, addressing postcards and letters, taking notes at meetings, and duplicating and distributing minutes.
— Ask the parent-teacher association to organize and conduct the house-to-house canvass, if this technique is employed in the campaign.
— Ask the parent-teacher association to organize election-day tasks, such as driving voters to the polls.

KNOWING THE COMMUNITY'S THINKING BEFORE THE ELECTION

After determining which groups can help in the campaign and the roles they can play, an early step should be finding out the community's thoughts and opinions regarding the need for the building. Too often school officials conduct surveys after elections to discover why the referendum failed. It is wiser to survey well before the elections to determine the best kind of campaign to wage. Surveys can elicit useful information regarding how much people know about the building, specific objections to the referendum, unanswered questions, and misinformation. Given this information, school officials can plan a campaign that answers the community's questions and helps eliminate misinformation. If, for instance, the survey unveils that a large segment of the community feels that additions to buildings would be preferred to a new building, much of the campaign will have to be directed to demonstrating that additions were fully considered but rejected. Reasons for rejection must be clearly stated and the rationale for the new building shown. School officials, acting on information from a survey, might want to reconsider their proposal before making the commitment on a referendum.

A survey can be conducted by the advisory committee, by the PTA, by service groups, or by school officials. It can be sent to all homes or to a sample of the community. The survey can also be done in personal or phone interviews, both of which lead to a solid percentage of response. If a written questionnaire is distributed, most public relations practitioners agree that the results should be made public. Hiding the results arouses suspicion, and suspicion and doubts are to be avoided at all costs. (See Chapter 3 for information on surveys.)

ADOPTING A THEME OR SLOGAN

Many public relations experts claim that a slogan or theme that captures public attention can serve as a plus for the campaign. It must be remembered, however, that a poorly chosen slogan can be a disadvantage. What works in one community could miss completely in another because of the different makeup of the public being served. If a theme is used, it should honestly represent what the referendum is all about. It should ideally focus on students and should somehow imply benefit for the community and, if possible, for the voter. The slogan should help voters remember the issue and the way that the educators would like them to vote. In California a picture of two small children was accompanied by the slogan

"For Jimmy and me, vote yes on 3." Another district used "The Child Looks to You—Vote Yes on 2." The slogan included the child, the kind of vote needed, and the date of the election.

Many campaigns are based on instilling fear; slogans such as "Save Our Schools" imply that ruin or disaster is imminent if the building is not approved. Yet following a defeat, the schools will continue to service children, perhaps in a less ideal way than if the building had been approved, but nevertheless in a way avoiding the ruin implied by the slogan. Slogans based on confidence and hope are usually more effective than those prompting fear. A campaign can effectively put across positive feelings in many ways—emphasizing a better curriculum, new kinds of learning resources, or more facilities for more people to use more frequently.

Certain statements lend themselves to positive impact, again depending on the public receiving the communications. Some worth considering for a building campaign follow:

- To parents, the public school represents their children's future; for all citizens, it represents the welfare of our country.
- Good schools produce taxpayers, not tax users.
- Poor schools are the most expensive tax burden.
- The schools belong to the people, and they must answer to the children.
- Inflation affects schools too.

Remember that few people are anti-children, and most Americans believe in the value of education. Thus, educators have a solid ground on which to build a campaign. Parents, especially, find themselves caught between two of their prized possessions—their children and their money. If they believe that the referendum will help their children learn better, usually they will opt for their children over the money.

PERSONALIZING THE CAMPAIGN

Too often administrators prepare a campaign aimed at a mass audience that doesn't exist. Although certain materials (newsletters, news releases, etc.) sometimes have to be written for the general audience, much of the campaign should be developed for specific targeted audiences. The first rule of any effective communications is: Know your audience. In the case of a campaign, this can be interpreted as meaning: Show voters how the referendum will help them in some way. Although many voters join the yes column because they are sold on the educational soundness of the proposal, many others are prompted to vote yes by one small phase of the building program. The following questions might be heard outside almost any polling place on referendum day: Where do I vote for the new gym? Is this where I vote so the CYO kids can play basketball? Many people are motivated by some personal need that will be met by having the building constructed.

"What's in it for me?" is the question many people ask themselves before committing themselves to a higher tax payment. School officials should make every effort to show how the new building will favorably affect different kinds of people. An early part of the campaign planning should be devoted to listing the various organizations and how they might benefit from the building. Similar lists should be developed for groups of people—the Golden Agers, the young voters, and so on.

KEEP IT SIMPLE

As in all communications from school to home, the message should be prepared in easy-to-understand language. This means eliminating educational gobbledygook and long polysyllabic sentences. Many taxpayers are befuddled by the conflicting tax increase information that is spread the few days before the election. To avoid this kind of confusion, educators should distribute simple fact sheets that clearly state the resulting tax increase if the referendum is approved. This means including an average house in the community, giving its market value and the tax increase.

Such specifics negate ill-founded rumors that invariably occur late in the campaign.

The basic facts are usually sufficient for most voters. The traditional pie-charts, graphs, and in-depth statistics are noticed by few readers and understood by fewer. Some campaigns have effectively used a gimmick for visual impact to communicate costs. One community used a pound of coffee in all literature, and speakers carried a pound of coffee to all meetings. This communicated that the cost to the average homeowner would be a pound of coffee a week. It is also important to explain what the new building will mean to the community. Lower maintenance costs should be communicated as well as increased community use of facilities.

WORKING WITH THE MEDIA

As noted earlier, rapport with media representatives should be established before the campaign. The daily and weekly newspapers are, in most communities, the main source of media news about the referendum. Superintendents who enjoy a sound relationship with local editors enhance their chances of gaining favorable editorials for the building. Early in the campaign, the superintendent or campaign director should meet with all editors to talk informally about the building and what it can offer the community. Such a meeting can encourage editors to check with school officials before printing negative editorials.

A series of articles prepared for all area newspapers about the building needs would be welcomed by many newspapers. Although some daily newspapers won't find room for them, they nevertheless should receive them. Weekly newspapers usually thrive on such information. Stories concerning the needs of the school district should begin appearing many months before the election; in fact, they should appear before the election is even announced. A survey of preschool children that would indicate future increases in enrollment can be the subject for one or several stories. Reports by the superintendent of schools to the board of education on enrollment trends, overcrowded classrooms, and dangerous or outmoded physical conditions in the schools should be publicized. Planned, continual newspaper publicity will furnish voters with an adequate background of the school district's needs and will thus make the proposal to meet these needs more acceptable. The appointment of the citizens' committee and its discussions and actions are newsworthy. If the newspapers have no representation on the committee, appoint someone capable of covering meetings of the committee and writing stories for the press. Develop a story on every talk made before service clubs and other community groups. Report each endorsement voted by an organization. Submit architects' sketches of proposed buildings, charts, graphs, and pictures for use by newspapers.

Capitalize on the community grapevine by working with key communicators to share information and dispel incorrect rumors during the campaign. Letters to the editor will be written by those opposed to the bond issue; school campaigners should have people writing pro letters throughout the campaign. Key communicators can play a major role here.

Radio and television stations should also be contacted early in the campaign and their support solicited. In most cases, provided the issues do not become political because of organized opposition, radio and television stations will assist school administrators in planning programs, spot announcements, and other types of publicity. Stations may be willing to donate this time on the air as a public service.

Radio call-in shows should be listened to in order to determine concerns of taxpayers regarding the referendum. In addition, school officials should appear, if possible, on community shows that allow questions to be called in. Cable television can be beneficial in many communities. As is the case with radio, materials must be prepared professionally because the reputation of the station, as well as the school, is involved. For help,

check with the staff of the stations. If television is available, an effective program could be a film or tape of the school system's budget or referendum needs followed by a half-hour or more of telephone calls from viewers with questions to be answered on the spot by school officials. The State College, Pennsylvania, school district did this effectively.

PUBLICATIONS CAN HELP

Information brochures are distributed to all registered voters of the district by mail or house-to-house canvass in most school districts. Brochures should be attractive and easy to read but should not appear too expensive. They should briefly explain the needs, the proposals for meeting these needs, and the cost to the average taxpayer. They should be prepared by someone who knows how to design an effective publication. Architects' renderings should be seriously considered before being used; often they contain embellishments that will not appear when the building is erected. And those embellishments (a lake or wooded surroundings) could lead readers to conclude that a palace instead of a school is being proposed. The floor plan can usually be deleted with little loss, except perhaps to the architect's ego. Few people read floor plans, and in most cases, they are reduced to such small type that they are illegible. A special feature of the building might be highlighted instead of a floor plan if visual impact is desired.

In all publications for the campaign, children should be featured. Too many school materials exclude pictures of what schools are all about—children. Parents especially appreciate photographs of children in schools. Publications should present information honestly and provide voting information, including a sample ballot. Because some new residents won't know the locations of polling places, the addresses should be given. Phone numbers of school officials and advisory group members should be included to encourage people with questions to call them. In at least one publication, different plans to meet space needs should be shown and the reasons for their rejection given.

SPEAKERS' BUREAU

A speakers' bureau should be organized as soon as the school bond election has been announced. The person designated to coordinate the activities of campaign speakers should be certain that speakers are thoroughly familiar with all aspects of the proposal. Informational kits, therefore, should be carefully prepared. Briefing sessions should be scheduled. Visual materials such as filmstrips, slides, charts, videos, and pictures should be furnished. Don't ask for volunteers; instead select only those board members, administrators, and laypersons who speak effectively.

As has been mentioned before, contact every local organization as early in the campaign as possible and endeavor to schedule a speaker for one of their meetings. Request each unit of the parent-teacher association to arrange for a meeting during the campaign when a speaker or a panel of speakers may discuss the school bond proposal. Arrange for talks over radio and television stations for your speakers. Prepare special letters to all religious leaders of the community inviting their support as "speakers" for the referendum.

ENDORSEMENTS

Obtaining endorsements from community organizations can be an effective campaign technique. These endorsements, often received after a speakers' bureau representative has talked at a meeting of the organization, can help in three ways. First, they communicate to members who missed the meeting that their organization is behind the referendum. Second, publicizing each endorsement can cause a bandwagon effect on the part of the community. Third, toward the end of the campaign, a list of organizations supporting the building can be distributed, communicating to the community that a broad spectrum of the district is behind the proposal.

Individual endorsements can also be helpful. Every time a school representative speaks to a group he or she can distribute an endorsement card—one that asks for permission to use the signer's name for publicity purposes. (See Figure 14.1.) Near the end of the campaign, a list of endorsers can be published in advertisements and publications. Undecided voters who see names of those they respect on the list might be convinced to cast a yes vote.

SMALL GROUP MEETINGS

The small group meeting has met with much success in many school districts. This kind of get-together allows six to ten people to meet with a school official or a representative of the citizens' advisory committee to discuss the bond issue. Such meetings can be held in homes of parents and other concerned taxpayers. Questions asked at the first few meetings might provide material for an inexpensive Q and A sheet later distributed to all residents. Questions that cannot be answered by school representatives at the meetings should be answered the next day by phone. Spouses who are working during the day—when most such meetings are usually held—might want to attend an evening meeting. Such meetings are conducive to attitude change and allow the all-important process of two-way communication to occur. When well organized, they reach large numbers of people and contribute much to the success of the campaign.

HOUSE-TO-HOUSE CANVASS

A house-to-house canvass of the school district, if properly organized and carried out, is an effective means of gaining support for a school bond issue. Below are listed suggestions for planning and conducting the canvass:

■ In districts with several schools, organize by school attendance areas, with the school principal

---

ORGANIZATION ENDORSEMENT

The Board of Education of the _____
School District has called for a School Bond Election
to be held on _____ . The amount of the
issue is $_____ .

We agree that additional funds are needed by the
school district to provide adequate housing for the
children and youth of this community. For this reason,
we endorse the proposed bond issue, we shall work
toward its passage, and the name of this organization
may be used in publicity during the campaign.

Name of Organization _____
Address _____
Signed by _____
Office in Organization _____

FIGURE 14.1 A sample endorsement card.

and the parent-teacher association president serving as cochairpersons for the canvass in this area.

— Divide each attendance area to be covered into several subdistricts and appoint a lieutenant to be in charge of the canvass in each district.

— Secure enough workers to have at least one canvasser for each city block. Block workers should be assigned to the neighborhoods in which they reside, if possible, thus giving them the advantage of approaching the voters as neighbors and friends. If workers know the voters' names, better impressions are gained.

— Arrange for an indoctrination meeting in each area for all those who will be taking part in the house-to-house canvass. At this meeting explain how the block plan works, provide a booklet of factual information to each worker, give instructions on how to make home calls, and answer all questions that may be asked.

— Have a sufficient number of reserve workers for each subdistrict. These people may be called on to make home calls in case of emergency.

— Home calls should be made no earlier than two weeks before the election. Probably the best time of the day to make calls in most districts will be between 6:30 and 8:45 P.M.

— Block workers should not spend too much time on any one call—approximately 10 minutes should suffice.

— All calls in the district should be made on the same evening; publicity can thus be given the canvass.

— If some people are not at home, workers should make follow-up calls the next evening. If no one is home at this time, the canvasser should leave the campaign materials and a prepared note stating that a parent-teacher association member has called to discuss the school bond issue.

— A second home call on the evening before election day is often made to remind voters of the election and to urge them to vote.

ABSENTEE BALLOTS

Especially important since the advent of the eighteen-year-old vote is the absentee ballot. As noted earlier, the young voter is seldom directly affected by property taxes. Young voters have also recorded yes votes in large percentages, frequently running as high as 90 percent. Thus, it is incumbent on campaign leaders to attract the absentee ballot, especially the ballot of the voter in the armed forces or at college.

A special committee of young voters can effectively undertake the project. Home addresses can sometimes be obtained from high-school yearbooks. A letter could be sent to the young man or woman at this address with a covering letter to parents asking them to forward the letter if necessary. The letter to the young voters should include information about registration and voting by absentee ballot. How to get a ballot, how to complete it, and how to return it should be spelled out in the letter. Although relatively simple, the ways to vote by absentee ballot are unknown to many people. By providing a step-by-step explanation, the school officials perform a service and also encourage a yes vote. Information about the bond issue should, of course, be sent to these voters.

Using a classmate who was popular to write the covering letter can be an effective approach.

This leader can also write letters to the editor urging absentee balloting and might prepare a news story for the local press, explaining how easy the process is.

ELECTION-DAY PLANS

Plans for election day should be developed carefully and carried out, even though the bond campaign appears to be successful with a minimum of opposition. Many elections have been lost by a few votes when campaigners became overconfident. Election-day plans should include telephone committees, transportation pools, and babysitting service. Some districts may wish to use poll checkers to record who has voted so that phone workers can remind potential yes voters to get to the polls and vote.

Each attendance area should be organized. Telephone committees should be thoroughly instructed on how and when to make calls. They should begin their calls late in the morning on election day and continue until they have reached everyone on the list of yes voters. Many people in surveys made after a bond election admitted that they failed to vote because they forgot. The telephone reminder eliminates that possibility.

The purpose of calling on election day is to remind citizens to vote and to offer transportation or babysitting service. No attempt is made at this time to influence voters.

CAMPAIGN TIMETABLE

The following suggested schedule for school bond campaigns may be helpful to school administrators when they begin making plans for conducting a campaign in their district.

Six Months to a Year Before Election

Determine future needs by studying current enrollments by grades, recent enrollment trends, adequacy of present facilities, and results of a survey of preschool-age children residing in the district.

Four to Six Months Before Election

- Study past campaigns and reasons for successes and failures.
- Survey the community to determine citizens' attitudes toward space needs and means to solve the needs.
- Develop a specific proposal and present it to the board of education.
- Explain and discuss the proposal with all school employees.
- Publicize the proposal and the reasons for making it.
- Organize a citizens' advisory committee to review the studies leading to the proposal and to assist in organizing and conducting a campaign.
- Name a chairperson for the campaign and apprise others to work with that person.
- Meet with the parent-teacher association to determine cooperatively what roles members can play in the campaign.
- Begin a campaign to register all parents of preschool and school-age children.
- Attempt to discover any possible opposition to the bond issue and to win it over or to neutralize it.
- Establish a timetable and budget.

Three Months Before Election

- The board of education should officially set the date of the election and announce the amount of the bond issue.
- Select a theme.
- Contact all organizations in the community and endeavor to arrange for programs concerning the school bond proposal.
- Organize a speakers' bureau.
- Prepare information kits for speakers and for house-to-house canvassers.
- Take advantage of every opportunity to publicize the bond issue in newspapers and over radio and television. Continue until election day.
- Have subcommittees of the citizens' committee begin work on all phases of the campaign.
- Prepare information for teachers and arrange for meetings with them to discuss the proposal and to invite their support.

➤ Begin soliciting endorsements from individuals and organizations, publicizing the fact each time an organization endorses the bond issue. Continue until election day.

➤ Begin preparation of campaign materials, such as brochures, posters, bumper stickers, billboards, letters, postcards, filmstrips, banners, slides, window displays, and newspaper advertising.

One to Three Months Before Election

➤ Organize workers for a house-to-house canvass.

➤ Organize and conduct small group meetings.

➤ Organize workers for election day. Prepare specific directions for every type of worker who will be employed on election day.

➤ Arrange advertising schedules with newspapers, radio stations, and television stations.

➤ Begin using motion pictures, videos, and other audiovisual materials before meetings of community organizations.

➤ Send absentee ballot information.

Three to Four Weeks Before Election

➤ Put up window displays.

➤ Distribute posters for placement in store windows.

➤ Distribute bumper stickers.

➤ Put up billboard advertising.

➤ Send letters to all religious leaders in the school district asking for their support of the bond proposal.

Two to Three Weeks Before Election

➤ Mail general brochures to all registered voters of the school district or distribute them through a house-to-house canvass.

➤ Schedule informational programs, such as panel discussions, for radio and television. Continue until election day.

➤ Obtain feedback (surveys, if possible) to determine feel of community; regroup final plans based on findings.

Final Two Weeks Before Election

➤ Mail special letters to all parents inviting their support on election day.

➤ Space newspaper, radio, and television advertising throughout this period.

➤ Mail postcards or pamphlets to all potential yes voters to arrive the day before election reminding them to vote.

➤ Publicize Hot Line (telephone number for citizens to call for information).

➤ Have "truth squads" counter misinformation that is disseminated in last stages of campaign.

➤ Continue small group meetings.

➤ Reprint favorable editorials for wide distribution.

Election Day

➤ Telephone committees should begin calling all parents and other potential yes voters.

➤ Check polls to determine which yes voters have voted.

➤ Offer transportation and babysitter services to those who haven't voted.

➤ Remind teachers and other school employees and students to vote.

Follow-up

➤ Write letters thanking all who took active parts in the campaign. Also write to newspapers, radio stations, television stations, businesses, and organizations that assisted in promoting the bond issue. The personal touch of a phone call is even better if time permits.

➤ Analyze the campaign as soon as possible after the election. Determine points of strength and weakness by talking with citizens, advisory members, parent-teacher members, school administrators, and others.

➤ Conduct a post-election survey to see why people voted the way they did. Record results for use in future campaigns.

➤ Send a financial report to all who contributed to the campaign.

RECOMMENDATIONS TO IMPROVE ELECTION-DAY RESULTS

The following recommendations are offered for the consideration of school officials. They have proved to be successful in school bond elections.

It is recommended that:

— The organization of a bond campaign be started not less than six months before election day.

— A complete survey of needs be made and publicized before announcing the possibility of a bond election.

— A citizens' committee be chosen with representatives from as many diverse groups in the community as may exist.

— This citizens' committee be permitted to study thoroughly the statement of needs and the tentative proposal to meet these needs.

— Everyone who volunteers to serve on the citizens' committee be given something specific to do.

— A voter registration campaign be conducted and efforts be made to register parents of all preschool and school-age children.

— Schools be utilized as places for registration and that school secretaries be deputized for this purpose.

— Every known community organization be contacted and asked to schedule a program concerning the school bond proposal.

— An effort be made to obtain endorsements of the bond proposal from all community organizations.

— Individual citizens be asked to endorse the bond proposal.

— Endorsements from organizations be publicized in newspaper stories or in advertisements.

— Newspaper editors or publishers and radio and television station managers be contacted before the campaign begins for advice and support.

— An effort be made to locate potential opponents and to win their support for the proposal.

— A complete handbook of facts be developed for use by teachers and other school employees, speakers, and members of the citizens' advisory committee.

— Teachers and other school district employees not be directed to participate in the campaign but that they be encouraged to volunteer their services.

— Religious leaders in the community be contacted and their support solicited.

— Pupils *not* be used in school bond campaigns.

— The final publicity campaign be no longer than two or three weeks.

— House-to-house canvasses be conducted in those attendance areas where principals and parent-teacher association members believe they will be effective.

— At least one carefully prepared brochure or pamphlet be developed and mailed to every registered voter or distributed to voters by means of the house-to-house canvass.

— Election-day machinery be planned which will get probable supporters to the polls.

— The cooperation of the parent-teacher association be solicited; that members be invited to conduct a survey of the district to discover preschool children; that they staff the election-day machinery; and that they conduct the house-to-house canvass.

— Administrators and members of the board of education play active roles in planning and conducting the school bond campaign.

— All potential yes voters be reminded of the election by a letter, postcard, or telephone call.

— Carefully selected media be employed to keep the election before the citizens of the community.

— A series of public meetings be avoided. Such meetings afford a platform for the opposition and often result in negative press.

— Polls be open when convenient for people to vote. A community with people on split shifts should consider the timing of the shifts and voting hours.

— The most trusted school official in a key position serve as official spokesperson.

— The date chosen for the election not follow the mailing of new tax bills, if possible.

— A year-round, two-way communications system be implemented to effect confidence in the schools. Confidence and pride in schools lead to positive votes.

▬ The bond campaign be financed by contributions and that no pressure be brought to bear on any individual or group for funds.

▬ Everything in the campaign be done in good taste and that nothing be done that might discredit the school district.

▬ Letters thanking everyone who participates in the campaign be prepared and mailed immediately after the election, regardless of its outcome.

ENDNOTES

1. George M. Beal, "The Communication Process in the Purchase of New Products: An Application of Reference Group Theory," paper presented at the American Association of Public Opinion Researchers, Chicago, 1958.

2. George M. Beal, "Validity of the Concept of Stages in the Adoption Process," *Rural Sociology* (1957), pp. 166–168.

3. Reprinted with permission of Macmillan from pp. 102–3 of *Communication of Innovations: A Cross-Cultural Approach,* 2nd ed., by Everett M. Rogers with F. Floyd Shoemaker. Copyright © 1971 by The Free Press.

4. Reprinted with permission of Macmillan from pp. 229–30 of *Communication of Innovations: A Cross Cultural Approach,* 2nd ed., by Everett M. Rogers with F. Floyd Shoemaker. Copyright © 1971 by The Free Press.

5. Don Bagin and David Lefever, *How to Gain Public Support for Your School's Budget and Bond Issue* (Glassboro, NJ: Glassboro State College Press, 1971), p. 9.

6. Richard F. Carter, *Voters and Their Schools* (Stanford: Stanford University Institute for Communications Research, 1960).

7. Don Bagin and David Lefever, *How to Gain Public Support for Your School's Budget and Bond Issue* (Glassboro, NJ: Glassboro State College Press, 1971), pp. 17–26.

8. Harry Karns, "Long Beach Defeats the School Shortage," *American School Board Journal* (February 1957), pp. 45–46.

15

SCHOOL PUBLIC RELATIONS AND THE SCHOOL CHOICE CHALLENGE

Call it CHOICE or a national chain of well-marketed schools. Whatever the challenge, the opportunity to select schools—public only—parochial or private—puts parents and their students in a buyers' position.

This means they'll want more information, expect more hard data, and pick schools based on reason and emotion. For school officials, it means simply this: If you don't attract students, you'll be out of work. Many staff members need to get this message, especially those who feel that public relations responsibilities are not theirs.

This chapter will present ideas on how to prepare for the impact of Chris Whittle's schools, the voucher system, and CHOICE as its proponents call it. The chapter will discuss leadership ideas that work—ideas that will encourage taxpayers, teachers, and colleagues to support school officials and their leadership; ideas that will work for them with or without the voucher threat. Also outlined in this chapter are some thoughts on how Glassboro (NJ) State College attracted 100 million dollars, and now high school officials might just want to go after some money that graduates and others might want to donate.

WHAT ARE THE CHALLENGES?

Before giving the positive possibilities of attracting money, let's take a look at the challenges of Whittle, the voucher, or CHOICE. One school administrator likened the challenge to the experience he faced when told he had cancer.

Authorities on cancer claim that there are a number of reactions when people learn that they have cancer. The first is *shock*. Superintendents have had that same reaction when they first heard of the voucher possibilities.

The next stage is *disbelief* or *denial*. "It won't happen to me" or "It can't be happening to me." Health authorities tell us that this is normal. They describe it as the morphine of the soul. It's a way we reject thoughts that are too painful to endure. Thinking about having to close a school, or greatly reducing the staff because of competition, has prompted denial among many educational leaders.

With cancer, denial is a normal defense mechanism. What happens is that people who keep denying don't seek early medical attention. And they have been known to reject medical advice and treatment. And some even "forget" to tell doctors of suspicious signs or symptoms.

The sooner the denial ends, the better off the patient is. The sooner school leaders accept the strong possibility that some form of CHOICE will come, the better off they and the people they serve will be. A natural question is: What impact will it have on me? On my schools? If a substantial voucher program or CHOICE occurs, ask how many students your school will lose: 50 percent, 25 percent, 10 percent, or 5 percent?

The next phase is usually *fear*. Many things frighten victims. They include the threat of death, pain, loss of bodily functions, and losing one's position of responsibility with the family or at work. The same thing can happen to school leaders in a different way. They see their position of responsibility lessening. They see all kinds of challenges they'll have to face when they have to compete for students. They fear having to let friends go if they must reduce staff.

The next stage is usually *anger*. Whether it's anger aimed at the doctor who provided the diagnosis or anger at family members just because they're near, the individual wants to be angry at somebody.

Many teachers and administrators feel the same way about the possibility of a voucher. They're angry because they don't think the voucher will work. They're angry because they think they're doing a good job. They're angry because they think that education overall will suffer as a result of this. They're also angry because they feel that their jobs could be threatened.

The next step is *anxiety*. People with cancer become anxious about not being able to pay bills. They become anxious about how their lives will be changed. They don't know in what way or how much they'll be changed. The unknown provokes much of the anxiety.

The same holds true for school officials. They really don't know what's going to happen. So they naturally become anxious. They're not sure when the changes will take place. They're not quite sure whether their state will be affected next year. They don't know if the federal government will come in and make some offers that some parents won't be able to refuse. The unknown is always a challenge.

The next step with cancer patients is usually *guilt*. They blame themselves for not being able to accomplish things that they could have accomplished before. They feel guilty when the treatment doesn't work the way it might. Many teachers and school officials aren't sending their children to public schools. They feel a bit guilty about the job that some of those schools are doing. And they share those thoughts with other people in the community. That doesn't help either.

The final step with cancer patients is frequent *depression*. When people get depressed, they withdraw from other people and they become moody. They feel helpless. They feel despair. All these reactions are common in people who have cancer. Many of them are common in people who

are concerned about the threat of the voucher system.

The good news, and it's getting better every year, is that more and more people who have cancer are beating it. The same will happen with many school districts if the vouchers come. Many cancer patients who conquered the disease went through lots of introspection. And they're better people leading fuller lives as a result.

COUNTERACTING A COMPETITOR'S MARKETING PLAN

It must constantly be remembered that perception is the key to all of these strategies. It's not what's happening in the schools, but what people choosing the schools think is happening.

Superintendents and principals will need to provide the kind of leadership that (1) builds confidence, (2) turns on teachers and others, (3) encourages ideas, (4) involves the community so people feel that they certainly don't want to leave their schools, and (5) values the parents' time.

School officials need to realize how important time is to parents. The research that marketers are conducting shows that time is one of the most important considerations when trying to develop a relationship with a customer. If people ordered something by direct mail, they know how important time is.

When you need someone to repair a refrigerator or a washing machine, you know how important time is. Remember the last time that you were told that someone would be there on Thursday morning and you or your spouse stayed home and the person didn't show up. Time is a most precious commodity, and school officials need to remember that.

Here are some things you might do to communicate to taxpayers and to parents that you do indeed respect their time:

▬ Schedule parent conferences in the evening so people don't have to miss work to attend them.
▬ Consider the reactions of parents when you have an in-service day and they need to get a child

watcher. Be sure you communicate the schedule of in-service days way ahead of time so people can plan.

– And you might want to go one step more. This suggestion comes from a superintendent, Bob Terrill of Washington Township, Gloucester County, New Jersey. Try to come up with assembly programs for students so that they can attend school while you're conducting in-service for 99 percent of the teachers. Whatever you can do to make it easier on parents' tough schedules by taking care of the children, do it.

– And here's an aside that helps people save time and it's something that only the parents of children who play sports would care about. Make sure the fields are clearly marked and directions to those fields are clear. Get one of your local business people to donate a thousand dollars so you could have some first-class signs made. Put those signs up too during basketball games so that when people are trying to find the right door to attend an away game, they won't have to walk in the rain for a quarter of a mile to get to the only unlocked door.

One of the most important things to realize is something that Glassboro (NJ) State College (now Rowan College of New Jersey) officials learned from the hundred million dollars that the College received. The press conference to announce the grant opened with questions from reporters. One of the reporters asked this question of the donor: "Mr. Rowan, you have no affiliation with Glassboro State College. You went to MIT. Why did you select Glassboro?"

The answer: "Because GSC selected me. Phil Tumminia from Glassboro State College was the only person who asked me for the money." The moral: You've got to ask questions if you want to succeed.

QUESTIONS TO ADDRESS

If school officials want people to choose their schools, they might capitalize on these suggestions:

1. Do we know now what people like about our schools?

School officials hear so much criticism that sometimes they don't think of the positive perspectives the public has of schools.

Do you conduct a formal survey of people in the community? If you're hurting for funds, you might want to consider using senior citizens to make phone calls for you. Bring in 20 senior citizens for breakfast every month or so. Have each of them make 10 completed phone calls, and you've got yourself a good feel for what the community's thinking. Ask some of the same questions each month so you can track trends that might be developing. Ask some new questions each time.

This will let you know what people think about your schools, not just people you socialize with, but the community as a whole if you properly select a random sample. What a good feeling it is when school officials are armed with information about what the community's thinking. This is especially true when someone stands up at a board meeting and makes an irrational statement about what the community thinks about the need for something school officials have proposed. They'll have the data and that data will be defensible. And there's a bonus. The folks conducting the survey feel that they are part of the schools.

2. Do we know now what people don't like about our schools?

Of course, you'll find out when you do the surveys mentioned above. But you might want to conduct an occasional focus panel where you bring in 10 people from the community to talk about the schools.

Also, start a Listeners' Bureau. This gives you some good insight on the community's thinking. One of the best ways of listening through the key communicator concept is described in Chapter 8.

A study done at Rowan College of New Jersey showed that people who served on an advisory committee or as key communicators became much more positive in their attitude toward the schools. This applies to critics especially.

3. How are we involving people in our schools?

Involvement, no matter how it takes place, is vital. People who are involved feel that they are part of the solution to any problems that come up. They are indeed shareholders in the schools.

For example, a parent of a second grader received a phone call from his daughter's teacher. She told him that he would be getting the traditional letter from the principal about American Education Week and that he should visit the schools. But she also said that she would like him to visit his daughter's school at a specific time to see a skit that his daughter's class would be putting on. She asked the parent if he could be there. He didn't want to turn down a personal request so he agreed to attend the skit.

After watching his daughter in the skit, the parent complemented the teacher on the fine class she ran and mentioned the excellent learning stations that were scattered around the room. At that time the teacher went to a closet for a packet with the parent's name on it and said, "Mr. Jones, you're our next learning station. Instructions are inside the package. Could you follow them and cut out the materials and paste them up by next Monday. We really appreciate it."

The parent felt he had been had, but in a good way—to help his child learn better. And that's the kind of good involvement that people want. They want to feel they're helping their children learn better. And it all started with a personal phone call.

How much better that type of phone call is. Wilt Chamberlain, the former basketball star for the Philadelphia 76ers, told reporters that he wasn't attending the celebration that the 76ers were sponsoring for the championship basketball team he played on a number of years before.

When the general manager of the Sixers explained to the reporters that Wilt had indeed been invited, he pulled out a copy of a letter he had sent to Chamberlain. When the reporters talked to Wilt, he said, "When you want me to attend something, call me; don't send a letter."

One of the consistent findings in market research is that if you can come up with ways to involve potential customers, you have a better chance of selling them and keeping them. Another consistent finding of research is this: People who have been inside a school building during the year preceding a bond election or a budget election tend to vote for the school's needs much more than people who have not been inside that building. So whether it's adult and continuing education, use of the basketball court or a meeting of the Lions Club, get those people in the schools. They'll support you more.

4. Do we do anything to recognize outstanding graduates of our schools?

Joseph Pollock, a former public relations director with the Philadelphia Public Schools and a former principal with the schools, suggests bringing back five outstanding graduates each year to a dinner in their honor. Each graduate is asked to select the teacher in the school who did the most to motivate the successful graduate. Pollock would then place the honored student's photo on the Wall of Fame in the school.

When a school does this, it certainly honors the outstanding graduates, but it also honors itself by giving some recognition to the fine teachers who are doing a good job. Word spreads in the community that something good must be going on there if so many successful people have graduated from the school. This pays off in a lot of ways.

5. What are we doing to ask people for money for our schools?

For some reason school officials equate public schools with only tax money. Schools can do something special. They can go after some money from outstanding graduates and people who have gone through the school system who have accumulated money.

If school officials think hard enough and they bring together some people in their organization and ask people on their school board and people who have been in their school district for a while, they'll be able to identify people with money. These people may not be active in the community. They may have never done anything for the schools before. But they might also be looking for a legacy. They might not want to give a sizable part of their estate to the government. Some of them don't like the way the government will use the money.

Asking for money for education can be an easy thing to do. Most people feel that an investment in education is worthwhile. School officials may be fortunate to find potential donors who just decided that their children shouldn't get all their money. They may want to have people learn to be better writers because of their contribution. They may have made their money because of their ability in math and want to earmark money to contribute to the math program for schools.

But school officials will never know unless they ask. The worst thing that can happen is that most of the people asked will say no. But all that is needed is for one to say yes.

Related to attracting funds, school officials enhance their chances by communicating a mission—a mission that all of their employees understand, a mission that the community can support, and a mission that's clearly linked to the school official as leaders.

It may very well be that the mission is to make sure that every person who comes out of the schools can speak and write effectively. It may be that the mission is to be sure that every student knows the important facts about health so that students will cut down on drinking and drug abuse and understand how AIDS is contracted. These are lifesaving topics.

6. Do we consider our employees our most important audience?

If school officials don't, they better reassess everything they do. Hal Rosenbluth of Rosen-

bluth Travel has gained quite a bit of recognition for a book he wrote. It's called *Customers: Our Second Most Important Audience.*[1] To most customer service experts, this statement would be heretical.

But Mr. Rosenbluth makes a lot of sense. He says that if you have your employee turned on to the organization—if your employees feel that their ideas will not only be heard but implemented when they're good for the organization—then your customers will indeed be taken care of very well.

In research studies on employee morale this question has been asked often: "If you had an idea to improve your schools and it would cost nothing to implement that idea, would you suggest it?"

In some schools, 70 percent of the people who work there would suggest the idea. In other schools, about 15 percent would suggest the idea.

A teacher in a school district for a number of years was asked if he would suggest an idea. He said, "No." And when asked why, he said, "Well, everybody listens to my ideas but nobody ever puts them into action. So I'm just going to coast out until retirement." He explained that he was just going to do the minimum job from then until retirement (22 years hence) because nobody really cared about his ideas. That's appalling.

Every school can identify employees who have been coasting out for years and will continue to coast out. And that's one of the things that's wrong with the schools. Somebody has to attack that. Somebody has to make sure that the people blocking ideas in the schools are counselled and if they don't stop blocking ideas, if they don't start encouraging ideas, then they shouldn't be serving in an administrative capacity.

Consider the gentleman retiring from a Fortune-500 company who grabbed the microphone after he was given his gold watch at the retirement dinner. He said to the audience that contained many, many managers, "You know—you blew it. For more than 25 years, you could have had my brain as well as my hands. But you never asked for my ideas. We could have done things better. We could have made more money. Everyone could have been happier. But you didn't ask. And what a waste.

One of the best ideas coming out of industry that can be applied to the school is a program called *effectancy*. It's an interesting word *effectancy*. It's a combination of *effective* and *efficiency*. A company increased the number of ideas it received from employees from about 22 in one year to over 1,800. How?

The company wrote about effectancy in its newsletter. It gave examples of employees who were indeed being *effectant*. It sponsored contests for ideas. Everyone who suggested something had an equal chance of being selected as a grand prize winner—for a trip for two to Hawaii.

School officials might say that it's just not in the budget. They might ask ten business people to donate the money to help the schools come up with better ideas. They'll get cooperation. But again they have to ask.

7. What are we doing to communicate with influential leaders in the schools and in the community?

Be sure to identify who these people are. If you're not sure, ask others in your administration to help identify them. Watch letters to the editor. Talk with reporters to help identify these influential people. Get a list of the leaders of the various groups in the community. Have a staff member do a research paper on the topic for a graduate course. Make sure you're communicating with these folks because they have tremendous clout in helping the community decide what it wants to support.

As you ask yourself these questions and come up with answers, you'll probably position your school system to be ready for competition that might come about—competition that doesn't exist now.

Consider a *Wall Street Journal* full-page ad featuring Chris Whittle's undertaking. It had a photograph of the former Yale president and some other well-regarded educators. The message was a simple one: We're going to put together a program for schools that will do the job better than the present schools are. Whittle told the Educational Press Association that his Edison Project is an attempt to start over and look at things as freshly as he can.

When asked why he's not collaborating with public schools as many foundations and business-school partnerships are, he said, "We have a better chance of achieving a radical redesign without the existing schools' involvement. Profits will exist only if we do our job right and if hundreds of thousands of parents say, 'Yes it's worth it to go to that school.' " And he's going to do it at the same cost per pupil. Only better, he claims.

He also said, "We've called it the Edison Project because it's as different from the traditional school system as a candle from a light bulb. Both produce light." "By the way, the light bulb is cheaper," he added.

A threat? Probably. In a debate between Whittle and the executive director of the National Secondary School Principals Association, the school official was adamant in telling Whittle and the audience that his membership certainly would not have TVs donated to the classroom if students had to watch ads. But we all know what happened. Thousands of school districts have chosen to participate in this program.

Public schools can't deny that this challenge will be coming. School officials can't hope, like a person does with the stages of cancer, that it will go away. It won't. It will be a real challenge.

And if school officials do all these things that are given above to get their staffs turned on and the voucher and CHOICE do not come to be and the Whittle proposal doesn't work, schools will be better. The efforts will not be in vain.

STATEMENTS A COMPETITOR MIGHT USE TO ATTRACT STUDENTS

If someone starting a chain of schools to compete with existing schools came to a public relations and marketing consultant to develop a plan to attract students, chances are good the plan would include many of the following 11 statements:

1. Our teachers are better than your teachers. Good ol' Mr. Davis was inept when he taught me; now he's making much more money, is still a bad teacher, and is teaching your kids. Our teachers won't get tenure.

2. We'll consider students and parents as customers. Example: If you request an A.M. kindergarten, we'll provide it.

3. We know your schedule is challenging. We'll provide child care from 7:30 A.M. to 6 P.M. if needed.

4. The former president of Yale will play a key role in our educational program.

5. Our schools will be similar all over the country. If you move, your children's adjustment will be appreciably easier.

6. Our technological expertise will allow children to learn in a current fashion—not with antiquated methods and materials. One possibility: Each student will have a computer and modem at home to access our Learning Center's encyclopedias and databases.

7. We'll provide up-to-date material and emphasize what's important—not what teachers are comfortable teaching. Example: We'll teach about AIDS, diet, alcohol, and drugs in a way that captures students' attention. We'll hire experts in these areas—not "phys-ed" teachers who really don't want to teach health.

8. We'll bring learning alive—using the best ideas of teachers nationwide. We'll identify our best teachers' best ideas and conduct TV training for all teachers teaching that topic via our electronic network.

9. Our schools won't be dull. One study shows that 25 percent of all teenagers report falling asleep in class at least once a week.

10. When you call us, you'll speak immediately to a helpful person. You won't have to invest three minutes in a menu maze of an electronic answering device.

11. Our schools will be safe. Period.

SUGGESTIONS TO GET PEOPLE TO CHOOSE YOUR SCHOOLS

In summary, then, here are a dozen ideas to get people to choose your schools when others are trying to get them not to:

1. Do an excellent job of teaching. Retain only good teachers.

2. Understand how people accept new ideas. Realize and capitalize on the fact that most people decide after talking to people they respect. Know and communicate with the respected people in your community. (See Chapter 6.)

3. Establish a key communicator network and communicate with key communicators. (See Chapter 8.)

4. Build a large, powerful high school alumni group.

5. Invite more and more people into school buildings. Expand adult and continuing education, host service group meetings, realtor luncheons, and youth sports events.

6. Emphasize to all employees that just about every community resident knows one school system employee and believes what that person says about your schools. Where do employees send their children to school?

7. Understand that the perception of discipline difficulties is often the key reason parents choose another school. Develop a campaign to assure that parents have a realistic understanding of discipline in your schools.

8. Be sure everyone is customer-service oriented. One example: Schools plan parent conferences for the convenience of parents, not teachers and administrators.

9. Develop a program to build pride in the schools. Send positive letters home, list in a newsletter students, staff, and volunteers who have achieved something special, and generally build a spirit of "We Care about Doing a Good Job of Teaching."

10. Involve as many citizens as possible in the schools. People who are part of the system tend to support it more.

11. Conduct focus panels with students and parents to determine what they like and don't like about the schools.

12. Brainstorm with staff members to come up with marketing and public relations ideas for the key audiences identified.

ENDNOTES

1. Also see: "Many Happy Returns," *INC., Magazine,* (October 1990).

16

ASSESSMENT OF THE PROGRAM

Assessment or evaluation is a vital step in carrying out a comprehensive school-community relations program. Characteristically it is an ongoing process that is applied during the planning and implementation stages of a program and after phases of the program have been completed.

As is true in other social sciences, many results in the study of school-community relations are intangibles that are difficult to quantify for evaluation. For example, public attitude is very difficult to measure, as is the impact a communications program has on it. Yet, even with this difficulty in measuring results, school officials must attempt to show the effectiveness of a school-community relations program.

School public relations practitioners and other school administrators, like public relations people in corporations, will increasingly be asked to verify that their efforts and programs are producing measurable results. Moreover, they will be asked to show that the results are in line with the cost of a program and that the communications programs are ultimately contributing to the overall mission of the schools—that of helping students learn better. In addressing the assessment of a school public relations program, this chapter will discuss the myths about measurements, the importance of evaluating a public relations program, approaches to evaluation, and appraising results.

MYTHS ABOUT MEASUREMENTS

The difficulty in quantifying the many intangible results of communications has led many practitioners to be swept up by some errors in assessing the provisions made for organizing and conduct-

ing the program and in appraising the results of it. Some more common errors follow:

Dissemination is communication. The assumption here is that any communications program put into action or any distributed publication communicates. School officials who subscribe to this don't consider the interest level, the educational background, and the reading ability of the targeted audiences.

Effort can be equated with results. There is no guarantee that a greater effort can bring greater results. But it can be true, if the effort is directed toward the proper goal. A school public relations specialist may be doing some task very well but he or she will not succeed if the task is not leading to the desired results. Peter Drucker, a management expert, said that it is better to do the right thing than a thing right.

Samples are representative. Many practitioners will listen to the thoughts of a very small sample of citizens with special interests and feel they represent the entire community. Often major decisions are made on these unscientific results, and much money and time are wasted. Or even worse, major crises result.

Increased knowledge means more favorable attitudes. Often feedback will indicate that the public has a greater knowledge of the schools as a result of a public relations effort. Some school public relations people erroneously equate increased knowledge with more favorable public attitude. It is often the case, but it also can mean that the public better understands the school district's position rather than that it holds a more favorable position toward the schools.

Everything positive is measured in big numbers. Evaluation techniques are often driven by numbers. And frequently, the bigger the number, the better the evaluation. For example, a large attendance at a back-to-school open house and a great number of positive column inches in the local paper are considered positive public relations results. But not everything positive can be measured by "big" numbers. Often stories that appear in the newspaper may be balanced rather than negative because of the efforts of a good PR person. And some stories may not appear at all because the school PR person persuaded "the press" to drop the story. Small attendance at the budget hearing or the school attendance area reorganization may reflect the positive, ongoing communication program the schools have in place. So big numbers are not always positive.

IMPORTANCE OF EVALUATION TO A PUBLIC RELATIONS PLAN

For effective evaluation of the process and the product of a public relations program to take place, *a total plan for a given period of time is mandatory*. With goals, objectives, and activities outlined, an evaluation of results can more easily take place. An evaluator, then, knows whether public relations activities are directed toward or are reaching an established goal. Lindenmann emphasizes that evaluation without predetermined goals and objectives is futile.

> All too often, public relations and public professionals who have been carrying out specific activities for a long time are suddenly asked to prove the effectiveness of what they have been doing. Does the approach being taken really work? In my view, practitioners who engage in such after-the-fact attempts to evaluate what they have been doing are getting themselves involved in an almost nonsensical exercise. The only effective way to evaluate anything is to establish a set of specific goals and objectives *before* any program is launched. You are only kidding yourselves if you try to evaluate a program and start

laying out the ground rules for evaluation *after* a project is already under way.[1]

Purpose of Evaluation

Four major purposes of evaluation are (1) to improve, add, or drop existing public relations activities; (2) to determine if the public relations program is achieving its intended results; (3) to determine if the results were worth the time and money spent; and (4) to bring greater visibility to the accomplishments of the public relations program.

APPROACHES TO EVALUATION

McElreath presents two models for public relations evaluations—closed and open evaluation systems, within which most measurement processes can be placed.[2] According to Baskin and Arnoff a closed system evaluation effort limits its scope to the messages and events planned for the public relations campaign and their effects on the intended public.[3] This system would include pretest and posttest designs.

Pretest. Once the methods of communication are determined, it is wise to check the methods in advance with a sample of the intended audience. A practitioner could get a reaction to an intended publication, a special event, a speech, or a visual presentation from a group of citizens prior to making it public. In this way, a school public relations specialist could measure public interest and acceptance of the intended message. Pretesting how well the public understands the message may indicate that it is written at a readability level that is too high or contains jargon that won't be understood.

Posttest. This design calls for research on how a message was received. Did the citizens read the publication? Did they like it? What effect has it had on their understanding of the schools? These questions could be asked of any method of communicating with the public—written, through the media, or in person. The results can be used not only to understand the public's acceptance or rejection but also to give the practitioner experience on how to improve subsequent messages.

The open system evaluation, according to Baskin and Arnoff, includes all the variables not included in the closed systems. Examples are unintended audiences, how well the school system is administered, the effectiveness of the organization of the school system, union activities, administration perceptions, and so forth. Many of these variables are outside the control of the public relations specialists, yet they can have a major impact on the closed system variables. The open system may require more sophisticated research procedures to show the correlation of some aspect of the public relations program and the variables mentioned above. In that case, it may be wise to seek assistance from an outside social research group.

Steps and Instruments of Evaluation

Some experts in the field of public relations evaluation offer steps to take, and others outline instruments to use. Jacobson offers seven steps in a systematic evaluation process: (1) select the rationale, (2) specify objectives, (3) develop measures, (4) administer the measures and collect the data, (5) analyze the data, (6) report the results, and (7) apply the results to decisions.[4]

Cutlip, Center, and Broom list three steps in the process: (1) implementation evaluation, (2) progress evaluation, and (3) outcome evaluation.[5]

Swinehart treats assessment differently by listing types of evaluations and then giving dimensions evaluated for each. His types are as follows:

- Appraisal and description by persons involved in the program
- Count of activities
- Outside expert appraisal of activities
- Volunteered reaction of audiences
- Solicited reaction from a sample audience
- Reactions of actual or potential audiences through small-scale studies

- Controlled field experiments or similar studies to assess actual impact of programs.[6]

Figure 16.1 graphically outlines Swinehart's treatment of evaluation. Process, quality, and objectives (intermediate and ultimate) are the three dimensions evaluated for each type given above. Under "process" Swinehart includes such factors as the nature of activities involved, the number of people working on a project, time required, and targeted audiences. The "quality" dimension includes the assessment of materials and programs for design, accuracy, clarity, and relevance for an audience. He separates the "objectives" dimension into intermediate and ultimate. The first includes the means to achieve a goal, such as placing news releases, media use of spot announcements, and similar activities. "Ultimate objectives," according to Swinehart, are changes in the intended audiences' attitudes, knowledge, or behavior.[7]

The evaluation instruments used in assessing the effectiveness of a public relations program are usually rating scales and checklists. If these instruments are designed properly and include the essential feature of a constructive and dynamic program, they are helpful in identifying strengths and weaknesses and in furnishing information that is useful in the redesign or modification of the program. Actually they are a convenient means for looking at the entire program either before it goes into operation or after it has been tried for a period of time.

Rating scales and checklists are widely used in evaluating public relations programs whether at the district or building level.

A comprehensive checklist with 168 items and an optional rating scale was developed by Bortner.[8] He divided it into seven categories: (1) program organization and administration, (2) school staff, (3) students, (4) parents, (5) community, (6) one-way communication (printed and nonprinted), and (7) school plant. Under each section is a series of statements which a practitioner can check if they apply to his or her school district. Bortner's list also provides space for a four- or

Some Types of Evaluation and Their Uses				
		Dimensions Evaluated		
			Objectives	
Types of evaluation	Process	Quality	Intermediate	Ultimate
1. Description and subjective appraisal by persons directly involved in program operation.	•			
2. Count of activities—number of materials produced, amount of material placed, films shown, inquiries answered, etc.	•		•	
3. Expert appraisal of activities or products by outside content specialists, media personnel, etc.		•		
4. Reactions of audiences or recipients of information—volunteered self-reports on usefulness of materials, etc.		•	•	
5. Same as (4), but utilizing reactions solicited from an appropriate sample of users rather than those volunteered by some users.		•	•	
6. Small-scale studies to obtain reactions of actual or potential audiences, with assured exposure and immediate assessment of reactions (e.g. small-group studies of films, pamphlets, TV, or radio spots).		•	•	
7. Controlled field experiments, panel studies, etc., to assess actual impact of programs or materials.			•	•

FIGURE 16.1 James W. Swinehart's types and dimensions of evaluation. Source: *Public Relations Journal,* July 1979, p. 14. Copyright © 1979; reproduced with permission.

five-point scale to assess a district's policies and practices. Figure 16.2 gives the first sixteen items on his checklist.

The benefit of this checklist is that it can provide an assessment of the total program as well as of sections of the program, such as the organization and administration of the public relations program and communication with students, parents, and the community. Additionally it provides ways of identifying weak and strong areas within each of these sections.

Another comprehensive checklist has been published by the National School Public Relations Association.[9] It was based on the Standards for Educational Public Relations Programs adopted by the association in 1968 and 1969. The checklist is still used with standards that have been revised since then.[10]

The National School Public Relations Program Evaluation Instrument measures the extent to which the school district has made provisions for organizing and conducting a final public relations program. It does not measure how good or how bad the school district public relations program is.

The instrument covers five areas of program concentration: (1) policy statements and procedure, (2) staffing, (3) budget and resources,

PROGRAM ORGANIZATION AND ADMINISTRATION   **COMMENTS**

____ 1 The board of education has a written policy establishing the purposes of and mandating a school public relations program.

____ 2 The board of education specifically delegates authority for developing and implementing the school public relations program to its chief executive officer.

____ 3 The board of education provides adequate budgetary support specifically earmarked for the school public relations program.

____ 4 The board's policy for school public relations provides for communication not only through information and interpretation but also through interaction.

____ 5 The school public relations program has long-range objectives which are reviewed periodically.

____ 6 The school public relations program recognizes the existence of and provides for two-way communication with the various publics of the community.

____ 7 The school public relations program is continuous while providing for timely changes in pace and procedure.

____ 8 Public relations are honest, factual, and objective.

____ 9 Public relations are comprehensive, presenting a balanced account of school programs and operations.

____ 10 Both the language and content of information about the schools are adjusted to the intellectual and interest levels of the public to whom it is directed.

____ 11 The school public relations program is organized and coordinated on both the central office and local school level.

____ 12 Duties of all staff members and committees having public relations responsibilities are clearly defined.

____ 13 A professionally qualified member of the superintendent's administration team serves as director of school public relations and as the system's chief counselor and consultant in public relations matters.

____ 14 The position as director of school public relations is full-time. (Exception: small district, under approximately 15,000 population, where there is a part-time director).

____ 15 The director of school public relations reports directly to the superintendent.

____ 16 The director of school public relations heads a specific organizational unit with supporting staff and funds adequate to the job.

FIGURE 16.2 First page of Doyle Bortner's instrument to evaluate school public relations. Source: *Journal of Educational Communications,* vol. 3, no. 2, p. 9. Copyright © 1979, Camp Hill, Pennsylvania, Educational Communications Center. Reproduced with permission.

(4) relationship of public relations professional to the governing body, administration, and staff of the school district, and (5) function of the public relations unit, internal and external communications, crisis planning, and long-range planning.

The instrument asks the rater to check yes or no after each response item. Each section is then assessed by the number of yes and no answers, which identify the strengths and weaknesses in the organization of the public relations program.

The National School Public Relations Association also offers a series of public relations checklists for board members, superintendents, principals, teachers, guidance counselors, and secretaries. (See Figure 16.3.) Once again, checklists measure only whether a function or activity is being performed. They do not indicate how well the function or activity is performed.

Yes	No		Yes	No	
☐	☐	1. The PR program has been assigned to an individual who reports directly to the chief executive officer and who participates as a full member of the administrative cabinet.	☐	☐	8. In-service professional growth activities relevant to the PR staff are supported at the same level of support as those provided for the general professional staff of the school district.
☐	☐	2. Recognition of PR as a management function of primary importance is demonstrated through the existence of a unit staffed by full-time professional PR personnel.	☐	☐	9. The salaries and fringe benefits of PR professionals are provided at the same level of support as comparable cabinet-level positions held within the school district.

☐ ☐ 3. The staffing of a PR program will vary according to a school district's size, needs, environment, and availability of resources. Staff size is sufficient to accomplish the objectives of the school district and to cope with the variety of inherent conditions and problems.

III. Budget/Resources

Operating budgets should include sufficient funds for the PR services and programs recommended in these standards. Provision for financing should be based on such factors as enrollment, total operational expenditures, and special communication needs of the organization. Major PR services to be financed, other than staff, should include:

☐ ☐ 4. The PR staff meets the National School Public Relations Association Standards for Educational Public Relations Professionals.

Yes No

☐ ☐ 5. Adequate clerical and support assistance is provided for the PR unit.

1. Materials and equipment.

☐ ☐ a. Sufficient supplies are provided for a program to meet the objectives and commitments of the PR unit.

☐ ☐ 6. A systematic procedure exists for sending professional staff members to professional PR meetings, including NSPRA seminars and conferences.

☐ ☐ b. Work stations (desks, chairs, bookcases, filing cabinets) are provided for all staff assigned to the PR unit.

☐ ☐ 7. The registration fee and expenses of the professional staff attending NSPRA national or special seminars are paid by the school district.

☐ ☐ c. The PR unit has adequate word processing and computer equipment available.

FIGURE 16.3 A public relations checklist from *Evaluating Your School PR Investment* (Arlington, VA: National School Public Relations Association, 1984), p. 8. Reprinted by permission.

With site-base management emerging in public schools, evaluative instruments designed to assess campus or school level public relations programs are becoming popular.

The Texas School Public Relations Association has developed a workbook for campus level public relations assessment. It provides for evaluation of the school's public relations program by the principal, the staff, parents, and students. Figure 16.4 and Figure 16.5 are examples of its rating scale. Each response item is accompanied by six-digits running from 5 = always or superior to 1 = never or inferior. One digit "0" is for unknown or not applicable answers.

A strength of this ordinal rating scale is that an average rating for each section and all sections collectively can be calculated.

APPRAISING THE RESULTS

In treating this aspect of evaluation, attention here is given first to conventional methods of gathering data—data that are used to judge how effectively the program is achieving its goal—and then to a public relations audit and to the built-in evaluation mechanisms of systems analysis and of management by objectives.

Conventional Methods

Before discussing the means available for appraising or evaluating program results, it should be acknowledged that evaluation is the least developed area in school and community relations programs. Despite this limitation, much can be done to make the evaluation of program outcomes more valid, reliable, and objective. The following list of methods and techniques is helpful in this respect.

Observations. Informal appraisals are possible through the careful and unbiased observation of program effects, even though the effects cannot be measured objectively. It becomes evident through observation that a program is producing good results when pupils and parents express more friendly attitudes toward the school, and when teachers wish to improve their skills in human relations, manifest a deeper interest in pupil welfare, or take a more active part in community life. It is not difficult to detect favorable changes in the tone of newspaper editorials, letters to the editor, and communications received from taxpayers.

Sound guesses may be made about the effectiveness of a program when parents and community leaders are more willing to sit down and discuss educational problems with school officials. Other opportunities for observing results include the reception accorded to school representatives who appear before civic groups, public reactions to resolutions adopted by the board of education and proposals made by administrators, citizen cooperation on school-community improvement projects, and general remarks by people about the school.

Records. Various types of records may supply evidence of program effectiveness. A running account of criticisms and complaints that shows both a reduction in number and a narrowing of scope may tell something of the impact of the program. Brief reports, written by staff members on a standardized form, telling of significant comments made by people with whom they have talked may give a picture of what is happening. Requests for publications and records of attendance at open-house affairs and parent-teacher association meetings provide signs of growing interest in the school. The problem-study committees formed during the year and the nature of their activities are evidence that the partnership concept is taking hold. Much can be learned from keeping systematic records of election returns and the distribution of votes on school proposals submitted to the voters of the district.

Telephone Surveys. Telephone surveys may be employed to check reader interest in newspaper stories and audience reactions to radio and television programs. A random sample of names is drawn from the telephone directory to make up the list of those who will be called. Brief interviews are conducted by telephone; respondents may be requested to state whether or not they read school news stories in the daily paper and, if so, the kinds of school news they prefer and any recent stories they can recall. A similar line of questioning is followed in seeking audience reactions to radio and television programs. Although

Principal Evaluation
Campus Level Public Relations Assessment

The Campus Level Public Relations Assessment Process is designed to assist principals and their staffs in evaluating their campus public relations activities and programs. As site-based management becomes more of a reality in the public schools, the public relations process will become more of a campus-level responsibility.

This assessment process has been developed through the efforts of elementary and secondary principals and school public relations officers from school districts throughout Texas. The format permits administrators to review a number of ideas which reflect the best theory and practice in campus-based public relations.

You may use the process in one of three ways:
1) as a confidential self-assessment process OR
2) as a means of gathering and organizing data to be evaluated with the assistance of a school public relations consultant OR
3) as a committee process in which staff and/or parents assist in the gathering and analysis of data. This third method is the recommended strategy, and forms of the assessment for different audiences are available.

Items marked with an asterisk (*) require documentation and samples of materials and procedures used currently.

The answers to the following questions as well as the packet of materials compiled to document those answers will serve as a springboard for thinking of ways to improve the public relations programs on a campus by campus basis.

The rating scale is as follows:

5= Always OR Superior   2= Rarely OR Marginal
4= Usually OR Strong   1= Never OR Inferior
3= Sometimes OR Satisfactory   0= Unknown OR Not Applicable

Internal Public Relations Program

The term "internal public relations" refers to communicating with the school's internal publics—employees and students.

1.   Rate the effectiveness of your recognition programs for the following groups:

students*	5	4	3	2	1	0
teachers*	5	4	3	2	1	0
other staff members*	5	4	3	2	1	0

List activities:

FIGURE 16.4 First page with rating scale from *Campus Level Public Relations Assessment Process,* (Austin, Texas: Texas School Public Relations Association, 1991), p. 5. Reprinted with permission.

2. Which of the following consistent communication
    devices do you use to communicate between
    principal and all staff members?

    newsletter/weekly bulletin?*   5   4   3   2   1   0

    memoranda?*   5   4   3   2   1   0

    public address system
    announcements   5   4   3   2   1   0

    other_____?*   5   4   3   2   1   0

    List activities:

3. Do you have meaningful decision-
    making processes which involve staff?*   5   4   3   2   1   0

    List activities:

4. Do you use planned two-way, interactive communication between:

    principal and staff?*   5   4   3   2   1   0

    team leaders and principal?*   5   4   3   2   1   0

    principal and students?*   5   4   3   2   1   0

    staff members?*   5   4   3   2   1   0

    staff members and parents?*   5   4   3   2   1   0

    List activities:

5. How often do you have scheduled "team"
    (grade level, department, etc.) meetings?*   5   4   3   2   1   0

6. Do you have staff development specifically
    designed for your campus?*   5   4   3   2   1   0

    Are all staff members involved in
    staff development?*   5   4   3   2   1   0

    List activities:

7. Does your school project a caring,
    friendly professional image?   5   4   3   2   1   0

8. Is your overall staff attitude caring,
    friendly, and professional?   5   4   3   2   1   0

9. Does your physical facility project a
    caring, friendly and professional image?   5   4   3   2   1   0

10. Does the telephone etiquette of your staff reflect a caring, friendly, and
    professional image?   5   4   3   2   1   0

6 * Campus Level Public Relations Assessment

FIGURE 16.5 Second page of Texas School Public Relations Association's *Campus Level Public Relations Assessment Process.* Reprinted with permission.

few school systems have engaged in telephone surveys of this nature, this type of survey is the quickest of the survey techniques and its cost is relatively low.

The Panel. The panel technique was described in Chapter 3, dealing with methods for understanding the community. As may be recalled, a panel consists of a selected jury of laypersons who are fairly representative of the population. Interviews are held periodically with individual members of the panel and opinions asked on a scheduled series of questions. An attempt is made to evaluate the intensity of feelings and to note trends in opinions. Commercial interests have enjoyed success in employing consumer panels to get reactions to products and advertising. These business concerns have found that for trend studies in opinion, the information supplied by a few panel members is just as reliable as that supplied by a large number of persons. Although there are definite weaknesses in the panel technique—the literature on this subject makes them clear—the advantages are strong enough to offset them. More use should be made of the panel for collecting evidence of program effectiveness and checking results against those obtained by other methods.

Questionnaires. Questionnaires are a widely used method for surveying public opinion and gathering data for judging the worth of it. The short questionnaire, in the form of a printed card, may be used when quick reactions are wanted to some activity or when opinion is sought on a particular problem. This type of questionnaire may be distributed to members of an audience attending a school event, with the request that they fill it out before leaving. It may be inserted in school publications to find out if they are read, what features are most appealing, and what the readers think of them. Printing the questions on the back of a stamped, self-addressed postcard ensures a greater number of responses; fewer readers are willing to reply if they must address and stamp the card themselves. When some measure of opinion is wanted at once on a particular problem

or issue under consideration, the postcard questionnaire may be sent by mail to a selected list or sample of residents with a request for an immediate reply. Usually a brief statement of urgency for reply brings a satisfactory response.

A more comprehensive type of questionnaire may be administered at regular intervals to staff members and pupils within the school when evidence is wanted on the nature of attitudes and opinions regarding existing policies and practices. Important changes may be discovered and leads disclosed for future planning by making comparative studies of the findings.

The mail questionnaire has been recommended widely as a desirable method of surveying parents and other adults in the community. It consists of a schedule of questions sent by mail to citizens on the survey list. These individuals are asked to fill out the questionnaire and return it by mail at a certain date. In some instances the questionnaire is either published in the local newspaper or else delivered in person to those on the list, and the request is made that it be filled out and returned by mail. The cost of preparing and distributing the mail questionnaire is relatively low, and it has the further advantage of permitting the recipient to answer it at his or her convenience. However, the returns are frequently low and scarcely representative of the sample to whom it was sent. More satisfactory returns are possible if the questionnaire is delivered and picked up after a reasonable period of time has elapsed. A well-constructed mail questionnaire can provide invaluable information in appraising the effectiveness of the program.

Checklists. Another means of gathering data on the outcomes of the program is the checklist. This instrument may be used for determining how much change has taken place in the attitudes and opinions of the public with reference to a problem or several problems receiving attention in the public relations program. The checklist consists of a series of multiple-choice questions arranged in sequential order. The questions are stated as problems, and each is followed by a list of from three to ten possible answers. The informant is asked to choose the answer most nearly representing his or her viewpoint, opinion, or judgment.

Rating Scales. Rating scales are somewhat similar in design to checklists. On these the informants are asked to choose from among three to five degrees of opinion or attitude intensity on a series of specific questions. The purpose is to obtain a quantitative expression of opinions and attitudes at the levels included in the scale. For example, the question might be asked, "How important do you think it would be for the board of education to establish a research program in the public school system—very important, only fairly important, not important at all?" Or the question might be presented in the form of a series of graded statements with the request that the informant check the one most descriptive of how he or she feels. Questions may also be presented in other forms that are more suitable for the type of inquiry being made.

The construction and interpretation of rating scales that attempt to measure attitude intensity demand expert attention. This work cannot usually be entrusted to just anyone on the staff. It should be assigned only to those who are familiar with social science research methods.

Opinion Polls. Opinion polls, using direct interviews with a stratified sample of the population, are one of the best methods open to school systems for ascertaining whether or not the views of citizens on selected problems and issues have changed as a result of the program. The nature and amount of change cannot be estimated with reasonable accuracy unless polls are taken at regular intervals and the findings compared. Chapter 3 discusses question development and wording, as well as the selection and interviewing of the population sample.

Communication Audit

Successful school-community relations programs are often the result of good planning based on periodic audits of the program. Many times they are conducted internally by staff members because of costs and experience. On the other hand, outside consultants are often employed to bring a greater degree of objectivity and more credibility because of experience or credentials. Whatever the case, it is important that periodic audits be conducted. An expert public relations auditor brings together many recognized appraisal techniques and applies them to all methods of communication and to all intended audiences. This, then, results in a comprehensive perspective of the effectiveness of the communications program.

Kopec defines a communication audit in this way:

> It is a complete analysis of an organization's communications—internal and/or external—designed to "take a picture" of communication needs, policies, practices, and capabilities, and to uncover necessary data to allow top management to make informed, economical decisions about future objectives of the organization's communication.[11]

A comprehensive audit will uncover communications gaps and suggest possibilities for improvement:

- Short- and long-term goals
- Priority of those goals
- Themes or issues to be emphasized
- Priority list of publics
- Community pulse on key issues
- Communication methods that are working
- New communication methods warranted
- A measuring stick for future evaluation.[12]

The scope of the audit varies. In school districts it could encompass all communications in the district, in a single school, in a department such as business, transportation, or guidance, or among teachers or other employee groups. Many times an audit is confined primarily to the public relations office.

A communication audit of the entire school district should be conducted every five to seven years. In the meantime, periodic monitoring of communication activities can provide information to modify or eliminate certain communications programs.

Audits are also helpful when a new superintendent or public relations director is hired. In addition, audits may be appropriate when (1) a new majority of the school board is elected, (2) major demographic changes are occurring, (3) employees are experiencing low morale, and (4) students are transferring out of a district or school.

The subjects covered in audits vary according to the purpose of the audit. An audit can focus on just internal and external communication, or it can be even more focused and assess a single issue—your school district's image.

Major topics covered in school district audits include:

- Communication philosophy: review of formal policies, management's openness, management's support of communication, role of PR office, centralized versus decentralized approach, etc.
- Community demographics: analysis of who is there now and who may be there in five years, activity or stability of the community, private school students, percentage of nonparents, etc.
- Objectives and goals of school district and PR office.
- Organization and staffing of PR office.
- Existing PR program: review of products, activities, and general program for internal and external public relations.
- Attitudes toward present PR program: internal and external public report on current program—its strengths and weaknesses.
- Needs and expectations: feedback from all consulted groups.[13]

The manner in which a communication audit is conducted does not vary much from school to school. Consultants or the district public relations specialist use essentially the same approach with slight variations. A worthwhile audit encompasses the use of the conventional methods of appraising a communications program listed earlier in this chapter—observations, review of records, the telephone survey panel, focus groups, questionnaires, checklists, rating scales, and opinion polls. These would be applied, where appropriate,

to the communications activities and to the intended audiences. The findings would be tabulated and summarized, and the results would be analyzed and interpreted. Along with suggestions for action, they become part of a written report.

Systems Analysis

In dealing with goals and strategies, systems analysis can play a part in the planning of programs. Evaluation is a necessary and vital feature of systems analysis. Evaluation should start with a precise description of the objectives sought in the program. Inasmuch as there are several types of systems analysis, the objectives are treated somewhat differently in each one. The objectives may be stated in behavioral terms, or they may be expressed in operational language or descriptions of a process that will take place. In some systems the objectives are accompanied by sets of performance criteria. These criteria help to produce evidence that tells how well an objective has been achieved. In all systems, however, the goal has to be measurable. Once a goal is stated clearly and unambiguously, skilled evaluators can measure a good many things. If necessary they can use controlled observations, tests, analysis of documents, laboratory experiments, questionnaires, and other instruments. If no quantitative measures can be developed, the goal may be a description of a condition that should exist when it is reached.

Management by Objectives

Management by objectives (MBO) was discussed in Chapter 4. MBO is a process of building into administration a continuing concern for purpose. At each organizational level, the administrators in charge work out the goals for the next budget period. They also ask persons who report directly to them to formulate their own goals and then to discuss them jointly. After the goals have been agreed on, they become performance targets for the year.

Certain criteria have been established for evaluating statements of goals or objectives prior to their adoption. Questions are asked such as these: Is the statement of each objective constructed properly? Is the objective measurable? Does it relate to the administrator's role and mission in the organization as well as to the objectives of the total enterprise? Is it realistic and attainable? Will the result justify the time, labor, and money required to achieve the objective? Is the objective in agreement with basic organizational policies and practices? Can accountability be clearly fixed?

As noted in these criteria, objectives must be realistic and measurable. To facilitate measurement, objectives are usually stated in quantifiable terms like percentages, weights, ratios, numbers, time, and volume. If quantification of some elements has been tried without success, then a descriptive statement is employed that points out the circumstances that will evolve when the objective has been reached.

At stated intervals or at the end of the year the administrator and his or her subordinate look at the objectives again and jointly review the evidence of the subordinate's performance in trying to achieve them. Rather than waiting a year before evaluating performance, some administrators meet with their subordinates either when promised milestones have been reached or at stated intervals. This latter arrangement serves as a further check on the soundness of the subordinate's objectives, and it permits taking corrective action if an objective has been improperly conceived.

These built-in evaluation mechanisms enable a school system to know what it is accomplishing in its school-community relations program and how the program should be modified in order to make it more effective.

ENDNOTES

1. Walter K. Lindenmann, "Hunches No Longer Suffice," *Public Relations Journal* (June 1980), p. 10.

2. Mark P. McElreath, "Public Relations Evaluative Research: Summary Statement," *Public Relations Review* 3 (Winter 1977), p. 133.

3. Otis W. Baskin and Craig E. Arnoff, *Public Relations: The Profession,* 3rd ed. (Dubuque, IA: 1992), p. 189.

4. Harvey K. Jacobson, "The Role of Evaluation and Research in Management," *Handbook for Institutional Advancement: Programs for the Understanding and Support of Higher Education* (San Francisco: Jossey-Bass, 1977).

5. Scott M. Cutlip, Allen H. Center, and Glen M. Broom, *Effective Public Relations,* 6th ed. (Englewood Cliffs, NJ: Prentice-Hall, 1985), p. 292.

6. James W. Swinehart, "Evaluating Public Relations," *Public Relations Journal* (July 1979), p. 14.

7. Ibid, pp. 13–14.

8. Doyle Bortner, "Benchmarks for School Public Relations," *Journal of Educational Public Relations* 3, no. 2 (1979), pp. 8–19.

9. *Evaluating Your School PR Investment* (Arlington, VA: National School Public Relations Association, 1984), pp. 7–15.

10. See "Standards for Educational Public Relations Programs," *1982-1983 NSPRA Membership Directory* (Arlington, VA: The National School Public Relations Association, 1982), p. 53.

11. Joseph A. Kopec, "The Communication Audit," *Public Relations Journal* (May 1982), p. 24.

12. *Evaluating Your School PR Investment* (Arlington, VA: National School Public Relations Association, 1984), p. 16.

13. Ibid, p. 17.

FURTHER READINGS

Agee, Warren K., Phillip H. Ault, and Edwin Emery. *Introduction to Mass Communications*. 10th ed., New York: HarperCollins, 1991.

Bagin, Don, Donald Ferguson, and Gary Marx. *Public Relations for Administrators*. Arlington, VA: American Association of School Administrators, 1985.

Bagin, Rich. "The Communication Audit: A Periodic Report Card Saves Time, Money and Boosts Productivity." *NSPRA Impact* (Fall 1986).

Baird, Russell, Arthur Turnbull, and Duncan McDonald. *Graphics of Communication*. 6th ed., New York: Holt, Rinehart & Winston, 1993.

Banach, William, and Bruce Bradway. *Mastering Marketing*. Blackwood, NJ: Communication Briefings, 1988.

Beach, Mark. *Editing Your Newsletter*. Portland, OR: Coast to Coast Books, 1988.

Biagi, Shirley. *Media Impact*. Belmont: CA: Wadsworth, 1990.

Black, Roger. *Roger Black's Desktop Design Power*. New York: Bantam Books, 1991.

Bland, Michael, and Peter Jackson, *Effective Employee Relations*. London: Kogan Page Ltd., 1990.

Bohle, Robert. *Publication Design for Editors*. Englewood Cliffs, NJ: Prentice-Hall, 1990.

Botan, Carl H., and Vincent Hazleton, Jr., editors. *Public Relations Theory*. Hillsdale, NJ: Lawrence Erlbaum Associates, Publishers, 1989.

Broom, Glen, and David Dozier. *Using Research in Public Relations*. Englewood Cliffs, NJ: Prentice-Hall, 1990.

Brown, Daniel J. *Decentralization and School-Based Management*. Washington, DC: The Falmer Press, 1990.

Caldwell, Brian J., and Jim M. Spinks. *Leading the Self-Managing School*. Washington, DC: The Falmer Press, 1992.

Center, Allen, and Patrick Jackson. *PR Practices: Managerial Case Studies and Problems*. 4th ed., Englewood Cliffs, NJ: Prentice-Hall, 1990.

Conover, Theodore. *Graphic Communications Today*. St. Paul, MN: West, 1990.

Conover, Theodore. *Graphic Communications Today*. 2nd ed., New York: West Publishing Co., 1990.

Crable, Richard E., and Steven L. Vibbert. *Public Relations As Communication Management*. Edina, MN: Bellweather, 1986.

Cravens, David, and Charles Lamb. *The Marketing Plan: How to Prepare It, What Should Be In It.* Homewood, IL: Business One-Irwin, 1990.

Creedan, Pamela J. *Women in Mass Communications: Challenging Gender Values*. Newbury Park, CA: Sage, 1989.

Cutlip, Scott M., Allen H. Center, and Glen M. Broom. *Effective Public Relations*. 6th ed., Englewood Cliffs, NJ: Prentice-Hall, 1985.

DeVito, Joseph A. *Messages: Building Interpersonal Communication Skills*. New York: HarperCollins, 1990.

Dilenschneider, Robert. *Power and Influence: Mastering the Art of Persuasion*. Englewood Cliffs, NJ: Prentice-Hall, 1990.

Dilenschneider, Robert L., and Dan J. Forrestal. *Public Relations Handbook*. The Dartnell Corp., 1987.

Doty, Dorothy I. *Publicity and Public Relations,* Haupauge, NY: Barron, 1990.

Fulginiti, Anthony J. *Power-Packed PR—Ideas That Work*. Blackwood, NJ: Communication Briefings, 1988.

Gedney, Karen, and Patrick Fultz. *The Complete Guide to Creating Successful Brochures*. Brentwood, NY: Asher-Gallant Press, 1988.

Goens, George A. and Sharon I. R. Clover. *Mastering School Reform*. Boston: Allyn and Bacon, 1991.

Grunig, James E., and Todd Hunt. *Managing Public Relations*. New York: Holt, Rinehart, & Winston, 1984.

Kruckeberg, Dean, and Kenneth Starck. *Public Relations and Community: A Reconstructed Theory*. Westport, CT: Greenwood, 1988.

Lesly, Philip. *Lesly's Handbook of Public Relations and Communications*. New York: AMACOM, 1991.

Newsom, Doug, and Bob Carrell. *Public Relations Writing: Form and Style,* 3rd ed., Belmont, CA: Wadsworth Publishing Co., 1991.

Oskamp, Stuart. *Attitudes and Opinions*. Englewood Cliffs, NJ: Prentice-Hall, 1991.

Parker, Roger C. *Looking Good in Print*. Chapel Hill, NC: Ventana Press, 1990.

————, *Newsletters from the Desktop*. Chapel Hill, NC: Ventana Press, 1990.

Rafe, Stephen. *The Executive's Guide to Effective Presentations*. Blackwood, NJ: Communication Briefings, 1989.

Reardon, Kathleen K. *Persuasion in Practice*. Newbury Park, CA: Sage, 1991.

Ross, Raymond S. *Understanding Persuasion Foundations and Practices*. 2nd ed., Englewood Cliffs, NJ: Prentice-Hall, 1985.

Samovar, Larry, and Richard Porter. *Intercultural Communication: A Reader*. 6th ed., Belmont, CA: Wadsworth, 1991.

————. *Communication Between Cultures*. Belmont, CA: Wadsworth, 1991.

Schockley-Zalabak, Pamela. *Fundamentals of Organizational Communication*. 2nd ed., White Plains, NY: Longman, 1991.

Schools/Community—Guidelines for Effective Communication. Harrisburg: Pennsylvania School Boards Association and Pennsylvania School Public Relations Association, 1986.

Shook, Frederick. *Television Field Production and Reporting*. White Plains, NY: Longman, 1989.

Smith, Alvie L. *Innovative Employee Communication*. Englewood Cliffs, NJ: Prentice-Hall, 1991.

Stevens, Art. *The Persuasion Explosion*. Washington: Acropolis Books, 1985.

St. John, Walter. *The Best Ideas in Employee Communication*. Blackwood, NJ: Communication Briefings, 1987.

Templeton, Jane. *Focus Groups: A Guide for Marketing and Advertising Professionals*. Chicago: Probus, 1990.

Tucker, Kerry, and Doris Derelian. *Public Relations Writing*. Englewood Cliffs, NJ: Prentice-Hall, 1989.

Walters, Dottie. *The Great Communicators*. Glendora, CA: Royal, 1985.

Weaver, Richard L. II. *Understanding Interpersonal Communication*. 4th ed., Glenview, IL: Scott, Foresman, 1987.

White, Jan V. *Color for the Electronic Age*. New York: Watson-Guptill Publications, 1990.

————. *Graphic Design for the Electronic Age*. New York: Watson-Guptill Publications, 1988.

Williams, Patricia A. *Creating and Producing the Perfect Newsletter*. Glenview, IL: Scott Foresman, 1990.

INDEX